GAY ROOTS

WINSTON LEYLAND
San Francisco, 1978
Photo by Stephen Lafer

GAY ROOTS

*An Anthology of Gay History,
Sex, Politics and Culture*

VOLUME 2

EDITED BY WINSTON LEYLAND

GAY SUNSHINE PRESS
San Francisco

1st Edition 1993

Front cover photo ("Kontiki") and back cover photo ("The Drink") copyright © 1993 by Steve Jensen. Cover layout by Rupert Kinnard.
George Washington, 1776 (p. 10). Painting by Charles Willson Peale (1741–1827) reproduced with permission from the collection of The Brooklyn Museum, Acc. No. 34.1178, Dick S. Ramsay Fund.

Publication of this volume was made possible in part by a grant from the California Arts Council, a State Agency.

LIBRARY OF CONGRESS # 91–33787

ISBN 0–940567–14–8 (hard cover: vol. 2 alk. paper)
ISBN 0–940567–15–6 (paper back: vol. 2 alk. paper)
ISBN 0–940567–16–4 (vol. 2 limited specially hand-bound cloth edition)

Gay Sunshine Press Inc.
P.O. Box 410690
San Francisco, CA 94141

For a complete, postpaid catalog of books send $1 to above address.

CONTENTS

*Front cover photo ("The Drink") and back cover photo ("Kontiki") by Seattle artist
Steve Jensen.*

Winston Leyland

INTRODUCTION

G AY ROOTS Volume 1 includes in its introduction an indepth self-interview in which I discuss the genesis of *Gay Sunshine Journal* and Press and the work I have published during the past twenty-odd years. Readers are referred to that introduction for a full discussion of the internal history of Gay Sunshine. Because of space limitations I was not able to include in that anthology all that I would have liked. I have therefore prepared and published this second (and final) collection, a complement to the first.

Some of the material in this volume 2 was first published in *Gay Sunshine Journal* during the decade of the 1970s and early 1980s. A brief note at the head of each piece gives pertinent bibliographical information. The main exception to this is the well-researched pioneering article "Washington's Gay Mess," written especially for the present volume by Professor Charley Shively—on the Board of Directors of the non-profit Gay Sunshine Press for many years, as well as being associated with Boston's *Fag Rag*. He currently teaches in the American Studies Program of the University of Massachusetts. Of the four pieces in this anthology by Rictor Norton—American-born but resident in England for many years—two appeared originally in the pages of *Gay Sunshine Journal* while the remaining two were first published by London's tabloid *Gay News*. Most of the poems in the present anthology are taken from unpublished manuscripts, while a few appeared originally in limited book editions now out of print. But all four poets have had work published by Gay Sunshine over the past two decades.

I am especially proud to be able to reprint Frits Bernard's pioneering novel, *Costa Brava*. First published in Dutch in Holland (1958), this was the world's first contemporary novel to deal with the theme of boylove. (A novel on the same theme from an earlier generation—Adolfo Caminha's 1896 Brazilian novel *Bom Crioulo: The Black Man and the Cabin Boy*—was also published by Gay Sunshine Press in 1982). *Costa Brava* appeared in English for the first time in Gay Sunshine Press' *Gay Fiction Anthology* (1982). That book is now out of print, and I am pleased to be able to introduce this novel to a new generation of readers.

I would like to take this opportunity to thank several people who have been supportive of Gay Sunshine over the years (in addition to those mentioned on page 27 of volume 1): Richard Yaxley, on the Board of Directors of Gay Sunshine Press, has been unflaggingly helpful, especially in the past five years; others to be thanked include Rupert Kinnard (who designed the layout for both of the *Gay Roots* volumes), Patrick Kearney of Santa Rosa (for his invaluable bibliographical work), John Karr of San Francisco, Tim Frick of Chicago. I also want to thank all those writers and artists whose work is printed in volumes 1 and 2 for being so cooperative.

Gay Roots Volume 1 won the Lambda Book Award for the best book published by a gay press in 1991. Reviews of that volume were overwhelmingly favorable, and quotes from a few of them will be quoted here as a fitting conclusion to this brief introduction:

John F. Karr wrote in San Francisco's *Bay Area Reporter*: "This radiant volume reveals the ancient roots of gay culture, its omnipresence, continuity and its ongoing ability to shake us up. *Gay Roots* proves to be thoughtful, provocative and entertaining reading."

Professor Robert Dawidoff (Chairman American Studies at Claremont Graduate School California) wrote in *Lambda Book Report*: "*Gay Roots* is one of those books I'd like all my friends to have. Then, when I visited, I could see where it opens automatically and I'd know my friends better . . . *Gay Sunshine* is the best known of the early 70s Stonewall-era gay liberation magazines. Under the inspired editorship of Winston Leyland, *Gay Sunshine* became a seminal influence on gay male culture. This hefty anthology of writings from the magazine and books published by Leyland's Gay Sunshine Press is a treasure."

Robert Friedman wrote in San Francisco's *Sentinel*: "Winston Leyland is one of the seminal figures in the history of gay publishing, steering *Gay Sunshine* from its days as a journal into an important advocacy and literary press. Now he has given us *Gay Roots*, a huge compendium of gay scholarship and literature."

And Jim Van Buskirk wrote in *The James White Review*: "The wealth of material in these pages is incredible. One is overwhelmed by the diversity of material ranging from fascinating historical essays to explicitly erotic poetry."

In *Gay Roots* Volume 2 I have tried to maintain the same high standards as those of its predecessor. I hope the contents of this anthology will have a catalytic, enlarging, joyful effect on you the reader. . . .

I

GAY HISTORY

*George Washington aged 44 (1776). Painting by Charles Willson Peale.
Courtesy of The Brooklyn Museum, Brooklyn, N.Y.*

Charley Shively

GEORGE WASHINGTON'S GAY MESS: WAS THE 'FATHER OF OUR COUNTRY' A QUEEN?

BLATANT LIES, OPEN SECRETS

WHAT YOU LEARNED in grade school—that George Washington chopped down a cherry tree and then confessed, "Father, I cannot tell a lie"—is a lie. And what your teacher never told you—that "Washington loved handsome men."—is true.

Evidence of Washington's love for men has been published before. Noel I. Garde in 1964 included a chapter on George Washington in *Jonathan to Gide, The Homosexual in History*. One of Garde's sources was J. V. Nash, *Homosexuality in the Lives of the Great*, Little Blue Book No. 1564, [1930], Girard, Kansas. The Kansas press had been founded by populist socialists who published the mass circulation *Appeal to Reason* and then switched to the famous Blue Books. Publication of *Homosexuality in the Lives of the Great*, like the original *Wizard of Oz*, attacked the sacred standards of its time. In Kansas—somewhere over the rainbow—they were fighting against the heterosexual standard as well as the gold standard.

Jonathan Ned Katz's *Gay American History, Lesbians and Gay Men in the U.S.A.* (1976) followed a populist impulse. He described his book as "significantly not a product of academia; it does not play it safe; it is rough at the edges, radical at heart." In the final section "Love: 1779–1932," he examines the correspondence between Alexander Hamilton and John Laurens, aides-de-camp to Washington. The notes to their love letters include references to Washington's drillmaster, Frederick Steuben and his Greek attachments. Katz, however, labels Garde as "unreliable" and of J. V. Nash, notes only that "The author and publisher of this pamphlet merit research." While Katz sidesteps the question of Washington, I follow him in viewing "homosexuality" in the broadest possible terms. "A sharp, either/or distinction between erotic and nonerotic relations is another common polarity by which puritan morality has mystified intimate same-sex relations."

Following these earlier hints of Washington's attachment to men, I presented a version of this essay as part of a course at the University of Massachusetts, Boston. My lecture distressed some members of the class. One student asked, "If what you say is true, why haven't we heard about it before?" Another objected that such a story would corrupt grade school (if not college) students. I then responded by surveying the class (about 70 students). Suppose my research is correct. And suppose that the cherry tree story is an out-and-out lie. Washington had a distant relationship with his father; the cherry tree myth surfaced only after Washington's death. Mason Weems's story is as fanciful as his claim that he was "parson" at Mount Vernon. Weems's fabrication, however, has had such staying power because of its heterosexual symbolism (as in breaking a virgin's "cherry") and like so many religious creations rests on evidence of things unseen.

If evidence of Washington's loving men is true and the cherry tree tale a simple lie, then should children be taught a lie about the cherry tree in order to teach them that telling the truth is good? And should they also be lied to and told that Washington was a conventional heterosexual family man? Rather to my surprise one third of the class favored lying twice: teach the cherry tree story and teach the conventional hetero-sexual lie. One third favored dropping the cherry tree story and also not mentioning the evidence of Washington's loving men (even though for the argument, they assumed it was true). And only one third favored truth all the way: drop the cherry lie and teach the fairy truth.

Eve Kosofsky Sedgwick in her *Epistemology of the Closet* (1990) examines some of the difficulties one has in opening closed doors: "In dealing with an open-secret struc-ture, it's only by being shameless about risking the obvious that we happen into the vicinity of the transformative." Some academics have been embarrassed by brazen queers and shameful predecessors. They denounce anyone as psychopathic who would iden-tify important figures who have been bisexual, gay or lesbian. Such debased queers would seek to uplift homosexuality and themselves by associating with the rich and famous. For instance during the fifties, thousands of men claimed to have had sex with Rock Hudson and/or Montgomery Clift. One flippant *Christopher Street* queen exclaimed re-cently: "You know how gays are always trying to make everyone and everything out to be gay!" The editors of *Hidden from History, Reclaiming the Gay and Lesbian Past* try to separate themselves from the "bad" gays: "It has long been reassuring for gay people, raised in a society offering them no positive images of themselves, to claim gay heroes, ranging from Sappho, Julius Caesar, and Shakespeare to Willa Cather, Walt Whitman, and Gertrude Stein, and much of the earliest work by historians simply sought to es-tablish in a more scholarly fashion the homosexuality attributed to certain respected historical figures."

The epistemological difficulties of the "open-secret structure" are endless. Not only the question of what is sex? homosexuality? bisexuality? heterosexuality? But also, what is the United States? Nothing of that name "existed" in Washington's youth and perhaps not even in his lifetime. And what is an "army"? In what ways have Alex-ander's, Caesar's, Cromwell's, George III's, Washington's, Napoleon's and Ho Chi Minh's armies shared a structure? And in what ways does the word "army" hide un-speakable differences? Even today, can we compare the Swiss army with that of the United States?

In *Discipline & Punishment, The Birth of the Prison* (1975, trs., 1977), Michel Foucault explored the relationship between the uniformization of armies with the contemporane-ous inventions of hospitals and schools: "the army, the school and the hospital" provided methods of studying obedience and of enforcing it upon "docile bodies." His penetrating analysis of French prisons and of Jeremy Bentham's proposed reforms, however, left many questions about how his analysis could apply to other times and other areas. Foucault explains that "Many disciplinary methods had long been in existence—in monasteries, armies, workshops. But in the course of the seventeenth and eighteenth centuries the disciplines became general formulas of domination." Foucault's formula-tions can be applied to Washington and his army less easily than to *fin de siecle* litera-ture. Nonetheless, the newly developed "domination" of the British army greatly alarmed the colonists in Massachusetts, Virginia and elsewhere. The American Revolu-tionaries opposed the growth so common in Europe "of professional standing armies led neither by a feudal warrior class nor by military contractors but officered by ser-vants of the state."

Academics have tried to appear judicious in traversing the shoals of so-called "responsible" research. Too seldom do they ask: "responsible" to whom? While academics have tried to become more responsible or at least more obscure, activists have pressed the issue of outing. Publications have taken names like *Outweek*, *Outlook* and simply *Out*. And much movement politics in the United States has come to revolve around closeted homosexuals inside structures of domination (like the military or the National Endowment for the Arts or even universities). Campaigns of exposure have been launched against closeted homosexuals who have used their disguise in order to eliminate other more open homosexuals.

Academia has become much safer for academics thanks to activists, who have risked everything to break their colleagues' judicious closures. Because of organized resistance to homophobia, dominant powers in academia now hesitate to fire lesbian and gay men. But the battle is only half won because few of the people of power would ever hire an openly gay or bisexual candidate. And few universities have lesbian and gay courses built into their curriculum or into existing courses. While the academy offers many opportunities for homophobes and more for reform, the distance between activists and academics seems to have grown rather than abated.

Like my own previous works on Walt Whitman, this essay on Washington attempts to bridge the gap between the activist and the academic community. Doubtless some of the same issues raised against my earlier books will again trouble some readers. Critics have attacked *Calamus Lovers, Walt Whitman's Working Class Camerados* (1987) and *Drum Beats, Walt Whitman's Civil War Boy Lovers* (1989) because the "evidence" was insufficient. In the face of a multitude of letters from Whitman's lovers which Gay Sunshine Press published for the first time, they complained that they had not heard any of this before. Understood in a heterosexual context, these letters, of course, are not evidence at all. In fact there can never be any actual "proof" of Whitman's having had sex with men. All the best biographers had argued the contrary. Even those who might accept Whitman as gay can't deal with male prostitution or boy love or drag. They would ignore Nicholas Palmer's letter asking Whitman about male houses of prostitution and instead speak of Henry James, whose judicious indirection has been a model for some queers.

What constitutes "proof" positive? The judicial model of British common law lingers in the back of many minds. Same sex contact is assumed to be a crime and the "burden of proof" requires evidence beyond "a reasonable doubt." And who decides? Straight white men constitute the judge and jury. I reject this model entirely. In the first place, if sex with males is a crime, then I celebrate the criminal. Second, I reject the idea that we have to prove something to straight people. Let them prove that they will not kill, maim or imprison us because of our love. I appeal not to juries who rejected the evidence of murder and mayhem in the Dan White or the Rodney King cases. Fuck their impartiality! I appeal to queers to judge the George Washington evidence. Assume everyone is homosexual until proven otherwise. Begin with our own experiences and use them to understand same sex love inside our society and its past.

Finally I reject the argument that examining male to male love in Washington's life offers too narrow of a focus. Whoever condemned John C. Phillips for being too narrow in his study, *George Washington Sportsman* (1928)? There are a multitude of very narrow monographic studies, which seldom arouse any anxieties. But any examination of homosexuality, gayness, queerness, bisexuality or even erotophobia drives fear into the heart of straightness. But those—homosexual, bisexual or heterosexual—who will not come out of their closets suffer immeasurably by their self-imposed dirty little secrets. Like Kafka's seeker, they stop at the door without daring to enter. This essay asks you the reader not to follow but to join your own liberation. Make history not an act of closure but an act of opening, continuing revolution and revelation.

ARMIES OF LOVERS

The military establishment provides an important context for George Washington's life. Today the United States armed forces are so militantly anti-gay that many can't imagine that the man "first in war, first in peace, first in the hearts of his countrymen" loved other men. With all the ROTC cadets and officers now coming out, some have concluded that the presence of mufti same sex love is something new. The openness is new, but the same sex experiences have been more common in the services than out. At one time I had never met an airforce man whom I did not have sex with (the first exception was the brother of a lover, who forced me to remain asexual around his relatives). Wayne Dynes in his comprehensive *Homosexuality, A Research Guide* (1987) notes that, "In Europe, from the 18th century onwards, there are documented cases of homosexual generals and military officers. Wartime experiences seem to foster the emergence of homosexual patterns of behavior."

Since armies began, the military has always included same sex love. The semimythical Amazons may have been the first armies of lovers. Gilbert Herdt has documented the way that Micronesian Sambians feed their youngsters a steady diet of semen so they can become men and then warriors. And in Greece, the Spartans kept their men separated from society. Spartan soldiers fought together as teams of lovers and later excited the young Alexander Hamilton to similar glory. Likewise the famous band of Thebes, the elite military group of that city formed as an army of lovers.

As a same-sex institution (like convents and monasteries), the military has long provided a refuge for those without interest in raising a family. Both women and men in service are seen as more powerful than their domestic brothers and sisters. And even now erotic commercials are run by Marine and Army recruiters emphasizing the sexual attractiveness of their limbs of service. And there has been such a continuous tradition of cocksucking and butt fucking aboard ships that boys entering the navy must be shocked that cruising in the Navy requires as much skill as among civilians. In a homophobic society, of course, all this must be vigorously denied.

In fiscal year 1987, the United States Armed Forces discharged 1,378 persons in "homosexuality separations" and currently they axe about 1,500 men and women a year. Those with special interests in uniforms and those wearing uniforms know that such a figure represents only a fraction of military activists. The services themselves know how inclined their recruits are since they publish lists of lesbian and gay bars which are labeled "off limits." When the *JFK* nuclear airforce carrier recently landed in Boston, the sailors used their navy list to find their way around town. Winston Leyland has edited two volumes of *True Homosexual Military Stories*: *Enlisted Meat* (1991) and *Warriors and Lovers* (1992). Miss Hush (a famous Boston Queen) during the Vietnam War received benefits from her sergeant lover who was a career officer. The sergeant kept a picture of Miss Hush (in drag) in his wallet to show the boys how straight he was. The Pentagon never checked Miss Hush's cock, which she also sold to other johns in her butch drag while hubby was away fighting to save the empire.

Kate Dyer and Rep. Gerry Studds (D-MA) have released some recently suppressed evidence of military queers in *Gays in Uniform, The Pentagon's Secret Reports* (1990). The Kinsey Institute studied queers for the report of Colin Williams and Martin Weinberg, *Homosexuals and the Military: A Study of Less than Honorable Discharge* (1971). Allen Bérubé has documented queer experiences in the United States armed forces in *Coming Out Under Fire, The History of Gay Men and Women in World War Two* (1990). And Lawrence R. Murphy uncovers some remarkable goings-on among sailors at Newport R.I. in 1919–1920 in *Perverts by Official Order, The Campaign Against Homosexuals in the United States Navy* (1988). And my *Drum Beats, Walt Whitman's Civil War Boy Lovers* (1989) tells something of the hidden lives of women and men in the Civil War who pursued love with their own kind. This essay would open up the Revolutionary army experiences of manly love.

WASHINGTON'S MODELS

Before Washington, a multitude of the great generals were same sex lovers. In 1759 Washington ordered busts of six figures to adorn Mount Vernon: Alexander the Great, Julius Caesar, Charles XII of Sweden, Frederick the Great, Prince Eugène of Savoy and the Duke of Marlborough. Major General Frank M. Richardson includes all these generals in his study *Mars Without Venus, A Study of Some Homosexual Generals* (1981). Contemporary sophisticates might argue that the word "homosexual" cannot be applied to men from such different times and societies. Nonetheless even in their own times and cultures their sexual impulses and their lives were queer. Washington chose these men as his heroes and their biographies provide a context for his own biography.

Alexander (356–323 BC), according to Athenaeus, was subject to unbridled passion for beautiful boys. A gay bar in Athens now carries his name. Lesbian and gay authors through the centuries have been moved by the story of his life. Roger Peyrefitte, Mary Renault and others have celebrated his lavender streak. The Hellenistic world, of course, differed from today's gay bars. Alexander, nonetheless, shares with today's queers a sense of being alienated from his father, from his contemporaries and from his society. His military campaigns carried him far beyond the limits of the Greek imagination. He marched as far as India and died in Babylon with little desire to return to his Macedonian birthplace.

Contemporaries and subsequent historians have debated his intentions. Certainly Alexander was no ordinary Greek. A Macedonian, he did not share the narrow Greek ethnocentricism but took a Persian eunuch Bagoas for his lover; and in the flesh pots of Egypt he allowed himself to be taken as divine. He's reported to have kept a book of poems under his pillow and to have wept that he had no Homer to record his glories. His campaigns were recorded by rather pedestrian historians, but Washington himself studied these accounts in search of Alexandrine secrets. Alexander's military genius (which any queen could imitate today) was demonstrated by his triumph in Phrygia. Here Gordius had tied so ingenious a knot that no one could untie it. Alexander cut the knot with his sword. Is this not an early illustration of the famed gay sensibility?

Julius Caesar (100–44 BC) fucked his way to the top. Warren Johansson writes in the *Encyclopedia of Homosexuality* (1990): "Exploiting his youthful good looks, together with the boundless charm for which he continued to be noted, he threw himself with relish into a scandalous liaison with king Nicomedes IV of Bithynia." According to a Roman witticism, Caesar was "husband to every woman and wife to every man." Whether military genius or not, he was a great publicist. Caesar's *Gallic Wars* recount the Roman conquest of present-day France and Belgium. (This text has provided a beginning text not only for Latin students but also for military cadets.) After conquering Gaul, Caesar crossed the Rubicon River, conquered Italy, overthrew the Roman Republic and was assassinated on March 15, 44 BC. Supposedly his dying words to his friend (and assassin) were, "Et tu Brute."

Alexander Hamilton, Washington's aide-de-camp, took the pen name "Caesar" for articles he wrote supporting ratification of the U.S. Constitution. Hamilton told Jefferson that "The greatest man that ever lived was Julius Caesar." Washington more often sided with Caesar's opponent Cato. Even so, his Fairfax patron wrote in 1756 that Washington was fortunate to have read Caesar and the life of Alexander so that he had "therein read of greater Fatigues, Murmurings, Mutinys and Defections than will probably come to your Share."

Alexander and Caesar would be on any short list of military conquerors, but Washington's choice of Sweden's Charles XII (1682–1718) demonstrates an admiration for queerness as well as cleverness. While a mere boy of fifteen, Charles began a largely successful defense of Sweden against Saxony, Prussia, Denmark, Poland and Russia. He made allies with Cossacks, fought in Turkey and died in a battle against Norway in 1718. Charles defeated or neutralized mighty enemies and provided a model of military strategy triumphing even with limited resources. His private life was less known to Washington's contemporaries and in parts remains obscure even today; nonetheless, everyone knew that he never married nor fooled with women. Charles lived with his soldiers; his immediate staff were not allowed to be married. Washington followed these policies and like Charles often slept with a chosen staff member. Voltaire called Charles XII "the only person in history who was free from all weakness."

Whether Washington knew the details of Charles XII's camp life is uncertain, but he received first hand information about Prussia's Frederick the Great (1712–1786) and his younger brother Prince Henry. Frederick Steuben served with both of these men-loving Germans and was part of their intimate households before he joined Washington at Valley Forge (see below). Lafayette, another Washington aide, later visited both Prince Henry and Frederick. Of the Prince he wrote, "I have scarcely finished breakfast when he comes to see me; we go for a walk by ourselves until dinner; we are close in the same way at supper as well . . . we are always together." He was likewise charmed with Frederick at Potsdam. He wrote Washington how surprised he was at the "softness of the most beautiful eyes I ever saw, which give as charming an expression to his physiognomy."

Historian, military strategists, German nationalists and hero worshipers alike unite in calling Frederick "great." While they say little about his love for men, the evidence of his dalliances is indisputable. An artistic child, Frederick fell in love with an older boy. Caught by his cruel father, the lover was executed before his eyes. A flood of protests came from other European monarchs against the advisability of executing Frederick, the heir to the Prussian throne. At the last minute the father commuted the boy's death sentence but sent him into semi-imprisonment. There Frederick developed a relationship (which lasted until his death) with a private named Fredersdorf. The youth was "tall, handsome, clever, silent and polite; and was a talented flautist." They played duets together; in his will, Fredersdorf was named as one of the few the king loved. Upon his father's death, Frederick went to take charge while he was in the arms of Francesco Algarotti, an Italian beauty whom he had snatched from Lord Baltimore (proprietor of Maryland lands whose family name also graces the Chesapeake Bay city). Frederick had his pick of international beauties and studs, whom the faithful Fredersdorf carefully guided in and out of the King's chambers, gardens and dining hall. "For company and jokes," Nancy Mitford writes of his final years, "Frederick had a jolly young Italian, the Marchese Lucchesini, an excellent acquisition. Someone said to the King that Lucchesini was clever enough to be used as an ambassador—Frederick agreed and said that was why he kept him in his household."

Prince Eugène of Savoy and the Duke of Marlborough (Winston Churchill's ancestor) were not lovers but they complemented each other on the battlefield. Beefy Marlborough needed the sauce of Eugène, whose preference for men was common knowledge. Known as "Mme l'Ancienne," Prince Eugène, "belonged to a small effeminate set that included such unabashed perverts as the young Abbé de Choisy, who was invariably dressed as a girl, except when he wore the lavish earrings and make-up of a mature woman." But the Duke of Marlborough got his position through his wife's liaison with Queen Anne. Anne herself appointed governor in New York a drag queen, Edward Hyde Lord Cornbury (1702–8) who claimed he dressed in women's clothing in order to honor his queen.

The busts of Alexander, Caesar, Charles XII, Frederick, Marlborough and Eugène which Washington had ordered never reached Mount Vernon. The London merchant tried to pawn off poets on an unwilling colonial customer. Washington's admiration for such a queer cast of generals, nonetheless, offers two important contexts in understanding his own same sex love sensibilities. First the figures provided reference points which suggest possibilities for his own behavior. While not well read, Washington had studied the lives of Alexander and Caesar and he knew people who had firsthand stories from the Swedish, Prussian and French courts. And he took his own training inside the eighteenth century British army. Secondly, these models provided him guides in forming what he called his "family"—the aides who helped him through the War for Independence against England.

BOY GEORGE

Washington's youth exemplifies the distant father/dominating mother pattern, which has often identified homosexual men. This paradigm describes some who are now called homosexuals much as the paradigm of rapist describes some heterosexual men. Without granting too much credence to such ideas, one can find clear evidence of father rejection and mother incorporation in Washington's life.

Among the more recent biographers, John E. Ferling, writes in *The First of Men, A Life of George Washington* (1988) that, "In all the millions of words that he ultimately penned, George Washington never mentioned his father." Augustine (Gus) Washington (1694–1743) was a predatory planter, land speculator, slave owner and iron maker. He bred his first wife into her grave and, after pocketing a handsome dowry, soon wed Mary Ball, George's mother. Born in 1732, George was Mary's oldest child; others followed in 1733, 1734, 1735, 1738 and 1739. (In 1736, Gus had visited England and left his son without a father in his tender Oedipal period.) By contrast George himself sired absolutely zero children. His father's compulsive heterosexuality was celebrated as part of the imperial campaign to drive the native peoples from their lands and was by no means unusual in eighteenth century Virginia. George's indifference or incapacity to be a stud was more remarkable. Gus died suddenly in 1743. On his deathbed he was reported as saying that he was glad he'd never hit anybody. "I am sure that from my remarkable muscular powers I should have killed my antagonist and then his blood at this awful moment would have lain heavily on my soul."

Mary Ball Washington (1708/9–1789) was even tougher than her husband. After bearing and raising so many children, she lived to see George elected President; however, she remained indifferent to her son's honors and considered them less worthy than hers as a mother. In notable ways, George incorporated Mary's commanding demeanor. A childhood friend recalled visiting the Washington plantation and being terrified by the mother. He "was ten times more afraid [of her] than I ever was of my own parents." In Mary's presence the noisy children became "as mute as mice." He compared boy George with Mother Washington: "Whoever has seen that awe-inspiring air and manner so characteristic in the Father of his Country, will remember the matron as she appeared when the presiding genius of her well-ordered household, commanding and being obeyed."

Washington came to incorporate so much of his mother within himself that his relation to her mirrored hers to him: "in childhood he was withdrawn; in youth, resistant; in maturity, resigned." He did not delete Mary Bell from his life like he did his father but, insofar as possible, he shelved her: "His correspondence with (and about) his mother reveals no emotion except exasperation (and perhaps a saddened tolerance); his visits to her after childhood were infrequent, reluctant, unrewarding, and short."

Throughout his life George Washington turned to men for love; his relations with women were friendly, even flirtatious, but always asexual. His relations with men were deeper, closer, more physical and perhaps even sexual. In *Love's Coming of Age*, Edward Carpenter argues that the differences between men and women have been vastly overemphasized—"that they rather represent the two poles of *one* group—which is the human race." So likewise with the differences between friend and fuck buddy: "as people are beginning to see that the sexes form in a certain sense a continuous group, so they are beginning to see that Love and Friendship—which have been so often set apart from each other as things distinct—are in reality closely related and shade imperceptibly into each other." Washington certainly never shied away from or repudiated homosexual love either in the Platonic or in the criminal sense.

Queers have been traumatized by centuries of persecution by church and state for putting a cock or tongue into another mouth, ass or cunt. Sodomy remained a capital offense in Christian countries until the French revolutionaries decriminalized the act. The Napoleonic code—now adopted in most of Europe and Latin America—retained the reform. In Virginia sodomy was a capital crime and remained so into the nineteenth century. Jefferson proposed castration instead but his "humane" reform was not adopted. Whatever the law, millions have taken great risks in order to enjoy such physical contact, and great numbers have twisted their minds and bodies in order to save themselves from such pleasures.

Even so, the criminalized and hereticized contacts have much less significance than friendships. In the right situations ("I was drunk; asleep; under the influence of drugs; etc.") anyone might (and multitudes have) tasted the pleasures of male-male or female-

female love. But we need to go beyond the clerics, judges and psychiatrists who have concentrated with such venom on the cock and cunt so that we can understand what kinds of love move a person's imagination. In this area, people fall along a scale of homosexual, bisexual and heterosexual. In Washington's time, people's behavior fell along these ranges even though such words had yet to be invented. And in those ranges, Washington's sexual interests in women were zero compared with his interests in men.

His love of men went through two distinct periods. As a young man, he searched for older men to love. He also sought them as escape hatches to break away from his own mother. While fleeing his mother, at the same time he related to his male lovers as she had related to him. Objects of his desire included his half brother Lawrence Washington, Thomas and William Fairfax (his neighbors and in-laws), Christopher Gist, an early Kentucky explorer and companion, and General Edward Braddock, under whom he served in the French and Indian War. Later as he became a commander, Washington became a mother to a long line of confused men to whom he provided love, direction and attention. George Mercer during the French and Indian War provided a transition; he became Washington's aide-de-camp after Braddock's death. About the same age as Washington, Mercer offered an imperfect model for later aides who were many years younger than the general. During the Revolutionary War, Alexander Hamilton, John Laurens, Gilbert Lafayette, and others were broken in to love and to war by their beloved companion/commander.

LAWRENCE WASHINGTON

Washington didn't meet his half brother until Lawrence was twenty years old. Taking Mary Ball as his second wife in 1731, Gus had quickly sent the boys from his first marriage off to England for school. Returning from his English boarding school, Lawrence quickly became inseparable from young George. Biographer Douglas Freeman explains: "As a result of his long and careful schooling in England, the young gentleman had grace, bearing and manners that captivated George. The lad quickly made a hero of Lawrence and began to emulate him." Washington Irving paints the relationship even more romantically: "There was a difference of fourteen years in their ages, which may have been one cause of the strong attachment which took place between them. Lawrence looked down with a protecting eye upon the boy . . . while George looked up to his manly and cultivated brother as a model in mind and manners."

Lawrence tried to wean George away from his mother Mary Ball Washington. The household underwent strain; Lawrence was sent off to run another plantation; Mary stopped having babies in 1739. The War of Austrian Succession or King George's War 1740–1748 stirred Lawrence's imagination. He received a commission and raised troops from Virginia who were picked up by the British Royal Navy, where they served under Admiral Vernon in an attack on what is now called Colombia and Panama. Lawrence returned home in time for his father's death and with his inheritance quickly married Anne Fairfax, whose family owned a great percentage of Virginia. They named their plantation Mount Vernon after Lawrence's beloved admiral.

Marriage quickly bored Lawrence; he displayed symptoms of tuberculosis. The older brother convinced George to accompany him to the Barbados for the 1751–52 winter so that they could escape family life. George contracted smallpox in the Barbados and recovered; Lawrence's tuberculosis, however, got worse. George returned to Mount

Vernon in January 1752; Lawrence tried Bermuda for a while, but in April he urged his wife and young brother to join him. Before arrangements could be made, Lawrence returned to Virginia for the Appalachian springtime and died July 16, 1752.

Lawrence Washington married well, had children and set up Mount Vernon, but he also had close contact with male to male sexuality. He spent about seven years in an English boarding school. He served two years under Admiral Vernon in the British Royal Navy, long known for its sodomy. R. R. Burg, *Sodomy and the Perception of Evil: English Sea Rovers in the Seventeenth-Century Caribbean* (1973) confirms the popular notion that men at sea tie knots with more than rope. There are no cum stained sheets or court records of George's ties with his brother, but in 1746 Lawrence did work out a plot to get George himself into the Navy. While not every boy joins the navy because of its reputation for sodomy, every boy must have been aware of the notorious reputation of sailors. In the generation before George, Cotton Mather's son joined the navy for just this reason and scandalized his Puritan father when he returned home wearing a leather jacket. And in a subsequent generation, Herman Melville went to sea just to find exotic male meat. In *White Jacket* (1850), Melville writes, "The sins for which the cities of the plain were overthrown still linger in some of these wooden-walled Gomorrahs of the deep."

In 1746 Lawrence sent George a letter from a Royal Navy recruiter whose ship was then docked in Virginia. Another letter in more general terms went to Mary Ball Washington asking for her permission (George was only fourteen). While George quickly packed and was ready to go, his Mother used stalling tactics and after a year of delay finally refused permission. She based her decision on a letter from her own brother claiming that "a common sailor before the mast has by no means the common liberty of the Subject; for they will press him from a ship where he has 50 shillings a month and make him take three and twenty; and cut him and staple him and use him like a Negro, or rather, like a dog." George's Uncle urged him to look for a wife and make his money from raising tobacco, slaves and children. George found the sailor's cutting and stapling not unattractive; but, if he ran away from home, he would have endangered his rights of inheritance which he would receive in 1753 when he turned twenty-one. He stayed in Virginia but his dreams of Gomorrah were not broken.

THOMAS FAIRFAX

While George had to give up dreams of sailing, his brother soon hooked him up with a wealthy friend. Thomas (1693–1781), 6th Baron Fairfax, attended Oxford and became an odd gentleman indeed. Fairfax mysteriously left his grand Leeds castle in County Kent England and permanently moved to Virginia in 1747. Since Thomas Fairfax never returned to England, he may have had reason to remain in exile; certainly backcountry Virginia was a long way from Oxford or Leeds. The Baron's estate in England was sizeable and his vast proprietary lands in Virginia included all of the land between the Potomac and Rappahannock rivers and west through the Shenandoah Valley—over five million acres.

Lawrence Washington had made his fortune by marrying a cousin of Thomas. To do this he had to butter up the men in the family and he in turn introduced Washington to this trade. Lawrence Washington and his father-in-law William Fairfax (1691–1757) used George as bait for the Baron. The elder men instructed the boy in winning the older man's attentions. William Fairfax (a cousin of the Baron) had himself come "to love George Washington like a son" and his advice on getting ahead was "to follow the methods he had himself pursued: an assiduous courting of the great." Cousin William had acted as the Virginia agent for Thomas, 6th Baron Fairfax, and had built Belvoir in 1741 within sight of Mount Vernon. George represented the best hope of retaining Thomas's favor. Thomas lived at Belvoir between 1747 and 1749; he then built a refuge sixty miles beyond the Blue Ridge, "Greenway Court" where he lived until his death in 1781.

The bait worked for a time: "Fairfax at once took a fancy to the boy. The old bachelor of fifty-seven was literary, philosophical, shrewd, and could hardly fail to be interested in this studious lad of fourteen." Between 1747 and 1749, George lived most of the time at the Fairfax Belvoir mansion. And when the Baron moved west, George often "made Greenway Court a second home." The Baron regaled the boy with stories of his own life in the navy and in the army. The family library contained a translation of Suetonius, *History of the Twelve Caesars*, which contains full accounts of the men loving men Roman emperors. George "enjoyed unrestricted access to the Proprietor's quite respectable library, and he derived 'incalculable benefits' from his association with the urbane, cultured Baron, both in the field hunting fox and deer, and in pipe-smoking, after-hours conversations."

Preferring only the company of men, Thomas Fairfax hated women intensely and avoided their company; supposedly he had once been jilted and never recovered. The old man took George into his intimate company and "was kind to the boy, who had such a way with horses." George early mastered the art of riding horses and was reputed to be most stunning when mounted. Lord Fairfax enjoyed the company of men, dogs and horses. George Washington interbred his dogs with the Lord's; in his diary, he recorded for August 28, 1769: "The young Hound Bitch Chaunter was lined [fucked] by Lord Fairfax's Rockwood (who appears to have the Mange) twice this day."

The Baron disdained fine clothing and dressed only for the outdoors; he took his pleasure in fox hunting. Even after twenty years, George would go alone with Fairfax as he recorded in his diary (November 19, 1768): "Went a Hunt[in]g with Lord Fairfax & catchd a Fox." Oscar Wilde described the English foxhunt as the unspeakable in pursuit of the inedible. Thomas Fairfax gave a queer twist to the sport. To horrify the ladies at Mount Vernon, he once took "to their doorstep his hounds and a fox in a bag so that, without effort, they could watch the kill."

In 1748 through the Fairfax influence, William and Mary College commissioned the sixteen year old George as official surveyor for Culpeper County. Between 1749 and 1752, Washington completed more than 190 surveys of landholdings in Virginia; through Fairfax's help the lad himself acquired vast landholdings. George received two thousand acres in the Shenandoah Valley alone; elsewhere he had picked up another four thousand acres through Fairfax's help. And with the Lord's help, George was elected to the House of Burgesses along with another favorite, Thomas Bryan Martin.

Although George Washington always retained the good favor of Thomas Fairfax, his relationship became less intimate after 1752. Thomas Bryan Martin (1731–1798) then took up residence in the Baron's secluded Shenandoah hideaway. Martin became Fairfax's land agent, always appeared with the Baron in public and never left his Lord's side. Although George Washington often visited, exchanged dogs and hunted with the couple, he no longer enjoyed the Baron's exclusive attentions. The great Proprietor cultivated the boys as he did his hunting dogs. Bryan Fairfax, a prodigal son of the family, gravitated to Greenway. A recent biographer writes that "despite the age discrepancy, he and Lord Fairfax got along famously. They exchanged visits, they hunted foxes together—in one letter, the Proprietor mentions leaving a 'tann'd' hound at Lees-burg for Bryan . . ." The Proprietor encouraged the boy in his wildness and when he ended up in jail George Washington rushed to bail him out. Bryan married, saw less of the Baron and named his first born after the old man. George Washington himself often went hunting with young Bryan.

While most of the Fairfaxes became open Tories and fled revolutionary Virginia, the old Baron stayed on with the dogs, horses and companions that he loved so well. Moncure Conway in his "A Lord and a Lad," wrote "There is a tradition that when the first gun of the American revolution was reported at the house of Lord Fairfax, Greenway Court, George Washington was dining there." Washington later sent the Baron a get-well letter from Valley Forge. The old man died in 1781; by then a celebrated general, Washington took time to send his condolences: "altho' the good old Lord had lived to an advanced age," he wrote, "I feel a concern at his death."

BAREASS BACKWOODS

From "the good old Lord" George himself learned the joys of living in the woods. First as a surveyor under the Fairfaxes he was broken in. The young kid was very green at first. In his diary, George describes the first night in the field: 15 March 1748 near present-day Berryville, Virginia, at Isaac Pennington's house: "we got our Suppers & was Lighted in to a Room & I not being so good a Woodsman as the rest of my Company striped my self very orderly & went into the Bed as they call'd it." Presumably he removed his pants, shirt and coat. Underpants hadn't yet been invented so he may have had a long undershirt or may have been completely nude. The boy soon discovered that his blanket and straw were filled with lice, fleas and other "Vermin. . . . I was glad to get up (as soon as the Light was carried from us) & put on my Cloths & Lay as my Companions." After that he remained dressed at night and chose "to sleep in the open Air before a fire."

Sleeping as George had in his shirt tail sometimes provided a signal for companions. In 1726, another Southerner had written to a friend: "I feel some inclination to learn whether you yet sleep in your Shirt-tail, and whether you yet have the extravagant delight of poking and punching a writhing bedfellow with your long fleshen pole—the exquisite touches of which I have often had the honor of feeling?" Washington had carefully studied *Rules of Civility and Decent Behavior in Company and Conversation* which taught boys not "to spit seeds" or "to scratch their private parts in public," but hadn't warned of the consequences of "stripping." Nathaniel Hawthorne (who Melville adored so fondly) once wrote: "Did anybody ever see Washington nude?" And he revealed more about himself than about Washington, when he answered, "He had no naked-ness, but I imagine was born with his clothes on, and his hair powdered, and made a stately bow on his first appearance in the world."

CHRISTOPHER GIST

Logically, George Washington should have taken a wife, since he had accumulated much land and showed great promise. Instead the good Baron obtained for the youth (as he approached his twenty-first birthday) a commission as Major in the Virginia army. Here he met Christopher Gist (1705–59), who initiated the young man into further mysteries of the wilderness. Gist, like Washington, came from the planter class but he, like Thomas Fairfax, also liked to go beyond refinements and walk on the wild side. Since people like Fairfax had grabbed the best lands in Virginia, the more adventurous and greedy looked further west, where they hoped to emulate the greed of their predecessors. In 1747 a group organized the Ohio Company, which soon hired Gist to explore the lands in what are now Ohio, Kentucky and Indiana. In 1751, he reached the Kentucky River and looked "as far as the eye could reach, over a vast woodland country . . . Kentucky lay spread out before him in all its wild magnificence; long before it was beheld by Daniel Boone." Of course, indigenous peoples possessed these lands which were also claimed by the French after LaSalle's trip from Montreal to New Orleans in 1682. The French claimed the whole Mississippi watershed for the King of France and named the land Louisiana. The Ohio Company represented the English entry into this imperial sweepstakes.

Leslie Fiedler brought attention to the underlying homosexual attraction in the stories of the west and western conquest: Natty Bumpo, Davey Crockett, Daniel Boone, Huck Finn, Buffalo Bill, Billy the Kid and all those lonely cowboys playing with and at being Indians. Christopher Gist was such a hero, but because he lived in the lingering world of eighteenth century nobility, his kind of backwoods, back-to-nature message was as little heard or understood as that of Thomas Fairfax. Christopher Gist, nonetheless, initiated Washington into the tough guy world. His and George's adventures parallel the *Song of the Loon* fantasy. In both the novel and the film two males go into the woods alone and make love there. George and Christopher romanticize each other and celebrate their being beyond all those sissies and women. And they even pick up an Indian on the trail.

Both men kept journals of their trip together in the winter of 1753–54. Sent by the governor of Virginia to warn the French to get out of Ohio, they travelled to Fort Le Boeuf (near Lake Erie) to present their message. The French replied that they owned Ohio. Gist, Washington and their company then started back to Virginia with news. The Virginians proceeded on horseback, but on the day after Christmas, Gist wrote that George "desired me to set out on foot, and leave our company. . . . I was unwilling he should undertake such a travel, who had never been used to walking." But after "he insisted," they then stripped down "like Indians." Then the adventures began. First they picked up a strange Indian who offered help. George was tired; the Indian offered to carry his backpack. When he offered to carry George's gun, the Virginians got suspicious and the Indian became sullen at their distrust. When his chance came, the Indian tried to murder the two Virginians. They overpowered the native and Gist wanted to kill him. But he wrote in his diary that George "would not suffer me to kill him." They let the Indian go but fearing others they split up and made two trails and rejoined after dark. "We encamped," Gist wrote, "and thought ourselves safe enough to sleep."

The next adventure was on the Allegheny River. Leslie Fiedler could have added this one to his "Come Back to the Raft Ag'in, Huck, Honey." On September 29, 1753, trying to cross the Allegheny River, they made a raft but had trouble with the chunks of ice rushing downstream. Washington wrote in his diary: "we expected every Moment our Raft wou'd sink, & we Perish; I put out my seting Pole, to try to stop

WASHINGTON AT THE AGE OF 25 (1757),
*from a miniature on ivory presented
by him to his niece, Harriet.*

LAWRENCE WASHINGTON (1718–1752),
*favorite half brother of George Washington
(see pp. 19–20). Mid 19th century engraving
by Benson J. Lossing from an original painting
attributed to John Wollaston.*

*Christopher Gist (1705–1759) (left) and George Washington, aged 21, crossing the
Alleghany River on their mission to Fort LeBoeuf, 1753. Engraving by Alonzo Chappel.*

the Raft, that the Ice might pass by, when the Rapidity of the Stream thr[ew] it with so much Violence against the Pole, that it Jirk'd me into 10 Feet Water, but I fortunately saved my Self by catching hold of one of the Raft Logs." Christopher adds in his own journal that Washington "having fallen in from off the raft, and my fingers frost-bitten, and the sun down, and very cold, we contented ourselves to encamp upon that island." After wading ashore in the frigid water to the island's safety, they were happy to awaken to find the whole river frozen over. They crossed easily over to the other shore.

Thomas Fairfax had taught George to love the wild west and Christopher Gist taught him to survive there. Their ideal of tough manhood—men alone against mother nature—prepared the way for the great imperial wars between France and England. The secret for winning the war in North America rested in the hands of the indigenous populations. Joseph François Lafitau, an eighteenth century Jesuit missionary in Canada, had written about some of the Indians that Gist and Washington encountered. Lafitau describes friendships between two men "maintained by mutual tokens of benevolence; they become Companions in hunting, in war, and in fortune; they have a right to food and lodging in each other's cabin."

The friendship between Gist and Washington resembled that of Indian warriors (or so they fancied). The couple also served together in the French and Indian War. In 1757, to promote Gist, Washington wrote: "He has had extensive dealings with the Indians, is in great esteem among them; well acquainted with their manners and customs—is indefatigable and patient. . . . for his capacity, honesty and Zeal, I dare venture to engage." Gist had been meeting with Indians associated with the Choctaws, of whom Jean Bernard Bossu had written, "most of them are addicted to sodomy. These corrupt men, who have long hair and wear short skirts like women. . . ."

Washington returned to the strategic juncture where the Monongahela and Allegheny rivers form the great Ohio. The French built Fort Duquesne there and under the English the site became Pittsburgh. With Gist's help Washington successfully attacked the French site, but, when the French counterattacked, the Virginians were forced to surrender. This incident launched the French and Indian War (1754–63) (called the Seven Years War in Europe). As one biographer notes, "Washington had, indeed, shed the first blood in the . . . conflict which, according to Frederick of Prussia, cost the lives of about 853,000 soldiers plus civilians by the hundreds of thousands." Both Gist and Washington fought during the war. In the course of scouting and negotiating with the native Americans, Gist himself contracted smallpox and died in 1759. Under General Amherst, the British had given smallpox-contaminated blankets to the Indians in order to kill them. Having immunity to the disease, Washington survived the war and emerged as the head of Virginia's forces. Washington never forgot his friend and later befriended his son Mordecai Gist who was reported to resemble his father.

SOLDIER BOY

Edward Braddock (1695–1755) provided Washington an example of command more powerful than anyone except his mother. Braddock's personality closely resembled Mary Washington's—irascible, narrow, obdurate and demanding. The mother tried her best to keep her son from going off to war but he quietly ignored her and chased after the older man. Washington's relationship to the general evolved inside a circle of men loving men in which the young Virginian fit like a glove. Braddock saw in the youth an unfinished country boy, a handsome and promising soldier. In Braddock and his circle Washington found a means to polish himself and advance his own career. The example of Braddock's "family"—the name he used to describe his circle of handsome young men—later provided the model for Washington's own circle during the Revolutionary War.

To fight the French, King George II had appointed Edward Braddock commander-in-chief of North America. The General arrived in February, 1755, at Alexandria, Virginia, with 1,400 British regulars. Through Fairfax and other connections, Washington met with Braddock right away. The older man liked the youth and allowed him very good terms for his service. To his brother, Washington wrote that he had found "familiar complaisance . . . from the General; who I hope to please without difficulty . . . [which] requires less ceremony than you can well conceive." "In Braddock's campaign the young surveyor and frontier soldier had been thrown," according to biographer Henry Cabot Lodge, "among a party of dashing, handsomely equipped officers fresh from London, and their appearance had engaged his careful attention."

Braddock's aides-de-camp, his "Family" of handsome young men embraced Washington, "and a cordial intimacy commenced between them that continued throughout the campaign." Like Braddock none of the aides were married, and only Morris, with whom Washington had the poorest rapport, showed great interest in women. George was closest to Robert Orme, described as "attractive and suave, a man of society, reared in the army." Another intimate of Washington, the young William Shirley wrote "I have a very great love for my Friend Orme." Some of the other officers disliked this circle. Even before they left Alexandria, there had been grumbling about the "young men" having too much influence with the General and one unhappy colonel vowed were he in command "he would dismiss the General's favorite [Orme] the very next day."

Many all male groups like the Boy Scouts or Armed Forces put on an exterior front opposed to sensuousness and intimacy. Yet inside these groups special friendships are cherished and the most elaborate ritual and finery flourish. Braddock's circle observed elaborate rituals. The General travelled in a chariot which was flanked by a body guard "of light horse galloping on each side of his chariot, and his staff accompanying him; the drums beating the Grenadier's march as he passed." He arrived at Fort Cumberland "amid a thundering salute of seventeen guns. When they had encamped, the General observed the strictest protocol among his men; every rank had to maintain their insignia and uniforms in tip top condition. Parades and reviews kept the men sharp looking and beautiful. Braddock's own circle retired to a convivial table which he maintained for Washington, Orme, Shirley and the boys. Braddock had the reputation of being a fine host who had with him "two good cooks, who could make an excellent ragout out of a pair of boots, had they but materials to toss them up with."

Braddock disliked women, colonials and Indians—more or less in that order. These three hatreds clouded his judgments and led to his downfall.

Braddock's objections to the women were primarily sexual, since they could seduce his men. His own troops had brought a large supply of "washerwomen" from England, who served both as nurses and sexual partners for the troops. Braddock bristled when these women demanded higher wages and "ordered that all those who would not work for 6d. a day and provisions should be excluded from camp." The skimping on mollies (as they were sometimes called) annoyed the men, but another measure taken against the Indian women alienated both the men and the Indian allies. Bright-Lightning and a group of Indian maidens entertained the troops in exchange for drink, beads and other gifts before Braddock ordered them out of camp. The Indians interpreted the General's anger and the attack on Bright-Lightning and her group as a rejection of their race and way of life. Washington through Gist had made friends with Bright-Lightning's father, White Thunder, who could have offered the English considerable assistance. "Most of the savages were offended by the severity of the camp regulations," and according to biographer Douglas Freeman, "the troops, in turn, were demoralized by the presence of native women." By "demoralized," he means they were "debauched," not that they disliked their company.

Braddock considered the indigenous people savages and the colonials little better. Washington, who had been brought into his charmed circle of love and affection, was exempted from the general's prejudice, but the elder did not take the boy's advice seriously. He considered the local settlers' unwillingness to supply food, wagons and horses as criminal. Their advice about the difficulties of travel along the wilderness road only showed faintheartedness or worse. When Indians friendly to the French attacked him, he offered a bounty of £5 for the scalp of any Indian. He distrusted Indians as scouts or as allies. Braddock didn't regret losing those Indians who had supported the English allies.

Washington fought with Braddock in the ill-fated expedition against Fort Duquesne (July, 1755), in which nearly two thirds of the troops were killed or wounded along with 63 of the 89 officers. (The battlefield on the Monongahela now forms present-day Braddock, Pennsylvania.) Recriminations flew back and forth after the defeat, but few noted that a French force half the size of the British had been successful because of their Indian allies. Since Braddock had alienated the allies that Gist and Washington has so carefully cultivated, he had no wilderness eyes to guard against his enemies. The French and Indians hid behind trees and mowed down the British as they advanced; officers in their fine uniforms were particularly good targets. Braddock and his beloved Orme were wounded on the field. Although suffering from dysentery, Washington rushed them from the field and helped rally what few troops remained. Braddock died and Washington buried him in the middle of the road so that the Indians couldn't find his scalp.

Had Braddock loved Washington's judgment as much as the youth's body, perhaps Queen Elizabeth would still reign over the United States. Washington like many other colonials saw that the British lion lacked claws. Consequently, the colonists could defend their own lives, liberties and properties. If the British objected, they too like Braddock could be defeated. The strategy used so successfully by the French and Indians later provided a blueprint for the colonial victory at Saratoga.

Handsome Robert Orme survived his wounds and in November, 1755, returned to England. He wrote Washington of their friendship: "Your amiable Character made me desirous of your Acquaintance and your Acquaintance confirmed the Regard and Opinion your Character had imprinted in my Mind." He assured his fellow companion: "my dear George Distance Absence nor change of Circumstances shall never alter the sincere Friendship and Affection which I have ever had for you." Looking back over his service with Braddock, he concluded, "I saw myself a Slave . . . serving of my Friends and the Man I loved."

Robert Orme loved Braddock but he was also a sexual adventurer like many of the young officers in the European armies who charmed both the generals and the women of the aristocracy. Orme was married but in 1756 he eloped with the wealthy daughter of Viscount Townsend. Orme's English wife reportedly went mad, while the couple fled to the continent with a maid, jewelry and a considerable fortune. The young woman became pregnant and according to one report "besides all her other infamy . . . [was] deeply in debt to all sorts of trades-people." They lived quietly abroad until she died in 1781 and "beautiful Orme" returned to Hertford, England, where he died in 1790.

GEORGE MERCER

George Mercer (1733–1784) resembled Orme in his sexual dalliance but his relationship to Washington was quite different. With Orme Washington had been a handsome colonial underling; with Mercer he became the commander. After Braddock's debacle, the governor of Virginia put Washington in charge of the state's troops. Mercer served as Washington's aide-de-camp from September 1755 until May 1757. In 1756 Mercer accompanied Washington to Boston where they negotiated the relationship of Virginia's troops to the British in fighting the French and Indians. Mercer went to South Carolina in 1757. After the war, he sat in the Virginia House of Burgesses (1761–65) and also acted as the London agent for the Ohio Company (1763–70). Briefly and disastrously, he served as Virginia's stamp officer during the Stamp Act Crisis (1765). Mercer then returned to London where in 1776 he eloped with a wealthy heiress. The couple lived from some time on the continent before Mercer's death in 1784.

Washington and Mercer undertook their junket to Boston during February and March, 1756. Governor Shirley of Massachusetts had become commander-in-chief of the British North American troops upon Braddock's death. Washington had a conflict with the head of the Maryland army about who should outrank whom at Fort Cumberland, built by the British, manned by Virginia but in Maryland territory. Washington had been a close friend of Governor Shirley's son, the personal secretary in Braddock's family. William Shirley, Jr., had died with his general in the battle. The elder Shirley did all he could for Washington and provided a letter giving him precedence over the Maryland commander at Fort Cumberland.

For this expedition, Washington spent lavishly for himself and his traveling companions, George Mercer and Robert Stewart. The latter elusive figure was "a favorite" of Washington, of Baron Fairfax and of the governor of Virginia; after the French and Indian War, he took up a "civil office in Jamaica." Stewart certainly knew how to butter up his superiors and had a grand time with Mercer and Washington. The trio gambled, drank, partied, went to entertainments, shopped and shopped some more in Philadelphia, New York City and Boston—all cities new, vast and marvelous to the Virginians. They traveled in royal style with three slaves and three horses in livery costume and themselves in splendid uniforms. Washington Irving wrote that "their sojourn in every city was a continual fête."

Meanwhile back in Virginia, the Indians launched Appalachian springtime and summer raids. Some puritanical white men were scandalized by Washington's carrying on. The Virginia *Gazette* (September 3, 1756) claimed that the commander and his officers "give their Men an example of all Manner of Debauchery, Vice and Idleness." The columnist accused Washington of promoting his boyfriends as "raw novices and rakes, spendthrifts and bankrupts, who have never been used to command, or have been found

THOMAS FAIRFAX (1692–1781),
6th Baron Fairfax of Cameron, who
preferred the company of men exclusively—
an early influence on young George.

GEORGE MERCER (1733–1784),
hot blooded gay rake, closely associated
with young George in the 1750s.

GEORGE WASHINGTON AS AN OFFICIAL SURVEYOR (ca. 1750
in his late teens). 19th century drawing by Felix Darley,
engraved by G. R. Hall for Irving's Life of Washington.

insufficient for the management of their own affairs." (Sounds like Mercer and Stewart.) Under such leadership, the army had supposedly lolled in lusts snuggled within their forts and had hidden from the indigenous warriors. "Men of Virtue and true Courage can have no Heart to enlist, and mingle in such a Crowd." And the few that may be of good character are "damped and mortified at the Sight of such Scenes of Vice, Extravagance and Oppression."

Among the examples of great armies debauched by vice, the newspaper lists Alexander the Great who was done in by the dark skinned people of the East. Himself debauched by a Persian boy, Alexander "suffered the army to debauch themselves in the same manner." The "effeminate" people of Tarentum likewise fell to the Romans because of weaknesses similar to Alexander's. (In 1795, a town near Pittsburgh in which Mercer and Washington had an interest took the name Tarentum.) Washington was being compared to homosexual rulers whose luxury, effeminacy, cruelty and sensuality had "unmanned many an army and enslaved or ruined many flourishing cities and kingdoms." The link of cruelty and effeminacy was common among eighteenth century critics. Such a link is less often made now. Nonetheless, occasional critics of Bondage and Discipline or Sadism and Masochism have linked homosexuality and cruelty in their analysis of the Nazis.

The work "debauchery" and "effeminate" as used by the Virginia *Gazette* would include both male and female (terms used then and now) and heterosexual, bisexual and homosexual (terms later invented). George Washington had a secretary inquire if friends thought the article referred to him. They all replied that that would be impossible. A friend wrote Washington: "Show your contempt of the scribbler by your silence, your watchfulness and care, and thereby disappoint him." Washington and most of his biographers have maintained their silence. All copies of the Virginia *Gazette* (but one) have been destroyed and that copy survived in the papers of a hostile British general.

The promiscuous and randy George Mercer does fit the model of a debauched favorite. He had written Washington August 17, 1757 that "The many Favors my dear Colonel that I have received at your Hands wou'd make Me blush at begging an Addition to Them, did I not know your Goodness in excusing such freedoms." In 1754 although "George Mercer was young and not burdened with domestic cares," Washington did not chose him to be one of the officers given to the French as hostages. Washington chose Mercer as his aide-de-camp and then took him as his companion for the trip to Boston. If Mercer had any military skills, they have been lost to history; he won favor not from his fieldwork but from his randy smile and his worship of his commander.

Sometime around 1759 Mercer wrote a remarkable physical description of Washington as "straight as an Indian." Six foot two; 175 pounds; light brown hair; grey blue eyes. "His frame is padded with well developed muscles, indicating great strength. His bones and joints are large as are his hands and feet." The man "is neat waisted, but is broad across the hips, and has rather long legs and arms." His mouth, lips and other "features are regular and placid with all the muscles of his face under perfect control, tho flexible and expressive of deep feeling when moved by emotions." A hunk in repose; in motion a god: "His movements and gestures are graceful, his walk majestic, and he is a splendid horseman." Mercer's description reads like a sex ad in one of today's gay papers. Both Douglas Freeman as well as the current editors of Washington's papers print the text but the original has not survived and this passionate description was once part of a longer document whose provenance is not known.

Mercer lolled in debauchery and sensuality, a condition common to the eighteenth century military men and Virginian planters. Such indulgence crossed the gender line without much thought. Thus Mercer could write Washington about his attraction to women to demonstrate his randiness and to displace his sexual warmth with Washington and other military men. From South Carolina, he wrote (17 August, 1757) about the women there: "A great Imperfection here too is the bad Shape of the Ladies, many of Them are crooked & have a very bad Air & not those enticing heaving throbbing alluring Letch exciting plump Breasts common with our Northen Belles." In the same letter he alerts Washington to "a Set of very genteel pretty Officers here" of the Royal British Army. Whether "pretty" is a slip of the pen for "petty" or was intentional cannot be determined, although Mercer generally spells well. At any rate, the "pretty" officers gave the Virginians "a polite Invitation to spend the Evening, & after to agree to keep Us Company." Nevertheless, Mercer remained "much on the Reserve as in any Place I ever was, occasioned by the Multiplicity of Scandal which prevails here."

One of the pretty officers Mercer mentions was perhaps James Grant (1720–1806) who had fought at Fort Duquesne as a major in the Highland Regiment. He had been captured there by Indians and held at Montreal until he was exchanged in 1759; he blamed his capture on Washington's aide Stewart; he returned to service in South Carolina, where as one of the "pretty officers" he renewed his friendship with George Mercer. Washington wrote on July 27, 1761, "The perfidious conduct of our neighbors, the Cherokees, have occasioned the sending of Major Grant with a detachment of his Majesty's troops and what forces the Carolineans could muster into their country on that side, while Colonel Byrd with the Virginian Regiment is ordered to penetrate it on this." Grant later became governor in East Florida where he invited the teenage Jack Laurens to elope with him to England, but Jack's father firmly but politely canceled that trip. Grant later fought against Hamilton and Washington at Brandywine in the Revolution and returned to England where he served in Parliament. His clear solicitation of Laurens as well as Mercer's attachment to him suggests something of the circulation of male bodies in the eighteenth century armies.

Mercer's subsequent career developed his lechery. His Don Juan character demonstrates a thinly disguised displacement of his attraction to men. Mercer's debauchery extended across genders (and generals) and across continents. Fleeing the wrath of the anti-Stamp Act colonials in 1765, he landed in England where he found a wealthy woman with whom he eloped. Mercer's startled father wrote that he thought "you were taken in," but a letter from the lady mollified the father.

In the prodigal's absence, George Washington and the father tended to the business affairs of the son. George Mercer neither returned to Virginia nor realized the great funds expected. George Washington had power of attorney for a Mrs. Savage who had "but a bad Time of it" in Ireland. Mercer wrote him in 1770 that the seventy year old lady was "denied the Use of Pen Ink Paper and Romances, and a frequent Use of the Strap is substituted in the Place of those Amusements." (*Colonial Series*, VII, 504). Here is not the place to trace all of Mercer's unflattering affairs. Douglas Freeman euphemistically concludes that his adventures "are precisely such as might have been written by Samuel Richardson." Richardson's *Pamela or Virtue Rewarded* (1740) might be less appropriate for comparison than Henry Fielding's *The History of Tom Jones, A Foundling* (1749). Tom Jones (both in the novel and the film) portrays something of the life of the English gentry in the eighteenth century. That fictional portrayal was remorselessly heterosexual but there were plenty of queers among the peers.

If George Mercer broke George Washington's heart, no record of the sorrow remains. But Washington's indulgence of him suggests more tolerance than he paid to any other man excepting possibly Alexander Hamilton. And Washington was known as a strict disciplinarian. Deserters were hanged; incompetents sacked.

Mercer not only broke a string of women's hearts, but he was also a totally incompetent soldier. In Virginia's last engagement at Fort Duquesne in 1758, he had his column of men shooting at Washington's. Fortunately the French were retreating, but this battle led one critic later to say that Washington's distinction in his first field command was to shoot down his own men.

The French abandonment of Fort Duquesne (now renamed Pittsburgh) ended Virginia's engagement in the French and Indian War. Washington retired to Mount Vernon and took a wife in 1759.

SISSY MAN

Washington was never a sexual adventurer like Orme but he did share with him the loose conviviality common among eighteenth century military men if not the whole society. Efforts to portray him as a lady's man, however, only demonstrate the eagerness of researchers to create (for them) a more comfortable heterosexual facade. An intense effort to heterosexualize Washington accompanied the United States emergence as an imperial power in the late nineteenth century. One of the founders of the Immigration Restriction League, Republican Henry Cabot Lodge waxed eloquent in his 1889 biography: "One loves to picture that gallant, generous, youthful figure, brilliant in color and manly in form, riding gayly on from one little colonial town to another, feasting, dancing, courting, and making merry." Democratic Woodrow Wilson tells more about himself than about Washington in his 1903 biography: "No young Virginian could live twenty-six years amidst fair women in that hale and sociable colony without being touched again and again by the quick passions; and this man had the blood of a lover beyond his fellows." Discounting the backwoods adventures, Wilson concluded that Washington, "had relished the company of lively women from the first, meeting their gay sallies sometimes with a look from his frank blue eyes that revealed more than he knew."

While an active sexual life with women does not preclude an equally active gay life, Washington's letters and journals reveal little interest in women. The letters between him and Lafayette are much more flirtatious than his letters with any lady. Women seldom were the object of Washington's desire. For instance, in the diary kept during the Barbados trip with his brother, he barely mentions females and then in odd contexts. For Guy Fawkes Day (November 5, 1751), the Washington brothers had "an invitation from Mrs Clarke & Miss Roberts to come & see the serp[en]ts fired." Serpents were fireworks; but the juxtaposition of women with serpents is suggestive as the entry a few days later: "Dined at the Fort with some Lady. Its pretty strongly fortifyed and mounts about 36 Guns within the fortification." Here "some Lady" suggests some barrier in his feelings which are restrained by the fortifications. There were thirty-six guns inside, but another fifty-one mounted outside. The Bridgetown serpents and fortifications aroused his imagination much more than the women there. (When

Washington became commander in the American Revolution, he prohibited celebration of Guy Fawkes Day.)

Washington's tastes in women generally ran to mothers and women attached to other men. His first amorous mention of a woman occurs in a letter to his boyfriend "Robin." Washington writes jokingly that Robin's "Low Land Beauty" had once aroused a "troublesome Passion," which he now wants to bury "in the grave of oblivion." Much has been made of his subsequent affection for Sally Fairfax. She like the unidentified "Low Land Beauty" was not available. George also remained a close friend to Sally's husband, the younger William Fairfax, a relation of his patron, Thomas Fairfax. Some of the letters to her are mildly flirtatious and hers to him are at best friendly. But closer examination of the relationship (if it should be called such) suggests that George was more interested in her than in her body. She taught him about plays, art, current music and gossip. Like many gay men George turned to womanly culture but that made him neither a woman nor a sexual partner of women.

With Sally Fairfax, Washington developed his love of theater, a pleasure he continued throughout his life. In camp his aides performed plays; and in the large cities he attended every play on the boards. At the Fairfax Belvoir mansion, he played a part in Addison's *Cato*. (Incidentally, Thomas Fairfax, who hated women but loved George for awhile, donated money for the publication of Addison's *Spectator*.) Whether Washington was a spectacular or only barely adequate dancer is a matter of historical debate. But he did dance and Belvoir provided him a place to perfect his steps. Being interested in the theater and being able to dance, however, are not commonly indications of burning heterosexual passion.

Martha Custis provided George Washington a perfect consort/cover. A very wealthy widow with two children from her first marriage, she was eight months his elder when they married in 1759. Both needed a ceremonial consort and both played the role remarkably well; their fortunes together made them perhaps the richest couple in what became the United States. (Ripley's *Believe It or Not* claims Washington as the country's first millionaire.) Washington once described his relationship with Martha as "more fraught with expressions of friendship than of *enamoured* love." And he advised a relative that a happy marriage "results from a combination of causes: none of which are of greater importance than that the partner should have good sense, a good disposition, a good reputation, and financial means."

There is some evidence that Martha at first chafed in the marriage, but the records of their relationship have been largely destroyed. Most of George's letters were carefully preserved with sometimes as many as two or more sets of copyediting by Washington himself. Since at least 1776, all of his letters have been collector's items of ever increasing value. After George's death, however, Martha carefully burnt all of their correspondence. Only two letters survive and they show little hint of passion or even closeness. After Congress appointed him to command the revolutionary army, George left Philadelphia for Boston. To Martha he wrote: (June 23, 1775) "I go . . . in full confidence of a happy meeting with you some time in the future. I have not time to add more, as I am surrounded with Company to take leave of me." Undertaking treason, risking his and her life, fortune and sacred honor, the commander is at best reticent.

Martha's and George's time together seems timeless. He was always the great public figure and she the faithful partner. Mount Vernon might sprout new additions; the number of house servants and slaves might increase; Martha might gain more weight; George might receive higher honors. But the household from 1759 to the present has remained a ceremonial pavilion. Between 1768 and 1775, they entertained some 2,000 guests. During the Revolutionary War winters, Martha entertained the troops (even at Valley Forge) and as the first First Lady she tried to set a high standard of entertainment. Some democrats thought she was too extravagant; both she and George loved beautiful clothing and furnishings; they continuously entertained. After retiring from the presidency, Washington wrote somewhat nervously, "Unless some one pops in, unexpectedly— Mrs. Washington and myself will do what I believe has not been done within the last twenty years by us,—that is to set down to dinner by ourselves."

The couple never had any children. George's mother had had a child almost every year during her marriage. That was not Martha's and George's model; they took the opposite path. Posterity has grappled with this fact of no children from the father of our country. An obvious possibility that he was not sexually attracted to women has seldom been entertained. One author claims he had mumps as a child and was rendered sterile but on what evidence is unclear. Impotence either acquired or congenital has had few advocates. On slender evidence adulterous liaisons have been suggested but no children of slave or free women have come forward to claim paternity. Natural children were less disgrace in the eighteenth century than now; Benjamin Franklin's illegitimate son became governor of New Jersey, and the governor's illegitimate son became Franklin's secretary during the Revolution. (Lafayette tried to pick him up as an aide). In 1786, Washington firmly said that even if Martha Washington should die soon, "there is a moral certainty of my dying without issue, and . . . whilst I retain the reasoning faculties I shall never marry a girl and it is not probable that I should have children by a woman of an age suitable to my own should I be disposed to enter into a second marriage." Like some gay men today he was attracted to women for other things than reproduction and sexual relations.

George Washington's heterosexuality resembles his religious feelings. He believed in Providence but little more. He disliked religion and had no clerical friends whatsoever. But he did not want to make an issue with such powerful and nasty people as clerics. Mason Weems, nonetheless, invented scenes of his praying; painters dutifully imagined them; and even today the religious claim him as one of the rocks of the republic. Weems even claimed to be a parson for a mythical Mount Vernon parish.

Washington was willing to conform socially up to a point. He was a vestryman and occasionally attended Church of England and later Anglican church services in his parish. But he did this only for social show. He approached religious people like military obstacles. When his aide Alexander Hamilton got in a fight with a loathsome Congregationalist, Washington soothed the minister's feelings and ignored him. When Lafayette returned to France after the war, he wrote Washington in 1785 for advice on trying to convince King Louis XVI to reinstate tolerance for Protestants. Lafayette supported Protestants because he hated the Catholic church not because he loved Protestants. The Edict of Nantes had established tolerance in 1598 but Louis XIV had revoked it in 1685. Washington responded cautiously: he wrote, "remember my dear friend it is a part of the military art to reconnoiter & feel your way, before you engage too deeply. More is oftentimes effected by regular approaches, than by an open assault; from the first too, you may make a good retreat—from the latter (in case of repulse) it rarely happens."

Washington disguised his true feelings and beliefs. And when he did rebel, he often did it quietly. He attended church (much as he had taken a wife and become head of a family) in order not to offend society; to fit in, to conform. Even after he had become the great hero, ex-president and simple farmer at Mount Vernon, he opposed the church passively. He resigned as a vestryman and never took communion. "After the minister, annoyed that when Martha took communion the President waited in his pew, preached a sermon in Washington's presence concerning the duty of great men to set a good example, Washington never attended church again."

So with his love of men he never made an issue of his desires like the Marquis de Sade, who shouted from the Bastille that they were torturing him. The people of Paris arose July 14, 1789, and tore the mammoth prison down, stone by stone. Washington would not have really understood either de Sade's glorious documentation of the many varieties of sexuality in his time or the Parisian attack on the Bastille. Lafayette sent him the key to the prison. But his use of religion and of flirting with boys was more subtle. When he was behind in his correspondence with Lafayette, Washington wrote, July 25, 1785: "I stand before you as a Culprit; but to *repent & be forgiven* are the precepts of Heaven: I do the former—do you practise the latter, & it will be participating of a divine attribute." I read this as Washington's making his lovers divine; someone else might read it as an example of his belief in original sin and the need for redemption.

SENSUALITY OF 18TH CENTURY

Randolph Trumbach argues that "Europe was switching from adult male libertines who had sex with boys and with women to a world divided between a majority of men and women who desired only the opposite gender, and a minority of men and women who desired only the same gender." Trumbach's generalization so far rests largely on research in London and might be tested in Naples, New York, Vienna, Athens, Potsdam, Paris, Madrid, Boston or Williamsburg, Virginia. For Washington's time three key figures might be Thomas Fairfax who initiated the boy (Fairfax could never be called a "fop," a "rake," or an "effeminate"; his influence on the young Washington has been discussed above); William Byrd II; and James Wilson (1742–1798), a close contemporary of Washington, whose diary shows that William Byrd II's behavior may not be so atypical as some have claimed.

Martha Washington was related to William Byrd II (1674–1744) and William Byrd III (1728–1777) remained a close friend of the Washington family. Martha and George were still teenagers when the elder Byrd died, but their relations were quite intertwined. They may even have had access to William Byrd II's writings. The elder Byrd did not typify Virginia planters because he could write so remarkably well. But he may have typified the Virginia Tobacco aristocracy in his sexual mores. Byrd recorded his lusty adventures in his *Secret Diary*, letters and other writings some of which still await publication. Using the pseudonym Inamorato, he described himself: "Never did the sun shine upon a swain who had more combustible matter in his constitution than the unfortunate Inamorato. Love broke out upon him before his beard . . ." His entry for October 4, 1718, suggests an active appetite: "I went to visit Mrs. A-l-n and committed uncleanness with the maid because the mistress was not at home. However when the mistress came I rogered her and about 12 o'clock went home and ate a plum cake for supper." In St. James park in London he took a woman into the bushes and fucked her.

Byrd read Petronius's *Satyricon* and translated one of the stories into English. In 1694, a translation appeared in London: *The Satyr of Titus Petronius Arbiter, A Roman Knight, with Its Fragments Recovered at Belgrade, 1688, Made English by Mr. Burnaby of the Middle Temple, and Another Hand.* "Another Hand" may have been Byrd; he was a friend of William Burnaby, a London playwright and translator. Washington could have read this translation or more likely knew another by his favorite author Joseph Addison. Through Lord Fairfax (Washington's patron) he may have been aware of the notorious "A Declamation against the Inconstancy of Women" included in the *Satyricon*.

The view of sexual intercourse portrayed in the *Satyricon* and exemplified in Byrd's life contains a remarkable acceptance of fate, the way things happen and are. Fellini's movie based on the book captures some of the acceptance of all forms of sexual love and lust. The only "problem" in the *Satyricon* is in not being able to become sexually aroused. Byrd himself addressed detumescence in his discussion of ginseng, which he raised on his lands. The herb's virtue gives "an uncommon warmth and vigor to the blood and frisks the spirits beyond any other cordial." However, he found it "of little use in the feats of love."

The *Satyricon* view of the world closely resembles that of both Martha and George in their acceptance of their sexuality, their position in society and the limitations of their compatriots. Theirs was never a romantic or Faustian affair; they always remained slightly detached. Martha's first marriage to a cousin of the Byrds could not be called a happy one but she demonstrated a willingness to go along. In contrast with her first husband, Washington was a vast improvement. Far preferable to cousin William Byrd III who provided an example of the limitations of the Virginian planter: "He eventually dissipated his inherited fortune by indulging his passions for thoroughbred horse racing, gambling for high stakes, personal luxuries, and fine houses."

In *About Time, Exploring the Gay Past* (Expanded edition, 1991) Martin Duberman has published a diary from 1773 attributed to James Wilson (1742–1798). Whether the diary belonged to the great Pennsylvanian writer, politician and Supreme Court justice has been questioned; but the authenticity of the dates, the narrative and the locale seem genuine. They demonstrate the diarist's very promiscuous and active sexual adventures. On January 7, 1773, he met a young woman: "Danced with her and aroused all of my passion. She resisted much, holding her limbs together, but my blood being up I thrust her vigorously and she opened with a scream." By April he reported "One testicle much swollen. Lucretia squeezed of it last night. I called to her to desist but she obeyed not." In May he met another woman "near the road and in some bushes. All over in ten minutes."

In the eighteenth century loose sexual morals were legendary. In Concord, Massachusetts, for instance, there was a remarkable change in the number of pregnant brides between the eighteenth and nineteenth centuries. At the time of the American Revolution a large percentage of the women who were married bore a child before nine months after their wedding; by the time of Emerson and Thoreau in the 1830s, most brides bore their first child only after nine months. The spread of Methodism and other religions combined with the developing cult of true womanhood which emphasized piety, purity and domesticity—all worked to reorganize the libertinism of the eighteenth century. Washington never lived into the Victorian world but his image and memory became transformed then into a religious, heterosexual cherry tree hatchet man.

While these changes swept the northern European community, their effects on men in the military services have not been explored.

REVOLUTIONARY WAR

George Washington and his compatriots grew up and acted within a world of eighteenth century values. Those values led them to resist George III's attempt to expand his empire. The Americans were alarmed to watch the growth of royal power; "between 1680 and 1780 the British army and navy trebled in size." As the monarch tried to force the colonies to pay for their subjugation, some believed they could live cheaper and freer without a monarchy. They launched a new republic. John Adams (first vice-president and second president of the United States) estimated that one third of the people supported the American Revolution; one third supported the king; and one third were waiting to see who won. With victory, the most rabid Tories fled, the fence sitters became the loud patriots, and the soldiers who fought the war returned home.

George Washington never wavered in his support of the new United States. As a young man he had hoped for advancement within the British army and had at first done well with General Braddock. After the general's death, Washington wrote to his successor in January 1757, that had Braddock lived, "I should have met with preferment agreeable to my wishes." The new commander Loudoun at first thought Washington was a French spy, and he had only contempt for the colonials. Washington's other great grievance was with the royal handling of the Ohio Company's land grants. George III in the 1763 Royal Proclamation had closed all land west of the Appalachian Mountains to European settlement. Good news for the native Americans was bad news for the Virginia land speculators.

In 1775 George Washington, ready to fight, attended the Continental Congress in full dress uniform. John Adams nominated him commander of the armed resisters who had fought the British in Lexington and Concord (April 19, 1775) and then on Bunker (and Breed's) Hill (June 17, 1775). Washington took command of the continental troops at the Cambridge Common, July 3, 1775; the rebel army in Charlestown, Cambridge and Dorchester kept the British bottled up inside Boston. After cannons captured from Fort Ticonderoga were placed on Dorchester Heights, the British evacuated Boston on March 17, 1776.

The American Revolutionary War was both long and bloody. Washington held his commission as commander from July, 1775 until December 1783, almost eight and a half years. Among United States troops a higher percentage were killed than in any other war excepting the Civil War. The British had overwhelming land and sea power but they were never able to focus their might at any one point against the revolutionary army. Whether from luck or strategy or both, Washington managed to keep himself out of the hands of the British. They occupied New York throughout most of the war (1776–1783) and with effort they could conquer any port town; however, they failed to take any ground inland. Even Philadelphia which the British held for awhile had to be abandoned as indefensible.

Washington had only to persevere to win. The British, however, could not just survive; they had to triumph. The Redcoats suffered their first great defeat in 1777 at Saratoga. Dashing General Johnny Burgoyne had attempted to sever the United States by an invasion from Montreal to New York City. United States backwoodsmen, regulars and Native American allies trapped him in upstate New York. They forced Burgoyne to surrender with 5,700 troops after he had been surrounded. Had Burgoyne's indigenous allies remained with him, he might have survived. Had his native allies stayed with him and the United States allies deserted, the results of the battle and of the war itself would have been reversed.

After the Saratoga victory the French signed an alliance with the United States and soon provided massive financial, military and naval assistance to the revolution. Even so, French support did not bring automatic victory. In 1779 the United States army under General Lincoln surrendered 5,000 troops to the British at Charleston, S.C. The British subsequently attempted to make inroads in the South, which they believed was filled with royalists. In 1781, however, Washington and Lafayette bottled Cornwallis up at Yorktown as the French fleet gained control of the Chesapeake Bay. Cornwallis surrendered with 8,000 troops on October 19, 1781. Scattered fighting continued until the peace treaty was signed in Paris in 1783 and the British evacuated their remaining troops. George Washington then retired from the army in December, 1783.

As a commander, Washington had used a relatively simple strategy: that of not getting caught. He escaped the British first in New York and then in New Jersey and Pennsylvania. When he had to abandon the nation's capitol (then in Philadelphia) for the winter of 1778, a Frenchman said to Benjamin Franklin (U.S. ambassador in Paris) that the British had captured Philadelphia. Franklin answered, "No, Philadelphia has captured the British." While many died, the United States avoided any grand defeats like Saratoga or Yorktown. In 1783 Washington correctly assessed his army in relation to the British: the Americans had "numbers infinitely less, composed of men oftentimes half starved, always in rags, without pay, and experiencing, at times, every species of distress which human nature is capable of undergoing."

One might ask whether Washington's military genius derived from some gay sensibility. The ordinary masculine thrust pushes forward and attacks, always asserting itself. The one rebel outward attack, that into Canada, was a total disaster. Washington proved a genius in avoiding direct combat with the great British army. He spun webs like a spider and from time to time captured the British. When they pursued him, more often than not, he disappeared. His greatest military maneuvers were his retreats: getting out of New York in 1776 with his army intact; and then in moving across New Jersey, where on December 26, 1776, he defeated the British mercenaries who were hung over from holiday celebrations.

Washington never played the role of angry and vengeful father, the role inevitable for the British and George III. Instead he played the part of the protective mother, gathering his children together, cuddling them here, spanking them there, but holding the army together. In *The American Revolution* (1985), Edward Countryman explains that "simply keeping the army intact was as important as winning battles. This, in face of enormous adversity, was George Washington's great achievement." His relations with the Congress likewise represent a careful exercise in indirect and passive accommodation.

Of course, Washington was not the only officer. There were many generals all vying for favors. Washington's relationship with the so-called Conway Cabal provides a model of the jealous queen outraged at some rival. True, Thomas Conway was an adventurer; true, he and some others criticized the commander. But Washington's notion that they were plotting to get his position rests more in his own fantasies than in their actions.

GEORGE WASHINGTON AT VALLEY FORGE, PENNSYLVANIA, 1778.
19th century engraving by J. McGoffin.

He fought for prominence and honor against a number of rivals such as Light Horse Harry Lee or Horatio Gates. In his battle with Conway and any other officer who might challenge his position, Washington emerged no less successful than he did over the British.

Washington worked closely with the Continental Congress (until 1789 there was no executive or judiciary). For instance, between December 23, 1778 and February 3, 1779, he lived with the President of the Congress, Henry Laurens along with his son John Laurens. They devoted many hours handling army patronage. Speculators made fortunes with army contracts. And a flood of applicants wanted commissions as officers in the army. Soldiers of fortune not unlike Steuben and Lafayette flooded into the United States hoping to sell their services. And Americans envied every appointment given a foreigner. Spunky John Adams snorted that they "Quarrell like Cats and Dogs. . . . military officers, high and low." And mixing metaphors a bit: "They worry one another like Mastiffs, Scrambling for Rank and Pay like Apes for Nuts." Washington steered through these political seas admirably. His favorite evening entertainment was cracking and eating nuts by the fireside with his boys.

UNIFORM FUN

Cross-dressing in the eighteenth century may have been less a problem than in later centuries as gender identification became stricter and stricter. In the eighteenth century cross dressing between genders was probably less scandalous than between classes. Thus if a commoner tried to dress like either a duke or duchess, crossing the class barrier would be a more frightful indiscretion than crossing the gender barrier. Nobles had then (and perhaps even now) wide berth for their desires. The famous Charles-Geneviève, Chevalier d'Eon (1728–1810), a contemporary of Washington, was celebrated and decorated in the court of Louis XV for work as an international spy, the James Bond of that time. D'Eon during most of his life dressed only in women's clothing.

Men taking women's roles may be less rare than the sparse record would indicate. "Mollies" served in Washington's armies; these were often classified as washerwomen. Braddock was unhappy in his 1755 campaign at Monongahela that so many washerwomen went with the army. No one seems to have checked whether these were indeed gender females. And the men themselves on occasion took the roles of women in dancing and in plays. Thus at Fort Cumberland (then under Washington's command) the 1755 Christmas festivities, of course, included a banquet and plenty of alcohol. They began dinner at three in the afternoon; ate, offered toasts, and "pass'd an hour in Singing and taking a Cheerful glass." But then they amused themselves "with acting part of a Play, and spending the Night in mirth, Jollity and Dancing." They parted "very affectionately" at midnight "remembering all Absent Friends."

Too seldom have the joy in wearing or making women's clothing been considered with the joy of wearing or worshiping figures in uniform. Washington and most of his fellow officers had a deep attachment to their uniforms. Those without or with incomplete uniforms or clothing were again and again referred to as "naked." While portrait painting at Mount Vernon in 1772, Charles Willson Peale was throwing the javelin with the boys (including the naughty Bryan Fairfax and Washington) and describes the group as "all stripped to the buff," when they only had their coats off "with shirt sleeves rolled up." Washington significantly did not strip "to the buff" for his throw. And at the end of the Revolutionary War, Washington wrote Congress that the troops had "patiently endured hunger, nakedness and cold." To be without a proper uniform was nakedness itself.

Washington spent hours fussing over his uniform, his hairdo, his sword and other military paraphernalia. One of his most stunning displays came in his trip from Virginia to Boston in February and March 1756. He spent four days in Philadelphia having all his clothes fitted just right. George himself designed the Virginia army uniform: "the coat to be faced and cuffed with scarlet and trimmed with silver; a scarlet waistcoat with silver lace; blue breeches; and a silver laced hat." Swords were festooned in gold and scarlet knots. In a letter, September 23, 1756, to Sarah Fairfax (taken by some to be evidence of a romance), Washington seemed most interested in fitting his shirts properly: "I have sent a piece of Irish Linnen, a piece of Cambrick, and a Shirt to measure by. The Shirt Fits tolerably well, yet, I would have the others made with somewhat narrower Wrist bands: Ruffles deeper by half an Inch: and the Collars by three quarters of an Inch, which is in other respects of proper bigness."

One of Washington's favorite aides, John Laurens, followed the general's lead in attending to uniform details. He wrote his father from Washington's Valley Forge headquarters during the harsh winter of 1778 requesting scarlet cloth, "hair powder and pomatum," a comb, "blue and buff cloth, lining, twist, yellow flat double gilt buttons" along with "corded dimity for waistcoats and breeches." Laurens also needed "A pair of gold epaulettes and a saddle cloth may be added, if not too expensive."

There is an odd conceit that only nudity is sexual. Clothing and costume, however, mean as much or more than the unmarked body. Likewise there is a conceit that clothing insofar as it is sexual is designed to attract the opposite sex. But in fact clothing is one of the ultimate forms of masturbation, a taking of joy in one's own self ornamentation. And after pleasing the self, most clothing is designed for one's own gender. Women dress to impress women and men to tickle men. Particularly in the armed forces, the men dress up for each other; they parade for their generals and sergeants. And the uniforms (not without attraction to the opposite gender, of course) primarily attract members of the same gender. The marine, army, navy ads mean to attract boys.

The use of the word "naked" differed markedly then from our own time. Generally "naked" now means displaying cocks, breasts, asses and balls. In Washington's time, "naked" meant not displaying one's proper rank. Today, we might say, I wasn't "dressed" for a funeral, graduation, swim-suit contest, or party. At Valley Forge in 1778, when they talked about the "nakedness" of the men, they didn't mean that their balls were hanging out. They meant they lacked proper uniforms so that you could distinguish ranks by a glance. When Horatio Greenough's statue of Washington was unveiled in the Capitol, public scandal erupted because he had given Washington a Michelangelean body draped only with a toga.

WASHINGTON'S GAY MESS

Like General Braddock, Washington assembled a group of very young men as his aides-de-camp. The "boys" lived, worked and slept together with their man who watched over them as closely as a mother hen. While he led a revolution, his "family" lived in a very eighteenth century way. During the French and Indian War, the Virginia *Gazette* in 1756 had uncovered "vice and debauchery" in Washington's headquarters. Before the American and French Revolutions, the aristocracy monopolized the officer corps who fostered loose habits. Although Washington maintained a Baron and a Marquis in his camp, there were few nobles in the American Revolutionary army. All were adventurers in that they had staked their lives against King George, but they were by no means ready to abolish all rank and privilege.

To various degrees Washington and his companions had mastered the ideology both of independence and of living without a king. Alexander Hamilton had written against the Tories. John Laurens had studied in Switzerland and absorbed the revolutionary teachings of Geneva's Jean Jacques Rousseau. In Prussia Frederick Steuben had lost his position at the end of the French and Indian War because his family was not noble enough and he had not been discreet enough with his boys. Thomas Paine's *Common Sense* had rung a cord in January 1776 both among the soldiers and throughout the country. Paine had denounced monarchy and called King George an ass. He called kingship "the most preposterous invention the Devil ever set on foot for the promotion of idolatry." The July 4, 1776, Declaration of Independence sealed the rebels' commitment to "Life, Liberty and the Pursuit of Happiness" to which they had mutually pledged to "each other our lives, our fortunes, and our sacred honor."

Love for each other drives soldiers as forcefully as their ideology. In his history of the war (*The Glorious Cause*), Robert Middlekauff observes that "The eighteenth-century battlefield was, compared with the twentieth an intimate theater, especially intimate in the engagements of the Revolution which were usually small even by the standards of the day." On the battlefield, soldiers need to know who will stand by their side; running was considered disgraceful; and to have come through a battle while all your beloved friends died leaves every soldier changed. To enter Washington's mess group you needed to be handsome (perhaps well hung like Alexander Hamilton). But you also needed to have proven yourself in battle. Washington had done that early and he gained fifteen minutes of fame in London for his 1754 letter, in which he wrote, "I heard the bullets whistle, and, believe me, there is something charming in the sound." Steuben, Lafayette, Hamilton, Laurens and all his intimates had stood up to fire.

Washington's group not only fought on the battlefield but also on the dueling fields. Washington himself avoided duels, which were commonplace in Virginia. But his aides all became embroiled in such affairs of honor. Lafayette and Laurens at different times challenged detractors of Washington to duels. Hamilton acted as second to Laurens in his duel with Charles Lee in December, 1778. Laurens challenged Lee's "grossest and most opprobrious terms of personal abuse, which He Col Laurens thought him bound to resent, as well on account of the relation he bore to General Washington as from motives of personal friendship." Laurens was slightly wounded and Lee seriously, but the latter was so moved by the youth's "bearing" that he exclaimed "he could have hugged the boy." Love has many different faces. Hamilton himself died in a duel in 1804.

Washington's mess group shared many experiences of comradeship common among soldiers. They differed, however, from other mess groups in being at command central which issued orders for the whole army. And they differed from American soldiers in later wars because they (excepting Steuben) had taken an oath of allegiance to the King of England. They now repudiated that oath, but many old habits lingered. Washington's "family" and "boys" called themselves "family" and "boys" as the circle around Braddock had done in Washington's youth. They had not yet adopted the nineteenth century masculinization, an odd and charming habit of men trying to prove they are not queer. When not issuing orders to the troops, the atmosphere in Washington's headquarters resembled something of a private boy's school. They vied in showing their love of each other and for demonstrating their love of art, music and literature. This milieu created a space and a freedom to be queer even within the obvious constraints of the battlefield.

While they broke their oaths to the King, many of the officers retained their view of class superiority. In many ways Washington and his boys continued to live the lives of those they were fighting against. The officers retained a class division between themselves and the common soldiers. Washington's boys might be primping with their hair and worrying about the stains on their uniforms while the common soldier lived less elegantly. These privates might not be to every queer's taste: "Soldiers throughout the war apparently disdained use of the vaults, as latrine pits were called, preferring to void wherever taken by the urge." And they had yet to master the nineteenth century gospel of cleanliness: "They also scattered food, scraps, carrion, and garbage throughout camps. They had to be forced to change the straw that served as bedding. And some had to be ordered to bathe."

In this context we need to read the court marshal of Lieutenant Frederick Gotthold in March, 1778. The Lieutenant was found guilty of "attempting to commit *sodomy*, with John Monhort, a soldier." In crossing a class line as well as committing a code violation, Gotthold had to be punished. Benjamin Holcomb had also been court martialed for crossing the lines. This Connecticut Lieutenant had displayed the rank of captain by "wearing a yellow cockade and mounting Guard in that capacity." In this case, his defense of ignorance saved him. Holcomb claimed he had not been aware of the proper officer designation. And, of course, he promised never to do it again.

Gotthold did not do so well. He didn't have a good English name like Holcomb and his crime may have been more serious than "wearing a yellow cockade." In most colonies then (except Pennsylvania), the punishment for sodomy was death. No one is known to have been executed in the eighteenth century as in the more religious seventeenth century. In Gotthold's case, his punishment was to be drummed out of the service. No great pleasure, being drummed out of the army at Valley Forge; nevertheless, not the worst fate ever to befall a queer. Perhaps they only allowed one obvious queer in the army then or maybe only one out queer German? Frederick Steuben who had had to leave Germany under cloud of sodomy charges against him suddenly appeared at Valley Forge to replace Gotthold.

COLD WINTERS, HOT BODIES

Modern readers should be alert to an important difference between warfare then and now. Before railroads, armies could hardly move during the winter because the horses could not get enough forage. Indeed the word "forage" means both "fodder" for horses and "to look for provisions." Feeding humans, for instance at Valley Forge, presented problems secondary only to feeding horses. Buying supplies created difficulties in the Revolutionary War because the supply was limited. There were only so many farms to produce grain and meat; once the frost hit there could be no more crops harvested until the next season.

The armies virtually retired during the winter months. Washington's Christmas attack at Trenton in 1776 and Cornwallis's unsuccessful Princeton response for New Year's 1777 were quite exceptional. In 1776 the season began only in late summer; in 1777 and 1778 in June. As the war concentrated in the South the fighting began earlier: in 1779 and 1780 in April and in 1781 in March. On March 4, 1782, the House of Commons voted to end the war and major fighting stopped.

Basically the soldiers and officers played with themselves between the first frost and the spring thaw. The winters were unusually cold then. During January 1780 New York harbor froze solid for the only time in its recorded history and the Chesapeake Bay froze solid to the mouth of the Potomac. Washington's very dull diary for 1780 only records the weather in his Morristown, N.J. headquarters: January 2nd, "Very cold— about noon it began to Snow, & continued without intermission through the day and night." Not much better on March 31st: "Snowing more or less all day & generally pretty fast." One of Washington's aides explained to a merchant that, "Winter quarters is to us what the stoppage of navigation used to be to you. . . . an increase in business in the way of paper, pens and ink."

In examining the papers—diaries, biographies and letters of Washington's circle—I am struck with what seems to me something extraordinary. Not a word about food (except for Washington's cracking the nuts). Braddock, at least, had a famous cook, but neither Washington, Mercer nor Gist wrote about the cook's creations. By contrast, William Byrd's famous diary has as much or more information about his food life as about his sex life.

Particularly Washington's *Diaries* are remarkable for the absolute absence of food. On this evidence alone I would argue that Washington's sexual interests were entirely anal. On the other hand, his great concern with his false teeth demonstrates some oral interests. His false teeth had been made in England but needed replacement parts which could come only from England. During the war his mouth suffered. Perhaps that's why he talked so much about this teeth and said so little about what else went into his mouth.

While Washington's mess group seldom mentioned food, a handsome youth was something else. John Laurens in February, 1778, spotted "a handsome young lad, who call'd himself Cope, and said he was an ensign in the 55th British." He said he'd had to flee because he'd killed another man in a duel. Lafayette latched right on to him. The mess group gathered a collection to help him, but he spent it on drink. A friend of Lafayette found him "making great noise in a tavern" and saying "so many indecent things" that he arrested Cope. Even so, Lafayette wrote the governor of New York that "the age of the gentleman and his being an enemy in our hands engaged me to indulge his going to Boston." Soon letters came from the English army "in terms very unfavorable to his character." And Washington himself reported the incident to the War Board suggesting the lad was probably not a deserter but a spy.

Hamilton in a long letter of October, 1780, explained to John Laurens the beauties of Major John André, the British officer who had been captured dealing with Benedict Arnold. Hamilton was won over by André's sweetness, which "united a peculiar elegance of mind and manners, and the advantage of a pleasing person." Moreover, he "possessed a pretty taste for the fine arts, and had himself attained some proficiency in poetry, music and painting." A perfect lover: "His sentiments were elevated and inspired esteem, they had a softness that conciliated affection. His elocution was handsome; his address easy, polite and insinuating." Washington despite the pleadings of the boy insisted not only on the death penalty but also on hanging rather than firing squad. Hamilton was profoundly moved by André's last words: "asked if he had any thing to say, he answered: 'nothing but to request you will witness to the world, that I die like a brave man.'"

Washington's headquarters differed from those today; he had no Pentagon. During the Revolution, Washington either rented (from Patriots) or confiscated (from Tories) the largest mansion in the neighborhood. In Cambridge, a big house on Tory row (later Henry Wadsworth Longfellow's residence) became his headquarters. Martha Washington joined him with a coach and servants in mid winter. She maintained a fast social life with concerts, dancing and entertainments. Dorothy Troth Muir identifies nearly a hundred houses where Washington camped in *General Washington's Headquarters 1775–1783* (1977); a third of these houses still stand, many now museums. They were not shanties.

Washington and his boys usually lived comfortably except when they were on the battlefield. At Monmouth Washington wrapped Lafayette into his coat and they slept the night on the field. More often there were beds. Nevertheless among the boys the quarters could become crowded. In October, 1777, John Laurens wrote that his companions were snoring and "are extended before the fire in the style which we practiced in the interior parts of So. Carolina." William Byrd of Westover in his description of the Carolina backcountry had written he was "obliged to lodge very sociably in the same apartment with the family, where, reckoning women and children, we mustered in all no less than nine persons, who all pigged lovingly together." Such close living creates conditions where men can get to know each other physically which offers a first step in knowing each other sexually.

During the war, Washington appointed thirty-three military secretaries or aides-de-camp. His relations with each one deserves study. The work of Emily Stone Whiteley, *Washington and His Aides-de-Camp* (1936), provides some fascinating clues to the gay life among Washington's boys. Recent publication of the Washington, Laurens, Hamilton, Lafayette and other papers offers even more suggestive leads. Some of the aides served only briefly. Aaron Burr, a beauty, was promoted in the spring of 1776 from captain to major but was quickly dismissed for his impertinencies. John Trumbull, appointed July 27, 1775, fled in August, terrified. Whiteley writes that, "As Aide it was his part to receive company and to do the honors of Headquarters to the most distinguished people of the country—'of both sexes,' he plaintively records, being evidently especially terrified by the ladies.' " She concludes, that "without drawing invidious comparisons, it is evident that General Washington had a warm friendship for all of his Aides, and for some a deep affection."

Here I am only going to examine the best documented examples of the men loving men in Washington's mess group. Alexander Hamilton, John Laurens, Frederick Steuben, and Lafayette interweaved their own lives with that of their commander. With the exception of Steuben, who was near the general's age, Washington took his boys in as he had been taken by Lawrence Washington, Thomas Fairfax, Christopher Gist and Edward Braddock. As a boy he learned from the older soldiers. In 1765 with George Mercer, he took his own aide; Mercer was near Washington's age. A poor student but a better profligate, Mercer was in some ways a transitional figure in Washington's relations. In the Revolution, Washington took on younger men and made them a family. During the Revolutionary War, Washington's mess group maintained a close intimacy. They went to battle together, they ate together, and at night blew the candles out together. Even after the war, the survivors maintained ties; some of them even set up house together.

ALEXANDER HAMILTON

"Washington's devotion to Hamilton was so marked," novelist Gertrude Atherton wrote, "that their enemies spread the story that they were father and son." However, none of the dates claimed for Hamilton's birth—1754, 1755, 1756 and 1757—coincide with Washington's 1751–2 visit to the West Indies. Court records nonetheless branded Hamilton as illegitimate, and dour John Adams dismissed him as "the bastard brat of a Scots pedlar." Hamilton's biological father abandoned his family, and his mother Rachel Levine died in 1768. She had been married to another man, who seized her belongings on her death but rejected the two Hamilton children. Although Alexander had gone to Hebrew school, he clung to claims of a noble Christian father and seldom mentioned his mother.

As a teenaged orphan, Alexander Hamilton had learned to cultivate the kindness of men; in his youth he had seen his mother working the rich men to keep her children and herself afloat. Alexander became a clerk on St. Croix for a merchant friend of his mother. Planter Thomas Stevens had befriended both Hamilton and his mother who may have lived with him before her death. Hamilton became something of a lover with the planter's son Edward Stevens, who wrote a decade later: "have you forgot-

ten those Vows of eternal Friendship, which we have so often mutually exchanged?"
On St. Croix young Hamilton also attracted the loving attention of Hugh Knox, a Pres-
byterian clergyman, apothecary and journalist who had fled a scandalous past in New
Jersey and Saba, a smaller island of the Dutch West Indies. Knox encouraged Hamilton's readings in poetry and Greek classics, and he may have helped him polish his
French. Biographer Broadus Mitchell writes that "An immediate sympathy sprang up
between them. Both had the taste for study and literature in a community more given
to ledgers and litigation."

Knox saw that Hamilton's vivid description of the hurricane of 1772 was published
in *The Royal Danish American Gazette*. And on the basis of that publication, the
clergyman organized a fund to send his protégé off to school. The older man later wrote
Hamilton, "I have always had a just & secret pride in having advised you to go to
America, & in having recommended you to some [of] my old friends." Hamilton advanced rapidly and soon entered King's (now Columbia) College where he joined his
boyfriend Edward Stevens. In New York City he lived with thirty-two year old
"bachelor" Hercules Mulligan, a haberdasher acquaintance of Knox. Hercules's shop
carried such decorative items as "gold and silver lace, with some half laces for hats" along
with "gold and silver buttons and loops," as well as "gold and silver treble French
chain." At the same time that Hamilton was living with Hercules Mulligan, the merchant got a woman pregnant. He married her and their son John W. Mulligan eventually became Steuben's secretary and later Hamilton's law clerk. During the war,
Hercules Mulligan served as a Revolutionary spy in New York City. When the British
evacuated and Washington reentered, the general took his first breakfast with Mulligan. Hercules later provided a "resplendent black velvet suit" to Washington when
he became President in 1789. Mulligan and Hamilton were still seeing each other as
late as 1796.

Historians have obscured or avoided explaining Hamilton's quick rise to become
Washington's aide-de-camp on March 1, 1777. The reason the couple took up together
is because they found each other handsome. Hamilton first captured the attention of
General Greene while working out in the New York City "Park (or Fields) where he
was attracted by the competent drill. . . . He sent to compliment Captain Hamilton,
invited him to dinner, and thus began their friendship." Greene in turn introduced the
youth to Washington. Another story has Washington himself picking up Hamilton
in Harlem: "After some conversation with him," Irving writes, "Washington invited
him to his marquee, and thus commenced that intercourse which has indissolubly linked
their memories together."

Despite his cockiness, Hamilton inclined more toward the feminine than any of
Washington's aides. In 1776 at New Brunswick, a soldier reported seeing Hamilton:
"a youth, a mere stripling, small, slender, almost delicate in frame, marching beside
a piece of artillery with a cocked hat pulled down over his eyes, apparently lost in
thought, with his hand resting on the cannon, and every now and then patting it as
he mused, as if it were a favorite horse, or a pet plaything." In a 1778 letter, childhood
friend Edward Stevens wrote that he "was tormented" worrying about Hamilton's
health since the lad had such a delicate constitution ("délicatesse de constitution"). And
as late as 1790, Senator Maclay commented in his diary on Hamilton's "very boyish,
giddy manner."

In Washington's "family" they called Hamilton the "Little Lion." His beauty sprang

ALEXANDER HAMILTON (*ca.* 1755/7–1804)
around the time that he joined the Revolutionary Army and first met
George Washington (1776). Hamilton, then barely out of his teens, soon became
Washington's Hephaestion. Engraving from the original painting by Chappel.

from his carriage which first drew Washington to him and his eyes which made him irresistible to some men and women. The attraction he and Washington felt to each other fulfilled a mainstay fantasy in Anglo literature and life: the dumb, dull fairskinned hunk linked with the Caribbean (or other exotic) wildflower. Beware of that "sparrow cock," Abigail Adams warned her husband, "I have read his heart in his wicked eyes many a time. The very devil is in them. They are lasciviousness itself." John Adams needed no warning, he had himself witnessed Hamilton's "debaucheries" and promised to keep clear of his "puppyhood." The Adams's might maintain their virtue but others willingly flocked to the devil.

The young Lion's handsome figure explains his entry into Washington's inner chambers; his wit explains the long relationship. Hamilton's and Washington's minds intertwined so that their writing, even their thinking becomes indistinguishable. Theirs was a symbiotic relationship that continued in the army and later in the new national government. Washington's mind moved slowly while Hamilton's moved in every direction, brilliantly erratic and unpredictable. Like the subject of his first teenage composition which brought him recognition, Hamilton was a hurricane. The mind may not have genders but it does have variety. Washington needed insemination; Hamilton needed direction and protection. Rather like the Duke of Marlborough and Prince Eugène of Savoy, their interaction conceived something more than the combination of its parts. Biographers of Washington claim that his writings are all his own; biographers of Hamilton argue they are written by Hamilton. But the biographers too often miss the essence of the collaboration in which two men in their love and commitment became irresistible.

Hamilton served as Washington's aide from 1777 until 1781; they both pushed for the Constitution under which Washington was elected President in 1789. He chose Hamilton as his Secretary of the Treasury and their two administrations ended with the famous Farewell Address in 1796. In those years, they had only one big fight, that in the winter of 1780–81. Hamilton married Elizabeth Schuyler in December; Washington responded to this marriage with more than his usual frostiness. Then in February, 1781, the roof fell in. Going to his room, George passed Hamilton going downstairs and told the lion he wanted to see him. The boy took his time while the General watched the clock. When the boy returned, Washington exploded: "Col. Hamilton you have kept me waiting at the head of the stairs these ten minutes. I must tell you Sir you treat me with disrespect." Hamilton replied: "I am not conscious of it Sir, but since you have thought it necessary to tell me so we must part." Washington came back with "Very well if it be your choice."

Typical lover's quarrel for the silliness of the issue. Washington apologized both in writing and through intermediaries. But Hamilton made demands: he would not come back as an aide and he wanted command of a field battalion. "I wished," he wrote the general "to stand rather upon a footing of military confidence than of private attachment." Washington replied that "Your letter . . . has not a little embarrassed me." What about all the other worthy contenders for commands? Hamilton stood firm and got everything he asked; he had a field command at Yorktown. His field service was satisfactory but brief; as the war ended he never got his opportunity to be a Caesar. To his father-in-law, Hamilton wrote "At the end of the war I may say many things to you concerning which I shall impose upon myself 'till then an absolute silence." He hinted that he had the key "to easily unlock the present mystery." If so, he took his "key" to the grave.

Hamilton was an adventurer who would sleep with anyone to further his career. Thus he married Elizabeth Schuyler because she was rich and her father influential. Apologizing to another boyfriend in the family, Hamilton wrote Jack Laurens that the marriage would not change their relationship: "as if after matrimony I was to be less devoted [to you] than I am now." He explained that from a wife he needed what Laurens could not give him: "I am a stranger in this country. I have no property there, no connexions. If I have talents and integrity, (as you say I have) these are justly deemed very spurious titles in these enlightened days." He invited Laurens to witness and to share the "final consummation," the breaking of his bride's hymen.

In Washington's family distinctions among homosexual, heterosexual and bisexual had less significance than between sexual and asexual. Hamilton's letters show him to have been (like Laurens, Lafayette and Steuben) very sexual. His love relations with Laurens will be considered shortly. His relations with Mrs. Peggy (Benedict) Arnold and Mrs. Maria (James) Reynolds likewise demonstrate powerful feelings. As disgraced women, they both resembled his mother Rachel and as Elizabeth Schuyler had fallen into his trap so he fell into their traps. When Washington and Hamilton caught Benedict Arnold's wife Peggy, she staged a grand scene of insanity (clutching her infant) in order to give her traitor husband time to escape. Washington was unmoved; Hamilton cried and pleaded her case. Hamilton also cried and pleaded for Major André, the stunningly beautiful British contact, who was captured while Arnold escaped. Washington insisted on hanging André as a spy. Hamilton wrote a detailed account of his attraction to Peggy Arnold and John André. He sent the account in his letters to friend John Laurens and fiancée Elizabeth Schuyler which evidently provided an extended part of his love making. Documents uncovered in the twentieth century show Peggy Arnold's pathetic scene was only part of the Arnold plot, while the Arnolds also duped John André.

The case with Maria Reynolds became quite physical as Hamilton fucked her over a year for $2,100. James and Maria Reynolds were married but they had a partner in Jacob Clingman. The team was busy selling Maria's body to Hamilton, extorting money from him, demanding positions in the Treasury Department and trying to sell the story to Hamilton's opponents. What won Hamilton over to Maria Reynolds was her sob story: she went to his office and begged his help "to reclaim a prodigal Husband who had deserted her and his Creditors at New York." The federal capitol and Hamilton's office as Secretary of the Treasury were then in Philadelphia; he conducted his later meetings in her nearby bedroom. After several visits, Mr. Reynolds appeared and demanded blackmail money. When that was paid, he demanded more money for each time Hamilton visited (alienation of affections). Strangely, Hamilton ended the whole matter by publishing all of their correspondence. Maria later divorced Reynolds and married Clingman.

In his *Federalist Paper #6* written to support ratification of the Constitution, Hamilton had denounced "loose women" and listed all the women "whose political intrigues led to religious persecution or foreign adventurism." That description according to his opponents described his own influence on Washington. In the middle of the Reynolds scandal, Washington sent Hamilton a gift: "a token of my sincere regard and friendship for you, and as a remembrance of me . . . a Wine cooler for four bottles."

In studying Hamilton's sexual/love life, the major question should not be whether he preferred men or women. The real question (which must be asked of any hustler or sexual adventurer): what if anything (beyond benefits) might be the object of his/her desire? Hamilton always said fame and glory, but such a pat answer sounds like the religious fanatic who claims divine love leads them to kill nonbelievers. John Adams called Hamilton "a proud-spirited, conceited, aspiring mortal, always pretending morality" but with totally "debauched" morals. Much has been written on the question of Hamilton's sincerity, but that question comes more from the Reformation than from the Enlightenment. Hamilton lived in the eighteenth century of courtly intrigue and never understood how scandalous his revelations and honesty about adultery would be to Puritans and nineteenth century romantics.

Hamilton's view of sex/love as manipulation with either man or woman caught him in a trap of his own design. Strangely, he blamed James Monroe (later fifth president of the United States) for his troubles in the Reynolds affair. In a wild bullying gesture he threatened Monroe to a duel. Monroe sensibly avoided that, but in 1804, Hamilton fought a duel on another issue but with Monroe's second, Aaron Burr. Burr killed Hamilton. Hamilton's own second claims that the young lion never fired at all. If this account is true, then Hamilton used the duel as suicide: he would rather die than retire to a quiet domestic life like Washington's at Mount Vernon.

JOHN LAURENS

Washington never chose an ugly boy to become aide-de-camp. He himself was a handsome man; consequently his boys could easily not only love him but also love each other. Hamilton's and Washington's relationship to Laurens, of course, contained a strong element of self interest. In the 18th century both friendship and love had to fill such a requirement. Between 1775 and 1777, John's father, Henry Laurens (1724–1792) led the revolution in South Carolina. From 1777 to 1778 he was president of the Continental Congress, which had the final say on military matters including officers' commissions. In 1779 he was sent on a diplomatic mission to Holland but was captured en route by the British. Held in the Tower of London until 1781, the elder Laurens then became a negotiator for the Paris treaty, which ended the war. Son John, consequently, provided a useful connection with his father. Nonetheless, had he been ugly John Laurens would never have been chosen as an aide nor have become Hamilton's bosom buddy.

John (or Jack) Laurens came from a prominent Huguenot family in South Carolina; his birthdate has been given as 1753, 1754 and 1756. He went to school in Geneva and studied law in England. Returned to the United States to fight in 1777, he immediately became Washington's aide-de-camp. In a South Carolina campaign in the summer of 1780 he was captured in the defeat of Charleston, but was soon released on parole (free but excluded from fighting). In December 1780 he went on a most successful diplomatic mission to France, where he obtained needed funds for the army. He returned, fought at Yorktown and was killed in a minor skirmish at Combahee Ferry, South Carolina, August 1782. Washington wrote, "No man possesed more of the *amor patriae.*"

John Laurens' father tried to raise his son straight but failed to save Jack from the 18th century sensuality. By all accounts Laurens was a stunning beauty. After meeting the boy when he was making a delivery in East Florida, Governor James Grant asked Jack to move to England with him in 1770. Father said no and the son reluctantly wrote the older man: *Nil est Tam difficile quod Solertia non vincat* [Nothing's too difficult for wit to overcome]. The governor was thirty years older than the teenage boy; he had served in the French and Indian War with Washington and had indulged George Mercer with him to South Carolina. Can we believe that Governor Grant asked for the boy's hand before he had enjoyed his body? As a General he later led British troops against the colonies; he almost captured Lafayette at Brandywine in 1778. After the war Grant became a member of Parliament.

His father warned John: "The Evil of *Prodigality* is not confined to the Loss of Money. Loss of time is a greater, & bad example possibly the greatest." In South Carolina Jack's French tutor formed "an attachment to a Trumpery Woman who Travels with him & whose quality is doubtful." Father Henry's warning to his son: "All, All, sacrificed upon the Knees of a little Freckled Faced ordinary Wench." And worse examples abounded in South Carolina. Jack's cousin Mary Bremar had attended her sister's funeral when the brother-in-law began an affair over the wife's coffin. Young Mary soon became pregnant and when the baby was due, the husband tried to sneak her out of Charleston, but before the ship left, the baby was born and the child died five days latter out of neglect. Henry Laurens wrote his son, "There's unnatural Adultery & I am afraid Murder. The Scene is Black. My Tears continue flowing & I can't describe it."

With all the debauchery and profligacy abounding, Henry Laurens decided London would ill serve his son for further education. Jack was sent to Geneva, a stern Protestant, democratic stronghold. Young Laurens did well there and then in 1774 entered the Middle Temple in London to study law. He soon impregnated the daughter of a family friend—the young woman's father later became a Trustee of the Bank of England. Jack married Mary Manning in October 1776, but he left for America by way of France in January 1777. More than revolutionary fervor to fight in the War for Independence or simple male callousness may have motivated Laurens (like Lafayette a year later) to leave their wives so near childbirth. To many men childbirth can represent a threat; a combination of womb envy and competition with the newborn for the woman's affection often bring out or intensify existing homosexual feelings. In any case, Laurens not only took off but he also hooked up almost immediately with a boyfriend, John White from Philadelphia who was then in Paris. They travelled from France, stopped in South Carolina, joined the Continental Army, went north and fought together at Brandywine, where White was killed in battle. Laurens rejoined his wife briefly when he went to France in 1781 but he was glad to return to the battlefield and avoid her.

Washington's aides-de-camp routinely knew French, Greek and Latin. (Lafayette and Steuben knew only a little English). In speaking to each other, they could use code to cover their libidinous intent. Thus on December 18, 1779, John Laurens in a letter to Alexander Hamilton casually dropped (using Greek letters) the phrase *kalos ka agathos*. Roughly translated, "the good and the beautiful," the phrase only came into use in the 5th century BCE, when the Athenian ideal of beauty (*kalos*) was linked (*ka*) with the Spartan ideal of valor (*agathos*). In English the term has been used among boy lovers as a code, while in Greece the usage is still understood among lovers. Recently I met a man in Athens' Harmony Square and we went to a by-the-hour hotel. He had beautiful thighs and a lovely cock; the room had wall to wall mirrors. I blew him and when we were lingering in detumescence, (he only spoke Greek) he said "how was I" and I answered *kalos ka agathos*. His whole body smiled and then I thought he asked "Do you want to do it again?" and as I went down on him he laughed and said, "No, no, I meant do you want to meet again." So we met again the next day.

LT. COL. JOHN LAURENS (*ca.* 1753–1782), AIDE-DE-CAMP TO GEORGE WASHINGTON
and probable lover of Alexander Hamilton. Painting by John Singleton Copley.
Courtesy of South Caroliniana Library, University of South Carolina.

Discussing the Greek tongues of Washington's aides, John C. Miller, in his 1959 biography of Hamilton, claims that, "The friendships thus formed in the army were compared by the young men themselves to that of Damon and Pythias, and they expressed their devotion in the high-flown literary language of the day." Many academics echo Miller's thesis that these phrases are only rhetorical, common conventions. Their argument is faulty. Neither Washington nor any of his aides referred to Damon, Pythias or Corydon, or other shepherds in Virgil's *Eclogues* and *Odes* who sang of their love of men. Such literary references may have provided polite or euphemistic designations of butt fucking and cocksucking. But does euphemism imply the opposite? Does the use of a nice word mean that what prudes consider nasty or unspeakable never happens?

"Hamilton and Laurens were not merely soldiers doing a job," according to Miller, "they were classical scholars whose thoughts and actions were colored by the grandeur of antiquity. They lived—and often died—by the code of the heroes of Plutarch." Hamilton kept notes on his reading of Plutarch from an English translation. He read with particular care the life of Lycurgus, the founder of Sparta; and in his spare time (while he was supposed to be doing the payroll) commented: "Every lad had a lover or friend who take [sic] care of his education and shared in the praise or blame of his virtues or vices. It was the same with the women." His misreading on "take" (should be "took") may be as significant as an inelegant pun of his. The Spartan's realm was called Lacedae-monia (from which the English word "laconian" for tight lipped); Theopompus of Sparta was called Philolacon. Philo, of course, means love; Hamilton then wrote "(La––d–s)"; Theopompus was thus a lover of lads. Hamilton's twisted philology (love of words) demonstrates minor wit and less literary flourish, but a clear understanding of the usage of "lads" in his army and in Sparta.

The letter John Laurens received from Alexander Hamilton in April, 1779, certainly contains the word "sensibility," but the passion for another man exceeds the demands of empty literary convention: "You should not have taken advantage of my sensibility to steal into my affections without my consent. But as you have done it and as we are generally indulgent to those we love, I shall not scruple to pardon the fraud you have committed . . . if . . . you will always continue to merit the partiality, which you have so artfully instilled into me." In his reply Laurens acknowledges and reciprocates Hamilton's love when he writes back, "how many violent struggles I have had between duty and inclination—how much my heart was with you, while I appeared to be most actively employed here."

In September, Hamilton writes "like a jealous lover, when I thought you slighted my caresses, my affection was alarmed and my vanity piqued. I had almost resolved to lavish no more of them upon you and to reject you as an inconstant and an ungrateful ––––." (Is "slut" the word left out? or is it a Greek word like *pornos*?) And again in September 1780, Hamilton replies to Laurens' desire for more letters: "I have conveyed your reproof to the lads. . . . Writing or not writing to you, you know they love you and sympathise in all that concerns you." And he closes with "My ravings are for your own bosom." And later again "The General and all the lads send you their love." In February, 1781 Hamilton wrote, "Do justice to my regard for you. Assure yourself that it is impossible more ardently to wish for your health safety pleasure and success than I do."

This 18th century language of sensibility may have been common among the army officers of the time (but where are the studies?). If so they represent neither latent nor suppressed but instead openly expressed homosexual feelings within the military. These letters were read to the whole group gathered around the general in the evening. Washington enjoyed hearing his boys read and chat while he cracked his nuts. Little reserve is observed and not much classical illusion. For instance, Hamilton wrote: "Cold in my professions, warm in my friendships, I wish my Dear Laurens, it might be in my power by action rather than words to convince you that I love you." This common literary conceit—words will never express my love—raises the question of what "act" exactly Hamilton had in mind.

While they flirted in Greek, Latin and French, Hamilton at least could call on the Anglo-Saxon. When writing to Laurens, Hamilton admonished him: "mind you do justice to the length of my nose and don't forget that I . . ." Here the manuscript has been mutilated so that the rest of the sentence is lost, but I would read "have a corresponding part." There is a folk tradition that men with big noses have big cocks. And Hamilton asked rhetorically: "After reviewing what I have written, I am ready to ask myself what could have put it into my head to hazard this *Jeu de follie* [crazy game]. Do I want a wife? No." This letter concludes; "Did I only intend to frisk? In this I have succeeded, but I have done more, I have have gratified my feelings by lengthening out the only kind of intercourse now in my power with my friend." Big cock—"lengthening"—our fucking—"intercourse"? These are not common rhetorical phrases such as "your obedient servant" but *double entendre*. Even so George Washington surprisingly gave that cliche a gay twist, when he wrote Lafayette that after the war, they could retire together to Mount Vernon "where I will endeavour . . . to shew you how much and how sincerly, I am, Your Affectionate and obedient servant."

In a letter dated September 16, 1780, to Laurens, Hamilton had distinguished between love *à l'americaine* and *à la française*. Hamilton's mother was French; perhaps he learned his French from her; certainly he was bilingual. As Washington's aide, his linguistic skills were particularly useful in communicating with Lafayette and Steuben (who at first knew at best tourist English) and with the French military. John Laurens himself was bilingual. Their mastery of French if not love *à la française* may account for Hamilton's and Laurens' making such quick and strong ties with Lafayette and Steuben. Lafayette either already knew or learned to play *jeu de folie* himself. He wrote May 25, 1778, sending his "warmest thanks" to Laurens' father for having "progenited a son like yours whose compagny and friendship is so agreable to me in camp . . . and tho' you dint think much of me when you did get him, I however acknowledge myself under great obligations to you for that so well performed work of yours."

GILBERT LAFAYETTE

All of the aides in Washington's headquarters loved him and vied for his affections. In his dealings with the lads the commander kept teasing them, leading the boys on and playing them off against each other. His closest ties, however, were with a young Frenchman, Gilbert Lafayette (1757–1834), whom in Gershwin-style George called "the man I love." Alexander Hamilton and Jack Laurens served as teachers, translators and interpreters for Lafayette after he joined Washington (July 31, 1777). A teenager when he left France, Lafayette's hazel eyes, red hair and puppydog obedience rapidly won Washington's heart. Lafayette's father had died when he was a child and his mother when he was a teenager. This orphan found his first family with his new commander in chief. He claimed Washington's "very intimate" friendship. When the couple went into the field, Washington kept an anxious eye on his movements. After the battle of Monmouth in 1778 the two spent the night inside the general's great coat snuggled together under a tree. By 1780, Lafayette could write the general that "my sentiment has increased to such a point, the world knows nothing about."

Lafayette was stunningly exotic to the Americans, who had grown up amid the long protracted wars between France and England. In the French and Indian War Washington had fought many battles against the French armies. France under Louis XIV (1638–1715) and Louis XV (1715–1774) had come to dominate Europe culturally, politically, and, in the Americas physically in the West Indies, Montreal and Louisiana. Lafayette unlike other soldiers of fortune traced his noble pedigree back to Charlemagne. And he was no younger son without prospects. Through marriage and inheritance the noble youth was one of the wealthiest men in France. His family had great influence in the court of Louis XVI (1774–1793); one relative was French ambassador to England; another first lady in waiting for the Queen, Marie Antoinette.

Among the earliest of his class to rebel against monarchy and aristocracy, Lafayette had defied a direct order from Louis XVI in coming to America in 1777. His foreign service, however, endeared him to Marie Antoinette and other French patriots; Lafayette became a popular hero in France like Franklin and Washington. When Louis XVI signed an alliance with the United States in 1778, as an aide to Washington Lafayette could build bridges between the ancien régime and the revolution. Of course, both the United States and France held exaggerated views (which he did not discourage) about Lafayette's greatness in the American Revolution and in France.

Marcus Cunliffe in his biography *George Washington, Man & Monument* (1959) concludes that "Washington opened his heart to Lafayette—there is a sprightliness in his correspondence with the Frenchman" absent from his other letters. In his own *Memoirs*, Lafayette wrote that the general's "confidence in other people always had limits, but for M. de Lafayette it had no bounds, because it came from the heart." Washington himself wrote the young boy (September 15, 1778) that "I think myself happy in being linked with you in bonds of strictest friendship." And Lafayette's tender expressions of love to the older man brought Washington to rejoice "at the happiness of my acquaintance with you." Washington took special care of the lad's horse when he was away, and as the lad was returning the commander expected to embrace him "with all the warmth of an affectionate friend when you come to Q[uarte]rs, where a bed is prepared for you."

Returned to France in 1779 for a furlough, Lafayette wrote that he was homesick for his general. "Happy in our union, in the pleasure of living with you," he wrote, "I had taken such a habit of being inseparable from you, that I can't now get the use of absence and I am more and more afflicted of that distance which keeps me so far from my dearest friend." The lad wrote of his fears for the health and safety of the General and complained when he was away that Washington didn't write often enough: "Let me hear from you. Write me how you do, how things are going. . . . Don't forget any thing concerning yourself, and be certain that any little event or Reflection concerning you . . . will have my warmest attention and interest."

In another letter to his commander, the youth asked for a picture from Washington and called himself his "sweetheart." Washington replied that he thought he was too ugly for the boy and feared to be considered vain if he had sat for a portrait to give

MARIE-JOSEPH-PAUL-YVES-ROCH-GILBERT DU MOTIER, MARQUIS DE LAFAYETTE
(1757–1834), aged about 20 during the Revolutionary War. Washington's Antinous?
Drawn by Alonzo Chappel, engraved by J. DeMare from an authentic portrait.

him. The commander wrote that "I really had not so good an opinion of my own worth, as to suppose that such a compliment would not have been considered as a greater instance of my Vanity, than a means of your gratification." Washington has such dread of appearing vain that he refused to assist potential biographers. He wouldn't allow extracts from his letters on farming to be published for fear some "officious tongue" would use "my name with indelicacy." Yet as a sweetheart, he could allow Lafayette intimacies denied all others.

The Frenchman speculated to Washington, "you posibly may laugh at and call woman-like" the desire for pictures, letters and mementos. "Woman-like" or not, Lafayette claimed that he would never conceal nor deny the true "sentiment of my heart." Washington sometimes did see Lafayette as a woman. And while these apparitions might be inside elaborate conceits or overdrawn jokes, their import is unambiguous. On his return to France in the fall of 1779, the youth had joked to Washington that his wife Adrienne Lafayette might want to make love with him. In reply, September 30, 1779, Washington asked (tongue in cheek?) "if you have not made a mistake, & offered *your* own love instead of *hers* to me?" Then he considers that they are separated by the Atlantic (that can be overcome) and by age (a greater gulf?) "Will you not remark that amidst all the wonders recorded in holy writ no instance can be produced where a young woman from *real inclination* has prefered an old man." An obstacle perhaps, but with Lafayette's own encouragement, Washington nonetheless promises to "enter the list for so inestimable a jewell."

Lafayette also became mixed in Washington's mind with his own wife Martha. Several times Washington called Lafayette to retire with him to his humble cabin in Virginia. After the war as a "friend & companion—I shall welcome you in all the warmth of friendship to Columbia's shore . . . to my rural Cottage, where homely fare & a cordial reception shall be substituted for delicacies & costly living." Just as Martha was conveniently forgotten in this fantasy, Washington scheduled Lafayette so that the two should seldom meet. On January 6, 1778, Lafayette wrote his own wife that "General Washington has also just decided to send for his wife, a modest and respectable person who loves her husband madly." But by a remarkable providence suddenly Lafayette received orders from Congress to take charge of a non-existent expedition to Canada. Washington claimed to be totally surprised. Lafayette went to Albany and spent the winter there (while Martha was visiting Valley Forge) in search of an elusive Canadian expedition. When Martha returned to Mount Vernon, Lafayette was quickly recalled. Likewise between January 12, 1779 and March 20, 1780 he spent the winter on a mission to France. And in November, 1780, as he was going South, he wrote, "I flatter Myself with the hope of Meeting Mrs. Washington on the Road." But alas, Martha Washington's itinerary was unexpectedly changed.

Both Washington and Lafayette shared a desperate passion for honor. All the boys shared this passion for themselves individually, for their leader and for the cause of independence. Thus Lafayette challenged Lord Carlisle, a British official, to a duel because he had besmirched the integrity of France. Jack Laurens likewise challenged Charles Lee to a duel over the honor of Washington. Thus the boys remained hypersensitive to any criticism of their general. One of the remarkable signs of Washington's love for Lafayette was his indulgence in Lafayette's support for Thomas Conway, a general who criticized the commander. Conway had been a colonel in the French army and Washington feared the French were plotting to overthrow him. While historians now find these fears groundless, Washington managed to squeeze Conway and all his supporters aside before the end of the war. Only Lafayette managed to get away with such outright disobedience.

Washington's view of honor (and of his officers) required proof on the battlefield. He demonstrated favor by offering his boys opportunities for glory. "Who is there," Washington asked, "that does not rather Envy, than regret a Death that gives birth to Honour and Glorious memory." The foreign officers, however, sometimes annoyed him because he feared that they and not the locals would get the glory and honor for winning the war. "It hurt his sense of honor," Edmund Morgan in his *Meaning of Independence* (1976) explains, "to have to rely so heavily on the French. . . . [Washington] had not counted on military assistance and would have been happier to win without it."

Like all Washington's aides, Lafayette wanted an independent command, the higher the rank the better. In 1781 it became clear that the British had decided to pursue the war in the South, where they saw greater opportunities to use their superior naval power. All the boys wanted Southern commands and they got them. Steuben, Hamilton, Laurens, and Lafayette displayed their glory against Cornwallis. Washington coyly asked Lafayette to stay with him: "It is unnecessary I trust, on my part to give assurances of mutual regard because I hope you are convinced of it, and as I have already put it absolutely in your choice to go to the Southern Army or stay with this [command. C]ircumstan[ce]s & Inclination *alone* must govern you." Washington did not in his anguish complete his thought after "this;" my "command" falters in the ellipsis. Lafayette struggled with the question in a letter to Hamilton: "He is going to be alone, you know how tenderly I love him, and I don't like the idea of abandoning him. On the other hand every Body, Laurens himself, advises me to stay." The Frenchman, however, had his mind set on action and glory.

The boys trapped the British at Yorktown in 1781 as Washington brought up the main body of his army; the French fleet temporarily controlled Chesapeake Bay. And Cornwallis had no choice but to surrender. When the two met on the battlefield, Lafayette kissed Washington from ear to ear several times "with as much ardour as ever an absent lover kissed his mistress on his return." The band played "The World Turned Upside Down." In Rembrandt Peale's painting of Washington and Lafayette at Yorktown, the General, sternly mounted with his dollar bill dignity, holds his hat in hand with his finger simultaneously pointing and the hat covering any view of Lafayette's crotch.

Lafayette returned to France in December 1781. In 1784 he finally got to Mount Vernon, but soon returned to Paris to participate in the French Revolution. On July 14, 1789, the Bastille fell; and the next day Lafayette became commandant of the Paris National Guard. He sent Washington the key to the Bastille, which had been totally dismantled by the revolutionary uprising. In 1792, however, he was impeached by the Revolutionary government and fled France. On the other side of the border he was captured by the Austrians and thrown into prison. Now President of the United States, Washington did everything he could to help his lad. In 1797, released from the Austrian prison, Lafayette soon returned to France where in 1815 as a member of the Chamber of Deputies, he led the movement for Napoleon's abdication. In 1824, he had a triumphal tour of the United States (he met Walt Whitman then only five years old) and returned to France where he was a leader in the 1830 revolution which overthrew the restored Bourbon monarchy. He died in 1834 in Paris.

FREDERICK STEUBEN

For his quartermaster, Washington chose Frederick Steuben (1730–1794) who had served
Frederick the Great as well as his brother Prince Henry of Prussia. Steuben claimed the
closest intimacies with these famous generals; his stories of being a baron and being so
close to the royal family like so many queen stories have a kernel of truth and a dash
of imagination. His letter to Washington declared, "Your Excellency is the only person under whom, after having served the King of Prussia, I could wish to pursue an
art to which I have wholly given up myself."

The French and Indian War (or Seven Years War, 1754–1763) created a need for
soldiers. Frederick Steuben had entered the Prussian officer corps when he was seventeen and advanced rapidly under General Mayr, a soldier famous for "debauchery and
profligacy" as well as a "riotous and daring disposition." In 1759, Steuben was captured
by the Russians and later returned to Prussia with the good news that with the death
of the Czar, Russia would end their conflict with Prussia. Steuben then caught the Great
Frederick's eye. The Prussian King enlisted him as an aide-de-camp and later enrolled
him in a small elite corps, whom the King personally drilled in the military arts.

After conflict with another of Frederick's favorites, Steuben suddenly left the service
and Prussia. With the war's end, the army was reduced; the King dismissed all officers
without firm noble pedigrees. Steuben's departure from Prussia, however, must have
entailed more than the usual military cutbacks since he never returned home. He next
went to Hechingen (one of the minor German principalities) where he served ten years.
When he sought a position in another principality, an opponent wrote, August 13, 1777,
that Steuben had been "accused of having taken familiarities with young boys which
the laws forbid and punish severely. . . . that is the reason why M. de Steuben was
obliged to leave Hechingen." He then fled to France. To his surprise, the French minister
of war financed Steuben's trip to the United States for service with Washington.

After Steuben's arrival in camp, Jack Laurens (one of his translators) wrote that "The
Baron Steuben has had the fortune to please uncommonly, for a stranger, at first sight."
Steuben's later portraits make him appear rather like a cartoon dirty old man, but the
boys saw him as handsome in his prime. William North remembers first seeing Steuben
and admiring "his graceful entry and manner in a ball-room, the novel splendor of his
star and its accompanying ornaments." And added curiously that no one had "reason
to be ashamed of him."

Steuben's entrance when he met Washington resembled a queen entering a gay bar.
Later recollections of the event may well be embroidered since the meeting occurred
during the harsh winter at Valley Forge. The German wore "a highly polished medal
the size of a saucer and a gargantual jeweled star" and was followed "by crisp aides and
a high-stepping greyhound, as a figure of striking martial aspect." Being a lover of dogs,
Washington particularly liked the greyhound. Steuben's own account dramatized their
meeting: "General Washington came several miles to meet me on the road, and accompanied me to my quarters, where I found an officer with twenty-five men as guard of
honor." Steuben responded, no, no, I'm only a humble volunteer. Washington
responded "in the politest words, that 'The whole army would be gratified to stand
sentinels for such volunteers'."

Steuben spoke virtually no English when he arrived. In his first interview, he spoke
French and Laurens "assisted in quality of interpreter." In regards to Steuben, Laurens

made a note on the French word for "boy": "Garçon being masculine, requires the article to be of the same gender; therefore, *une*, which is feminine, makes a false concord; take away the *e* final and make it *un*, all will be right." Had the new guy in camp used the feminine when convention called for the masculine? Bruce Rogers' *Gay Talk* (1972, 1979) and Hérail & Lovett's *Dictionary of Modern Colloquial French* (1984) both recognize the sexual connotations *Garçonnière* (boy house). *Garçonnière* is feminine and unlike the more general *Garçon* has only sexual connotations.

Steuben wrote that he "was fortunate enough to find a few officers of merit, who gave me every satisfaction; they were General Greene, Colonel Laurens, and Colonel Hamilton." Hamilton and Laurens immediately took up with General Steuben and found him boyfriends and assistants. Laurens wrote of "the pleasure of Baron Steuben's acquaintance. Nothing that depends on me shall be wanting to make his stay in camp agreeable." Alexander Hamilton sent an invitation to the German to celebrate Lafayette's recent return: "We have heard from the Marquis. He will be here at Dinner. Will you dine with us also? The General requests it." For the rest of his life, Hamilton looked after the affairs of Steuben and his spendthrift boyfriends.

By 1780, Lafayette had become attached to Steuben as well as Washington; the two fought together at Yorktown. Lafayette usually wrote Steuben in French as he did in July 1780: "Feeling with great pleasure the new obligation I shall have toward you . . . I hope I do not need to assure you of my tender affection." Relations between the two became somewhat strained when Lafayette was promoted over Steuben at Yorktown. The German, nonetheless, retained his good humor. When Steuben jumped into a trench to avoid a shell, Mad Anthony Wayne landed on top of his ass. Turning to Wayne, Steuben said, "I always knew you were a brave general. . . . You cover your general's retreat in the best manner possible."

Washington and Steuben who were about the same age understood each other at once. Steuben needed a job, boys, honor and an army, which the American commander provided. Washington needed the German's military prestige and his intricate knowledge of military drills. The marching servicemen constitute a masculine equivalent of the female chorus line and both perhaps provide the discipline necessary for assembly line production. In any case, Steuben began drilling the Yankees at Valley Forge. In an often quoted letter to a German friend, Steuben wrote, "The genius of this nation is not in the least to be compared with the Prussians, the Austrians or the French. You say to your soldier, 'Do this,' and he doeth it, but I am obliged to say, 'This is the reason why you ought to do that,' and then he does it."

Steuben with the help of his translators compiled the first edition of *Regulations for the Order and Discipline of the Troops of the United States*, basically the drill manual in use today. In a 1937 biography, John McAuley Palmer claimed that, "If you would catch the still surviving thrill of his personality, go to West Point some morning in mid-June when the new yearling corporals are drilling the plebe recruits. They do not know it, but each of these young drillmasters is doing his best to follow the Baron's example."

Steuben called his American boys *sans culottes* (without breeches or *culottes*, the tight pedal pushers Washington always wore). Steuben thus coined the term later used for radicals in the French Revolution. Doubtless Steuben had studied the soldiers' asses and crotches closely and was curious at his *sans culottes'* physical modesty. In so-called developed countries, the relatively modest trousers (or *sans culottes*) have covered men's bottom (better?) half ever since the French Revolution. In his quarters at Valley Forge,

FREDERICK WILLIAM, BARON VON STEUBEN (1730–1794).
He loved and lived with handsome young soldiers from Washington's army.
Engraving by Chappel from an original painting.

Steuben held a gay themed party centered on pants. He invited a select group of hand-some young officers to dine with him "on condition that none should be admitted that had on a whole pair of breeches . . . torn clothes were an indispensable requisite for admission, and in this the guests were very sure not to fail." There is no record of who worked the door for this event. But Steuben's party may have given rise to the legend of soldiers in rags at Valley Forge.

Steuben himself quickly assembled his own family, which dined two or three times a week with Washington's but maintained their own house, tent or hut. His two most intimate aides were Ben Walker and Billy North. North described the general's meet-ing with Walker: he was doing drill and Walker volunteered to help: " 'If,' said the baron, 'I had seen an angel from heaven, I should not have more rejoiced.' . . . Walker became from that moment his aide-de-camp, and remained to the end of the baron's life his dear and most worthy friend." Likewise Billy North joined the family "until death do us part." Palmer in his biography rejoices at the "relation between an old general and an ideal aide-de-camp that is closer than the relation between father and son. When this rare bond is once formed it is one of the closest and tenderest ties in all human relations." On the general's birthday in 1787, the fifty-seven year old man fondly watched Billy cut their names "in a Big tree" at the Baron's new mansion in upstate New York.

Steuben never married and never had any children. After the war, he maintained a loose and extravagant household that sometimes worried Alexander Hamilton, Billy North and Ben Walker. The latter two lived for some time with him in his New York City Mansion "The Louvre." Here Billy's picture hung prominently in the entrance and guests were asked to speculate which was more handsome the soldier or his pic-ture. Steuben lived beyond his means with a "chariot," "front carriage," as well as a "steel-spring sulkey." He had an expensive habit of picking up stray boys. For instance in Connecticut Steuben had met Jonathan Arnold, whom he convinced to drop the "Arnold" (because of Benedict) and had the boy take Steuben's own name; in turn good Jonathan later named his children after Steuben's boyfriends North and Walker. The Louvre served as a magnet for loose boys needing a job or a place to stay.

Steuben and his circle in New York pioneered in house remodeling and in the in-troduction of French architectural design into the United States. Roger G. Kennedy in a recent study, *Orders from France, The Americans and the French in a Revolutionary World 1780–1820* (1990) documents a busy group of architects, designers and engineers, whom Steuben indulged. Pierre-Charles L'Enfant, for instance, served with Washington and after the war was hired to renovate the Federal Building in New York City and then commissioned to build the whole District of Columbia in 1789. Washington and Hamilton both supported their boy L'Enfant, who had shown up at Steuben's tent in 1782 and served with him for a time in a 1783 military expedition.

Steuben's extravagances overtook him and he was forced to move into less elegant quarters, owned by another friend James Tillary at the southeast corner of Broadway and Wall Street. Tillary wrote Hamilton that the old general "is still in my debt, but such is his delicacy & his honor, that I could as soon offend the former, as suspect the latter." Alexander Mitchell his roommate valet was spending money wildly and dress-ing "like a beau, with his silk stockings and waistcoats." Indeed, the old man was skid-ding down: from mansion to flat and finally out of town.

Debts and extravagant boyfriends forced him to move upstate to the present-day

Steuben, New York. Some of the Indian lands there had been granted to the general for his army service; the Iroquois even attempted to kidnap Steuben. But they failed and his name survives in the state park as well as Steubenville, Ohio. A French architect Pierre Pharoux came for a visit and designed an elaborate estate, which centered on "a little pond in the English style to receive all the waters" drained from the meadows. At the time of Steuben's death in 1794 he was living on his as yet undeveloped estate with a young Columbia graduate John W. Mulligan; his final house was little more than a log cabin.

Mulligan's history provides further evidence of a same sex circle of lovers. The youth received his M.A. from Columbia in 1791 and then served as Steuben's "secretary and companion." In 1794, Mulligan received Steuben's last words: "Don't be alarmed my son." Billy North described Mulligan at the funeral as "the young gentleman, his late companion," and himself as "one on whom for fifteen years his eye had never ceased to beam with kindness." Mulligan returned to New York City, where he served as a law clerk for Alexander Hamilton and was admitted to the bar in 1795. John Mulligan subsequently held minor offices in New York City such as justice of the peace, clerk of courts and similar patronage positions, then he landed a queen's dream of an appointment in 1848, United States consul in Athens. He died in 1864.

Steuben's life presents every evidence of male to male love and he even demonstrates some secondary characteristics often only associated with gays in the 1980s. Who could dare say he was "heterosexual" or even "bisexual"? His tastes and desires were hardly a cause for disguise or shame, although he did have to flee Germany and he did flirt with men regarding their wives (not unlike Washington). At a tea, he told Martha Washington that he had been fishing in the Hudson; she asked what he'd caught; he replied, "a whale." And he wrote the wealthy Richard Peters who had a mansion (Belmont) in Philadelphia that he wanted a house like Belmont but he lacked two things: money and a wife. On money he gave up. "As to the second, it is my hope that you will not insist upon living forever, and then—But why in the devil should I tell you all my secret plans?"

To the end Steuben remained faithful to Washington and Washington to him. Steuben organized the Cincinnati group of officers who celebrated the great general. While Washington resisted their effort to make him or anyone else king, he tended to accept worship from his army comrades as Alexander had among the Egyptians. And when Washington was inaugurated as the first president, Steuben was at his side on the platform. Steuben's carrying on provides a thread through the Virginian's camp and even his life: loving the boys could be perfectly acceptable as long as it remained within certain boundaries (among officers and officers, for instance, but not between officers and enlisted men).

As Commander of the Revolutionary Army, Washington's last official act was to sign an encomium for Steuben. His expression of "regard and Affection . . . Sincere Friendship and Esteem" was the last document he signed before he retired to Mount Vernon: "I wish, to make use of this last Moment of my public Life," the commander wrote, "to Signify in the strongest terms my intire Aprobation of your Conduct, and to express my Sense of the Obligations the public is under to you for your faithful and Meritorious Services."

A QUEEN BUT NOT A KING

Washington's love of boys and men means more to the United States than a little gossip. Had he had lots of children (like the Kennedys) he might well have been tempted to become king for his descendants' sake. But he resisted that temptation. In a draft for his first inaugural, which was not delivered, he (or Hamilton) had written "that the Divine Providence hath not seen fit that my blood should be transmitted or my name perpetuated by the endearing, though sometimes seducing, channel of immediate off-spring. I have no child for whom I could wish to make a provision—no family to build in greatness upon my country's ruins." Washington thus recognized that perhaps his greatest gift to the world was in his not siring children.

But what about his "lads?" As a group they unfortunately tended towards the monarchical more than the republican party in the politics of the early United States. Jack Laurens died in battle in 1782, but Frederick Steuben, Alexander Hamilton and even Gilbert Lafayette had connections with monarchy. Today such inclinations lack fashion. United States historians shun the topic of monarchical tendencies in the early republic almost as firmly as they ignore same sex love.

Even within the lesbian/gay community monarchists have been largely ignored. There are contemporary homosexuals who admire monarchy, but their position goes far beyond the imagination of lesbian/gay politicos—whether anarchist, Marxist or mainstream. Royalist queers, nevertheless, abound. They follow closely the fortunes of various pretenders to deposed royal families—in Romania, for instance, not to mention Russia or France. Elizabethan historian A. L. Rowse celebrates monarchs in his *Homosexuals in History, Ambivalence in Society, Literature and the Arts* (1977). Few of his critics even seem aware that his monarchism makes the book so ditzy; they say the book lacks context when in fact it has a context, but one very alien to their lights.

In hindsight, the United States rebellion from monarch George III represented the opening shot in making the world safe for democracy. But at that time, many royalists expected that the independent United States would want and need a king. Lafayette, DeKalb, Steuben and a whole slew of European officers had encouragement from the secret services of the day. Henry of Prussia, younger brother of Frederick the Great allowed the possibility that he might be available. As recently as 1714, George I from Hanover had become king of England without being able to speak English. In 1832, newly independent Greece took first a Bavarian and then a Danish king. The idea of a king for the United States was far from impossible in 1783.

Thomas Jefferson (second vice president and third president) wrote the first draft of the Declaration of Independence and consulted on the French Revolutionary Declaration of the Rights of Man in 1789. Returned home to become the first Secretary of State in 1790, he was dismayed to find: "Some officers of the army . . . trained to monarchy by military habits, are understood to have proposed to General Washington to decide this great question by the army before its disbandment, and to assume himself the crown, on the assurance of their support." Jefferson identified Steuben and Hamilton as active leaders first in the Newburgh Revolt which would have made Washington dictator or king until he repudiated them. And then they supported subsequent intrigues to recruit European monarchs. Steuben corresponded with Prince Henry of Prussia to take the throne after Washington refused, but Washington's refusal to support another king completely destroyed any chances of their success.*

Jefferson gave Washington credit for saving the United States as a republic or democracy. He wrote in 1784 that "the moderation and virtue of a single character has probably prevented this revolution from being closed as most others have been by a sub-version of that liberty it was intended to establish." Among revolutions, in England Charles I had his Cromwell; in France Louis XVI had his Napoleon; in Mexico Hidalgo had his Iturbide; in Russia Czar Nicholas had his Stalin; in China the last Emperor had his Mao Tse Tung; and in Cuba Batista had his Castro. Virtually every revolution but one has ended with a military dictator.

In examining Washington's uniqueness no one has given due credit to his sexual ambivalence. Some say he turned the way he did from his love of Addison's play *Cato*. But if so who but a queen would live their life from a play? When the French Alliance was announced to the troops in 1778, Washington set aside May 6, as a day of celebration. "Prisoners convicted at courts-martial were granted pardons. An elaborate *feu de joye* was arranged, in which cannon salutes were followed by a running fire of musketry for each of three cheers—to the king of France, the friendly European powers, and the American states." Steuben had his boys show their stuff with elaborate marching drills, and to finish off the week of festivities, Washington's officers staged Addison's *Cato*. Cato fights for the Roman Republic and against Caesar. Addison's play ends with Cato dying on his sword: "These are thy triumphs, thy exploits, O Caesar!/ Now is Rome fall'n indeed!" Washington to paraphrase John Wieners was "in only one play, still living it, through his loves, acting himself, writing it, staring it and directing it." ("A Casket Before Dark?") Steuben later named Utica after Cato's hometown.

FREEDOM'S JUST ANOTHER WORD

The role of the lads in improvising a monarchy failed to thrill Washington perhaps because they assigned too great roles for themselves. While he always took care (in so far as possible) of his lads, he did not want them to outshine or outrank him. Washington's man/boy/love circle impacted history in two important ways: first, in the premiership of Alexander Hamilton and second, in the circle's opposition to slavery.

Historians have been unable to explain satisfactorily the close alliance between Hamilton and Washington in the new national government. Hamilton as Secretary of the Treasury represented a very different group than Washington's Virginia friends. In-

---

*Wisely for his country, George Washington did not choose to become a monarch. Had he done so, however, America would have had a ruler with a bloodline as noble (if not more so) as that of Washington's nemesis, king George III. And since Washington *did* become president, our first holder of that office surpassed in antiquity of traceable ancestry the Hanoverian usurpers on the British throne. The Washingtons probably descend in the direct male line from Maldred, lord of Cumbria, an eleventh century Scots noble and younger brother of Duncan II, king of Scots from 1034 to 1040, when he was deposed by the historical Macbeth. According to the eminent, contemporary historian Sir Iain Moncreiffe, both brothers in turn descend in the direct male line through many generations from Niall of the Nine Hostages (died A.D. 438) pagan, sacral high king of Ireland. Ironically, then, George Washington had a better claim to be king of Scotland and Ireland than George III, who was almost totally of German descent. It was only in the 20th century, however, that modern historical research unearthed Washington's royal ancestry; it was apparently unknown in his own time.

It is interesting to note also that George Washington's very distant cousin, Prince Charles Edward Stuart (1720–1788), the "Bonnie Prince Charlie" of the ill-fated military invasion (1745–46) to restore his family to the thrones of England and Scotland, was contacted in his Italian exile (ca. 1775) by a group of Bostonians to make him figurehead of a provisional American government—perhaps even to be elected as constitutional, democratic king after independence had been won. (See Frank McLynn, *Charles Edward Stuart, A Tragedy in Many Acts*, 1988, p. 519) —Editor (*Winston Leyland*)

deed in the first cabinet a division between Thomas Jefferson from Virginia and Alexander Hamilton from New York presaged the two-party system in the United States and the division between agrarian and commercial interests. Washington's aligning himself firmly on Hamilton's side can be explained by his love for the lad. Jefferson never understood that love and most historians have remained perplexed. They might just cut the Gordian knot.

The other great division in United States history has been between the "free states" and the "slave states"—labels used at the time and subsequently. I certainly would not want to argue that homosexuals are less racists than other people, although miscegenation has less meaning for us than for biological families. On the issue of slavery, his boys may have helped Washington because they to a man opposed slavery. Jack Laurens from a large slave-owning family wrote his father from Washington's table at Valley Forge: "I have long deplored the wretched state of these men, and considered in their history, the bloody wars excited in Africa, to furnish America with slaves—the groans of despairing multitudes, toiling for the luxuries of merciless tyrants." Lafayette, Hamilton and Steuben likewise joined in opposing this "peculiar institution." John Brown in his famous 1859 raid on Harper's Ferry used Washington's sword in his effort to free the slaves in Virginia.

In the 1820s Lafayette visited Monticello, Jefferson's plantation. Jefferson sired seven children with his slave Sally Hemings. One of Sally's children who acted as coachman overheard Lafayette ask Jefferson how he could reconcile slavery and freedom (as in the Declaration of Independence). Hemings listened closely for Jefferson's answer, which the master nearly whispered, that the slaves weren't ready for freedom; they still needed education. When Jefferson died, he owned about two hundred slaves; he emancipated only his mestizo children. The other slaves were willed to his white children.

Washington wanted Laurens to go slow with abolition, but he never himself favored slavery. He encouraged slaves to enlist in the army in return for their freedom. He thanked Phylis Wheateley, the Boston slave who wrote a poem for him, and he may have entertained her at tea. With Hamilton at his side, Washington "was known to favor the gradual emancipation of slaves 'by legislative authority,' a position that he clung to until the end of his life." At his death he owned 124 slaves; he willed them to Martha with provision for their emancipation on her death. In confronting slavery, Washington responded as he had to the English and to the church people and to other enemies: cautiously and slowly. The nineteenth century historian George Bancroft wrote of Washington "that placed upon the largest theatre of events, at the head of the greatest revolution in human affairs, he never failed to observe all that was possible, and at the same time to bound his aspirations by that which was possible."

MYTH OF THE AGES

Washington despised religion and pedlars of religion. In this he was an Enlightenment man. Steuben had struck the fitting classical image in naming the soldier's society, Cincinnati, after the Roman general who had left his farm to fight a war and then returned to his crops and animals. But history has been unkind to Washington as the various forces he hated most have obliterated his life.

Religious writers have deformed Washington to have him constantly saying his prayers before battles. Only after Washington's death did Weems tell the fable of

Washington's praying at Valley Forge. A soldier spies him "in a dark natural bower of ancient oaks" going down "on his knees at prayer!" As religious revivals swept the country and claimed a monopoly on virtue, they incorporated Washington as one of their own. Soon "Washington had become America's new center and circumference a naturalized version of both the Old Testament father and New Testament savior." By 1832, the centenary of his birth, a congressman declared that "Mount Vernon and Mount Calvary will descend to posterity with coextensive remembrance." And Catherine L. Albanese treats Washington as indeed coeval with Christ in *Sons of the Father, The Civil Religion of the American Revolution* (1976).

The heterosexual image of Washington distorts him as profoundly as the religious image. Finished only after the Civil War, his monument in the city named after him represents Washington as one big cock. Seen as a super stud in the age of imperialism he has come to symbolize male dominant heterosexuality. The cock represented republican virtue or imperialism equally well, but Washington with his uniforms and boys ill fitted the cock and balls image. In our own twelve step time, Washington has even been made into an amiable family man. Miriam Anne Bourne wrote *First Family, George Washington and His Intimate Relations* (1982); here "intimacy" can only be heterosexual. Jay Fliegelman in *Prodigals & Pilgrims, The American Revolution Against Patriarchal Authority, 1750–1800* (1982) makes Washington into a "sensitive" straight man who led families in his own new age bliss: "Parents who embraced the new childrearing felt a deep moral commitment to prepare their children for a life of rational independence and moral self-sufficiency." Fliegelman reconciles the big cock and no children contradiction in Washington's life by giving him mumps as a boy: "At an early age Washington was rendered sterile by a case of mumps." Fliegelman uses the word "rendered" in an interesting way.

Ideology in Washington historiography had recently been overwhelmed with advertising: the Presidents' Day automobile sales and shopping sprees. In keeping with our times, there are a flood of "image" books. Historians now care less about controlling the records of wars, politics, ideas or economies; they flow where the real power seems to be: in perception. These secretaries of perception have turned out useful studies like Barry Schwartz, *George Washington, The Making of An American Symbol* (1987). And Karal Ann Marling carries Washington into his ultimate depths as a consumer item. *George Washington Slept Here, Colonial Revivals and American Culture, 1876–1986* (1988) ends on "a cold afternoon in the 1980s when Ronald Reagan dragged Washington into his inaugural festivities as a mark of his adherence to a never-to-be-defined credo of traditional American values."

To argue that Washington was not his monument may be to shout against the wind as well as to speak the obvious. My evidence may not be universally compelling, but that is not the fault of either the evidence or the messenger but of the poisoned networks of communication imposed on us. Without the independent Gay Sunshine Press this essay would never have appeared and would probably not have been written. Even homosexuals too often assume that because we have been boxed into limited ghettoes that everything beyond that ghetto must be straight. When lesbians, gays and their friends marched on Washington in 1979, they gathered by the Washington monument but not one person I met talked about what the general might have been doing down on his knees at Valley Forge.

The queer who understood the position of George Washington best may have been

Jean Genet in his play *The Balcony*. Here customers come to a bordello to imitate or have imitated various figures in their sexual fantasies. Outside the house a revolution occurs; the respectable figures of society—Bishop, General, Judge, Rebels, etc.—have all been killed. The sexual palace image-mavens instantly replace the dead by their imitators. Washington thought he was living and acting in *Cato*, but instead he was in *The Balcony*. In that play Irma urges everyone to prepare their disguises:

> Prepare yours . . . judges, generals, bishops, chamberlains, rebels who allow the revolt to congeal. I'm going to prepare my costumes and studios for tomorrow . . . You must now go home, where everything—you can be quite sure—will be falser than here."

The notion that "Washington slept here" now takes on another meaning for gay revolutionists—when they tell you to go home, don't listen. And don't ever "allow your revolt to congeal."

ACKNOWLEDGMENTS

I give special thanks to those who encouraged me first to continue and publish this essay on Washington. In April, 1990 Eugene Rice invited me to present my work in progress to the Columbia University Seminar on Homosexualities. Chris Wittke, *Gay Community News* features editor, published an early version in *Gay Community News* (Boston) (July 1–7, 1990). In December 1990, William A. Percy, chair of the American Historical Association Committee on Lesbian and Gay History, assembled a panel at the AHA annual meeting where I presented my research on Washington and Gist. And Winston Leyland by encouraging me to finish this work helped pull me out of my despair and depression from these waves of dying friends. If not the best revenge, publication can be gratifying. Thanks to William Andrew Jones for letting me read his play, *Friedrich*, based on the life of Steuben. Warren Johansson, Michael Bronski, John Mitzel and others have offered me some good leads, but one of my best informants ("Deep Throat"?) wrote that "if anything develops from research further, credit to inspirer is not only not sought but explicitly rejected." That important gay historian must remain anonymous.

SOURCES

Intended for the general reader, this essay does not include author's footnotes, endnotes or bibliography. Claiming to be easily distracted, sensitive readers have complained about notes at the bottom of the page, embedded in the text or included at the back of the book. Their instincts are correct: most authors use such paraphernalia to intimidate and belittle the reader. "Look how many marbles I've got," the authors shout. Those interested in the marbles can write the author with ten dollars and will receive an annotated copy of the text with bibliography. (Charles Shively, American Studies Program, University of Massachusetts, 100 Morrissey Boulevard, Boston, MA 02125–3393.) Also any complaints, leads to unused sources or other suggestions would be appreciated.

For those who can't wait or don't have the fin, my sources should be obvious. There are standard and recent biographies of most of the figures here. For Washington himself the best short biography is Marcus Cunliffe, *George Washington, Man & Monument* (1958) and the best long biography, Douglas F. Freeman, *George Washington: A Biography* (7 vols. 1948–57). *The Papers of Alexander Hamilton* have been published by Columbia University Press in twenty-seven volumes; Lafayette's papers, *Lafayette in the American Revolution*, have been published by Cornell University Press in five volumes; *Henry Laurens Papers* (with many of his son John's letters) are in progress with University of South Carolina Press. *The Writings of George Washington from the Original Manuscript Sources, 1745–1799* were published (1931–44) by the U.S. Government Printing Office in thirty-nine volumes. And collecting his work has again been undertaken by the University of Virginia Press, whose twenty volumes are only a fraction of what will be the completed work.

Despite the monumental efforts to commemorate the founding fathers, much has been lost. Martha Washington burnt a vast body of the Washington correspondence including all the letters between her and George excepting only two letters which she had missed; and in the 1920s J. P. Morgan was reported to have burned a batch of Washington's "smutty" letters. On the other hand, a cottage industry keeps busy forging romantic letters from Washington to women. The heterosexists, however, don't really need evidence to spin their tales. In 1989 Bill Moyers with General Motors celebrated the 200th Anniversary of the President by having Barry Bostwick, Patty Duke, Jeffrey Jones, Penny Fuller and Richard Bekins redo Washington's life as a soap opera. The Kansas City *Star* called this "a lesson in American History more enlightening than a dozen speeches on the Fourth of July." Few things could be *less* enlightening than a dozen Fourth of July speeches, but this General Motors production may qualify.

Rictor Norton

THE HISTORICAL ROOTS OF HOMOPHOBIA
FROM ANCIENT ISRAEL TO THE END OF THE MIDDLE AGES

This article appeared originally in four parts in Gay News *(London, England), 1975–1976. Part Five is appearing here for the first time. Rictor Norton is an American-born free lance writer who has lived in England for several years.*

PREFACE

*I*N THE EARLY days of gay liberation there emerged the slogan "We are not so much fucked up as fucked over," and as usual the slogan contained more than a germ of truth. But however important it is for us to come to the full realisation that we are quite normal rather than sick, it may be equally important in the long run to come to an awareness of how sick a good many heterosexuals are. There is in fact a sometimes-not-very-subtle form of neurosis, often reaching the proportion of mass hysteria, underlying most of the institutions and attitudes used to oppress and degrade homosexuals.

I readily admit that in current usage the concept of homophobia (invented by Dr. Wainwright Churchill in *Homosexual Behavior Among Males*, 1967—though his actual term was 'homo*eroto*phobia') is often little more than a political metaphor used to put down people who dislike homosexuals, and users of the term ascribe anti-gay attitudes more to ignorance than to actual phobia. But homo*phobia* does indeed exist as a specific classifiable mental illness, ranging from mild anxiety to paranoia, with physiological symptoms such as an involuntary gag-reflex, dilation of the pupils, and a shrinking in penile volume upon seeing a naked male—all of which have been scientifically measured in sporadic experimental studies though as yet there has been no large scale research into the subject. Tentative studies nevertheless indicate that anti-gay prejudice is very deeply seated in the western psyche, quite irrational (usually consisting of excessive fear tantamount to castration anxiety), and a clear indication of how difficult it will be to achieve homosexual equality at the level of merely rational argument for legal reform.

My own belief is that homophobia generally originates in primitive taboo customs which are now largely subconscious, which is why I think that a specifically historical investigation of the subject is important to an understanding of it. At the same time, however, I recognise that on many occasions anti-gay laws were enacted solely on political rather than moral or phobic grounds, as when the English law against buggery was enacted by Henry VIII primarily to deprive the Ecclesiastical Courts of their temporal power. I'm interested in how irrational homophobia has been very much supported by the specifically political oppression of homosexuals, which again I think is usefully revealed by historical investigation.

So in this "History of Homophobia" article I use a combination of psychological and political analysis, usually resulting in a 'radical' analysis since I wish to discover the 'root' or *radix* of what is one of the most complex problems of modern society, a disease that ultimately threatens heterosexuals as well as homosexuals.

One final prefatory note: I'm especially intrigued not so much by homophobia in general as by specific anti-gay attitudes, such as the curious notion that homosexuality is contagious (which I think originates in primitive superstitions about the Evil Eye), and it's for this reason that I want to examine its 'history' at some length and in some detail, for we need much more than an appreciation of prejudice in general if we hope to eliminate all of its ramifications in society.

I
HOMOPHOBIA AND THE ANCIENT HEBREWS

*I*T'S COMMONPLACE to say that anti-gay prejudice is "a medieval Christian attitude." Although it's true that such prejudice was certainly expanded and cruelly enforced during the medieval Christian ethos, homophobia nevertheless began long before Christ or the Church Fathers, and is quite specifically Jewish or Hebrew.

In comparison with other ancient legal codes, Mosaic law was relatively lenient—it listed a mere 36 crimes which were punishable by death. But of these 36 crimes, exactly one half were 'crimes' involving sex, so in contrast to other legal systems the Hebrews gradually extended the notion of 'crime' into the personal and private affairs of people rather than limiting it to the social and public level (such as the public crimes of theft of property). Further, there rather quickly evolved the notion that crime and sex were intimately related. Unlike their contemporary Greek, Egyptian, and other civilisations, the Hebrews held the view that sex, the sex organs, and nudity were shameful.

In Leviticus 18.6–19 there are as many as 12 prohibitions relating entirely to nakedness ('Thou shalt not uncover the nakedness of thy father'; 'Thou shalt not uncover the nakedness of thy aunt'; etc.) and most of the other death-deserving laws are in the context of condemning "the uncovering of one's nakedness," whether for erotic purposes or not. In Exodus 20.26 and 28.42 nakedness is forbidden within the precinct of their cult deity, Jahweh or Jehovah, and the priests of Jahweh are commanded to wear linen breeches (the ephod): "from the loins even unto the thighs they shall reach."

Whereas the Greek term for the male genitals, *medea*, was an entirely neutral term having no positive or negative connotations, the Hebrew term for the male genitals, *erva*, means "hideous flesh." Virtually every psychologist, anthropologist, and student of comparative religion now recognises that the Hebrew ritual ceremony of circumcision is a muted form of castration and a symbolic attempt at genital mutilation having virtually no justification in terms of hygiene. In Leviticus 15.16–18 semen is declared to be "unclean," and men are admonished to bathe after they emit semen, and any garments or the skin of other persons upon which semen has fallen are similarly considered to be "unclean."

This attitude towards sex, the male genitals, and nudity seems to provide evidence for a pathological anxiety, a barely-suppressed paranoia that may have been a national trait of these tribes insofar as it extended even to highly regulated dietary habits revealing severe alimentary prudery. However, a strong political motive contributed to this attitude. The texts containing these prohibitions date from the seventh century BC, at the time when the Hebrews had returned from the Babylonian Captivity. It was a time of a wave of nationalism when for purposes of political survival the Hebrew leaders were attempting to distinguish themselves from the Babylonians, Canaanites, Egyptians, and Assyrians. One of the predominant features of the religions of these other cultures was "ritual nakedness" in the temples and ritual masturbation before the idol of Baal as a kind of symbolic fertilisation of the deity. Thus a major goal of the Hebrew national religion came to be the stamping out of such heterodoxies in their people. It is entirely plausible, even probable, that this sex-loathing was not so much emotional and irrational as originally political and religious.

It's also quite likely that the prohibitions were more theological, more theoretical and formal, than practical or actual, for there is no evidence whatsoever that any death penalties were ever inflicted. The Mishnah and Talmud prescribed stoning to death (as does Leviticus), and in due course there were discussions among the rabbis resulting in agreement that 13-year-old sodomites (i.e., minors) were not guilty of a crime because the Biblical phrase "*men* with *man*-kind" referred only to adult males. This was a purely theoretical discussion amongst the rabbis, and never applied.

This attitude toward sex, the male genitals, and nudity not only forms the background, but is directly linked to, the laws specifically against homosexuals. Unfortunately for us, homosexual rites were included in the religions of the Assyrians, etc., that the Hebrews felt constrained to renounce. It was common practice for the Assyrian priests to be homosexual, to often don women's clothing and thereby acquire the magical powers of the Mother Goddess Ishtar, for the higher priests to castrate themselves in religious imitation of the god Attis, and for the lower acolytes to ritually prostitute themselves to all men who came to the temple (symbolically to collect fertilising semen for the deity, practically to collect money for maintaining the temple). They were called *quadesh*, which means "holy ones"—that is, those blessed or consecrated for this divine service. This term was used by the Hebrews as an exact equivalent for "sodomite," and the term for the female temple prostitutes, *qedheshah*, was used as an equivalent for "whore" (see I Kings 14.22–24, 15.12, 22.46; Deuteronomy 23.17–18; Leviticus 19.3, 24–30, 20.23, all of which relate specifically to Egyptian and Canaanite religious homosexuality).

What is really interesting in this respect is that the identical male homosexual religious rites were commonly practised in the Temple of Jerusalem itself, and were an integral part of early Jewish worship (see II Kings 23.7). But, burning with anti-Assyrian nationalistic fervour, the good King Josiah (640–609 BC) zealously burned out the room of the *quadesh* in the Temple, scattered and reviled them (though again there is no clear evidence of them being killed), and began the campaign against homosexuality that has never ceased since.

So militant homophobia began in what was basically the historical accident of a local sectarian feud. Unfortunately this prohibition of a specific religious practice quickly became a prohibition of male homosexuality in general, and we are left with Josiah's anti-gay law such as "Thou shalt not lie with mankind, as with womankind: it is abomination"; "If a man lie with mankind, as with womankind, both of them have committed abomination; they shall surely be put to death; their blood shall be upon them" (Leviticus 18.22, 20.13), passages which occur in what is known as the "Holiness Code." The actual Hebrew word not very correctly translated as "abomination" is *to'ebhah*, which the Hebrews understood to mean "unholy" in the sense of being related to a "sacred" practice of a non-Hebrew religion, but which is derived from an Egyptian word meaning "holy"; it is simply a matter of philological inversion which becomes a prime means of degradation. *To'ebhah* occurs 116 times in the Old Testament, virtually always in the context of idolatry, though sometimes in terms of sexual metaphor such as "lust-ing after strange gods."

The other relevant laws are in I Corinthians 6.9–10 and I Timothy 1.9–10, which specifically condemn *malakoi*, most often applied to men who perform the receptor role during anal intercourse, not very correctly translated as "effeminate men," and *arseno-koitai*, most often applied to men who perform the insertor role during anal intercourse, not very correctly translated as "abusers of themselves with men." (*koitai* means "to lie with"; *arseno* may come from the Ionic *arsen*, meaning "man, to be made wet with semen" or from the Doric *orson*, meaning "arse, buttocks"). Romans 1.27 condemns men who "leave the natural use of the woman, and burned in their lust one toward one another," which may relate primarily to heterosexual men who go gay in a deliberate rebellious attempt to be perverse and lecherous, etc. Romans 1.26 condemns "women who changed the natural use into that which is against nature," which is extremely vague and probably refers to non-conventional heterosexual practices or positions. Biblical scholars tend to agree that lesbianism is nowhere mentioned in the Bible. The Talmud, however, mentions lesbianism, considering it as a mere obscenity that disqualifies a lesbian from later marrying a priest.

The translations of the very influential Revised Standard Version of the Bible use the word "homosexual" in the passages mentioned above. This is a grossly unjust distortion of the text, for it extends the prohibition to *all* male *and female* homosexual practices *and personalities* rather than what is really prohibited—anal intercourse between men, this and only this. But this perpetuation of intolerance comes much later in the history of the spread of homophobia.

(Likewise, the story of Sodom and Gomorrah at this early date had not yet acquired a homosexual interpretation. This developed around 100 AD, and will be discussed when we reach that phase of the history of homophobia.)

The most remarkable fact in the history of the ancient world is that only the Hebrews condemned homosexuality. From this mere mutation in the history of humankind, from the petty local jealousies of a small nomadic tribe, we have inherited a tradition that has mangled half the world on an unprecedented scale, an anti-gay and anti-sex tradition that is presently spreading into the Eastern and Arabian cultures. Aside from making me sick with loathing, what impresses me most, with a kind of helplessness, is that it was largely an accident of historical circumstances that brought upon homosexuals the wrath of Jahweh.

Homophobia was originally a condemnation of male to male anal intercourse, which was a feature of Assyrian and other religions and usually symbolised humility, though the Hebrews regarded this as humiliation. Laws proceed by precedent, and more than a millenium would pass before the "crime" was extended to include male oral copulation, and not until our own century could mere male to male kissing in public be prosecuted as lewd behavior. One historical lesson we'll discover during this history is that as homophobia loses its direct link to its religious origins and becomes more secular, it becomes more subtle, all-inclusive, and increasingly prohibitive through the law.

Law proceeds by precedent, so likewise lesbian practices are rarely prohibited—not merely because "what women do doesn't interest male lawgivers" (a superficial feminist analysis), but because lesbian practices were not part of the religious rituals originally prohibited by homophobia. The Hebrew degradation of women, however, began simultaneously with their religious-based homophobia, for the male temple prostitutes worshiped Astaroth, Ishtar, Isis, Cybele, and other of the Mother Goddesses in the matriarchal cultures, and Hebrew patriarchalism busied itself with burying Cybele in order to elevate Jahweh. Men such as the *quadesh* who freely subordinated themselves to Cybele, etc. became anathema to the new dogma of male supremacy, and here begins the castration anxiety and impotence anxiety (which despite Freud's errors is much more common among male *hets* than male gays). In a related area, male transvestism was condemned because it represented the *quadesh's* worship of the Mother Goddess.

Homophobia originally had nothing whatsoever to do with a prejudice against people who refused to procreate. In spite of the general opinion today, (male) homosexuals were *not* condemned on the grounds that they refused to "be fruitful and multiply." There is simply no evidence to suggest this modern interpretation of the Biblical attitude, and this particular homophobia doesn't occur until much later. Even "the sin of Onan," which came to be a condemnation of masturbation, derived originally from a prohibition against ritual masturbation before the idol of Baal, not because it violates a "law" of procreation. The phrase "against nature" in this 'phase' still meant only "as a heretic" or "as an idolator," and wouldn't be interpreted as "against 'natural' procreative 'law'" until much later. More specifically, "against nature" always meant "as an apostate," one who goes 'against true nature' in the sense of betraying and renouncing the true religion. In fact the trend of the Hebrew, and later the Christian, priesthood towards celibacy is a reaction against the fertility cults of which homosexual rites were an integral part.

Homophobia originally was a condemnation of idolatry, the worship of the phallic deity Baal in which homosexual rites happened to play an important part. I think this is still the essential factor of homophobia: that it is so firmly rooted in the psyche of contemporary people that homosexuals are still seen as heretics and foreign/strange/queer worshippers of a system not held by the majority. (More evidence for this will be adduced when we get to the active persecution in the eleventh century). In this context Dr. George Weinberg's definition of Homophobia as "acute conventionalism" is quite accurate, more than metaphorically derived from the Hebrew's acute nationalism.

II
THE DESTRUCTION OF SODOM AND GOMORRAH

THE STORY OF these two ill-fated cities of the plain is the single most influential vehicle for the transmission of anti-gay prejudice. The sad irony is that the story originally had nothing whatsoever to do with homosexuality.

The account—told in *Genesis* 19.4–11, and repeated in *Judges* 19.22—in a nutshell goes thus: Lot decided to settle in Sodom, a city reputed to be as wicked as its neighbour, Gomorrah. In order to determine the truth of this reputation, God sent two angels to investigate. These two foreign travellers were met at the gate of the city by Lot, and they accepted his hospitable invitation to sojourn at his home. That night the inhabitants of Sodom clamoured round Lot's house, pounding on his door and demanding: "Bring the visitors out unto us, that we may know them." Lot refused to comply with this 'evil' request, and instead offered them his two daughters. When the Sodomites wouldn't relent, the angels smote the crowd with blindness. The next morning Lot fled the city with the angels and his family, and God let loose a torrent of fire and brimstone to consume these wicked cities of the plain.

The difficulty of interpretation is that the 'sins' of Sodom and Gomorrah simply aren't specified in the Bible. Christians with no linguistic expertise assume that "know" means "engage in coitus." But the term for "know"—*yadha*—is used in the sexual sense only 10 times in the Old Testament and all of these cases are heterosexual. *Yadha* is used in the sense of "get acquainted with" 924 times. Thus the odds against the homosexual usage of this term are nearly 1000-to-one, and most modern Biblical scholars have now abandoned this theory.

The interpretation now accepted by most Biblical scholars (excluding the Festival of Light and other evangelical sects) is as follows: Lot was a *ger*, a sojourner, a resident alien in Sodom. He had certain civic obligations in return for the protection which the city offered him, and there are indications that he was unpopular in the city. He did not have a right to open his house to foreigners, and the citizens of Sodom were merely demanding to see the credentials of these two foreigners, i.e., to "know" whence they came and their intentions. Lot had to refuse, however, because he himself was under the obligations of the Jewish code of hospitality to his guests. He offered the Sodomites his daughters as the first appeasement that came to his mind, *not* as a heterosexual substitute for a homosexual demand. The cities were then destroyed for not recognising the obligations of hospitality, and the whole story is a moral allegory on the dire effects of inhospitality.

The sins of the Sodomites may have been great and grievous in the eyes of a wrathful god, but the Bible doesn't cite homosexuality as one of them (cf *Genesis* 13.13, 18.20). *Jeremiah* 23.14 suggests adultery and lying, and *Ezekiel* 16.49–50 suggests pride and sloth and idolatry. Since the word for "idolatry" is *to'ebhah*, and one form of it could have been homosexual temple prostitution, it is remotely possible that homosexuality was included, but it must be emphasised how *remote* this possibility is. If it was believed to be an example of homosexuality, it is remarkable to the point of being an inconceivable omission that Sodom is never mentioned in any of the Biblical condemnations of homosexuality that I discussed earlier. The Apocrypha demonstrates the standard interpretation: "Whereas the men of Sodom received not the strangers when they came among them, so the Egyptians made slaves of the guests who were their benefactors" (*Wisdom* 10.8, 19.8, and *Ecclus.* 16.8).

Why is it, then, that the "sins of Sodom" have become the prototype for "sodomy"? Basically it is the result of the same kind of nationalistic fervour that we have seen much earlier. The Palestinian Jews and Jews of the Dispersion during the period from about 100 BC to 100 AD, confronted by pagan Hellenistic 'immorality' alien to them, deliberately foisted a homosexual *mis*interpretation upon the story. They began reacting against "the ways of the Gentiles" just as they had earlier reacted against "the ways of Canaan" and "the ways of Egypt."

The Palestinian Pseudepigrapha, particularly the *Book of Jubilees*, a product of the most rigid and conservative Jewish orthodoxy, specified the sins of Sodom and Gomorrah as fornication, uncleanliness, and "changing the order of nature." The *Testaments of the Twelve Patriarchs* (109–106 BC), particularly the *Testament of Naphtali*, says that the Sodomites "changed the order of nature," and *Jude* says they "went after strange flesh." This is still rather vague, but by 50 BC the Rabbinical interpolators had more or less agreed that the Sodomites were "sodomitical."

The Book of the Secrets of Enoch, written in Egypt before the middle of the first century by a Hellenistic Jew, says that the Sodomites committed "abominable lecheries, namely one with another" and "the sin against nature, which is child-corruption after the Sodomitic fashion, magic-making, enchantments and devilish witchcraft." This is nonsensical embellishment when compared with the actual Biblical text, and obviously a result of coming into contact with the 'underworld' of first-century Alexandria, where pederasty and homosexual prostitution existed alongside competing mystical sects, astrology, fortune telling, and cults involving castration and transvestism.

Philo during this period gives us the full-blown story we're familiar with today: "Not only in their mad lust for women did the Sodomites violate the marriages of their neighbors, but also men mounted males without respect for the sex nature which the active partner shares with the passive; and so when they tried to beget children they were discovered to be incapable of any but a sterile seed. . . . little by little they accustomed those who were by nature men to submit to play the part of women" (*De Abrahamo*, 26). A similar account of the Sodomites is related by Josephus (died about 96 AD), who emphasises the rape of beautiful boys. In very short order this false story superseded the original.

The Fathers of the Christian Church would eventually adopt this homosexual misinterpretation of Sodom and Gomorrah lock, stock, and barrel, and when the first Christian Emperors formulated it into the highly influential Roman Law Code, we arrive, by 600 AD, at the anti-gay legal attitude that is still in effect today in most western societies.

It's a bit misleading to suggest that the homophobia of the Christian/Roman Empire was the direct result of adopting this attitude of the Jews of the Dispersion, for there is plenty of anti-gay satire in works by Juvenal, Suetonius, Martial and others, particularly criticism of the cult of Cybele which first entered Rome in 204 BC. Quite independent of the Jews, the early Romans had the similar beliefs that copulation was an expression of violence that had to be controlled, that the 'active' somehow conquered over or perpetrated a crime upon the 'passive'. Women were 'protected'—i.e., oppressed—as 'defenceless creatures', and men who assumed a so-called 'passive' sex role were often ridiculed.

But early Roman anti-gay attitudes weren't so severe as to require official condemnation or legal sanction. It's not until 226 BC that we come across the first anti-gay law, the *Lex Scantina*, so-called because a tribune of the plebs named C Scantinius Capitolinus was charged with homosexuality before the Senate and heavily fined. The meaning of the law and the tale of its origin is open to dispute: it isn't likely that the law takes its name after a criminal defendant. It was several times invoked against political enemies, particularly during the reign of the Emperor Domitian (81–96 AD), but there seem to have been no convictions, and it seems to have been obsolete by the late fourth century. Most important, it forbade homosexual intercourse between freeborn men and slaves, an indication that it merely *regulated* relations which crossed class barriers rather than totally condemned all homosexuality.

During the first four centuries AD it is difficult to differentiate between the anti-gay attitudes of the Church Fathers and the Roman Emperors. St. John Chrysostum emphatically denounced male homosexuals for having "devised a barren coitus, not having for its end the procreation of children," and equally denounced lesbians, "for women ought to have more shame than men." Discussion about this "barren coitus" is really interesting when we realise the folklore behind such prejudice.

Clement of Alexandria condemned homosexuality because it meant *coitus per anum*, and he justified his condemnation by referring to Moses' injunction against eating the flesh of the hare (*Deuteronomy* 14.7). It was a commonplace belief that every year the hare acquired an additional anus, and its superabundance of orifices led to its proverbial promiscuity. The *Epistle of Barnabas* condemns pederasty for the very same reason about the hare, and proceeds to condemn fellatio by referring to *Leviticus* 11.29 wherein the weasel is described as an unclean animal because it was believed to conceive through its mouth. If homosexuals were compared to such mythical hares and weasels, little wonder that we were called "unnatural"! Today we've lost the folklore, but retained the epithet.

The supposed relationship between homosexuals and hares and weasels is broadly relevant. "Sodomy" is usually condemned in the same breath as bestiality. And the Jewish/Christian/Roman view that male homosexuals resemble women is related to the view that women are mere animals. St. John Chrysostum said: "among all savage beasts, none is found so harmful as woman." Even as late as 585 the Council of Macon debated the question "Are women human?"—an affirmative answer won out by a majority of one vote. One of the roots of sexism is not so much a separation between men and women as a separation between men and animals (in which latter category are we homosexuals and hares and women and weasels).

To this list of unclean animals must be added the dog. The Jews called the Gentiles "dogs," *kunes* (from Greek *kuon*, dog, modern term: canine), and the priests of Cybele were called "Gallic hounds," or *cinaedus*, from *canus*, 'dog'. The frequent Renaissance epithet was "you Sodomite dog"—and the modern equivalent is "you son of a bitch."

So again, as in Part I, we find the very same combination of religious and political motivations behind anti-gay prejudice, determined primarily by the need of the Jews to assert their separateness from foreign cultures. There were three important additions to the repertoire of homophobia in Phase 2: First, the belief that homosexuals are pederasts and child-corruptors. Second, a pronounced anti-feminism: an explicit degradation of women, the first explicit condemnation of lesbians, and the view that male homosexuals are 'deformed' by assuming a 'woman's role' in 'passive' intercourse. And third, the first direct equation of "unnatural" with "non-procreative"—but not so much "refusal to procreate" as "an attempt to procreate like the hares and weasels do."

The major point here, of course, is that what amounts to a deliberate *lie*—about Sodom and Gomorrah—was created in order to justify such prejudices. That story hasn't changed much since 100 AD, except that the man in Trafalgar Square who carries the sign 'Repent Ye Sinners' probably believes that sodomites lived in Sodom and lesbians lived in Gomorrah.

III
THE LATER ROMAN EMPIRE & THE EARLY MIDDLE AGES

HELIOGABALUS, the last truly pagan Emperor, was an initiate into a Syrian sun-cult, and, like the followers of Cybele, he frequently engaged in homosexual temple prostitution. After his murder, his cousin Emperor Alexander Severus (AD 222–235), son of a Christian mother, resolved to put a stop to such decadent pleasures. He deported homosexuals who were active in public life, and heavily taxed the *exsoleti*—homosexual prostitutes and camp-followers who had a thriving trade in Rome—as well as heterosexual prostitutes and procurers.

Severus refrained from totally suppressing the *exsoleti*, only because he feared losing the tax revenues for the restoration of the Circus, the Amphitheatre, and the Stadium. After his death, Rome was in a nearly constant state of civil war, running through a dozen emperors in as many years. Nearly two-thirds of the Empire's population was Near Eastern—Syrians, Jews, Iberians, and a significantly large number of people who worshipped Cybele. Society became radically fragmented and unRoman.

The Emperor Philip (244–249), himself the son of a Bedouin chief and a Christian mother, attempted to stem the tide by altogether outlawing the *exsoleti*, the most visible practitioners of unRoman practices and 'exploiters' of the immigrant population. So once again homophobia is essentially a (semi-)Christian's fear of 'foreign ways'.

The organised Christian Church began to pass its judgment. In 305–6 the Council of Elvira forbade the giving of last rites to pederasts. In 314 the Council of Ancyra in Asia Minor excluded all homosexuals from receiving the sacrament, and unhappily their decision became the authority for all later ecclesiastical laws. In 323 the Emperor Constantine was converted to Christianity, and the doom of homosexuals was sealed.

His worthy sons, the Emperors Constans and Constantius, who ruled respectively the Eastern and Western Empires, in 342 jointly decreed that "the law must be armed with an avenging sword" to rid the land of 'passive' homosexuals, "those men who marry men as if they were women." The two doughty sons continued the suppression of the seemingly irrepressible *exsoleti*.

Church regulations became equally severe. St. Basil in 375 and Gregory of Nyssa in 390 demanded of homosexuals a 15-year penitential of self-mortification while going without the sacrament—along with those who committed adultery, pederasty, incest, bestiality, idolatry, witchcraft and murder. In 385 Pope Siricius decreed celibacy for all priests.

Down in Africa, Augustine's boyfriend Alysius died in 386, and Augustine repented of the love which had once been more intense than his love for God. He ceased being a Manichaean, converted to Christianity, sublimated his emotions towards Christ, and exhorted everyone else to do likewise.

In 390 the Emperor Valentinian decreed burning at the stake as a fit punishment for homosexuals—in memory of the purifying flames which devoured the cities of Sodom and Gomorrah. Five years later the Emperor Theodosius outlawed all other religions besides Christianity, and codified the laws against heresy, treason, and homosexuality.

But the Roman Empire was collapsing; in 410 Rome was sacked by the Goths, then re-sacked by the Vandals again in 455. Did that mean that things would get better for homosexuals? Of course not. The Barbarians adopted the laws of the conquered, and in 506 the Visigoth Alaric II decreed burning at the stake for homosexuals. Roman/Christian attitudes pervaded the nearly defunct Empire, i.e., the whole of western civilisation.

The Byzantine Emperor Justinian in 529 closed the Platonic Academy in Athens, bringing to an end the era of classical learning. Justinian preferred superstition: he believed firmly that the tale of Sodom and Gomorrah was an example of how God destroyed cities with homosexual citizens.

So he decided to salvage the Empire by the methodical suppression of homosexuality.

In his 'new laws' he says: "because of such impious conduct cities have indeed perished. . . . Because of such crimes there are famines, earthquakes, and pestilences" (*Novellae* 77, 538 AD). In 543 a plague swept through the Byzantine capital of Constantinople, and probably as a terrified reaction to this, Justinian the following year issued another 'new law', exhorting the "sodomites" to repent: "There will be no relaxation of enquiry and correction so far as this matter is concerned" (*Novellae* 144). Justinian ordered the Prefect to arrest any homosexual who refused to repent, and to subject him "to the extreme punishments."

The punitive correction was brutal: first the convicted homosexual's testicles would be cut off; then sharp reeds would be thrust into his penis; then he would be led—or dragged—naked through the streets for public humiliation; and finally he would be burned at the stake. The Bishops Isaiah of Rhodes and Alexander of Diospolis were so mutilated, and dragged in agony through the streets before the frenzied populace.*

Procopius in his contemporary *Anecdota* says that Justinian's laws were carried out ruthlessly and recklessly—that slaves were forced to falsely accuse Justinian's political enemies, and that the streets were filled by mutilated, castrated, and humiliated victims of his fanaticism. The records are too scarce to positively demonstrate a 'massive persecution', but the scale on which Justinian performed such public services may be imagined by the fact that he once 'converted' 70,000 people in a single campaign.

The full weight of such cruelty rests not alone on the Emperor's shoulders. His underling bishops exerted equal zeal to gain the favour of this temporal Pope. And his good wife the Empress Theodora indulged in a variety of extraordinary pleasures including masturbating while watching men being castrated and tortured. Homophobia may be primarily a masculine sport, but not entirely. It isn't even entirely a heterosexual sport, for some of Theodora's relationships were homosexual as well as incestuous.

Despite Justinian's 'corrections', the Roman Empire continued to 'fall' for several centuries thereafter, and its Christianised fragments kept on splitting through the period we are about to enter now: The Dark Ages. This era really is not so 'dark' as we used to believe, but for homosexuals it held out few bright spots. The Sins of Sodom and Gomorrah were irrevocably associated with ideas about the corruption and decay of the state, and "sodomites" were regarded as a threat to unstable medieval societies.

Again, however, written records of persecution are scarce—possibly because when a sodomite was burned at the stake, all of his books and papers and the trial records were burned along with him in order to prevent contagion. Many of the anti-gay laws during this period may be merely re-enactments of older statutes, and theoretically legal dead wood. Occasionally, nevertheless, we find clearly new laws, which probably were applied.

This is especially likely in Gothic Spain, the strongest foothold of Christianity, where, for example, kindly King Kindasvinth in 650 issued an edict against the "execrable moral depravity" and ordered that both partners in a homosexual act either repent or be excommunicated and castrated. It was a very practical law, treating the convicted homosexual as legally dead, and allowing a wife, if any, to remarry, and sons, if any,

---

*We doubtless have here an early proof of the high percentage of secret homosexuals among the Christian clergy (smiting the wicked sodomites in the public pulpit and sucking off young men in the privacy of their chambers—a phenomenon which carried through successive centuries up to and including our own). See my comments in *Gay Roots* Vol. 1, p. 15. —Winston Leyland

to receive his property. Good King Egica at the 16th Council of Toledo in 693 urged further curbing—apparently homosexuality was gaining ground—and the criminal was forced to have his hair shorn and to receive 100 stripes, after which he was castrated and sent into exile.

In due course homosexuality became a civil crime throughout Christianised Europe, a phenomenon aided greatly in the eighth century when the Emperor Charlemagne condemned "sodomy," and Alfred the Great, under pressure from the Church, condemned the "disgusting foulness . . . as contagious as any disease." The real contagion was of course homophobia.

The most interesting development of homophobia during this period is the Penitential System which illustrates a better awareness of exactly what homosexuals do in bed, even though the disapproval of such activity is still blinded by prejudice. The authors of the handbooks of penances—written mostly in the puritanical Celtic Churches of Ireland and Wales, then spreading their influence to England, France and Germany from about 569 to 1008—seem to know what they are talking about, and clearly specify the previously ambiguous 'sins' of Sodom.

Every act is ranked according to its degree of sinfulness. The basic penance consists of exclusion from the sacraments, self-mortification—though younger boys were beaten with rods at the hands of older clerics—fasting on bread and water on holy days (which included *most* days), and general discomfort. The major difference between the penances was the amount of time they were required.

The Penitential of Theodore the Archbishop of Canterbury in 670 required 1 year for inter-femoral contact (penis between thighs); 3 years for all lesbian activity, undifferentiated; 7 to 15 years for anal intercourse; 7 to 22 years for fellatio; and, for comparison, 7 to 10 years for murder; 15 years for infanticide—reduced to 7 years if the mother was a pauper!

If caught kissing, boys under the age of 20 were subject to 6 special fasts; 8 fasts if it was "licentious kissing"; 10 fasts if it was "kissing with emission"; more if it involved mutual masturbation; and much longer if they were over the age of 20. Sometimes the penance was greater for the insertor than for the receptor. It should be emphasised that all of these penances are for acts between consenting persons.

It's interesting that the penances were usually greater for "those who befouled their lips"—as Columban described fellatio in 600—than those who used their or others' bums. When Theodore says that fellatio is "the worst of all evils," he quite literally means just that—that it's worse than murder (maximum 15 years) and deserves up to 22 years of penance and even a lifetime for the habitual offender. Probably this severity is due to the belief that the mouth was ordained to receive the eucharist, whereas the arse plays no special role in Christian ritual. Or perhaps it's just a regional Celtic oddity, for it's strange that so many British gay men today have similar feelings, that oral intercourse is somehow 'worse' than anal intercourse.

Well, now we're getting into a history of homosexuality rather than a history of homophobia. Or more precisely *male* gay sex, for it's not until the eleventh century that Bishop Burchard of Worms gives more detailed penances for lesbians, and even then it's still from the 'penis-sex' male point of view: women who use an artificial penis are given a penance of 1 year if used alone; 5 years if used with another woman; 7 years if used by a nun—who, as a Bride of Christ . . . commits adultery by using a dildo!

The Penitential System (of which I've noted fewer than 5% of the handbooks) documents the fact that medieval gay men did virtually the same things as modern ones; it also suggests that medieval gay love was widespread enough to be fairly accurately observed. In the context of a history of homophobia, it demonstrates the official anti-gay attitude of the Christian Church towards brotherly love (kissing) as well as sex. But there is little evidence that these penances were severely applied in actual practice: in a closed monastic community, the confessor may well be as 'guilty' as the confes-see; the penances may well have been light. The only real indication that this attitude was effectively suppressive is the fact that joyful expressions of gay love became increas-ingly rare in medieval poetry while at the same time anti-gay satire increases. Most of the friendship in literature demonstrates that the clergy followed Augustine's advice and attempted to repress their emotions in favour of 'spiritual love'. In 960 St. Dun-stan, Archbishop of Canterbury, began a moral reform of the Church and society, and under his influence Church law became the core of civil law, and 'penances' were en-forced as sentences through the law courts.

The Penitential tradition itself came to a head in 1051 when Peter Damiani published *Liber Gomorrhianus* (derived from 'Gomorrah'), an entire book devoted to condemn-ing homosexuality in the most horrifying rhetoric imaginable, urging the maximum penance for every homosexual activity (except fellatio, which he unaccountably forgot). His exposure of 'rampant vice' among the clergy raised a storm of protest, and his intemperate zeal was rebuked by Pope Leo IX. Leo urged the clergy to apply the penances carefully, with attention to the age of the sinner, whether or not it was habitual, and similar extenuating circumstances. Leo questioned only the severity of the penances, not the anti-gay attitude itself, so his epistle codified the Church's homophobia rather than challenged it.

The important point to note is that quite ordinary homosexuals—e.g., boys who kiss, rather than the mythical monsters of Sodom—came under the vigilance of the Penitential System. Doing penance is a remarkably effective way of *internalising* the stigma, and this is one of the origins of the guilt and shame of the homosexual per-sonality. To be castrated is to be a victim of oppression; to be forced to repent daily is the beginning of self-oppression.

IV
GAY HERETICS AND WITCHES

*T*HROUGHOUT ITS early development, the Christian Church was under con-stant threat by the religious teachings of Mani, born in Persia in 216 AD. His system—now called Manichaeism—held that 'evil' was as powerful as 'goodness', con-trary to the Christian view that Goodness is all-powerful, and it acquired an immense number of believers, no doubt because common sense tells us that Evil is indeed a power to be reckoned with in the real world. During the early middle ages cults of this religion spread throughout Egypt, Asia Minor, Constantinople, northern Italy, southern France, the Balkans and Bulgaria.

Of greatest importance to us is the fact that many of these Manichaean groups per-mitted homosexual intercourse. They not only tolerated homosexuality, but went so far as to advocate its superiority over heterosexuality, on the grounds that the latter enslaved humanity in a chain of procreation which bound us to the earth and hence to

Evil. They thus held in varying degrees of esteem all the nonprocreative sex that the Christian Church condemned: masturbation, male and female homosexuality, anal and oral sex between men and women, and group sex-play that wasn't designed to produce offspring. The Church's condemnation of them as homosexuals as well as heretics was not only inevitable, but to a large extent accurate.

Nevertheless the condemnation still had more to do with church politics than with morality. Most of these heresies the Albigensians, Paulicians, Patarenes, Bogomiles, Cathars, etc. were rather puritanical in non-sexual areas and appealed not only to the common people, but to wealthy burghers and the nobility. The Cathars—meaning 'the pure'—were openly supported in France by the counts of Toulouse, Foix and Bezier, and the king of Aragon, and the princes seized Church property on the 'religious' authority of the Cathars. It's hardly surprising, then, that the Church branded these people as heretics, and used the homosexual charge as an effective weapon in its crusade against them. Any defeat of heresy meant the confiscation of more property for the Church.

When Manichaeism entered France by way of Bulgarian immigrants in the eleventh century, the word *bougre*, meaning 'Bulgarian', became synonymous with both 'heretic' and 'sodomite'—which survives in the English language as 'bugger'. Nor is it insignificant that the Inquisition's official term for heresy was 'heretical pravity', having much the same meaning as 'depravity'.

The first explicit allegation of homosexuality against the heretics was made in 1116, concerning the Henricians. From that time onward we hear more and more frequently that the heretics copulated 'vir cum viris' (man with man) and '*Femina cum feminis*' (woman with woman). In 1209 Pope Innocent authorised the Crusade against the Albigensians in France, a policy which resulted in nearly total genocide throughout the southern part of the country, and by the time the Inquisition would finish its work in the seventeenth century, several million heretics and homosexuals had been burned at the stake. But let's pause for a moment and look at the first well organised persecution, that against the Knights Templars.

This Order was founded in 1118 by Hughes de Paynes and eight French knights, followers of Godefroy de Bouillon. Their religious function was to defend the Holy Sepulcher, and to safeguard pilgrims to it. But due to the constant intermingling of cultures in that area, they quickly became adherents to the great heresy, just as quickly took up the sexual practices tolerated in the East, including homosexuality, and at the same time acquired vast wealth and property as traders and bankers. By the beginning of the fourteenth century, the Order comprised 15,500 Knights, an appropriate number of squires and lay brethren, more than 150,000 gold florins and over 10,000 manors, plus a few fortresses and Temples in every major city in Europe (including London, on the site now occupied by The Temple on the Embankment).

In other words the Knights Templars were almost as powerful as the Holy Roman Church. Recognising a threat when he saw one, Pope Clement V persuaded king Philip le Bel in 1307 to issue an arrest order, accusing the Knights Templars of sodomy, heresy, general abominations and criminal acts. Philip himself was gay, but he stood to gain much wealth by outlawing the 'heretics'. On October 13 of that year, Jacques de Molay, Grand Master of the Order, was arrested along with 140 Knights. They were hideously tortured, and confessed to heresy, sodomy, cannibalism and a host of crimes. More than a hundred of them were then burned to death, and 51 more were cremated in 1311. The Order was formally abolished by the Pope in 1312, and on March 18, 1314, Jacques de Molay and his friend Guy D'Auvergne were burned. Just before dying, Molay ordered his persecutors to join him within the year 'at the tribunal of God': both Pope Clement and Philip accordingly died before the year was out. But before their deaths they had totally demolished the Knights Templars.

There is a great scholarly controversy over whether or not the Knights Templars actually were gay. It is impossible here to sum up the evidence for either side of the argument, and I can only note the tendency in the most objective recent scholarship to conclude that they were not cannibals, etc., but that they were indeed 'heretics' as defined by the Church, and that they did indeed engage in homosexual sex. Their initiation ceremony is well documented and has the ring of truth in spite of being extracted by torture. It involved such things as stripping oneself naked, kissing the high priest or leader on the mouth, anus and penis as a sign of fealty, and engaging in homosexual group sex as a symbol of brotherhood. Like the other heresies, they were theologically opposed to marriage and procreation, and taught that erotic tensions were better relieved with one's brothers than with women.

Such ideas were intolerable to the Christian Church, and the commonly-held view (whether true or not) that the Templars were gay strengthened the Church's already deeply ingrained prejudice against homosexuals. This charge became a major weapon in the arsenal of the Crusades and the Inquisition. In 1209 Pope Innocent began the Crusade against the heretical and sodomitical Albigensians in France. It was a wholesale slaughter. In Beziers alone nearly 20,000 heretics perished by the sword. Several thousand heretics who had fled for refuge to the Church of Mary Magdalene were massacred after the Crusaders had amused themselves by gouging out their eyes. Within twenty years a million heretics were exterminated. The Cathar movement was similarly expunged.

It's against this political background in which heresy and homosexuality were so closely aligned as to be virtually identified—that the great Church Father St. Thomas Aquinas (1225–1274) formulated his Christian sexual ethics: "right reason declares the appointed end of sexual acts is procreation", and declared that homosexuality was one of the gravest of the *peccata contra naturam* or 'sins against nature', which is still the official view of most Christian Churches.

Though it is not documented with certainty, some commentators believe that the term 'faggot' as applied to homosexuals is derived from the bundles of sticks or 'faggot' that were used to burn the heretics. The heretics were easily identified with the fuel used to burn them, for symbolic faggots were embroidered on the garments of those who refused to recant: hence the phrase 'to fry a faggot'.

For nearly a century 'heretical pravity' included only the subcults of the Manichaean heresy, but in 1320 Pope John XXII gave his permission to the Inquisitors of Carcassone and Toulouse to prosecute witches. Whereas the Manichaean heresy was an eastern religious import, witchcraft was native to western Europe and the survival of a pagan cult. The heretics often came from the upper middle classes in urban centres, while the witches often came from the lower classes in rural areas relatively untouched by new-fangled religions, either Christian or heretical. Nevertheless the very widespread witch cult was a stumbling block to the enlargement of Christendom, and had to be similarly destroyed once the more powerful heresy groups had been gotten out of the way. I share the view of the Margaret Murray school of anthropological study which argues

Modern engraving illustrating the execution of a gay man by the burning of faggots.

that the witchcraft persecutions were primarily the result of a class war, or a new Christian culture stamping out a witchcraft culture. Many scholars now agree that witchcraft did indeed exist, perhaps as a folk or pagan religion, and is no figment of a hysterical Christian imagination.

The important point for us to note is that the witches, like the heretics, seem to have often approved of all forms of non-procreative sex, partly because they simply were not prejudiced against any form of erotic pleasure, and partly because the production of offspring was inimical to a peasant population which couldn't afford more mouths to feed or further divisions of limited agricultural areas through inheritance.

Homosexuality was often an important feature of the witches' initiation rituals and the communion we now mistakenly refer to as the Black Mass. We have very well-

Tortures for the sin of Lust from Taddeo di Bartolo's medieval fresco of Hell at San Gimignano, Tuscany. An adulteress is lashed by a horned demon, while a sodomite is impaled on a stake from anus to mouth; one end of the stake is held in the mouth of another homosexual, while a devil turns the other end over the fire. Illustrative of official Church homophobia continuing to our own days.

documented evidence—freely given instead of extracted by torture concerning the practice of one rite sometimes called the *osculum infame*, the 'shameful' act of kissing the anus of the 'Devil' or leader of the coven. It is first recorded in 1303 regarding the Bishop of Coventry, and is especially found in the records of the sixteenth century, for example: "le besa de derrier" (1563); "chacun de l'assemblee luy va baiser le derrier" (1567); "puis un chacun luy baisoit le derriere" (1574); "the deuel . . . caused all the company to com and kiss his ers" (1590); "They kiss'd his Backside" (1594); "he wold hold up his taill untill we wold kiss his arce" (1662); "Satan offers his back-parts to be kissed of his vassal" (1617); and not only his back parts: "que le Diable lui faisoit baiser son visage, puis le nombril, puis le membre viril, puis son derriere" (1609). Today the term "kiss my arse" indicates a kind of humiliation, but then it was any act of humility and fealty. This 'kiss of shame' is still found in primitive initiation rituals and even in college fagging.

After everyone in the coven had kissed the Devil's or Leader's arse, and sometimes his erect penis, they would have sex with one another without regard to gender. Then followed the Black Mass, which in the most authentic accounts is merely a Feast of Communion that is more hearty and friendly than demonic.

My major argument is not that the Christian Church was justified in persecuting heretics and witches, but that it *was* justified in believing that the heretics and witches approved of and engaged in homosexual sex. Today so much sentimentality and polemic has obscured the witchcraft persecutions that we can barely credit the existence of witches, that we believe that all witches were women when in fact very many of them were men, and that we think the fertility rites were heterosexual when in fact they often contained a goodly element of homosexuality. Traditional historians steer clear of this nasty topic, and even contemporary compilers at the trials would give only a few details "as a warning to all Christians to take no part in these abominations," and then draw a prudent veil over the rest, "and God fordid that curiosity should lead anybody to explore them." Nevertheless there remains enough evidence to justify our feeling a sense of brotherhood with the witches.

In the book *Montaillou, village occitan de 1294 a 1324* (Gallimard), based on records taken during a heresy investigation in a village in southwest France from 1319 to 1324 (now deposited in the Vatican), Emmanuel Le Roy Ladurie, one of the most distinguished French historians, establishes that homosexuality was 'far from uncommon', and that the medieval villagers were very "permissive" regarding sex outside marriage. One of the 'false priests', and a homosexual as well, was Armand de Verniolles.

Little purpose will be served by reviewing yet again the slaughter of the witches throughout Europe and the tortures of the Inquisition. Once Pope Innocent VIII issued his *Bull Summis desiderantes affectibus* on December 5, 1484, giving the Inquisition full power to seek out and destroy witches, the sickening note in the margin of the courtbooks is always the same: *Conuicta et combusta*—convicted and burned. We all know that the tale is even more horrifying than that of the Nazi concentration camps, and the death toll may have been as high or higher. This story has been told many times, and we're all aware how thoroughly and perhaps irremediably the Christian Church disgraced itself, how amply Christians made recompense for their own persecution under the Roman emperors centuries earlier. The story that has never been adequately told—is how the persecution of witches is relevant to a history of prejudice against gays and women. [This story has since been told in Arthur Evans' *Witchcraft and the Gay Counter-*

Culture, FagRag Books, Boston —Editor]

What began primarily as a straightforward political ruse to wrest economic power from the Knights Templars and the heretical cults, eventually became a mania so immense as to challenge our powers of comprehension. A number of things can be explained in simple economic—even Marxist—terms. For example female witches were vehemently opposed by the medieval medical profession who were their economic rivals in herb-lore and midwifery.

What is more difficult to understand is what some historians refer to as the 'anal obsession of the Middle Ages'. For nearly half a millenium the Christians of western Europe were obsessed with a fear of everything associated with the anus. Luther defined the Devil as a giant anus, and in much iconography we see Evil and Sin personified by farting, shitting and sodomy. There is no satisfactory explanation for this anal phobia, though no doubt it had something to do with what we now call the 'anal-retentive' personality of authoritarian types, as opposed to the 'anal-expletive' personality of, perhaps, tolerant pagans and witches. All we know for certain is that this variety of homophobia wreaked havoc on all things 'sodomical'. Very strong pressures —e.g., the stake and thumbscrew—were brought to bear to 'properly' align the husbandly penis with the wifely vagina, which meant not only the suppression of homosexuality, but the enforcement of gender-defined clothing (witches were often persecuted for transvestism, for which 'crime' Joan of Arc died), strictly-controlled marital groups as opposed to the brotherhood and coven groups of the heretics and witches, and a gender-defined labour force. In other words, both homophobia and sexism were even more rigidly entrenched than in earlier centuries.

V
THE MEDIEVAL BASIS OF MODERN LAW

ALTHOUGH THE Middle Ages, extending from about the twelfth through the fifteenth centuries, is not a single cohesive epoch, the copious citation of trials and laws would merely accumulate evidence of homophobia rather than give us insight into its causes. Throughout this period antihomosexual attitudes and stereotypes changed only in so far as they became more rigid, and were used increasingly to bolster certain social institutions such as the papacy and state governments. The real reason for the persecution of the Templars—the most powerful crusading order of its time—derived from political and economic hostility, greed and envy. The Church and the State defeated a real threat to their authority, confiscated their great wealth, and achieved an "object lesson" which struck terror into the hearts of much less powerful potential enemies. The unquestioned authority of Church and State was reaffirmed.

Since medieval asceticism was virtually identical with an obsession about sex, it was inevitable that charges of heresy and treason were always accompanied by charges of sexual deviation. Popular writers such as Dante used the same technique to attack their personal enemies. It is embarrassingly clear that certain men are condemned as sodomites in his *Inferno*, Canto XV, simply because it was a convenient smear tactic. Most of those literary men and clerks assigned to the seventh level of hell were Dante's political opponents; some, such as Guerra, Rusticucci, Aldrobandi, Latina, and perhaps Borsiere, were Guelfs, those responsible for Dante's exile from Florence.

Nor should we ignore the role that homophobia plays in the denunciation of intellectual nonconformity as well as religious heresy. D. Stanley-Jones has interestingly argued that a hidden battle over homosexuality paralleled the struggle to introduce Aristotle at the University of Paris in the thirteenth century. Aristotle was tolerated and eventually accepted as the lesser of two evils as opposed to neoplatonic idealism and its associations with Platonic homosexuality. His argument is overstated in lieu of definite evidence, but those of us who have ever worked in an academic department know how effectively a homosexual rumour can damage a teacher's reputation without ever finding its way into a printed record. In any case, at a later date we do know that intellectual heretics such as the "Averroists" were condemned at the University of Paris and charged with sexual vices. The University of Paris played a major role in the trial of Joan of Arc for heresy, the main charge against her being that she dressed in men's clothing.

The most famous professor at the University of Paris in the thirteenth century was of course St. Thomas Aquinas, who in his *Summa Theologica* established a rational basis for antihomosexual prejudice by defining the *peccata contra naturam* as the greatest sin of lust, specifically founded upon pleasure rather than procreation. He declared that "right reason" would always see procreation as the purpose of intercourse, and his philosophical condemnation of homosexuality became the precedent for all theological and intellectual discourse upon the subject. His views are the foundation for the most recent declarations against homosexual acts by the Church of England and the Roman Catholic Church.

In order for the Church and the State to maintain control over what they perceived as a disorderly population, medieval people were increasingly forbidden to deviate from the right path in anything. Religious orthodoxy, political orthodoxy, and intellectual orthodoxy were all firmly bolstered by the savage imposition of sexual orthodoxy. Medieval secular law almost universally deferred to ecclesiastical law, in ever more rigid sanctions.

In French legislation, in Beauvais sodomites were burned and their property confiscated; in Touraine-Anjou, they were burned and their goods fell to the local baron. In Italy, in such cities as Perugia, Bologna and Ancona, lay confraternities were created in 1233 and entrusted with the task of ensuring religious and sexual conformity with particular attention to sodomy. In Perugia, the law provided for 40 men—eight from each of the five sections of the city—to investigate and denounce sodomites. At Ascoli Piceno a bounty was given to those who denounced sodomites. At Pisa, people who harboured sodomites were fined 100 lire. At Bologna, whoever dwelt in a building where sodomy was practised might be burnt along with the house. In Sienna, if a sodomite could not pay the 300 lire fine for a first offence, he was suspended by his genitals.

In fourteenth- and fifteenth-century Florence—whose reputation was such that the Germans dubbed pederasts *Florenzer* and their act *florenzen*—the laws were precise with a vengeance: pederasts were castrated; consenting boys under 14 were beaten, driven naked through the city, and fined 50 lire; youths between 14 and 18 were fined 100 lire; houses or fields where the act took place were laid waste; men found in suspicious circumstances were presumed guilty; torture could be used to elicit a confession; conviction resulted in burning at the stake. The chief city officials could investigate, punish and torture in any way they saw fit, and could ban suspects from the city; even songs about sodomy were fined 10 lire. It is not much of an exaggeration to call this a campaign of extermination, although the penalties were gradually lowered towards the end of the fifteenth century, and a fine was often sufficient for those enforcers of the law who were more interested in money than in morals.

The persecution of homosexuals was one of the tools in the repertoire of repressive measures by which the Inquisition strengthened the Church and contributed to the centralization of the papacy. Modern defenders of Christianity, who point out that canon law emphasized the punishment of homosexuals within the clergy, usually ignore the fact that the lay confraternities and mendicant orders had a brief to seek out and punish homosexuals in all sectors of the community. The fact that the ecclesiastical authorities turned over the heretics/witches/sodomites to the civil authorities for execution was of course a pious hypocrisy. The Inquisition's spawn of lay confraternities and the mendicant orders established sexual oppression throughout much of northern Europe as well as Italy, and every "secular" law justified itself with references to the Church Fathers, Scripture, and the papal decrees. Burning at the stake, and laying waste the fields where sodomy occurred, were directly inspired by the Christian interpretation of the story of Sodom and Gomorrah, and the severity of the antihomosexual secular laws was a Judaeo-Christian inheritance.

The more specific detailing of homosexual crimes and punishments may be due to the rapid rise of political democratization in Italy, the reduced power of the oligarchy and the ethics of the petit bourgeois—though again, the Church's unaccountable hatred and fear of material pleasures formed the basis of this morality.

The Penitential System had a devastating effect upon the laws of England (and subsequently the laws of America). In 960 St. Dunstan, Archbishop of Canterbury, began a moral reform of the Church and society, and under his influence ecclesiastical law became the core for civil law. Thus "penances" came to be enforced as "sentences" in the courts of law. The eleventh century court of the Norman William Rufus and Robert Duke of Normandy was believed to have been rife with homosexuality, and the successor King Henry I set about cleaning it up. At a Council in London he laid down new penalties for "those who commit the shameful sin of sodomy, and especially for those who of their own free will take pleasure in doing so." Homosexual clerics were to be expelled from their orders, and homosexual laymen were to be deprived of their civil rights. His orders were moderated by Archbishop (later saint) Anselm (himself probably at least a repressed homosexual, to judge by his letters), who directed the clergy to exercise discretion: "It must be remembered that this sin has been publicly committed to such an extent that it scarcely makes anyone blush, and that many have fallen into it in ignorance of its gravity".

The first significant reference to civil laws against homosexuality in England occurred in 1376, when the Good Parliament unsuccessfully petitioned King Edward III to banish all "Lombard brokers" because they were usurers, and other foreign artisans and traders, particularly "Jews and Saracens", accused of having introduced "the too horrible vice which is not to be named" which would destroy the realm. But it was not until 1533 that a statute was actually enacted against homosexuals. The Act—25 Henry 8, chapter 6—adjudges buggery a felony punishable by hanging until dead. The Buggery Act was piloted through Parliament by Thomas Cromwell in a effort to support Henry's plan of reducing the jurisdiction of the ecclesiastical courts, as the first step towards depriving them of the right to try certain offences, which supported his policy of seizing

Church property. Thus it was defined as a felony without benefit of clergy, which denied homosexuals in holy orders the right to be tried in the ecclesiastical courts, with the result that a conviction entailed loss of property to the Crown. The statute was re-enacted in 1536, 1539 and 1541 under Henry VIII; it was repealed in the first Parliament of Edward VI, along with all new felonies established by Henry, but re-enacted in 1548 with amendments which no longer forfeited the felon's property to the Crown, and stipulations that indictments had to be framed within six months of the commission of the alleged act, and that no person who would benefit from the death of the accused could give evidence against him; with Mary's succession in 1553 it was repealed, along with many other statutes, thus giving jurisdiction back to the ecclesiastical courts; in 1563 it was revived by Queen Elizabeth I, in the harsh terms of the 1533 Act rather than with the amendments of 1548, because according to the Preamble, since the repeal of the Act in 1553 "divers ill disposed persons have been the more bold to commit the said most horrible and detestable Vice of Buggery aforesaid, to the high displeasure of Almighty God." Historical evidence fails to reveal any such excessive "boldness" for the years 1553 to 1563, and the only circumstance which prompted this severe reaction of Elizabeth's ministers was probably Elizabeth's desire to establish her claim to the throne as direct heir of Henry VIII; always politically astute, she naturally re-enacted her father's laws rather than those of intermediate monarchs.

The immediate effect of the 1533 Act is unknown. It was on the books primarily as a symbolic token of the supremacy of the secular courts over the ecclesiastical courts. The prosecution of homosexuals was relatively infrequent during the sixteenth and seventeenth centuries, and as far as one can discover, homosexual acts were not prosecuted with vigor until the second and third decades of the eighteenth century. The first recorded instance of any legal action was in 1541—one of the years in which the Buggery Act was re-enacted—when Nicholas Udall, headmaster of Eton, was convicted of buggery; but strings were pulled in high places, and he was set free within a year. Homosexual prosecutions throughout the sixteenth century are exceedingly sparse; in 1570 John Swan and John Lister, who were smiths and servants of the same master, with whom they lived, were charged with sodomy in Edinburgh, and in 1580 Matthew Heaton, a clergyman in East Grinstead, was prosecuted at the Sussex Assizes for a relationship with a boy in his parish. Fewer than a dozen prosecutions are recorded up through 1660, though this may reflect inadequate research into the subject.

Convictions and punishments in other countries seem to have been more frequent and more severe. When William Lithgow visited Malta in 1616 he "saw a Spanish soldier and a Maltese boy burnt in ashes, for the public profession of sodomy", and by the end of the following day more than a hundred young men had fled to Sicily for fear of suffering a similar fate. In Geneva there were frequent prosecutions for sodomy from 1560 to 1610, linked to peaks of religious revival; a typical case was that of Pierre Canal, who in 1610 was tortured for high treason and murder, and before this inquisition was finished he had accused some twenty men of sodomy. Most of the sodomy charges throughout this period of Genevan history were levelled against French religious refugees. In Ireland, in 1640 John Atherton, Bishop of Waterford and Lismore, and his lover and tithe proctor John Chile were convicted of buggery and hanged.

One of the tragedies of the New World is that it took over much of the legal system of the Old World. The Buggery Act of Henry VIII (as re-enacted by Elizabeth I in 1563) was adopted, sometimes verbatim, by the original thirteen Colonies, and buggery was punished by death. The records of convictions are scarce, but were not systematically recorded and are therefore difficult to discover. In 1624 Richard William Cornish, Master of the ship *Ambrose*, anchored in the James River, Virginia, was hanged for committing sodomy with the 29 year old cabin boy William Couse. We know that sodomites were prosecuted in Plymouth Plantation in the 1640s. In 1646, in Massachusetts Bay Colony, William Plaine was executed for having committed sodomy with two persons in England; and in the same year, in Manhattan, New Netherland Colony, Jan Creoli, a negro, was sentenced to be choked to death and burned to ashes for a second offence of sodomy. In New Netherlands Colony there is a reference to attempted sodomy by N. G. Hillebrant or Hillebtantsen in 1658; and to alleged homosexual rape by J. Q. van der Linde (or Linden) in 1660—he was tied in a sack and drowned in a river, while his supposed "victim" was whipped and "sent to some other place." In 1674, in Massachusetts, a young man named Benjamin Goad was castrated for a crime which seems to have involved masturbating himself in front of, or with, other boys. The death penalty was gradually replaced by whipping, imprisonment, castration, and forfeiture of all lands and goods, though in several states the death penalty was reintroduced.

Indeed the reform of antihomosexual laws has been exceedingly difficult despite the increasingly liberal attitudes of more recent times. The Judaeo-Christian abhorrence of homosexuality and the buggery laws are likely to be with us for a long time to come, exacerbated by the fear of AIDS. In March 1991, during the debate in the parliament of the Isle of Man as to whether or not to decriminalise homosexual acts in accordance with the British Government and the European Convention on Human Rights, the majority of the Council of Ministers wished to retain their law against homosexuality. The argument of the select committee which rejected a proposal to bring their law into line with the rest of Western Europe pretends to be modern in its argument that private homosexual activity should be banned in order to protect public health by preventing the spread of AIDS, but the vocabulary of prejudice has not changed over the centuries. It is summarized in the words of Mr. Edgar Quine, opposed to reform of the Manx laws, who said "Dress it up as we will we are still talking about the unnatural offensive and abominable act of buggery."

SOURCES

BAILEY, DERRICK SHERWIN. *Homosexuality and the Western Christian Tradition*. London and New York, 1955.

BULLOUGH, VERN L. "Heresy, Witchcraft, and Sexuality", *Journal of Homosexuality*, 1, 2 (1974), 183–201.

GOODICH, MICHAEL. "Sodomy in Ecclesiastical Law and Theory", *Journal of Homosexuality* 1, 4 (1976), 427–434.

GOODICH, MICHAEL. "Sodomy in Medieval Secular Law", *Journal of Homosexuality* 1, 3 (1976), 295–302.

HYDE, H. MONTGOMERY. *The Other Love*. London: Heinemann, 1976.

KATZ, JONATHAN. *Gay American History: Lesbians and Gay Men in the U.S.A.* New York: Thomas Y. Crowell, 1976.

MCNEIL, JOHN J., SJ, *The Church and the Homosexual*. London: Darton, Longman & Todd, 1977.

MONTER, E. WILLIAM. "La sodomie à l'epoque moderne en Suisse romande", *Annals: E. S. C.*, 29 (1974), 1023–1033.

NORTON, RICTOR. "The Biblical Roots of Homophobia" and "A Rejoinder", in *Towards a Theology of Gay Liberation*, ed. Malcolm Macourt. London: SCM Press, 1977, pp. 39–46, 57–60.

II

GAY SEX AND POLITICS

Rictor Norton

REFLECTIONS ON THE GAY MOVEMENT

This article first appeared in Gay Sunshine Journal *22 (published in 1974 with Boston's* Fag Rag *as a fifth anniversary celebration of Stonewall). See also Rictor Norton's essays in the history and literary sections of the present anthology.*

▽

THE PRIMARY CAUSE of the modern gay liberation movement is the massive invasion of privacy characteristic of modern western culture. It isn't so much that we are coming out of the closets, but that our closets have been invaded and there's little else we can do. For fear of subversive revolution, the police state in America has broadened its definition of the public domain so as to extend its control over private life styles—a form of behavior typical of dying regimes. Teachers are being trained on the principle that their right to teach (i.e., their right to propagandize) extends from the public classroom into the private home, where parents weren't socializing children as effectively as the state required. One of the motivations behind the community involvement of progressive university programs is the need to divert the growing unrest of the potentially revolutionary lower classes.

The masters of the media have exploited bedroom/bathroom activity not merely to increase the market for deodorants and sex-aids, but to mould the patterns of private behavior into predictable, and hence controllable, outlets. Psychiatrists/psychologists/sociologists, through their official affiliation with educational/business/governmental agencies, have crippled the vital strangeness of intimacy, and have brought us to a poverty of the private self that forestalls revolution just as effectively as does abject economic poverty. The starving person is kept working for tomorrow's daily bread, or tomorrow's lay, rather than going without for the sake of next year's revolution. Civil police agents have become plainclothes decoys and private investigators into criminal activity, vice, drugs, conspiracy, and other phenomena of the countercultures and subcultures that a rapidly-decaying culture can no longer afford to ignore in self-confident security.

Whether such developments are good or bad, or can or should be reversed, is beside the point. The point is that the old-line homophile ideology of the right to privacy was no longer tenable to those of us who recognized that privacy is virtually non-existent in modern culture. Of course we still talk about the right to privacy, and it's a useful concept when arguing the fine points of constitutional law. But it's an ideal whose substantive reality can never be reclaimed. The modern gay liberation movement had little recourse but to proclaim, in effect if not in rhetoric, a right to publicity, and developed an ideology of coming out as a matter of course. The closet was becoming so intolerably delimited by the claims of an open-orientated society that it was becoming virtually impossible to live a double life of which half could still remain a secret. Somewhere in our educational/military/credit dossier is a note indicating that someone knows about our closet; gone are the days when homosexuals could have a large circle of friends who could provide a security nest if one had to leave town quietly.

My point is that we didn't come out; we were squeezed out by those very same forces that heretofore had tried to keep us in. "Come out!" need never have been shouted so loudly. Whether they like it or not, more and more people will be forced by society to join our ranks. This suggests that we will have larger resources from which to draw in the future. We would be foolish strategists indeed were we to waste these resources by channeling all of our energies towards any specific goal, such as a gay civil rights amendment to the Constitution. A great many rivulets will be emerging, and we've got to avoid damming them up as we did at the outset of the movement.

At this grass-roots/popular level of people who are out of the closet simply because of circumstances rather than political choice, the general mood will be conservative. This was also true at the beginning of the movement, and our failure to recognize it prevented us from effectively facilitating the growth through the reformist stage towards the revolutionary stage. There will be increasing numbers of us gamboling about looking for something to do, and hopefully we will be able to accommodate *all* workers. An ideology of "Never trash thy brother or sister" must become a categorical imperative. And at the same time we must recognize the difference between "trashing" and "using," between "exploiting" and "facilitating," so that we can develop strategies of implementing the functionally subversive potential of even the least radical thrusts of any part of the movement.

I wish we could postpone the revolution. I wish we could quietly spend our leisure time developing a sound ideology of liberation, while we spend much of our gay activist time engaged in humanistic reform. The simple humanitarian task of gay liberation is immense, so immense as to almost preclude the possibility of a large enough popular base for a program of revolution. Most of us still get barely enough sex/love/friendship to sustain us: the fifty-year-old homosexual priest still has his problems about coming out and getting old and being Roman Catholic; most of us still don't know what to do about our parents; and our ideology, such as it is, is thoroughly enmeshed with the American Dream.

Because we've been squeezed out at this particular time and place, the Healthy Happy Homosexual seems likely to conquer the gay liberation movement. More and more healthy happy homosexuals, quite ordinary blokes (like the ad says, no freaks, fats, fems, drugs, dopes, or leeches), are getting it together as couples, and together happily buying houses and cars and cameras, washing their underwear and "keeping it clean," preparing joint income tax returns like most other just plain folk in America, and healthily dancing to funky rock 'n' roll at healthy happy homosexual discos. When I discovered that most of us were mediocre instead of different, and that, if given half a chance, we would indeed become these healthy happy homosexuals instead of pure perverts, I wasn't at all liberated. I wasn't happy; I was a bit bored. When I discovered the existence of proud practicing pederasts, and sadomasochists, and drag queens and genderfuckers—*then* I was liberated.

When I first became active in the movement, I was always arguing that the age of consent should be lowered to three (i.e., I was hoping that the oppressive distinction between "child" and "adult" could be replaced by the revolutionary concept of "person"); and that total consent wasn't really absolutely necessary for determining the morality of an act; and that orgy was grand and S/M was fine (and maybe even water sports were okay). But people started yelling at me for upsetting the apple cart and killing the horse. Like most supersensitive adult male homosexuals, I shut up. I began my dutiful stint of appearing on campus panels to present the case that we all—every goddam last one of us—were normal, middleclass, respectable, and non-pederastic. I constructed such a perfect gay mirror-image of the American Dream that I almost believed that maybe we *were* normal, middleclass, respectable, and non-pederastic. The thought filled me with utter horror, so I ceased being an active gay activist. I became instead something of a "humorist gay historian" in public and a radical ideologue in private. I'm peeping out again.

THE HUMANITARIANS

In terms of submovements within the movement, the most significant development during the past five years (1969–1974) is the increased humanitarian emphasis within local communities. Telephone counseling services, child-care programs, community service centers, half-way houses, crash pads, etc. are noticeably increasing, paraprofessionals who've abandoned the sickness theory of homosexual love are being effectively recruited, and the antihumanitarian aspect of homophobia in straight institutions is being challenged more and more successfully. Within this humanitarian movement there's a great deal of sloppy sentimentality, a great many silly notions about health and happiness and the key to the scriptures, and many do-gooders who attack the symptoms rather than the causes of oppression.

In the very long run this humanitarian movement, like all movements with strictly humanitarian goals, is doomed to failure (the Red Cross never stopped a war). Appeals to sentimentality, pity, and charity tend to reinforce condescending and patronizing attitudes which backlash when it comes time to demand one's rights; health and happiness is *the* normative pattern of the American dream; do-gooders tend to be moralists. But I'm still glad that the humanitarians are very much on the scene. For one thing, they are valuably concerned with the age extremes that the liberationists and the reformists have tended to ignore, much to the detriment of the gay community. We've exploited our elderly for financial donations from behind the scenes, and abandoned our young for fear of a pederastic image. People at the age extremes are ipso facto conservative if not reactionary, and it's quite true they can be stumbling blocks for any ethnic revolutionary group.

Revolution becomes increasingly difficult to the degree to which advanced cultures can preserve the presence of their older members and prolong the dependency of their younger members—I take that to be a neutral fact with which all revolutionary movements must somehow cope. I'm not sure how to cope with it except on the humanitarian level, which can be condescending, but I do know that it's crass and barbaric to ignore or exploit or repudiate the elderly for the sake of an imaginary future generation. The increasing number of under-age coffee-houses, crash pads, and parental advisory services to a great extent have a specifically Christian religious motivation which is anathema to any ultimate liberation. But it's at least a start towards meeting the needs of a steadily increasing number of homeless young gay people.

In spite of the basically reactionary home/family/childhood concepts that humanitarians tend to approve, their parental advisory services tend to weaken the nuclear family unit just as heterosexual marriage/family counseling generally fails to hold families together while creating a more realistic situation in which they separate amicably. Regardless of the conservative nature of most humanitarian ideals, their activity itself is functionally subversive, if only because modern humanitarians tend to espouse slightly more radical ideas than their Victorian forebears. Most important, however, they broaden the base of functional people—people who are no longer helplessly hamstrung by their fear/guilt/oppression/isolation/loneliness, who will have more time and ability to contribute to the more liberationist part of the movement. All things in due course.

THE REFORMISTS

The reformist movement is proceeding about as well as we can expect it to proceed. The women's rights movement channeled all of its energies into the single issue of obtaining the vote, and after fifty years of hard work they achieved the vote and found that it didn't make much difference. I imagine that the gay civil rights movement as such will take the same course, but that, given the more rapid pace of society, it will attain its dubious achievements more rapidly. I'm exceedingly relieved that the reformist front is being taken over by the professionals. It's unsufferably tedious for the gay liberationist to argue the fine points of any specific anti-gay law when the concept of "law" itself is an incarnation of oppression and of course has got to go. And the gay humanitarian is always frustrated when he or she leaves the courtroom or legislature. The reformists persevere because of their worldly wisdom "it's all in a day's work," and that helps the morale of the gay populace. We can conserve our energies while the experts handle things. Exactly what is being accomplished I'm not quite sure, and it's somewhat preposterous to argue for *civil* rights within the context of the death of *civil*ization (hasn't anybody noticed?). It's rather hard to argue that gay teachers should be allowed to be role models for gay students, when the concept of "role models" is almost as archaic as the "leadership model" of education, and educational systems are wobbling on their last legs.

It's feasible that the great education campaign of the reformists has inadvertently educated our oppressors as to the options open to them for effecting our oppression. If we had not attacked the sodomy statute on the grounds that the phrase "unnatural and abominable" was void for vagueness, the legislatures wouldn't be listing oral-anal and oral-scrotal acts to make everything crystal clear. But I don't blame the reformists for this—I think it was an inevitable reaction to the dying police state. Right now I think the reformists are functioning as a diversionary tactic, distracting society from the revolutionary principles at the core of gay liberation.

THE LIBERATIONISTS

What really upsets me is that the liberationists haven't developed a radical ideology. For a variety of reasons, GLF groups are collapsing everywhere (are there any left?). The gay liberation movement that began in 1969 is now defunct, a matter for historical research, and we left-over liberationists have scuttled mostly to the humanitarian ranks, wondering why things happened the way they did. We didn't hold firmly enough to a "never trash thy brother or sister" philosophy. When inner-directed guilt was transformed into outer-directed anger, we weren't quite prepared for the fact that such anger automatically attacks the nearest available object instead of the enemy-at-a-distance. So we kept getting into these incredible bitch fights. We might have gotten things under control if we hadn't run off to Washington and Cuba and conventions of other oppressed groups. But there's no use lamenting the passing away of what could have been.

But, being an incorrigible ideologue, I'm still disappointed that nothing of ideological significance has appeared since Carl Wittman's *A Gay Manifesto*. In that document—the most important document of gay liberation so far—Wittman made a number of very important points, including the following: "kids can take care of themselves, and are sexual beings way earlier than we like to admit"; s/m *can* be a "highly developed artistic endeavor, a ballet"; "we shouldn't be apologetic to straights about gay people whose sex lives we don't understand or share." Since then, we have internalized our oppressors' ideology to such a degree that Dennis Altman in *Homosexual Oppression and Liberation*, can by a curious doublethink, call himself a liberationist and still utter these thoroughly establishment sentiments: "My personal belief (hope?) [his parenthesis] is that transvestism/sexism would disappear were our social norms not so oppressive of men who exhibit 'feminine' traits and vice versa. Similarly I suspect sadomasochism is a product of a screwed-up sexuality that is also likely to pass. The relationship between gay liberation and those who practice both transvestism and sadomasochism, usually stigmatized within as well as without the traditional gayworld, is one of the real challenges faced by the movement." Altman confesses that he wasn't able to meet the challenge in 1971, and by 1973 it still hadn't been met: in *The Gay Liberation Book* Len Richmond and Gary Noguera acknowledge that they weren't able to collect any essays on S/M or transvestism. And we hardly hear a whisper about that other radical challenge: pederasty. Our ideology is going practically nowhere.

Of course there is such a thing as "a symptom of internalized oppression," but that's a very broad idea, and we tend to carelessly apply it before engaging in radical analysis. It is only superficially apparent, for example, that pederasty imitates a dominant/subordinate exploitative power structure. Radical analysis reveals that pederasty challenges the child/adult dichotomy imposed by western culture, and it would certainly be to our tactical advantage to foster pederasty because of its relevance to a radically transformed child-rearing. (I know PTA mothers will holler, but PTA mothers are obsolete.) Of course there are exploitative patterns in pederastic relationships, but it can be fairly well documented that such patterns were created by the oppressive "school" concept invented in the nineteenth century (and nothing in modern life had *not* been corrupted by this "school" tradition), but the root itself is still revolutionary. We've handled transvestism in a similarly superficial and dismissive manner. We should have noticed that drag queens do not "imitate women"—the difference between drag queens and women should have been obvious to us, and not just because some drag queens are inept with their greasepaint. The "women" imitated by "female" impersonators are not "women"—they're "famous stars," usually Amazonian/lesbian type women who are self-defined and *not* simply an extension of The Man. Of course there's a lot of sexism in a lot of drag shows, which just means that sexism may have corrupted something that was not inherently sexist. If sexism originates in patriarchal culture, as it does, then it is indeed strange that transvestism and transsexualism originated in the matriarchal culture of Asia Minor around 3300 B.C. Homosexual marriages (formal "mateship" contracts recognized by law) also originated in matriarchal cultures, and it's not the "pure and simple truth" to suggest that homosexual marriages "imitate" heterosexual marriages (there's some evidence to suggest exactly the contrary). It's been said that sadomasochism is one of those dominant-subordinate things that will magically pass away when liberation comes. Any honest leatherman will tell you that he's neither sadist nor masochist but both, alternately and simultaneously, and a clear pattern of oppressor/oppressed or the master/male/active exploiting the slave/female/ passive exists to the degree that it exists only because it has been corrupted by a society that demands sexist role-playing.

The primary ideology that's been developing lately is a very vague concept that Altman calls "androgynous bisexuality." The theory that we will all become androgynous bisexuals lacks a materialist basis and is frighteningly normative. We've fallen into the subject/object trap of heterosexism/dialectism, and wrongly defined "the polymorphous" in terms of sex stimulus rather than sex gratification. Pansexuality, a proper liberationist goal, simply means that one's entire body becomes erotically responsive (e.g., as in the case of "cuddle freaks"), regardless of the gender of the stimulus (male, female, child, animal, vegetable, coke bottle, porn pic, what not). Such a goal can be achieved entirely within the context of exclusive homosexuality, though some of us are copping out to a "humansexuality" that still bears the traces of The Man's definition of (hetero)sex.

I don't think anyone has done much with our most radical idea of liberation: perversity. That's because it's our most dangerous (non-reformist, non-humanitarian) ideology, an ideology that even goes beyond cautious liberationism. Altman refers to Mick Jagger as a symbol of the androgynous bisexual goal, without mentioning that Jagger is also a symbol of Lord High Satan. If we're hearty radical analysts we should be able to go beyond androgyny (a mixture merely of male and female) to a mixture of human and animal. The great god Pan, symbol of pansexuality, was half-goat, and Satan has goat feet. Well, I'm becoming metaphoric. But I don't believe that revolution will be possible until we can open up the abyss, or that Satan can be transformed into bright Lucifer until we can climb upon him and achieve our desire. I don't mean to frighten away our humanitarians and reformists and cautious liberationists, but as a radical ideologue I simply can't close up shop at the point of humanism with its false dichotomy of human/inhuman, which is the origin of the false dichotomy or natural/unnatural.

THE STRATEGISTS

I'm disappointed that there hasn't emerged a fourth group of gay strategists who might set about seeking ways to interrelate the activities of the humanitarians, the reformists, and the liberationists. Probably one reason for this lack is that we've been so excessively abused as non-persons that we justifiably refuse to use/exploit others in an impersonal manner. However, all known revolutions have required the Machiavellian manipulation of bodies of people, both one's own and one's enemies', often to their hurt and with full cynical knowledge that every revolution has its casualties. Herbert Marcuse in *Eros and Civilization* (1955)—a book that increasing numbers of gay liberationists are referring to—says quite bluntly that cultural revolution will first of all require an interim dictatorship in which the oppressors are eliminated and their repressive ideologies are purged. That's a bit heavy for young idealists, and most of the time we use the phrase "cultural revolution" strictly as a metaphor. I'd really like to know if anyone's preparing a contingency plan just in case a real revolution comes, guns and all.

Of course guns are phallic symbols, and that raises the specter of male power structures. But not necessarily. In strict symbology, a gun is no more phallic, and no less phallic, than a television tower, and even the purest women's liberationists have not advocated *not* using the media because of its inherent power/influence structure. A gun is simply a tool like any other, which can be abused as an exploitative tool, or used for corrective repair. In some of my more "what's-the-use" moments, e.g., in response to a story about the use of the drug prolixin to "cure" homosexuals by inducing acute anxiety death panic, I envision a holocaust that seems the inevitable outcome of our collective rage, and I hope someone's around to direct that rage upon the nearest available heterosexist institution. My entire personality is so imbued with the influence of the humanist educational tradition that I can't come to grips with questions relating to revolutionary violence as an instrument of change, so maybe it's just as well that the reformists and humanitarians are keeping us busy with committees and more committees and campaigns and community projects.

But I think it would be wise for us to at least give some careful attention to the potential revolutionary strategies inherent in the gay situation itself. Whereas women cannot persuade men to become women, and blacks cannot persuade whites to become black, gays can certainly persuade straights to go gay. I see absolutely nothing wrong with proselytizing; to cringe under the accusation of proselytizing probably is a symptom of internalized guilt, and certainly exhibits a lack of gay pride. Proselytizing could be used to slightly swell our ranks, but mainly as a subversive tactic to play upon the self-doubt of machismo males. There's no better way to destroy machismo than to fuck it in the ass. We have a reformist ideology of the function of the secret voting booth; what we need is a radical revaluation of the function of the closet—certainly our invisibility would make for excellent saboteur tactics, if such become necessary. Some really interesting possibilities come to mind once we start thinking about it.

FINAL COMMENTS

The consciousness-raising flurry at the beginning of the gay liberation movement held out the promise of transforming society by the aid of our heightened consciousness; i.e., it held out the hopes that a raised consciousness would automatically reveal ideologies and how to implement them. Because of our learned behavior for introspective analysis, we quickly digressed into encounter therapy, encountering each other instead of confronting society, and at best achieved a temporary alleviation of loneliness. The radical gay media have become an extension of this encounter-therapy model, and the papers are filled with many short testimonials and personal statements that don't really go anywhere. This is an important period for us men—and the gay movement is mostly a male gay movement—to go through, in order to release pent-up sorrow and discover fraternal tenderness. But now that we've told each other our sob stories, several times, with variations of rage, pity, joy, anger and other of the primary emotions, we're discovering a gnawing emptiness because we men, as men are presently defined/oppressed, still need that abstract idea to keep us going. On our road to gay liberation we've stopped long enough to weep over the slain. Insofar as our status for several hundred years has been that of anti-persons (demons, anti-social criminals, anti-religious sinners, unnatural/*contra naturam*/against nature, perverts) rather than merely inferior persons with the second-class citizenship of women and blacks, it was inevitable for us to clasp onto the very personal as a part of our liberation. And it is part of our liberation. But our emphasis upon the dignity of individual personality, particularly our obsessive insistence upon "personal" rather than "theoretical" discussion, indicates that we're becoming trapped by the false dichotomy of public/private constructed by our oppressors.

I hope that gradually we begin re-recognizing that "dispassionate objective radical anal-ysis" can also be an effective path to liberation. Personal self-affirmation and the joy-ful exuberance of first coming out has sustained us, but *only just* sustained us, for the grim and earnest tasks that lie ahead.

▽

EDITOR'S NOTE:

Upon re-reading this article prior to my choosing it for the present anthology, I was struck especially by how relevant it remains almost twenty years after it was written. There have been major changes, of course, in the gay movement during the past two decades—especially the emergence of gay groups serving particular parts of our community (e.g., Asians, African-Americans, students, seniors, countless others; a perusal of the national edition of Frances Green's superb *Gay Yellow Pages* will prove my point). Yet there has not been a similar profound development in the ideology of gay liberation during the same period. The "reformers" seem to have largely prevailed over the "liberationists" (I say this without denying the liberationist aspects of certain areas of gay reformism; and in the last two or three years the pendulum of gay activism has swung at least partially away from reformism and back to a "liberationist" approach with the emergence of right-on groups such as *Act-Up*). The internalized oppression detailed by Rictor Norton in his essay is just as much with us now as it was in 1974, and indeed in some aspects it may have deepened. (For ex-ample of such internalized self-oppression, see my comments on p. 336 of *Gay Roots* Volume I; also John Mitzel's article "Wit vs the Ward Heelers" elsewhere in the present anthology.)

Whole areas of gay sexuality, such as S&M and boylove, have been long confined to sub-ghettos by the reformist seekers of straight acceptance and mores within our gay com-munity. Only within the last year or two is S&M finally beginning to emerge into the main-stream of the gay community. As for boylove, it is perhaps even more repressed and oppressed within our community than it was twenty years ago. An example of this oc-curred in the June 1992 liberation day parade in San Francisco (of all cities!) where the small boylove contingent (N.A.M.B.L.A.) was booed and forced from the parade by certain gays masquerading as liberated, but actually the moral equivalents of a Jesse Helms (yes, I speak harshly and needfully so!). We are still very much "on" the road to the true gay libera-tion limned by Rictor Norton in the preceding article.

—Winston Leyland

Clark L. Taylor Jr.

SEX IN THE MEXICAN BATHS

This article appeared originally in Gay Sunshine Journal _29/30 (1976). It was part of a larger study of Mexican male homosexual social life sponsored by the Department of Anthropology at the University of California, Berkeley, through a Lowie Graduate Scholarship. In accordance with the provisions of this study, all names of participants and places have been changed._

Clark Taylor teaches at San Francisco State University and the Institute of Advanced Study of Human Sexuality, 1523 Franklin St., San Francisco, CA 94109. Dr. Taylor's article "Mexican Gaylife in Historical Perspective" appeared in Gay Roots _[Volume 1], and it would be beneficial to read that piece before beginning the present article._

▽

DUE TO LIMITED plumbing facilities, unreliable water pressure and a scarcity of hot water heaters, public baths have been very popular in Mexico for many centuries. The yellow pages of the Mexico City phone book [mid 1970s] list 166 baths, and _Swingers Over Seas_ states "There are over 225 baths in Mexico City proper. They range from dirty little dumps to elegant, spotless monsters . . ." The layout of baths is fairly standardized throughout Mexico. There is a private bath section with individual suites containing a dressing room, shower and a steam room; then there is a general bath section for men. The private bath section is very popular with families and couples, or people looking for a place to go have sex together. However, it is in the general bath section that men most commonly meet and make dates or have sex on the premises.

In _The Homosexual Matrix_, Tripp has stated that there are more homosexual baths in Mexico City than in all the rest of North America put together. Nothing could be farther from the truth. There simply are no bath houses built explicitly for a homosexual clientele, much less Gay baths featuring orgy rooms, sex mazes, sex movies, homoerotic murals and novelty shops which sell sexual appliances. Sex in a Mexican bath house is most similar to sex in a public restroom. Though it may occur in the public section of any bath house occasionally, only five baths were consistently listed by respondents in my study as particularly frequented by homosexuals. Here we will describe the two most popular baths in Mexico City, and perhaps the Gayest baths in all Mexico.

LOS BAÑOS DE ORO

Los Baños de Oro is a large marble and tile bath house in the center of Mexico City. On a quiet side street surrounded by small businesses, the bath no longer has a large residential clientele, and is too hidden to attract many down town people who might want to take a casual afternoon bath during siesta break. It has survived economically, however, because of its continuing homosexual customers. According to Don Antonio, an elderly masseur, the public bath section already had a homosexual clientele and reputation when he began working there in 1936.

Typical of other bath houses throughout Mexico in design, there is a place to buy a ticket to either the private or general baths, check valuables, buy soap, a scouring pad ("sacate") and other bathing accessories. A ticket to the public section costs about 70¢ U.S.

Inside the general bath section, there is a waiting room. At one end of the room is a mirror which allows those waiting to discreetly exchange longing glances and flirt with one another and those bathers who happen to be in the adjoining hallway. In an alcove next to the waiting room, a shoeshine boy or old man sits on a stool working on customers' shoes. He is customarily dressed in a swim suit or long towel wrapped like a diaper or loin cloth. The bath manager, usually clothed in loose fitting cotton street clothes, takes tickets and assures that people are properly attended and that the rooms are not used for sex (unless, perhaps, it is with one of the personnel for money). Additional attendants are a man who shows clients to their rooms and generally sees to the clients' initial needs, various masseurs who approach prospective clients offering their services, and cleaning attendants. While the manager is modestly salaried, the other workers receive only a small fee, work for tips, prostitute themselves, or any one or combination of these.

It is very important to cultivate the friendship of the bath personnel, for they warn good customers when the police are on the premises, help smooth over trouble if a homosexual naive bather becomes scandalized over observing sex, help arrange for clients occasionally to have sex in their rooms and are generally useful. Likewise, bath personnel can be formidable opponents, informing the police, making it impossible to find sexual privacy and spreading malicious gossip (such as that a client is a secret policeman, or has a venereal disease). Of all the bath personnel, it is the masseurs with whom customers have the most contact, and consequently about whom the customers like to gossip the most. Below are some of the kinds of information customers exchange about the masseurs at Baños de Oro.

THREE MASSEURS

DON ANTONIO

At seventy-three, Don Antonio ("El Viejito"—"the nice little old man") is the oldest person working at Baños de Oro. He is married, has three adult children, and has been working at this particular bath for the last forty years. He is bisexual, and continues to have an active sex life, (some claim, though Don Antonio denies, that his days of prostitution are almost over). When strangers question him about the baths, Don Antonio pretends to be senile; not to know what is happening. After he has watched a man or boy in the baths, and is reasonably sure the person is engaging in sex with the other customers, Don Antonio is likely to give the client a test or initiation. During the massage, he inserts his finger into the patron's anus and massages the prostate gland. The act is skillfully done and so ambiguous, that it is not possible to say for sure whether the act is erotic or only part of an obscure massage routine. The act is unusual, but then; as the Mexicans say, at his age, El Viejito has a right to be unusual. If the customer relaxes and allows El Viejito's finger free entry, he passes the test, and Don Antonio confides to him the lore and gossip of the baths. He identifies those who are homosexual, those about whom he is uncertain, who to watch out for, and who likes to do what with whom. Sometimes El Viejito also acts as a match maker. Patrons joke about Don Antonio's custom, and when more anal massage is performed than is "in the line of duty," they tell him so. For example, a very masculine young friend told El Viejito, "next time I want more massage and less fingers in my ass hole" ("culo").

Don Antonio's children are educated and have left home. He expresses concern for some of the younger men who work at the baths and must try to raise and educate their children in these times of inflation. He enjoys his job. It gives him security and companionship in his old age; he gives a good massage, and serves an important function to homosexual people who come to the baths.

TOMÁS

Twenty-four years old, Tomás is very macho, nearly six feet tall and robust. The following excerpt from my field-notes is typical of Tomás and his kind who work at the baths:

> Tomás made a crude remark to an elderly gent who limped and painfully held his back. When Tomás asked the old man if he wanted a massage, the gent said, "no." Tomás said derisively, "You'll feel better after some 'uh-uh' "—jerking his head in exaggerated motions indicating sucking cock. The manager corrected him mildly with "El Pobrecito" (the poor little old man).
>
> After about twenty minutes, a customer, Renán, came from his dressing room wearing red woolen tartan flaired baggie pants and plastic bangles. When Renán was combing his hair in the waiting room before departure, Tomás grabbed him by the waist in front of the other patrons and told him how hot he is for him, pulled open his swim suit, wagging his half erect cock at Renán, telling Renán how eager his cock was for Renán's ass and was generally begging for it when Renán broke away. The staff and other customers laughed, but Renán was humiliated.

Of course, from Tomás' point of view, there is always a good reason for his lack of diplomacy. For example, Tomás and others say that Rénan is a big sex teaser. As one of Rénan's friends remarked, "He is the type who will invite you to his home panting and then tell you his mother is waiting inside and not so much as give you a good night kiss."

One afternoon, I met Tomás and a masseur from another bath at a corner store (or "tiendajón"), where he likes to have a few beers during work break. In our conversation, I learned that Tomás is bisexual, was born in Ciudad Victoria, in Northern Mexico, and was in the Mexican Marines. While in the service, he visited San Diego and Los Angeles, California where he learned about and participated in the leather scene. Tomás and his friend discussed their massage techniques with enthusiasm, each, of course, exclaiming his own virtuosity.

Though he intimidates people sometimes with his crude remarks and macho games (like including a face and neck shave with a razor blade held only between the fingers as part of a massage), Tomás is an essentially harmless person, and a dependable friend.

JAIME

Jaime had been working at the baths for three years and is now seventeen. Bathers often comment on his slender good looks and warm personality. Jaime says he is heterosexual only. And though he receives many offers for sex and prostitution, he has a reputation for turning them down but offering friendship instead. His quiet ways and polite manners type him as a "bueno hijo," or "good son." Jaime works an afternoon shift at the baths and studies at school in the evenings. He is a favorite of the customers and gets along well with his fellow workers. But he is not really a part of his co-workers lifeway, for he is socially upward bound, while one has the impression that the others will probably be working at Baños de Oro for the rest of their productive lives (like El Viejito and several of the older men have).

AN AFTERNOON AT BAÑOS DE ORO

The following composite vignettes from my field-notes are typical of events one can expect at Baños de Oro during a two or three hour visit on a moderately busy day:

I was shown to my dressing cubicle. A lad next door (perhaps 20) had ordered a coke, and was standing naked in his doorway waiting for the attendant to bring it to him. He was short, slender, well built and very Indian in features. My attendant threw a towel out on the floor of my dressing room, asked if I wanted my shoes shined, and inquired to make sure I didn't still have any valuables with me (thereby relieving himself of blame in case of loss or theft). After undressing, I walked down the hall and entered the main part of the baths.

First I passed the restroom. There were about eight guys standing around. That is where the heavy sex action is for those who want to have sex in pairs in semi-private in the stalls. In the shower room, fifteen guys were showering, soaping up, eyeing each other, or pretending not to notice one another.

I went down the hall into the steam room, but nothing was going on sexually, or more likely, my arrival probably caused everyone to stop what they were doing. Then, after a few minutes of exchanging glances, watching my reactions to their flirting and generally sizing me up, a slightly fat young man began to masturbate, then another, and soon four of the six men on the bench of one wall and a man standing against the opposite wall were masturbating. Then a dark skinned man next to the one who initiated the masturbation knelt down and sucked off the pudgy man. Someone then entered the steam room. Everyone stopped their sexual activity immediately and pretended that nothing sexual had been going on. After a few minutes, when everybody was sure that the one who entered was safe, the activity began again. I left the room.

Back in the shower room, I struck up a conversation with another customer and Don Antonio. We joked with Don Antonio about his magic finger. Then the old man confided that police agents had arrested three guys the day before. They were in the toilet. However, it was safe today except for one man whom he didn't know. He cautioned us, however, to be very careful. I related to the other customer how Don Antonio had initiated me into the inner circle at the baths first in 1960, but how he had repeated his actions again recently. After learning that I was studying the baths as part of my doctoral dissertation research, Don Antonio took the opportunity during my next massage to insert his finger deep into my ass and leave it there for a long while. They he bent down close to me and whispered in my ear. "Don't snicker or talk bad about us. We are good people." Naturally I assured him I would not.

Later in the shower room, a dark skinned, curly headed young man with a medium build came over and introduced himself. His name was Guillermo. He grew up in Nogales and had visited California for two years. We chatted a few minutes, then went into the steam room. When we entered, a man who was whistling stopped for a moment (until he recognized us as safe participants) and then resumed his melody. Two men in the center of the room were fucking standing chest to back. The one standing in back had his arms gracefully and tenderly draped around the chest of his friend. (Mexican homosexuals call this position 41 because of the resemblance of the actors to the numerals.) Guillermo asked in broken English, "you like?" and motioned to the fucking. I answered yes, but that I didn't want to have sex at the moment. He asked if I were bashful. Laughingly I replied, "Are you kidding? We have sex in front of and with hundreds in the baths of San Francisco!" We contented ourselves with pulling each other's hair (an activity the Mexicans seem to enjoy very much). In a few minutes, a young man entered with his small son (perhaps six years old). Everyone played like sex was the least thing on their mind and enjoyed the innocence of the boy. The father was either aware of the bath's reputation or sized up the situation, for he winked and thanked the group for their sexual continence when he and his son left. A couple of men grumbled a little that it cut into their sex time, but even they had enjoyed the event. Eventually, Guillermo and I parted company.

In the shower, the young man who had ordered the coke was soaping himself and flirting with another patron. Eventually they went into the steam room together. Tomás passed me and called, "Hey, you wanna pay me go fucky fucky?" I told him that if anybody paid it would be him. We both laughed.

In the bathroom next to the water fountain, a guy rattled the door of a toilet cubicle, and complained, "Chingados Hombre" (Fuck Man). He and his companion wanted to use the cubicle for sex and felt the man inside was alone, not eliminating his bowels or using the place for "proper" sexual activity.

After another half hour of observation, in which I saw several more people engage in anal intercourse and various other people masturbate, I dressed and left the Baños de Oro.

LOS BAÑOS DE ARGENTINA

Baños de Argentina is about ten blocks away from the Baños de Oro in a less prosperous section of downtown. It is behind a large food market next to a popular square where musicians hire out to play "Mariachi" music. It is definitely less sanitary and luxurious than the Baños de Oro, the most homosexually active bath house in the city and the most dangerous.

Going to the Baños de Argentina involves the danger of being exploited by petty criminals and the police, as both are aware that there generally is an orgy in the steam room from six in the morning until nine in the evening, when it closes, and make the most of the fact. Before entering, I customarily had imaginary discussions in which I prepared smart actions and answers for any problems. First I walked down the street checking out the cars and market for any suspicious characters. On the day described below, all seemed safe. It was cold and rainy, near lunch time (unlikely conditions for a police or extortionist stake out; or so it seemed to me).

The bath attendants at Baños de Argentina are usually surly and aloof from the customers. Though they know that sex goes on in the steam room, they seem to strongly disapprove. At least, they were never observed being friendly to the patrons. At first glance, the only thing which distinguishes Baños de Argentina from other baths is a sign at the entrance to the showers and steam rooms which reads, "If there is a complaint of moral irregularities, the parties responsible will be turned over immediately to the authorities." The sign proved to be slightly humorous, for inside the steam room, the orgy was consistently the largest I have seen in Mexico for many years. Obviously no one was complaining of irregularities that afternoon.

In the showers, two men were singing a beautiful Mexican melody in parts. In the steam room, about twenty men and boys were seated on the benches along the sides. The room was brightly lit and sunlight filtered into the room through windows at the top. There was little steam. After about five minutes of no action, one man began to masturbate discreetly under a towel. I caught eyes with a young man with a very muscular, lithe build, very white skin and straight black hair. I thought he was very masculine when I first saw him, but then I got my first dose of "ultra loca," ("super effeminate," literally "ultra crazy girl"). He stuck his cock between his legs so that it looked like he didn't have one and began to charm me with homosexual stereotypes of the nelly queen begging for sex from a super macho. I explained that it was my first time to these baths and that some of the people looked "buga" (homosexually naive) to me and I didn't want to disturb them.

In the shower, the men were still singing. A dark, robust, masculine adolescent with a hippie haircut was showering also. While I was showering, the "ultra loca" approached, put his arms around me and said, "Ay, papacito, mi amor, ay papa, cuanto me gustas, te quiero, dame tú verga, papacito, por favor." ("Ah, little daddy, my love, ah daddy, how you please me, I love you, give me your cock, please.") I politely disentangled myself both flattered and embarrassed, by telling him that he was lovely, but that it was not the time and place for our great love. I did not mention that it is almost impossible to have sex and take field-notes at the same time.

Back in the steam room, the lights were out and the orgy was beginning. Steam and darkness—mystification . . . men touching, kissing, some sucking and many fucking. I went to the darkest part of the room, where an exceptionally large muscular man had laid back another exceptionally large muscular man with a mustache and was enthusiastically engaged in anal intercourse to the admiration of four or five men who watched and masturbated. When the man fucking backed off, another man took over, first sucking the balls and dick of the man with the mustache, then fucking him. To one side, a slender, muscular adolescent (perhaps sixteen), was sucking off a very corpulent gentleman in his fifties. A younger, better built man wanted to participate with them, but the teenager pushed him gently and firmly away. There were moans and many other sounds of sexual ecstasy.

CONTRASTS

One goes to Baños de Oro to socialize and meet new friends more often than to have sex on the premises. On Friday and Saturday evenings men often go to Baños de Oro to find a companion for the evening or weekend. When sex occurs, participants make sure that no one present objects. The activities at Baños de Oro are typical of bath house cruising throughout Mexico. In contrast, at Baños de Argentina, there are so many people involved in sex that it is next to impossible for one to keep note on who has been participating in the orgy and who just came in. This is particularly the case in the evening when the lights are occasionally out and the crowd swells to sixty or more participants. Thus, any chance bathers who enter Baños de Argentina not knowing about the bath's homosexual reputation and not wishing to participate in the activities are obliged to retreat to the showers and forego having a satisfactory steam. Baños de Argentina approaches being a Gay bath house as we know it simply because there are consistently more homosexual clients at the bath than Straight ones, and participating in the orgy is the usual thing to do in the steam room.

Sexual activity is usually tolerated at the Baños de Oro. Indeed, the bath house attendants help clients to make contact and insure that sexual participants are not accidentally observed by unsympathetic eyes. However, the situation at Baños de Argentina is often called a "desviación de homosexuales," (a scandalous homosexual deviation), by Straights and Gays alike. The size and regularity of the orgy attracts petty thieves, who select prosperous appearing clientele and "shake them down" when they leave the baths. Sometimes they also intimidate or physically attack the poor. The bath attracts the secret police who are said to have a standing order to arrest homosexual participants. Compared to the United States, the fine for engaging in public sex is very small ($4.00 U.S., or 15 days in jail and/or deportation for foreigners). However, the fears of exposure in Mexican society as a "depraved homosexual" and the fear that one's family will find out about one's sexual activities are both real and serious. Tough baths with a homosexual reputation are sometimes closed in Mexico, Baños de Argentina manages to stay open. It is said the management pays off the police. Gays endure the insults of the bath attendants, and the dangers of police and thieves simply because there are almost no other places to go in Mexico City for immediate sexual gratification. From everyone's point of view, to close Baños de Argentina would be "to kill the goose that lays the golden egg."

GENERAL OBSERVATIONS

Despite ample historical evidence to the contrary, there is a common Mexican notion that homosexuality is a preferred sexual activity of people in the United States, and that we are purposefully exporting homosexuality in order to subvert the Mexican morality. For example, in an article, "Imperialismo y Homosexualidad," in a major daily newspaper, *El Dia*, José Santos Valdes claims that homosexuality is being promoted by the United States to control population in "Third World" countries and that when "capitalism declares war on something, it declares total war in the mode of the Nazis. For this reason, I reiterate, the diffusion of homosexuality is another grand weapon in the war against the population explosion." If this were the case, one would expect to find U.S. homosexual institutions and customs in Mexico. However, the types of places Mexicans cruise, the slang they use and the customs they observe (i.e., the rules of the game), are authentically Mexican. Perhaps the most striking contrast between Mexican and United States homosexuals is to be seen in culturally distinct sexual positions preferred in public sex. Mexicans are much more anally oriented in sex than we are in the United States. Not content to settle for a blow job, Mexicans have evolved a number of special sexual positions which allow them to discreetly engage in anal intercourse in public. Though I have observed these positions in public places throughout Mexico, they are not particularly common in the United States. For example, in Mexico it is very common for one partner to sit on the lap of the other while fucking so that he can quickly stand or slide to one side should a stranger enter the area of sexual activity. The 41 position discussed earlier allows partners to disengage quickly and hide their erections from anyone coming through the door.

Though some Mexican homosexuals expressed a strong desire for places like ours, where men have the opportunity to safely relax sexually with one another in public, others preferred the traditional Mexican bath system despite its dangers and furtiveness. The major advantage seen in the traditional system is that homosexuality is not totally isolated or divorced from the rest of ordinary daily life. Thus people can flow in and out of homosexual activities and view themselves as homosexual rather than as "a homosexual."

Though Mexicans have sexual ideal types and judge one another on criteria such as age, masculinity, femininity, physical shape and social class, in the baths they find that these ideals often have little connection with what people actually do sexually. For example, one participant in my study noted, "The Mexican baths are our schools about homosexuality. It is there that our sexual stereotypes are broken. They teach us things about each other that foreigners often learn at Gay bars, in magazines and sex movies." Another participant states, "The general mingling and diffused eroticism one sees in the Mexican baths is not a product of free choice or general male agape; it is really just a product of acute frustration." Whatever the cause, one commonly sees young people chase the old, the slender chase the fat, the fat chase the fat and all kinds of behavior which is not in keeping with commonly expressed Mexican ideals of masculine sexual attractiveness. In short, one gains some comprehension of the Mexican saying: "En gustos se rompen géneros y en petates buenos culos." (In personal tastes stereotypes are broken, and on the sleeping mat good assholes are broken.)

John Mitzel

Sports and the Macho Male

Portions of "Sports and the Macho Male" appeared originally in Gay Sunshine Journal *18 (1973). It was reprinted in 1976 as a booklet by Fag Rag Books, Boston. Author John Mitzel is a Boston gay activist, writer.*

For: Mr. Cruzman, my 6th grade gym instructor

▽

I HAVE ALWAYS loathed compulsory sports, no matter what the sport and no matter what form the coercion took. Whether it was the daily after-dinner game of "catch" my older brother prodded me into as a youth, or the required courses in "physical education" through high school (and amazingly at many universities), to the obsessed chatter of my fellow adult men about professional sports, I have held them all in extreme contempt and done my best to avoid inclusion—even to the point of suffering harsh consequences.

Initially, I assumed my dislike of organized team sports and the fanaticism sparked by athletic competitions was merely a matter of personal taste. I *did* wonder at the extent to which sports commanded such a huge and intense following among other men. It seemed a trifle odd that my personal preference would be in such a tiny minority.

I noticed this obsession with sports crossed all age and class lines, as well as occupational and racial ones. In earlier years, it rarely crossed sex lines (though lately "jockey" women have become a pet of the media—and "women in sports" has become a "social issue," the aspect of the women's movement which is most willingly accommodated). Were all men this way? Had I missed out on something?

There appeared to be no escape from this ubiquitous kowtowing to the Sports Obsession. One was just as likely to be bombarded with sports trivia in a lower-class workingmen's tavern as one would be in an elite club or college fraternity house, just as likely to be asked about the Big Game on the assembly line as in a posh corporation board room. Most surprising of all to me was the admission by members of the intelligentsia that they harbored an enthusiasm for professional sports. (Can you really trust a writer who admits he stops writing to watch a football game?)

At some point in my life it became clear to me that an interest in sports and the incorporation of as many men as possible into some contact with the system of values promoted by the sports—either as player, coach, "booster" in the stands, or TV viewing fan at home—was deliberate and calculated policy for recruiting and maintaining males in a sexually-repressed, ego-fragmented, homophobic macho manner of living.

This grip that sports holds over our male population is staggering. It permeates every social gathering; it complements every militaristic or industrial structure; it's foisted on us constantly by the agents of control to transmit the values and behavior which most benefit *them*. This system called "sports" in our society is methodical in its enlistment of males and rigorous in its maintenance of a code of behavior among them. At our institutions of "higher learning," for example, one could more successfully suggest the curtailment of library services, or even their elimination than if one were to suggest the same for the football team. In the fall of 1975, when the city of San Francisco's public school system faced a money shortage, "sports" (football, particularly) were slated to be eliminated from the curricula. The outroar was heard across the nation. And through private subscription and other means, Saturday afternoon gridiron savagery was rescheduled and "education" was returned to normalcy.

Competitive team athletics are used by Macho Straight Men to concentrate, stereotype, and enforce their superficial heterosexuality, their *actual* state of sexual repression, and their power-obsessed interpretation of masculinity. Sports are important instruments which daily rekindle the repression and competitive drive a Macho Man needs to fend off fears about the kind of masculinity he has so tightly adopted for himself. Sports remain the socially-approved pattern of the vestiginal need of men to form into assaultive gangs—Lionel Tiger's turf.

The kind of behavior most highly valued among Macho Straight Men is found in clear, uncomplicated form in team, competitive sports. Sports are a projection of the collective image of how Macho Straight Men *wish to see themselves*—a kind of fantasy in other words. By examining the attitudes and values which support professional sports in particular, those which fire the Macho Man's Sports Obsession, we will get a better understanding of why men behave as they do in our society, and *misbehave* to the extent they do and are certain they can get away with such thuggery.

Sports become a symbol for all those aspects of Macho Masculinity that American men seek to embody or at least identify themselves with. Since most men are unable, either through sloth, physical ineptitude or consumed with the frantic pursuit of the elusive dollar, to make it a full-time job possessing these Macho Masculine qualities in a flashy, developed form, they settle for displaying an aggressive *attraction* to these characteristics as they are embodied by "professional men" and I mean *professional men*, guys who are paid to represent society's Ideal of masculinity to other men. These "stars" are the actual carriers of machismo and sexual repression which they are paid to offer up as a desirable lifestyle to the masses, and they are paid handsomely for it, this meat, and curiously even allowed, as part of their reward, some exemptions from the rigidity of the role they promulgate.

Before proceeding too far, I'd like to define or at least narrow down the use of some of the terms employed in this discussion.

By "sports" I will be referring to the system of team competitions and all it involves. This includes the values and process used in selection and elimination of those who get to play (how many maudlin American household dramas have unfolded to tearful conclusions just because Sonny didn't make The Team?), the training used to mold individuals to fit expectations, the discipline and subservience required of the individual to form a part of a collective obedient unit, and the promotion and exploitation and manipulation of men, women and children to make them into "fans" (pep rallies, e.g.).

In this discussion I have in mind college and "professional" sports like football, hockey, baseball, basketball, those sports in which the greatest number of people "involved" are merely spectators. I also include the vast network of neighborhood leagues, Catholic sports programs, tot team competitions, all those activities which model themselves on Big Time Teams and which boldly proffer behavior which is expected to form the core of a life.

But I direct most of this criticism at the most visible and potent of the sports agents: professional teams, these men who are "owned" by corporations and whose lives are used to bend and shape and exploit social attitudes for private monetary gain. The Macho attitudes of the fans—already extant by their being "fans"—are pandered to by profes-

"I'm not crazy about football . . . but I like big, butch
guys shoving their hands in my crotch."

sional sports; their visions of themselves as Tough Guy upholders of Macho Straightness are reenforced and exaggerated if they are willing to pay the price of admission and make the psychological commitment, which of course they are, no matter how personally bumbling and ungraceful they themselves may be. *Identification with the gang is sufficient.*

But as exploitative team sports become increasingly established as *the* ideal enactment of Macho projections, lesser levels of group activity mimic them: minor leagues, schoolboy sports and little leagues, picking up the corruptions even the name "professional sports" denotes to a person who realizes what physical exercise and expression might otherwise be all about. To quote a review of some sports book which appeared in the Sunday New York *Times* book section 7 January 1973: "At a Midget League football game I watched recently, I saw a man berate a little lineman for missing a block until the boy wept. Like too many American men these days, that parent took the game too seriously." All too true, sadly. The guy probably screamed at the kid even more, once they got home, for crying in public.

I will not include a criticism of voluntary, participatory sports here, that is those physical activities organized and held in the right spirit and not simply enacted as one more manifestation of compulsory aggressive competitiveness to assert a sexually-repressed form of masculinity. (How could I *dare* say anything nasty when the newest gay group in Boston is the Gay Recreational Activities Committee—GRAC—which organizes gay men and women for soccer, bowling, handball, swimming, volleyball, etc. In fact, the leaders of GRAC carried a volleyball net as their "sign" in the 1975 Gay Day Parade!)

I believe in physical culture and the necessity of regular exercise. I admire a well-disciplined body and an elegant and exercised physique. But exercise need not be "sports," and it need not be competitive. Athletic activity shouldn't be streamlined to serve the needs of social repression, political reaction, and become a feeder system for profit-making concerns which exploit their players for vast profits. Against the background of present-day American culture, professional sports cultivate and excite attitudes and behavior among the masses which would better be left unstirred.

So when I attack Sports Obsession and the Sports-Fan Mentality, I am not automatically demeaning the Tuesday night bowling league, or the group that convenes on Saturday morning for a few rounds of golf. Though, having worked as a bowling alley manager in the depths of South Boston, I observed first-hand how "bowling leagues" were almost always organized out of churches, industrial plants or offices as part of the church's or company's policy to use recreation to keep church control and to keep production high on the assembly line.

I also exempt "individual sports," like golf, tennis, boxing, swimming, etc. from this discussion. Even though some of these contests have large followings and may see the award of great amounts of cash, it seems to me that these sports are in a period of general eclipse as the mass audience spectator sports continue their ascendancy. Also, there is a level of abstraction that makes a considerable difference between identifying oneself with a specific man or woman of achievement in an individualist sport and identifying *with a team.* Individuals grow old, retire, lose their competence, display human characteristics; a team endures all by replacing its members with an occasional overhaul, just like an industrial production. In addition, a successful athlete in an individualist sport has no protection from the fans turning on him; his can be more like a tragic condition—something for which there is no place in modern, mass-marketed, standardized society. Take Big Bill Tilden, world tennis champ in the 1940s. His arrest and conviction for having sex with teenaged boys not only ruined his career and his life, but it added to the stigma that tennis was a "sissy-boy" sport, a reputation it has only lately begun to shake. This room for tragedy is why Patricia Nell Warren, in her two-hankie weeper, *The Front Runner*, chose to make her gay, doomed athlete of the individualist stripe and not, say, a hockey goalie or football liner. The youth's isolation and fate seem greater since he's standing Out There Alone Against The Prejudice Of The World and does not try to mitigate his condition through a teamful of buddies.

My targets are, then, to list them in concentric circles starting at the center and moving out: the professional team itself, its players, coaches, managers, owners, and all they aim to exploit in our society; the dedicated "fanatics" who attach great importance to everything that happens to the team and who adopt their own system of coercion to get others to follow their model; the system which establishes Macho Straightness as the only acceptable form of masculine identity and then exploits the demand that *all* men associate themselves with this system; the network of popular press, educationalists, politicians, and churchmen who support and celebrate the values promoted by competitive team sports (a network which often adopts the terminology of sports to win support for their own manipulative policies).

By "Straight" and/or "straightist" I do not refer to the incidental fact that someone is heterosexually-oriented in his social/sexual behavior. (This fact, by the way, is more often an effect of his being a straightist.) The words "gay" and "straight" are not exactly interchangeable with "homosexual" and "heterosexual" respectively, despite the common incorrect usage to the contrary. To label someone Straight in this context takes into consideration other aspects of a man's social attitudes and behavior beyond publicly-acknowledged sexual orientation and activity. (And God knows, there's plenty of homosexualists around today—I've been meeting lots in the leather & denim bars—who could hardly be tagged as gay.)

I offer the idea that there exists a social imperative which sets very strict perimeters on all male behavior; one's socially-admitted sexual behavior is only one function of that imperative. As *actual* sexual performance is not so important to the Macho Straight Man, so it is not to us in labelling him. He is more concerned with gaining power for himself through whatever means are available to him.

His being Straight means that he has done little honest and independent thinking about his sexual nature and what he should do with his Eros energy beyond the pap he has accepted as handouts of the institutions of the society. Sexual tension, to the extent he is free to exercise it, is used as a tool for maximizing his power over others of both sexes. The Macho Straight Man is not acquainted with the extensive outlets for erotic energy in his life. He is profoundly embarrassed by open displays of sensuality. To the straightist, sex is only one more battlefield on which he must be sure he triumphs. And he is angered, threatened, and thoroughly challenged by any greater competence in sexual technique, either in men or women, especially in a peer situation.

What makes a Straightist is his unquestioning adhesion to a standard of conformity which keeps him uninformed (or detesting) of his natural capacities. After all, the Straightist spends so much of his time following the minutiae of sports—feeling he maintains an elevated masculine status by doing so—he just doesn't have a great deal of time to concern himself with some of the more real forces in his life, e.g., his condition of repressed sexuality, his economic exploitation, his sexist attitudes. Life is short enough as it is; to spend it becoming a compendium of locker-room statistics seems a pathetic way to speed it along.

The Straightist is repressed often without even knowing it, anti-sexual, anti-sensuous, anti-expressive, preferring rather to see destructive behavior flourish than permit "deviant" and unharmful expression unfold. Not only is he repressed, he lives in dread of lifting his repression. He sees far too much to lose *vis-à-vis* his Macho Masculinity. He bought a flashy but shoddy lot of goods, and his pride is so mixed up in it by the time he realizes what he got stuck with that he refuses to relinquish what he possesses. This is also an accurate characterization of the militarist, and that these two types of gent overlap is no coincidence.

What are some of the specifics so appealing about the way sports depict Macho Masculinity to their susceptible audiences?

First and foremost, professional sports glorify The Team. The Team has always been the traditional authoritarian technique for abnegating the responsibilities of the adult ego and fleeing into child-like irresponsible collectivity. The team is the place where one's individuality is subsumed to the welfare of the whole which in turn acts as the instrument of some other collectivity's will. Every team obeys a tight pecking-order of authority. There are rookies, veterans, captains and co-captains; there is always the coach, the figure of the higher authority, usually an older man to whom "the boys" are subservient, and behind him are the cigar-chomping, nickel-counting owners and front men.

Competitive sports mimic the military in this regard among others. And why not? Good athletes make good soldiers. Both are conditioned "properly" to serve the powers that be, in our case, to the glory of an expanding empire and its Imperial Male Heroes.

The boys on the team wear uniforms, whereas the coach is not required to. The coach rarely gets dirty, engaged or actively involved. He is the father figure on the sidelines, representing a patriarchy and its values in the process of perpetuating itself, symbolically sending his sons into combat to defend the "honor" of the school, the city, the region, etc. This, I suggest, is the classic pattern of how males must relate to other males in a culture of repressed homosexuality. If you succeed in knocking the opposition's teeth out, your buddy may let you pat him on the ass. The "boys" may share the homosexually-inspired camaraderie in their role as subservients but not that of equals in pursuit of it for its own sake.

To digress for a minute, it's refreshing that that horrible phrase "latent homosexuality" has all but vanished from common usage. It was largely a bogey raised in the 1950's, that decade of revered psychoanalysts and perceived threats, political and psychological, from within. "Latent homosexuality" was some scary demon one had to fear might be lurking within oneself without knowing *for certain* if it was really there! *Repressed* homosexuality, on the other hand, has a certain measure of dignity and personal control involved in it; it acknowledges the possibility of homosexuality, but puts one on top of it and at the reins, and the Macho Straightist can be proud of keeping it under control. As Norman Mailer wrote: "Any man who has successfully repressed his homosexuality has earned the right not to be called a homosexual." In other words, close the hatch, man, and welcome to the club; now let's chose up sides for the game! What I like in this current view is the implication that any and every man, given opportunity and instruction, is potentially a successful homo-erotic.

The main reason for two teams to be meeting on the field or court is so that one may beat the other. *To beat one's opponent* is the culmination of all ambitions of Macho Straightists, a clear establishment of power. Hence the importance of "standings." In our Macho-obsessed society, in which males enforce a hierarchical concept of the *thoroughness* of one's masculinity, "standings" are very important. To be *too low* in the standings suggests a defect in a man's or team's collective virility.

The early years of the New York Mets baseball team raised this problem: they were constant losers. But the team managed to slip into the role of deliberate buffoons and by this ruse temporarily increased their popularity. Failing at being Tough Guy Conquerors, they became stunt men and clowns. Fortunately for them, they ultimately vindicated themselves by asserting their potency and winning the so-called World Series.

(This "World Series" business is often quite visibly a case of not only biting off more than one can chew but attempting to swallow it as well and winding up barfing up the whole mess. The World Series of Little Leagues at one time actually encouraged international competitions. Alas, the Taiwanese team kept winning the title year after year, which finally provoked the American sponsors to *forbid* any foreign teams from entering "World Series" contests, thereby assuring that the winner would *always* be an American team. Late in 1975, no doubt on account of the turning of the historical tide in Southeast Asia, the Americans relented and allowed the world back into the event named after it!)

The playing field, then, is a battlefield manqué. It is kept under stricter supervision. Where the battlefield is the real thing in being indiscriminate in its allowing for destruction as the test of masculine superiority through violence, the playing field is more selective and ritualistic. (If Eton and Waterloo share a metaphor, let's throw fear of the bedroom in there too.)

"Manliness" through the force of power and conquest, and the constant threat of these, is what Macho is all about. It's the outcome of The Game that's important to Macho Straightists. Calling what occurs between the two Big League teams a "sport" is like calling I.T.T. a "business"; it's not totally incorrect, but it's wildly misleading; it leaves the truth of the matter undetailed.

The game is essentially one of power. The professional clubs may have begun with what was once an amusement for participants and their friends, but they have perverted this purpose and offered what they do as a litmus paper test for affiliation with Macho Straightness.

Apropos of this, one little-publicized fact about the visit of the American ping-pong team to the People's Republic of China in the spring of 1971 was that the printed accounts of the games themselves did not boast of the final scores, Team A "slamming" Team B (though, of course, the Americans lost). The Chinese press mentioned the good-natured spirit of the games and the enthusiasm of the spectators. But the scores and the victories were not triumphed. This would be unthinkable in popular American competitions.

On the same note, in May of 1975, an American track and field team wound up two weeks of competitions in the P.R.C. and at a final dinner, hosted by the highest-ranking Chinese "sports dignitaries," men on the American team got drunk on mao tais and started beating on tables, screaming and clapping during the speeches. New York *Times*: "One American was particularly unruly. Finally, three U.S. weightmen picked him up and carried him to the team bus . . . Bruce Cummings, a hurdler from

Philadelphia, described this display as 'terrible,' adding: 'I was embarrassed at the way some of our men acted. I thought it was discourteous to the Chinese'." Why the dummies freeloading on the payroll at the U.S. Dept. of State *imagine* that sports teams can well represent U.S. citizenry perplexes me. Anyone who's seen male teams from the outside *or* inside knows one thing for certain: you can count on them being unruly, violent, drunk, and thuggish. Teams like this sent abroad might *typically* present U.S. behavior, but certainly not diplomatically put a best foot forward.

Professional team sports are short-order, comparatively neat, highly-stylized forms of organized violence. *As* violence, they again mimic the military. In this active physical encounter, whether restrained or brawling, those patterns of behavior most adored by Macho Straightists poseurs come to the fore.

Among the mass spectator sports, we can observe a definite order of preference. Though all of them overlap in their appeal to the Sports Obsessed Macho Straightist, each sport reaches its own depth in the "souls" of American men. The recent sharp rise in the mass popularity of professional football can be partly explained by the physical violence promoted by the rules of that game. The shocking number of routine injuries, disabilities and even deaths that result from the game's brutal demands, as well as the public's indifference to these, only enhance its hold over Macho Straights as the "sport" which best represents their Ideal of American manhood. I contend that as our social life becomes more fragmented, as the distance grows between people and the sources of power which affect their lives, and as they themselves are increasingly separated from any active involvement in the expression of their desires and ambitions and must turn more and more to merely relating to abstractions in symbols of what they fantasize about themselves, the greater is the toleration for pain and mutilation as "entertainment." They increase proportionally; it's an old story.

Similarly, the tremendous expansion in the professional hockey leagues in recent years further testifies to the male's appetite for fast-moving, body contact sports, seasoned with a heavy measure of cruelty. When I grew up in Ohio, "hockey" meant field hockey which was a girl's sport and no self-respecting macho-aspirant boy would be caught *dead* swinging a hockey stick. Was I shocked when I moved to Boston to discover that every lower-class thug and tough and street corner gangster wanted to *be* a Boston Bruin hockey star! Now, of course, many middle-western cities have professional hockey teams (with their talent imported from Canada). It just demonstrates how marketable are lower-class body contact sports when merchandisers can give their goods a macho pitch; in this case, they switched the whole gender of a sport!

The simultaneous levelling off (and relative decline) of interest in professional baseball—"America's National Pastime"—shows just how our society's tastes are changing. Our sensibilities have undergone a drastic alteration in the last three decades, with the nastier strains in our collective character being stimulated far more than our gentler capabilities. Baseball now appears as a slow, pokey, old-timers' game, not as team-oriented as football, not as violent as hockey, not really requiring the "test of a man's abilities," and it lacks great suffering on the part of the players. Baseball's decline and the ascent of the faster, more violent sports is partly a reflection of how our television-addiction has affected us. We are now more willing to tolerate physical violence, first in its depiction, and later in its reality (the exception being Jackie Kennedy who flees the room any time a shooting sequence flashes across her TV screen). And, too, there has been an increasing overall brutalizing of the quality of life in our society as a product of the militarization required for maintaining our empire. Military procedures are idealized, and one of these is the role of force in the making of policy with its attendant acceptance of the consequences of exercising force. Those sports which are increasingly popular happen to be "games" in which "unsportsmanlike" fistfights, assaults and brawls break out between players of opposing teams and/or players and fans. The fans dearly love these moments when even the rules of the violent game are ignored and indiscriminate fighting triumphs. Brute force reveals the real face of "civilization" and just listen to the fans squeal! *That's* what they pay their bucks to see! John Foster Dulles and Hank Kissinger would be pleased: when you can't get what you want by the rules of the game, punch the other guy in the face! Such international assaults are not to be laughed off: in early 1976, the Russian Army hockey team was shipped off to the U.S. as part of the exchanges of Détente to play the American teams. While playing the Boston Bruins (and defeating them handily), one Bruin slugged a Russki player in the gut with his hockey stick which moved the usually sports-lapping Boston *Globe* to editorialize: "The Russian Army team gave the Bruins a hockey lesson the other night and reminded us what a wonderous game hockey can be when played without the macho mayhem that has brought some district attorneys running . . . The message could not have been clearer than when the Bruins' Wayne Cashman, looking more like a bully boy than an athlete, levelled Russia's Boris Mikhailov with his stick in an act of retaliation that's become standard fare in the National Hockey League. The way to play winning hockey is not by learning to be a goon on ice . . ." *Wrong* you are *Globe*-writers! The Russkis may have beaten the Bruins, but at the same time, Boston's bears are the top team on the ice in the N.H.L.

As the editorial informs, District Attorneys are also looking into this new popular violence. Dave Forbes, another stud on the ruff 'n tumble Bruins team, was actually *indicted* in the fall of 1975 for assault in Minneapolis as a result of a clobbering he gave a member of an opposing team *during* a game. He beat the rap, but this new concern of law enforcement agencies in the felonies that take place under the protective umbrella of "sports" is a whole new development. And what worried sounds emanated from the sports claquers when it looked as though "the law" might spoil "the fun"!

When a small democracy has expanded into a military empire, as has the U.S. of A., it is surely the spirit of democracy which must suffer. The network of supports which legitimates and propagates the military ethic undermines democratic attitudes and impulses. "Sports," in their current metamorphosis, serve this function, handmaiden to empire, the military ethic passed off as civilian "leisure," to tune folks up for teamwork on the assembly-line and to send their sons and daughters off to war. It is in this role as agents for undermining what's left of democratic attitudes and behavior that I attack sports and accuse them of being the most visible part of the effort which is hurrying the demise of what has been good in the American social experiment.

In the May 1975 issue of *The Match*!, an anarchist journal, I came across an article "Not Just For Sport," reprinted from the April 1946 issue of *Why?*, also an anarchist journal, now defunct. Its author, identified only as "D.D.W.," argues along similar lines and I am pleased to quote: "One thinks of the degeneration of the Grecian sports into 'practices designed to gain the oak-leaf.' The very word, athletics, means prize-getting in the original Greek . . . By definition athletics must be rejected; there is no way to reform such practices . . . It is revolting to think of natural activities utilized by governments in order to stabilize their oppressive institutions." As to what is to be done: "A frontal attack upon games as they are played by youth, with a scathing, persistent expose of the neurotic character of athletics, can at least suggest a solution."

Always remember: Good Athletes Make Good Soldiers.

D.D.W. recalls the words of Mussolini as he addressed a group of athletes on their way to an international competition: "Athletes of Italy, remember when you fight outside the borders of Italy, you carry the honor, the sporting prestige of your nation in your muscles, bodies and souls!"

The "tougher," the more violent the sports with which a Sports Straightist identifies, the more Macho will he want to appear in his social behavior. In fact, one could forward this rule of thumb: The more machismo displayed in a sport with which a fan identifies, the more repressed he is likely to be personally, and the more likely it is that his social personality will be merely an agglutination of popular clichés, right-wing politics, traditionalist "solutions" to social problems, and typical authoritarian patter. He is satisfied with what's processed through to him as *abstracted* Macho Straightness; he is, alas, a sideliner under the delusion he's right up front for manhood and freedom!

We can find some interesting examples of this successful repressed personality type. Ex-president Nixon, surely one of the most physically uncoordinated of the recent occupants of the White House—ever notice how he frequently dropped things in public (other than bombs, of course)? Baseballs, pens, medals? And how he hired the model of Dr. Strangelove to be his "right-hand man"?—has called himself America's No. 1 Football Fan. Never a bride but always a bridesmaid, Nixon was a second-string benchwarmer at Whittier College for four years. No "touch" football games on the White House lawn à la J.F.K. (to whom athletic prowess and "toughness" in world affairs went hand-in-hand; remember the fifty mile hikes?). No horse-riding or speeding in cars and throwing around beer cans like L.B.J. Hell, Nixon didn't even play golf regularly like Eisenhower. He just sat on his butt in the Oval Office and watched football games maniacally, phoned congratulatory messages to naked, wet jocks in the locker rooms, and provided coaches with specific plays.

Nixon (as has his successor) even took over the lingo of the playing field and applied it to domestic and international policy. Hence, a cabinet is a "team," emphasizing its subservience to its "coach," rather than accenting the alleged integrity of these men and women who should be leaders—good-bye Wally Hickel, Robt. Finch, Eliot Richardson, *inter alia*. Imperialist diplomacy becomes "game plans." Elections are the Super Bowl of politics, and even *they* are rigged.

The successor actually *did* make the team back in school days. And Jerry Ford's stint as a college football hero was in that season when Michigan's varsity sustained its losingest record in years. No matter; follow Nixon's lead; one Mayagüez will make up for it. Yet, isn't it curious how he *too*, despite his much-publicized dedication to exercise and physical fitness, keeps falling down, bumping into things, klutzing about? What Lyndon Johnson *actually* said was: "Jerry Ford can't *fart* and chew gum at the same time!" And, after 5 years of a clod like Nixon, a nation resents it; it's no wonder those California ladies tried to gun him down.

Also interesting to note is that both football and hockey involve apparel which makes men appear considerably larger than they are naturally, visually re-enhancing the association between "manliness" and sheer physical size. Men in football or hockey uniforms recall the huge papier-mache dummies in Jean-Claude van Itallie's wonderful play, *America, Hurrah!* The larger a man appears the greater it's assumed is his potential and *will* for violence, and the greater the "respect" he commands in our society. With football uniforms particularly, most traces of individuation among the players are hidden under bulky helmets, shoulder pads, numbered jerseys and padded pants. At most, one can catch only a glimpse of flesh, black, white or brown on the limbs, and by this identify the player's race. The covering of physical individuality is but one of the functions uniforms serve, as we shall discuss later. But speaking of race, we should point out here that professional spectator sports only began to be racially integrated at approximately the same time as were the American armed forces: both in the late 1940s. Why was this such an important achievement? Because it was finally an admission by White Macho Straightists that the "toughness" of Black men was on par, officially at least, with that of whites. Interesting though that desegregation was proclaimed as having made its biggest advances in Macho enterprises: uniforms, group discipline, violence, subservience, and guns, the inner sanctum where white men re-enacted their masculinity by rituals of force. Blacks were accepted on the playing field and in the army before they were accepted as equals in public schools, in housing, and in public accommodations, in other words accepted in matters where obedience and achievement for the team is rewarded but not where parity and activism is the norm.

Still, as integration had to come, it is consistent that upwardly aspiring members of ethnic and racial minorities should have to prove their loyalty to the values of established Macho Masculinity before being accepted on whatever terms, proving they can duplicate and even exceed in the worst and self-denying of masculinist expectations, not the best. As players, members of minorities were as qualified for professional competition as whites ever since "sports" began. What was so disturbing to White Macho Straightists was the idea that Blacks and others were going to be included as *symbols* of Macho Straightness, and that the sex-repressed energy of the sports fans would, ultimately, have to be tied up with these dark-skinned stars. Would they let Blacks possess the honor of embodying the sexually-charged symbolic behavior of Macho Masculinity? Integration as an issue in sports was one of the first times that it became obvious to many Americans that the playing field, despite hypocritical claims of it being an apolitical, unifying aspect of American life, was actually a hotbed of politics and racism. Well, integration came to sports—with prominent exceptions in the South—but the "problem" of Blacks as symbols of Macho Masculinity remains unsolved for many men to this day. Witness the threats and insults to Hank Aaron just as he was to break Babe Ruth's record as Home Run King. To have a Black man as "the best" of some achievement is still very unnerving to many white Macho Straightists.

That team sports serve the symbolic function of representing how men want to see themselves in their idealized roles is underscored by the obvious fact that the image of a society which the teams proffer is one in which *women are deliberately excluded*. Team sports are exclusively the domain of males—and Macho males at that! Team sports are atavistic remnants of a social separation of the sexes which is now obsolete; to celebrate this separation by games in a ritual of violence, in fact, glamorizes and enhances social reaction instead of moving to accommodation and resolution of social problems. *The male team sports are examples of the height of the arrogant principle and practice of male prerogative.* Women who do succeed in athletics are virtually all involved in the individualist sports, and compete almost always against other women, and the few women's teams which do exist are rarely brought to public notice, except as "human interest" stories.

What has been the *conventional* role of women in the lives of Sports Obsessed Males?

Ex-First Lady Pat Nixon advises "grid widows" how to behave: "They should get in there and join him—that's what I do," she told the Associated Press. Apparently, it was just a terrible burden for all of them—and such confusion!—for as the President was trying to pay close attention to The Big Game, there were those damned interruptions—Washington under seige, buggings, break-ins, his staff and cabinet being indicted. What could she do to help? "When he has to go to the telephone, I make it a practice to try to keep up with what is happening so I may fill him in."

Of course it is endlessly amazing that in American life if a phenomenon and its consumers operate in some kind of equilibrium, if they block out criticism, and if they attempt to pressure virtually everyone to join their fold, they smugly regard themselves as "non-political." Being non-political is regarded in our society, for some reason, as a *virtue*, or so say the Authorities, as I guess anything non-political is no threat to their status in power. Being *not* non-political means that one must be *critical* of the present order of life in this country, and being critical is . . . well . . . *harpy*, don't you think, and not *lots* of fun. It is rarely observed that the stresses, tensions, and wastes produced to support the structure of any particular social arrangement should be properly regarded as the domain of politics and open to any kind of shots lobbed its way.

Sports are always presented as "non-political." In the last few years, there have been many groans over the "introduction of politics" into "The sporting arena," as though the very symbol of a society—its games—should be prissily exempt while all other institutions in our society are scrutinized, attacked and destroyed! When two American Black athletes, Tommie Emith and John Carlos, gave a raised fist salute during the American national anthem at the 1968 summer Olympics in Mexico City, "sports fans" were outraged. They were merciless in their collective cry for punishment. When Arab terrorists kidnapped and killed members of the Israeli team at the summer Olympics in Munich, 1972, conventional world leaders and press clucked over this intrusion of international hatreds into the playing field. What amazed the more disinterested among us at the time was how people failed to understand the Olympics as extensions of nationalist competitions. After all, weren't the teams representing *states*? They did not represent interest groups, athletic associations, peoples, or least of all themselves; they were carrying the flags and hopes of political states! And as such, who's to be surprised they end up squashed beneath the foot—and for the reputation and glory—of Leviathan!

Mr. Avery Brundage, then the chairperson of the Olympics Committee and a fairly perfect case of the Sports Obsession and the strange distortions it inflicts on a man (and now mercifully deceased, no doubt calling the plays from the sidelines in Hades), was notorious for his iron fist, iron heart, and iron head when it came to maintaining rigorous subservience among participating States' teams and enforcing a strict interpretation of the Olympics as an international *competition*. Lacking a mind, however, he failed to reason how what he upheld could only lead to violence. Brundage even had the temerity, while speaking at the memorial services for the slain Israelis, to blame for the tragedy those nations which weeks earlier had demanded the exclusion of racist Rhodesia. These nations had, he asserted, established the precedent for "introducing politics into sports" which "culminated" in the terrorist action.

In a more recent, similar incident, two Black members of the E. Michigan University track team continued their warm-up exercises during the playing of the National Anthem at a Knights of Columbus game in the Nassau (N.Y.) Coliseum. New York *Times*: "The commotion started during the playing of the anthem when several fans began shouting from the stands. At the conclusion of the music, most of the 8,551 spectators joined in the booing. Some chanted 'Throw them out!' Others shouted racial epithets at the athletes, who were Black . . . As the booing continued for more than a half hour, Referee Ed Swinburne disqualified the team." What is the lesson to be learned from this? If you don't show respect for the trappings of the State, you can't play!

More clucking was heard too when team men like Jim Bouton and Dave Meggysey wrote books detailing the extent of human exploitation and brutality that owners and managers inflict on players and which the spectators consume without protest.

I do not deny that there is some "entertainment component" in spectator sports. It is very little actually, less than some drab TV soap opera, and certainly there is not enough to maintain viewer interest on its own merit for an entire season, especially when you consider the effort and expense to the fan who attends the games in person. What little entertainment there is in watching and shouting at sports matches is marketed by owners as "giving the fans what they want," always offered as "a reason" by people selling *anything* in American society. But it is not the entertainment quality which keeps Macho Straightists returning to the stadium week after week or glued to their boob tubes eating junk foods. No, what attracts them in mobs is the weekly display of the Macho values to which they feel they must bear allegiance, the ritual re-enactment of the establishment of masculinity through violent encounter and the ultimate humiliation of someone losing, and just the plain old pitch to their basest anti-social frustrations: "Kill the Ump!"

Much of the resentment against men like Bouton and Meggysey was occasioned by their public disclosures of the damage this "entertainment" inflicts on men and how contrary professional sports actually *are* to the image the hired sportswriters project. They told of the administration of drugs before and during games, the degrading personal discipline and pettiness of authority, the disregard for serious physical injury sustained while in a game, and the indifference to the general "burning out" of men in professional sports by age 35. Owners and managers, of course, did not want this seamy side of their business exposed. Reality had no place in the fans' conceptions of their favorite teams and how they worked. Fans do not want to be made aware of the dirty mechanics of the system of sports. Bouton and Meggysey were "unsportsmanlike" to have tarnished the *image* of professional sports this way. Or, like they used to say in another area of exploitation: "If you didn't come in to work on Sunday, *don't* come in on Monday." Sports won't tolerate golden boys who go rusty; everyone must keep up *in spirit*. Pep! Pep! Pep!

In 1974 and '75, we've seen a new development among the players—football players in particular—the emergence of, if not class consciousness, at least a surge of trade unionism, and the economic and organizing use of the strike. Though one may well question the strike as a tactic in a superficial and "luxury" industry like professional sports, these confrontations with the bosses brought the guts of the sport, i.e., the intake and outflow of dollars and the slavery conditions of the players' contracts, into public lights, much to the embarrassment of the fat cats of the leagues. And the bosses were quick to denounce striking players as ruining the image of the game for milions and, again, taking the "fun out of sports."

The bosses are right, in a way. The fans—their expectations already displaced from reality through their Sports Obsession and the fantasy it serves—don't really want to know the *actuality* of a team member's life in professional sports. They content themselves with the sportswriters' jibberish. Since athletes are presented at the summit of what it means to be a Man's Man, it's naturally assumed that they are tough, that they can take it. Tough He-Men aren't supposed to whine and complain; that's the route of panty-waists. So if these guys can't take it, then *get out*, because there are plenty more waiting in line who'd love to suffer every minute of the agony and humiliation and ephemeral triumphs. If the truth were generally admitted about the life in college and professional sports, the Macho attachment of the fans might be called into question; they might get upset or become uneasy, disquieted by the confusion of it all, and that might hurt the box-office. And this must never happen. The reality that men need a *humane* masculinity, that they cannot be tapered into self-sufficient machines for competition and conquest and quick disposal without inviting perversions of Self, must not be conceded by those who gain by maintaining the status quo.

Part of Lance Rentzel's ignominious fall from favor can be understood when put into context of this system of duplicity. Rentzel, a star with the Dallas Cowboys football team, became an overnight pariah in the sports world and an object of pity—*pity*! Ick! The very antithesis of what Macho Straightness aims for!—after he was arrested and charged with indecently exposing himself to some pre-teen girls. Though, granted, this is not the healthiest kind of sexual behavior on the market, it is surely not uncommon among males, especially those who are sexually repressed. Other well-known and well-loved ball players have kinkier interests and obsessions than Rentzel's. Rentzel was a victim of hypocrisy more than anything else. As a pretty-boy glamor-guy in uniform, it was an unspoken part of his job to represent to fans not what men *actually are in their behavior* but rather how they want to see themselves in their ideal and in front of others—The Macho Male Leader of the Tribe. Had Rentzel been hired for the team *just to play ball*, his having exposed himself to girls would have in no way altered his skill at the game. By being apprehended, however, he gave the fans grounds to revoke *their belief in him* as an embodiment of the Butchie Ideal of Macho Masculinity. He was flawed and got caught at it. He had lost control over events. He had been publicly humiliated, had allowed reality to become complex; these are things that any person who is chosen to represent the treasured fantastic projections of the fans must never permit to happen.

Sportsmen are, in their way, expected to be the chorines of their sex: bubble-headed, not too bright, cliché-ridden, ready for a good time, ready for sex in a healthy way, and total strangers to the world of ideas and independent thinking. Bill Walton, vegetarian star of Portland, Oregon's basketball team, while mixed up with the Jack Scott-Patty Hearst-SLA imbroglio, made some remarks in a press conference about the abuse in the grand jury system, etc., which were immediately pounced on as "unAmerican." He was duly spanked in the press and dressed down by his bosses.

In the summer of 1975, the *Advocate*, the West Coast gay fortnightly, published an exchange between them and the Minnesota Twins baseball team front office. The *Advocate* had been seeking info about the members of the Twins club reputed to be gay. The Twins' press lackies freaked out, denounced suggestions that any of their fine, outstanding players was gayola and told the *Advocate* to cease and desist any further communication.

Well, of course there are faggots in baseball land, and I'd say their situation today parallels that of the gay movie stars vis-à-vis the studios in their heyday in the '30s and

'40s. They're kept under tight observation and allowed no opportunity to create "scandal" or fuel rumors. But I predict that as 1974 saw the start of coming out among politicians (Elaine Noble, Allen Spears), and as 1975 saw the military coming out (Sgt. Matlovich, WAC Pfc Randolph—and don't forget Oliver Sipple, the ex-Marine who saved the Prez!), so 1976 will be the time of the coming out of the athletes.

And, my dear! Barely did my pen leave the page after writing the above but the trusty Boston *Globe* hits the stands with this front page item: "Ex-Grid Pro Admits He's Homosexual," just totally jumping the gun on my prediction. Though not actively involved in professional sports now, Dave Kopay, "thought to be the first pro football player to admit his homosexuality openly, stepped forward in an interview with The Washington *Star* after reading the initial installments of the newspaper's current series on gay athletes . . . Homosexuality is never discussed in the locker room, he said, not even among the players who know one another to be gay. 'You were fearful of being called a faggot or getting kicked off the team,' he said. 'It's so hidden'." So move over Rep. Noble and Lenny Matlovich! Here's one more face soon to hit the lecture circuit; tonight's topic in our Howard Brown Memorial Lecture Series is "How Coming Out Can Perk Up a Waning Career."

To be included with the acceptable males in our Macho society, it is requisite that one should admit to possessing an interest in sports. Whether feigned or real, this interest establishes one's consent to the role of the Sports System in our culture. This mandatory assent is how American men "sniff each other out," their way of spotting if another male is "safe." If a male were not to admit to accepting the primacy of the Sports Obsession, other questions about him would quickly be raised. But assenting to the Sports Obsession gives other males a fast way of affirming that one shares with them a whole set of attitudes and behavior. They wear it like an identity card.

Put any two American males in a closed room and it is more than likely that within minutes they will start discussing sports. Hand an American male a daily newspaper and he will probably turn directly to the sports pages. It is a fundamental assumption in our society that "sports" figures foremost in the "minds" of American males.

Once again, the strange case of ex-President Nixon provides us with an excellent example of this compulsive singlemindedness.

After the American invasion of Cambodia in 1970 and the murders at Kent State, and during the siege of Washington which followed, Nixon, wearing make-up, met with student demonstrators at the Lincoln Memorial at 4 AM. After finding out which universities they came from, he asked them how the football teams did that year. They were trying to end the war and Nixon wanted to know football scores! Incredible? The best is yet to come: Nixon even remarked that had he his life to live over again—grim thought!—he'd like to end up a sportswriter. Sportswriters! Ugh! Talk of camp followers! They remind me of drag queens in beauty contests; both tramp from town to town, carrying little overnight bags, the sportswriter his portable typewriter, the drag his cosmetics, living off the handouts of promoters, each in search of some elusive ideal, two sides of the same coin, really, given currency by those fleeing genuine eroticism into the superficial stylization of a repressed sexuality.

One needn't actually *be* interested in spectator sports; one must only admit to it publicly and make the effort to be tolerably well-informed about each day's Big Game to exchange sports-talk banter with the guys to pass muster with Macho Straightists.

But, then, this is the pattern of much behavior in our land. The social function of hypocrisy is to allow one to appear to be what one *isn't* when convenient. This is necessary for many people because our society proscribes some very reasonable and expectable components of human behavior. One needn't really *be* heterosexual, say, in one's desire for regular sexual activity; it is only required that one *appear* to be so. Appearance is all. Like cancered cells in the body, one hypocrisy births others, and people keep smiling, nodding and never noticing the pathology.

Since a Macho tilt in masculinity requires the repression of vast potentialities of expression, Macho Males' obsession with sports provides them with something to occupy the vacuum created by their affiliation with Macho values. (The other approved subject for conversation is The Pursuit Of The Dollar. Macho men rarely talk about women *as* women. Women only enter into their conversations and lives as components necessary for OK-heterosexual coupling which will lead to the maintenance of The Family which enhances their personal power. Women are the "other" through which they build and secure the stature of their male prerogative.)

The identification with competitive team sports begins very early in an American male's life. The old gag about the proud new father giving his offspring a football is not so funny in this light. Mother can help too. Little boys are dressed in coats with baseball or football team insigne stitched on them. Here in Boston, it appears that every other male child wears a blue windbreaker adorned with a capital "B" emblem of the Boston Bruins hockey team and a knit cap bearing the same. They identify with teams, yes, but given the option of identifying with one of many teams, they pick the winningest team and/or the most brutal. This patterning is as uniform as the "uniforms."

As team members have the same uniform, so fans, though under no official compulsion—except that they volunteer by their allegiance to the Macho system—clad themselves in similar costumes. In fact, "fans" wear the badges of their fan-dom proudly, boastful, though God knows why, of being "players in abstraction," i.e., spectators. This kind of visual "social skin" is a particularly proud identity for lower-class males. Their garb is their public projection of an identity they have internalized as personal and private. These clothes remind them that they belong to something that they think means something—the Club of approved Macho Straight Masculinity. The loss of individuality (never so great a sacrifice for interchangeable people in an industrial society) is more than compensated for to them by the reward of belonging to The Gang with its implicit power and threat of violence. They can pick one another out in a crowd, or, as is more likely the case, in the crowd of OK males, they can pick out the ones who have chosen not to conform to their system of Macho coercion.

And, as one who has long been interested in uniforms and their possibilities (and male gear of all types, really), I am always pleased and, I suppose, titillated in a way when I observe teen boys on the Boston subways in their football or hockey uniforms, attire more suited for sex orgies than the slush of "practice" on the field. But more about uniforms later, yet having become a solipsist somewhere along the way, I fancy that their "practice" will be eventually utilized to serve my pleasure.

Instead of being just a spectating fan, it's best to be involved in some team sport, at whatever level, so that one may publicly identify oneself in this capacity. Sport Straightists love to wear jackets with their bowling league name stitched over their tits or on the upper sleeve. Their position is even more favorable if they've actually *defeated* someone, other males. Then they can have "Champs" added to their Butch Identity!

Adult men will costume themselves in other garments of sports attire when in public. Many men affect the baseball cap, most noticeably the American astronauts, surely Butch subservient figures if ever there were any (and didn't they all freak out or turn sour once released from their "duty"?). In the case of the Astronauts, they actually *were* military men being passed off as civilians.

In the last 10 years, another popular butch-identifying article of apparel (often favored by female "jock groupies") is the grey T-shirt with the legend "Property of Touchdown U. Athletic Dept." printed across the chest.

A word should be offered here in explanation of the recent self-awareness of Macho Straightists as "Jocks." The word "jock" when used to refer to a Sports Obsessed male was at one time not too long ago considered an insult, belittling, if not an outright derogatory slur. But in the last few years, the word has become respectable. Sports Obsessed Macho Straightists proudly refer to themselves as Jocks. In the early '70s a slick commercial sports magazine began publication (and promptly folded) called *Jock*. Headline writers now use the word without a second thought. And it's even common to hear women refer to women athletes as "jocks," which still makes me wince.

What has happened to bring about this change?

The elevation of the word "jock" to acceptable public usage came about because Sports Obsessed Macho Straightists grew to realize that they were on the defensive. Yes! Staggering as the idea was to them, it could not be denied. Their lifestyle, which they thought was eternally triumphant, had eroded in its grip over males in the 1960s and was no longer absolute in its "authority." Young men were growing up *who didn't idealize sports stars* and all they represented. Large and vocal minorities were proliferating who were indifferent and/or aggressively hostile to the system of Macho Values. Anti-war demonstrators, though not opposed to sports yet per se, did attack War and—good grief!—"sports" as but the farm system to war, from the original Greek Olympics that prepared Hellas for the slaughter of the Peloponnesian War to the football scrimmages at the American base at Danang which were meant to keep up the fighting morale and spirit. To attack war is getting awfully close to home. What next? Hippies! Drug-users! The social order was mass-producing its antithesis—certainly trying its damnedest, as it looked like good business—in what has since been called "the counterculture." Not only were members of this counterculture not characterized by a Sports Obsession, some even had their doubts about *all* Macho attitudes as well. Then came the feminist wave, challenging masculine prerogative itself! And then gay liberation with those faggots thinking men should dance, and suck cock and wear those tight pants! This was just too much too fast. Reaction was the only response.

As one by one the assumptions of the Sports-Military Macho Straightists met assailants striking closer and closer at their repressed core with reason on their side, Sports Straightists retrenched, regrouped and made a more brazen, more forward declaration *of just where they stood.* They were going to hold tight to what they believed in. No quitters, they! No slobbery criticizers! No pantywaists! No sissy longhairs! They became JOCKS—almost with a vengeance, self-admitted, pushy macho men, trying to defend something (they were never able to put it into words) which they knew was under attack. Their position became more self-consciously defensive, since now they were only one of many public factions. The liberation of others made them very nerrrvous, and they retained the brain-set as if they were still absolute in the world of men even though in fact their attitudes and behavior were being challenged from many directions. It's hell for Repressed Straightists to have to defend themselves against criticism that they never expected would arise in the first place once their conventional supports fall away. Talk of your rats in corners, my dear. They can only come out slugging away!

Possessing no argument, they fall back on posturing, and *that's* something Jocks have always done well and played on for sympathy, support, and intimidation. The posing in a locker room far outstrips that in any gay leather/denim bar hands down; yet both share a kind of heavy oppressiveness in their atmosphere, even though the one is totally closeted, whereas the latter openly appeals to erotic desire.

Now that the Absolute Reign of Macho has been publicly challenged, now that there are visible and creative public alternatives, the Jock, né Macho Straightist, has had to admit to the changing circumstances in his own way which, in itself, becomes an undermining of his repressed identity. All these sports stars and their loyal male fans with hair dryers! I don't understand it. Are they supposed to be Knute Rockne or Veronica Lake, or something in between? Macho Straightism has failed to impose totality. Hence, its "magic" is gone forever—assuming that in every generation there will be large numbers of men and women who genuinely know, recognize and act on their own best self-interest. And even as they become more pushy as "Jocks," look how they become so fashion-following. Long-haired males 10 years ago were *automatically* "hippies" and "faggots." Yet today, who's got the over-the-shoulder hair-dos? The *Jocks*! Watch the ads during a football game! Besides the hair-dryers mentioned above, the Macho Straightist has become a veritable beauty shoppe of rinses, nets, curlers, Quiana fancy clothes, make-up, colognes, beauty aids. The gay boys these days are wearing short-cropped hair and are getting into being mannish; the sports fans are now totally stylized and becoming "ladies." What a bunch of hypocrites they are! It's so characteristic of these kneejerk authoritarians: they become what they hate—after an appropriate cultural lag. I even saw Joe Namath on TV modeling a pair of pantyhose!

Men are also proud to be known as Coaches, whether it's just a school-boy sport, a neighborhood league, a college or, best of all, a professional team. In fact, the name "Coach" has assumed a place of honor among acceptable nicknames for Tough Guy Sportsmen along with Bucky, Butch, Buzz, Champ, Legs, Stretch, Skeeter, Scooter & Woody.

The coach has much the same relationship with "his boys" as did the abbot of yesteryear with his young monks. It is obviously a homosexual one, though expressive manifestations of this cannot be allowed or the superior would lose his authority. The coach's interest in the boys is, allegedly, "for the good of the boys," for their proper development and as their socializing agent. The asceticism of their relationship requires the repression of sensuous intra-sex interest, and the energy which would have normally been channeled out this way gets released in violent, painful, self-sacrificing body contact "sports" for the victory of the team.

It is my contention that intra-sex interest is there nonetheless; it is up to men to deal with it reasonably or flee it in fright. Boys want to love men in positions of instruction, men with whom they are secretly affectionate anyway, men whom they seek to please with their young bodies in competition with other boys ("To Sir, With Love").

Similarly, the coach harbors the desire to take his avuncular relationship with his charges to a further expression, something more than just a pat on the ass, a chuck on the chin, an arm across the shoulder (viz. P.N. Warren's *The Front Runner*, again). The relationship cries out for a closeness between men of different generations, for expressions of the need our society wrongly and fiercely quashes. Why not embrace the boy with affection? Why shouldn't a man in charge of developing a boy to physical grace and beauty encourage a thorough appreciation of what is happening, happening both to the youth and *between* the youth and his mentor?

This refusal to acknowledge openly the homosexual passion that exists in the coach-athlete relationship (as a paradigm for inter-generational contacts) invariably perverts the form that intra-sex desire takes when it finally breaks through to expression in some form. This accounts for the stories one hears of coaches arrested in bus station tea-rooms, the Boy Scout leader caught fellating male hustlers in cars, the scandalous Navy Admiral with his entourage of swishy young sailors, etc. It's all too familiar. When these men are barred from an honest and open recognition of tender passion between males, and when they can no longer hold back their desire, it is these tawdry and/or coercive forms with which they are left. Surely it must be conceded that in our present structure of society, the ethic supporting the Sports Obsession has little room for eroticism of *any* kind, excepting perhaps some little corner in a sportsman's life marked SEX which usually involves the "conquest" of women or some brutish quick encounter with a "cocksucker." There is of course lots of eroticism involved in each ballplayer's relation with his teammates as well as with his coach, though you won't catch any of them admitting it. Why can't they acknowledge what it so obvious? Why must it be the job of others to educate individuals to identify and accept what they already know by another name? "Buddy-ism" is simply a rudimentary, adolescent form of homo-eroticism on a very covert plane, packaged and sold in the mein of Butch Tough-Guyism. That's the only way society will tolerate homosexual connections between males. Men gather with other men because they like to do so. It's that simple! But where do they go from there? Our society forbids instruction in homosexual encounters, hence men usually find some excuse to give "purpose" to their assembly. That they frequently choose "sports" as their excuse is the final paradox of the sportsman's interest in other males; his fascination can only approximate expression as long as some males are striving to conquer other men. It boils down to this: a boy or man can be interested in another man or men so long as that man or men exert their physical powers of force to overcome men designated as "opponents." For *that*, they become objects of admiration, and it's *then* OK to say so.

Another oddity:

Entire cities are identified by the privately-owned teams which play in them and call them "home." Where this may have once meant something as, say, in baseball's early days when a hometown boy might make it big on his town's team, today's athletes are good corporation lackies; they will move anywhere for that promotion, greater salary, or to fulfill a contract. They are traded as rapidly as are the bubble gum cards on which their pictures appear.

As Americans themselves become increasingly more mobile, the emotional attachment to the concept of "hometown" diminishes. What we are encouraged to believe belongs to the city and its citizenry remains the "private property" of a corporation. Ask "fans" in Brooklyn how they felt when the Dodgers picked up and left.

As Super-Fan Nixon said: "I always make it a practice to root for the hometeam"— where have you heard *that* before?—"and Washington is my hometown now." Is he boosting or *boasting*? But then, like chasing commies one year and sipping tea with Mao another, in the 1972 Super Bowl, he boosted the Miami Dolphins; in 1973 he was be-hind the Washington Redskins. (Incidentally, the team he supported each year lost.)

As local connections break down and dissolve, these identifications with abstrac-tions, such as with ball clubs in municipalities, have to carry a greater significance as a symbol. In this regard team athletes foster a narrow chauvinism which has nothing to do with normal local pride, and it is a competitive chauvinism promoted for the private profit of the team owners. The team of one town must defeat and ideally humiliate the opposition or the fans will be disappointed in them.

It's hard to convey my dismay when in early adolescence I learned that my home-town baseball club—the Cincinnati Reds—*did not belong to the town*. They were "owned" by cigar-chomping wheeler-dealer types! And though I was never a gung-ho sports nut as a youth, it seemed an important gesture to support what I thought was a municipally-owned effort as a symbol for a city I rather liked then. To subsequently hear rumors of the team's leaving because pickings were better elsewhere shocked me deeply, and I quickly understood more of the *nature* of capitalists and financeers than any ensuing booklearning offered. And how really queer, I thought, that so many people (sports fans) could be so intensely involved in an activity over which they had no control—except to pay the salaries—one which, in turn, makes no commitment to them, and one in which their only role is as consumer and exploited. That, too, led me to see the result of personality fragmentation in industrial society. Indeed, sports did, as high school coaches promised me, prove instructive.

The *names* of sports teams always intrigued me; different ways of identifying them seemed to come in and out of fashion. First came social characteristics or distinctive ar-ticles of clothing—Yankees, Redstockings, White Sox; then came a vogue for animal names—Bears, Tigers, Bruins, Colts, Dolphins; most interesting is the recent trend of identifying teams with a city's or region's leading industrial product—Pistons, Steelers, Oilers, Supersonics, etc., further demonstrating the deliberate complementary functions of modern team sports with consumer capitalism.

Speaking of names, sports stars, once they've proved their competence, are allowed certain privileges in violating Macho expectations—flashy, even swishy clothes, the appearance of gross sexual promiscuity, rumors of drugs, etc.—as long as they remain in good standing on the team. I've always been surprised with the *tolerance* shown for what I regard as "feminine" and/or cutie-pie names for rugged Men In Sports: Jo-Jo, Gayle, and there was even a guy named Nellie Fox! These are not my idea of what macho sports fans *expect* their heroes to be called. How could a kid identify with his sports hero if his hero is named Nellie? You'd think the front office would have made him change it! There's only one name acceptable to red-white-'n-blue sports fans, and I just happened to find a picture of this fellow in the papers—your favorite and mine: BUTCH DEADMARSH. Second place goes to the L.A. Kings' hockey star: BUTCH GORING.

The operation of privately-owned mass spectator sports teams directly encourages anti-social behavior among the fans. Team owners and players rarely accept responsi-bility for the disruptive passions they provoke. Fans are fanatic by their own admis-sion; they need little to excite them to acts of unreasonable violence. No outlet it provided for these passions once they are stirred at the stadium. The aroused fans are just dumped back into society to do their damage. To my mind, it's always a bad idea to gather X-thousand of Americans together in one arena for any event, and especially so if they are Macho Straightists who zealously anticipate some sort of disruption and vandalism as part of the festivities.

Name-calling, fistfights, even stabbings are not uncommon at Big Games. High school football leagues in most large urban areas don't pass through a season without some sort of increasingly armed battle between school antagonists, often a front for racial conflict. At the municipal level, should a team win a pennant or cup or league title, the price of the "celebration" will be paid in damage to private property—stolen cars, smashed plate glass windows, rock tossing, gang assaults on by-standers. "Victory" invariably leads to mayhem. This kind of excitability and irrational violence is a *necessary part* of the Macho personality, completely expectable of repressed males once they accumulate in mobs and can let go without guilt. And though the results of this vicious behavior are given lip-service concern by Macho authorities, the perpetuation of the Macho Straightist interpretation of masculinity demands that this damage be tolerated without punishment. Many Macho Straightists don't even perceive this kind of rowdy behavior as despicable and anti-social. To them the concept of "having a good time" has *always* involved some kind of destruction: hunting, lynching, wife-beating, demolition derbies, barroom brawls, etc. Why, for example, is it customary for the fans to tear down the goalposts while "celebrating" the conclusion of a football season?

Fat-cat owners and promoters get rich by arousing base behavior in the susceptible parts of the population (mostly male) and by inciting threats to you and me. I'm always appalled by "sports commentators" who tsk-tsk at the prevalence of drunks, thugs, fist-throwers and gang violence at sports stadia. They lament these "fringe elements" with their "misconduct." Nonsense! Rowdies are the *thrust* of sports fans; they're only picking up on the cues given them by the game itself; they want to tear the place up!

Opposite to the majority culture of repressed Macho Straights, we find that gay males have little psychological commitment to organized, competitive sports. Being openly gay frees men from the compulsion to have to maintain bubble-surface interest in these games. Of course, there is some participation in some sports by some gay men, mostly, however, the individualist sports. And there is certainly some interest in the superstar professional athletes themselves, partly as conversation items resulting from the massive and adoring attention given them, partly because they are attractive, well-built men who are presented as symbols of sexual potency, albeit repressed, and partly, too, because some of them are actively homosexual and feed the gossip grapevine.

There is nothing particularly odd or eccentric in this overt sexual attraction for the athletes by gay males where it exists, even if the value systems of the two life-styles are in opposition. After all, the men who select athletes for professional teams are just as conscious as are overtly gay males that they prefer pretty faces to fill those uniforms. It is no coincidence that big name talents just happen to be "lookers," as are rookie cops for the very same reason. They are selected not for their athletic excellence alone, but also with an eye for their marketability as symbols of saleable Macho Manliness. Best they be ruggedly handsome, but they can get away with being downright *pretty* as long as they're good ball players.

The sex lives of these beauties are much whispered about in private and in the press. Stories constantly circulate through the mill. Superstars like Joe Namath, Derek Sanderson and Bobby Orr, we must suppose, are pleased to have their observable prowess in athletic competition flow over into the assumed prowess they must show in the bedroom—or wherever they have sex. But is this rumored sexual wonderfulness fact or fiction? The athletes themselves care only as long as they increase their circle of power and prestige.

Gay men are simply not hesitant to articulate their overt sexual interest in Butchie Symbols, be they Macho or otherwise, though admittedly the carryings-on of the Macho Man will quickly dampen the passion. (It's damn hard to have good and regular sexual fun with a repressed man. Ask around.)

Teams constitute symbols, and though there are certainly many athletes who handle themselves well on the playing field, the jobs go to the beauties first. What has accelerated this process of selecting the most handsome men for professional sports is Television with its merciless close-up and its demands on a Celebrity's private life. It is an unpleasant truth to admit, but facially or physically repugnant men, no matter the extent of their athletic achievement will simply not make the team, just as they are no longer "qualified" for high public office in this post-Kennedy era of stylish electables.

The necessity of sports stars being sexually inviting physically is becoming somewhat more openly admitted by players and press alike. The February, 1973, issue of *Pageant* magazine features a cover story: "We Pick THE TEN SEXIEST MEN IN SPORTS!" Several of the men, including Cover Guy Terry Bradshaw, posed undraped to the waist. Said Bradshaw, in an attempt to smudge his tracks lest there be those who think he went too far, "People might say I've gone to the dogs! But it's all for fun. I don't think women will be trying to grab me!"

WHAT?

As an example of how exploited repressed eros attracts new recruits for the Sports Ethic, Victoria Pelligrino, who edits *Pageant*, says after selecting and interviewing these Ten Sexy Superstars: "I've never been a big sports buff, but now I've become a fan!" You bet! Skin sells tickets, as I know well. Yet she continues: "Interestingly, during our interviews it emerged that practically all of their attitudes toward women were on the conservative side . . . Almost all of them felt they wanted to dominate their women and that women, indeed, *want* to be dominated."

Pellegrino finds these attitudes surprising. Why? A representative of the Macho Sports Ethic couldn't think or believe otherwise. Of her ten Sexy Superstars, a majority—six—are unmarried. A peculiarity of their profession? Not necessarily so. The Sports Ethic is exclusive of women, and the repression of sex energy and its rechanneling into Team Sports favors a spartan existence—no matter how great the press plays up the "hi-living" angle of a sportsman's life. This is one reason why young boys have such an enormous affinity toward the lifestyle of teammates as presented by professional sports. These men in uniform on the gridiron are the archbishops of modern-day brutality; theirs is a life's calling to which all of life's other activities must be subsumed for the duration. There are no women around, except when and if you choose, and you set the terms. Women, it is assumed, would require "civilized" behavior of them, and that's a compromise. And though this lifestyle is fundamentally homosexual (i.e., all male) in its orientation, the team's *raison d'être* prevents them from having to deal rationally with the real questions of *how* men behave in groups and, more importantly, *why*.

This channeling and molding of erotic energy is a way of maintaining a specific order of authority, either for the benefit of an individual or a hierarchy of individuals. One can enhance the power of a system of values by connecting with and manipulating the erotic needs and responses of the masses, if one can excite them the right way. Sports heroes play a major role in containing the libidinal energies within the established system of values. They act as lightning rods for attracting males and then as conduits for absorbing them into the celebration of the Sports Ethic, then passing them on to the Military which, in turn, prepares them for "civic participation" in a "liberal democracy." If a male can be made to fear for his masculinity (after you've defined that masculinity very tightly), you can get him to do just about anything to save himself from being thought "queer" and "unmanly."

Let's take as an example the case of the handsome high school football captain (whose steady is—or at least was in my day—Miss Tits 'n Prom Queen). It is tacitly understood that what makes him a "leader" is not solely his assumed potential for physical violence; were that to be his sole base of authority, he'd be just a bully. But the legitimizing aspect of his power over other students comes from the fact that he is the *approved* representative of ideal masculine behavior, the pet of the coaches and the administration. He can "charm" the girls, and he does. And the other boys as well. Since he has the strongest hand in Force and Eros, other youths seek alliances with him to gain some reflected eminence, thereby setting up a hierarchy of preference with him as king-pin, and by this method the sports system of values perpetuates itself in majority that allows no active opposition.

If there happens to be a more handsome youth in the class who shows little interest in sports, the football captain can never really be top dog. In this case, eroticism for its own pleasure has a representative, and there will be those who are attracted to it as a principle embodied. Creative self-expression and selfless obedience to authority thus become split and antagonistic forces, and once the authority of force and the pursuit of pleasure are made separate and distinct, it's the brute who comes off poorly. The two forces when combined in the same person are always a winning combination for maintenance of the status quo; once divided each reveals its true character. Hence, one of the purposes of having attractive sports stars is to guarantee the combination of the two in the same person or group of persons.

The power of perverted eroticism is mobilized for violence in at least two ways in team spectator sports. It is made precious by the very rules of the game which impose formal limits on the ways men may connect. Violence becomes erotically charged when it is constrained in a controlled set of circumstances, like in a courtship or in a duel. Too, we know at the outset of the game that one team will win and that the other will lose—God forbid they should tie—and there's something profoundly comforting in knowing this. In our culture, the encounter of men against other men on the playing field, sweating in physical exertion, banging into one another to *overcome* one another is about as obvious a substitute for passionate sexual intercourse as we can find anywhere, the weird substitute society encourages. In place of thanatic orientation, let the fuckers wrestle, and likewise let the wrestlers fuck!

Without a comprehensive, *inclusive* view of how eroticism affects our total lives, men will continue to live fragmented, frustrated lives, leaving themselves wide open for corrupting appeal for manipulation and the perversion of behavior we now see as essential to the continuation of the Sports Obsession.

The uniforms that athletes wear are another means of drawing the ego-less, authoritarian-conditioned libidinal interest of spectators into celebrating brutal competition of men. The uniform disguises individuality, reduces players to "numbers," and makes them part of something larger than the sum of its parts. The uniform stimulates us to a certain degree, on whatever level of consciousness (we all, alas, have this Prussian streak in us which responds to elegant symbols as tools of subservience), but this erotic stimulation—which under more healthy conditions would be permitted a creative, self-fulfilling expression—is subsumed by the culture's imperative of ritual violence. It is no coincidence that the armed forces have traditionally had uniforms best cut to the masculine physique. The more articulated the uniform (while still closely detailing the male physiognomy) the more the uniform will successfully cover the individuation of each player and the more it becomes a focal point for repressed and rechanneled sexuality. Sexual involvement is invited, but it is not on an overt level; it is abducted and made to serve another purpose. The implied sex with a guy in uniform is the pitch to fuck with strangers, always easier in ways than sex with friends.

With the football uniform, for example, the head is enclosed, the face is guarded, but the massive forearms and calves are gaudily displayed, as is the bulbous derrière. While the eyes and mouth are hidden—traditional repositories of the "soul"—the ass and crotch are more accessible and solicitous than, say, on a man in a business suit who's all head and hands. Normal proportions are severely altered. It is this combination of high stylization with the gross accent on visibility of the distorted male physique with implications of violence which make uniforms achieve their most outstanding purpose. John Mitzel in a uniform is no longer just John Mitzel, ego; he's closer to pandering both to an Ego Ideal as well as drawing on the lewdness and lasciviousness of the Id.

The hockey uniform covers a man from his neck down with layers of cloth and heavy padding. The goalie of a team may as well be "Mr. Machine" for all you can see of him. And don't discount the attraction of males to the presentation of other men as total automatons (note the respect for Marines who'll do any- and everything their masters order). *Six Million Dollar Man* meet *Bionic Woman*. A hockey player ends up looking like a little boy dressed in too many snowsuits (which is perhaps why young hockey players look better in uniform than do their older teammates).

Baseball uniforms have become a little more stylish in recent years and more attentive to the male body. But they still remain too prosaic, too much like any man's acrid sweatsuit, to provoke a strong erotic interest. Fortunately, however, baseball players— who are much more head, hands, and feet than other ball players—have become hairier about the face and by this making a more direct sexual appeal than that of the clean-cut baggy-uniformed stars of the drab '50s.

Basketball uniforms are skimpy though often visually provocative by being made from erotically-associated materials like silk or nylon. Still, you've got to like skin to be a basketball fan. One might dare say that part of the reason professional basketball commands such a poor ranking among interests of Macho males is that there is something almost consciously embarrassing about seeing adult males—men intended as Straight Macho authority and its values—running around in front of *paying* customers in garments not dissimilar from their skivvy shirts and drawers. It is difficult to take a naked man seriously as a figure of authority in our culture, and nearly naked persons, in this case basketball players, face some degree of this problem.

And, yet, it was perhaps on account of this overtness of skin and hint of available sex that Le Jardin, the allegedly gay discotheque (but now largely patronized by AC-DC swingers and gawking straights) garbed their bartenders and bar men in slinky basketball uniforms. What a sensation! As with The Playboy Bunnies, it was definitely Look 'n Enjoy But Don't Touch.

Basketball is also a warm, indoorsy sport, and though this doesn't automatically make it a *sissy's* sport, it . . . well . . . lacks the quality of those sports played outside, where men battle not only each other but Nature as well. That's why it was an arguable mistake for Houston, Texas, Macho Capital of The World, to construct its glorious Astrodome. It closes out Nature's weather with its dome and even usurps Nature's grass with its synthetic Astro-Turf (which promotes players' injuries). Which is Butcher? Having Technology and MONEY enough to circumvent Nature? Or playing football in the elements? Houston, city to technology and money, saw something too feminine in the changes of the fickle weather and decided to close her out entirely and create an all-male *controlled* environment.

It's interesting to note that soccer has never caught on in this country, despite massive attempts at promoting it as "a major league sport." As I grew up I always regarded soccer as a "preppie" sport, as both of my older brothers went to private boys' schools with snotty brats from Shaker Heights' industrial-wealth families, and they had soccer teams, and I consequently thought of soccer as a game for the children of the elite. To then discover that "futbol" was the world's most favorite sport, beloved of the working classes everywhere, came as a surprise. It seemed only a matter of time and publicity before the American Sports Fan got addicted to this one as well.

But it didn't come to pass, partly I think because 1.) there was no "open season" left for it to cultivate a following without having to compete for audience with the junkies of another sport; 2.) it wasn't a game invented and/or modified in America and was thought to be a "foreign" pursuit, offensive to our strong nativist sentiment; and 3.) since *hands* are the least valuable instrument in the game of soccer, Americans, "do-it-yourselfers" from way back—as well as being physically awkward vis-à-vis The Old World, refused to accept this largely Third World sport. Hence, the audience at the soccer games which do transpire in the USA consists almost entirely of Europeans and Latin Americans.

The erotic stimulation caused by athletes in their uniforms becomes conscious among gay men, though it remains repressed in Macho types. To these latter the uniform is not so much a symbol of repressed and rechanneled sexuality as it is a manifestation of elective conformity and acceptance of the Sports System. To them the uniform represents the quality of repressing sexuality to band together with like-minded repressed, authoritarian men for the purpose of defeating and humiliating others. The thrill for them is not the erotic charge made conscious and utilized for self but rather the power of the brotherhood whose goal is to conquer others. The professional team becomes the male equivalent of the chorus line with billy clubs, decorated, disciplined, an attractive narcotic for the fan; it's an instrument for arousing sexuality then diverting the energy into creating and exercising the use of power. The repressed sexuality of athletes gladly becomes a subservience, and anyone among the males who's been in a uniform and not felt a tingle in his mind and prick when ordered about by a beefy older male in a position of authority is either terribly obtuse, conditioned to abuse, or lying. And with what speed and eagerness boys from authoritarian backgrounds and "educations" jump into uniforms given the chance. What is needed is to make this thrill more *self*-serving in erotic terms and less obedient to instituted authority.

The overtly homosexual sado-masochistic encounter is partially a distillation of this model, though admittedly it is wholly voluntary and outside social approval. It is comprised of many of the same inputs and remains to be fully explored and thoroughly explained by any theory: boys in uniforms which designate roles, some sort of stylized physical exertion, a clearly delineated dominator and a dominated. (And don't these sports-loving Boston Irish make splendid sado-masochists when they finally get into it—which, alas, they never really do since it's the pain, guilt and violence they relate to and not the transcendence into pleasure in it all.) But in the refining process of moving from Sports Fan Obsession to homo Sado-Maso encounter, the impurities have been removed, including the notion of defeating the opponent, the fear of failing, the necessity of keeping up one's Macho masculinity, and the compromise of being team-minded. In the gay S&M scene, Eros is the force served, not Thanatos; and one man will gladly be humiliated by the other and suffer the limit of pain his partner will inflict on him since it's a joy for both of them—as well as teasing and overcoming the set of "Do-Not-Trespass" perimeters we're all mind-fixed with as youths in this culture. These obstructions have been pared away and we are left with the essence of homosexual behavior become affectionate, though left in forms which may appear to the uninitiated as antithetical to affection, at which point we must remind ourselves that the expressions of love may take strange forms. It is a transcendence of taboo; at its best it is men totally at comfort with their bodies and their minds' masculinity. It is a kind of homosexual behavior made overt at long last, finally recognized as an end in itself. As Gore Vidal has sagaciously pointed out, the locker room after the game is the most ideal setting for a homosexual orgy. A lovely thought. But it's highly unlikely, because the attitudes which put the men in the locker room in the first place are the same ones which prevent them from sharing overt intra-sexual acts with their buddies, coaches and desired objects (see Dave Kopay's quote above). The team itself is a way for them to share what they see as their *strengths*. How could they violate the spirit of that by openly sharing what they are instructed to perceive as weakness, i.e., overt and sympathetic homosexual passion?

It might be said that the homosexual S&M experience and the Macho Straight's Obsession are not far apart. Both are overwhelmingly masculine-oriented in conventional symbols and terms. Both *apparently* seek the Butch Ideal of Manliness. It might even appear that the S&M encounter or relationship is only a further evolution of the sports-military fetish.

But in fact there is a qualitative difference between the two which puts them in separate worlds—certainly as far as the Macho Straightist is concerned. The homosexual encounter is an overt recognition of the pleasure to be taken in honest, open sex between men even if fantasy's games are being enacted. And the roles they assume are no inhibition to their pleasure; in fact, they're far from it. But, then, it's the contrary that's true: for the many who enjoy this pastime, they come to the experience already more liberated than their repressed macho brethren, already aware *and ready to act on* the highly, erotically charged uniforms and games of dominance and subservience. They use leather, military customs, disciplinary action and talk as *instruments* not as *goals*. The more specifically detailed the scene, the greater is the totality of the pleasure. I meet more and more guys who refuse to strip for sex and want to do it with their gear on. As they have learned, partners stimulate each other on many other levels as well as that of the skin. The uniforms, the sex-discipline, and the *methods* of the sports-military world are turned into *props* over which the partners have control for the expression of intra-male sensory pleasure. This very directness of *getting at* what they want is antithetical to the rigidity, alienation and abstration of libido characteristic of The Sports Fan. The props are just instruments in satisfying the human need for contact with others through like-minded sympathetic self-expression. They are not means for reducing one's individuality, as they are for the team players and/or soldiers. They are no longer the Macho male's manifestations of self-repression to the end of destruction, his outward and visible sign of inward and spiritual corruption. No, they are metamorphosized into devices for increasing pleasure; and creative pleasure cannot be long subservient to *any* outside master. For those who accept overt homosexual affection as a part of every man's life, these props are used to bring release from sexual stimulation and excitement. The game is played with all participants aware of their roles *as* roles, the props *as* props, the game as transitory, and with an unspoken equality even more solidly established between them when it's all over. Sports Fans would find themselves totally befuddled if they wandered into Whitman's omni-erotic democratic vistas.

To the sportsman, be he spectator or athlete, the uniform, the discipline and the other specifics of Macho male behavior are forms required by the *ethic* of the sports-military system. The cornerstone of this ethic is the demand for the repression of overt, unfettered, intra-male sexual possibilities and the rechanneling of this same energy into approved forms of social and personal aggression for the betterment of the team's positioning, the brotherhood, and the futurity implied by the power of its collective force. This ethic forbids the recognition of affectionate, desirous, non-brutal homosexual potential within each man, requiring each male to cut himself off from the source of some of his greatest inspirational energy.

Of course, this repressive ethic is rarely achieved in its perfect state. Homosexual contacts occur between males who are athletes just as they occur among the fans. But the ethic is still enforced and maintained and supported as the Ideal, and failing to keep up to it is definitely viewed as "deviance" and slippage." The Macho Straightist prefers men banded together in groups for the socially-approved ritual of destruction to the ritual of sex between and/or among men which might involve a measure of enjoyable submission, utilizing some other part of their bodies than their cocks for fun, and *that* is anathema to any Macho Straightist. A Macho Male is *so* obsessed with the awareness that his every action, his every public posture, his confrontation with other men must in some way reflect his sense of his own power that his ideas of love, sex, friendship, and sociability are seriously, if not permanently, warped.

There is a determined and deliberate effort to de-eroticize or repress the recognition and the impulse of the homosexually-encouraging aspects of "sportsmanship" that yearn for genuine, satisfactory release that find themselves again and again frustrated in "sports" by the mandatory rerouting into group-subservient collective violence. There is the fear among those who maintain the present system that homosexual acts, if allowed to flourish, would lead to homosexual affection, and *this* would undermine Macho masculine enterprises. Team owners, managers, and their puppet athletes are not in the business to encourage men to be affectionate with each other and deal responsibly with the erotic, personalist feelings they arouse in other men. They're there to foster competitiveness on the obvious plane, and to support symbolically gangsterism on another level for the end of present and future power. The prosperity of those behind the status quo depends on the continued repression of overt, familiar curious homosexual desires. Their profit is generated by pandering to the distorted personality of the Macho

Straight Male, encouraging him to believe that he is complete *as is*. The knowledge must never surface that, in truth, the repression of urges for tender homosexual contacts leaves a strange corrosive fissure across the breadth of a man's life and personality. He connects himself, as do all authoritarians, with those superior and inferior to him unlike a democratically-instructed person who connects horizontally with everyone, whom he views as peers.

The Sports Ethic demands lust for power over others. It requires constant encounters to reassert Macho Masculinity through conquest. The Sports Ethic is an impediment which blocks awareness, urgency and the possibility of intra-sex libidinal release. Others as well as I can testify that sexual contact with a "sportsman" is never very satisfying. Unlike that of exuberant gay men, an interest in the pleasure-maximizing specifics of sex is not part of the stuff of their lives. Nor are they thoroughly comfortable with the idea of making a coupling equally satisfactory to both parties, be it heterosexual or homosexual. Sex for them is largely a matter of swift orgasmic gratification, with maybe a soupçon of humiliation heaped on the partner ("cunt" or "cocksucker") if possible. They are restrained from being comfortable in homosexual contacts (even while having them) by their Macho masculinity which insists all the while that they are conventionally heterosexual in their behavior. Hence, your typical sports fan requires large quantities of alcohol before he can temporarily circumvent the repressed state of his sexual identity. In their expression, the threat of socially-approved, "morally"-backed violence must always be present. Such men are unable to disentangle their own self-interests in their actions from their acting as *agents* for institutional authority.

Yet, just as a point of behavioral interest, whenever it is suggested to a Sports Fan Type that it is repressed homosexuality which accounts for much of his sports obsession, he issues a raucous, beery laugh—perhaps just a little *too* loud—and threatens to punch you in the mouth (though I must say that Tough Guy Mouth Punching seems to be out of style these days, perhaps another sign of Macho's flabbiness). And then comes the automatic separation of *them* as socially-approved Macho Straightists from anyone who would dare to oppose them. "Only a faggot would say that," they counter. Precisely. *That's* the point! Who else would have the width of vision, the lack of fear, and the personal integrity?

Matters of sex remain deeply embarrassing for our Macho Straightist and contrary to his sports-obsessed lifestyle. Many sex words are taboo for him, and he fears that even mention of the sound of some of them will in some way compromise his "standing," even though he fancies himself satyritic—though incapable of describing it (verbal pornography being largely a solitary, middle-class male's pleasure). He has some dim awareness that he is inadequate in his erotic capabilities, but rather than begin to change, he zips up, forgets his inadequacies, and joins with the other sports fans who prefer the routine violence of the playing field. Ball players, team men and their fans are like B-girls, strippers and bunnies; they're big on the tease but cheap on the come-through. Folks are scandalized by the suggestion that team members should be lovers of each other and/or public love objects up for grabs.

Yet, apropos of this, I noticed for the first time in my life how overt this buddy-cum-buddy appeal is as I sat in a smokey haze in the *chi-chi* closet queen bar at the wonderful Hotel Essex, across from Boston's South Station Terminal. It was the 6th game of the 1975 "World Series," pitting the Boston Red Sox against the Cincinnati Reds. The bar was jammed with cigar-chomping straights and the usual percentage of quiet gay guys, and boy, was I surprised to see the fags get so *worked up* over a goddamn baseball game. So I paid close attention to try to find out why everybody was so excited. A standard TV shot of the game is from centerfield, and because TV flattens out distances, the relation between the pitcher, who was standing on his mound, legs apart and hands on hips, and the catcher, down squat on bended knees and *waiting to receive* is a classic representation of the position of fellator and fellatee in the act. Having noticed this lovely image-orthicon juxtaposition, my interest in the game immediately perked up!

The primary contradiction in Macho Masculinity as it exists in America today is: if a member of the sports-military ethic is really supposed to be attached to the Macho Butch Ideal—all those handsome, virile fellows doing their things were what sucked him in initially—how can he satisfactorily *express* this attraction without compromising his newly-gained Macho status? He is recruited as the result of his individual impulse; once caught he can only maintain his "privileged" status through group conformity and obedience to the hierarchy. He must even repress his sexually-charged attraction to the embodiment of Repressed Masculinity in his revered Macho Butch Ideal models. To express *any* kind of individual interest in other men except inasmuch as they represent a closed, uncommunicative Ideal is suspect. To go too far in appreciating Macho Masculinity *unmans the male*; it contradicts the set of values one is supposed to be upholding. Mr. Sports Fan's belief notwithstanding, there is only a fine line between being thought an ardent Sports Fan and being thought some kind of faggot, and exactly where that line is, or to where it shifts season after season, has been and remains a great puzzle to me, but wherever it is, you can bet that just a hair on the *safe* side is the epicenter of the orbit of lower-middle-class males' vision of themselves at their most desirable.

Is it because the Macho male community is not one based on eros—or even genuine self-interest—but on the power of intimidation and eventually its toadying to Thanatos that this contradiction arises? Surely, a Macho Straightist prefers the company of other repressed Macho club members or aspirants; he needs them for support. The presence of an "effeminate male" makes Mr. Sports Type *very* nerrrvous. But what are the borders of his acknowledgement of attraction for Macho in others? How honest can he be in his liking of other men and still stay in the club? How friendly can his courtship of other men get? *Really* friendly? Hold on, pal, not *that* friendly! As soon as it becomes clear that any man's interest in his fellows is not that of a repressed sexuality responding to a similar condition, out he goes!

The Straight Macho Male's ethic—and sports is the best place to find it on a large civilian scale—is one based on exclusion and hierarchy. Men are never sure of where they stand with relation to other men unless it is through explicit exercises of some kind of power.

By contrast the gay alternative is one of open, honest self-expression. It is inclusive of others, emphasizing the similarity among men and the affectionate bonds they can build among themselves. It does not accent their differences nor does it use as incentives rewards some can gain at the expense of others.

The acknowledgement of homosexual eroticism, and the insertion of this phenomenon into a place of dignity in our society, if permitted to express itself in a healthy, unneurotic manner can't help but make the standard of intra-male activity, in the main, affectionate, erotically curious and friendly.

We can also begin to understand why so many institutions which support society today profit from the fragmented, alienated, repressed Macho personality—The Roman Catholic Church and its impersonators, the armed forces, agencies of the state, economic bossism, e.g.—and why they often join together to praise competitive team sports as universally desirable pursuits for males. Representatives of these coercive institutions gladly crow about the "apolitical" function of sports and how it "molds good citizens," and how sports act as a unifying symbol in which diverse parts of our society can come together in "harmony." And yet, to my ears, every cheer I hear arising from the mob at the ball bark is one more buttress for a system of exploitation, one more success for those who advance off the segmented, twisted lives of the athletes and their spectators.

In their current American interpretation, sports are a "unifying symbol" to the powerful institutions of the social superstructure because they're all in the same business: they share a common disregard for individual development, democratic means of organizing, and the need to construct co-operative means for maintaining and improving social action. Sports are *not* a symbol of unity; they are a measure of how badly infected a democratic society has become with authoritarianism. Consequently, I do not agree with short-sighted "sports critics" of the accommodationist sort who only wish to rid athletic competitions of the big business predators who bleed big profits from the game. I seek to undermine and destroy not only "sports" as a symbol for all the corruptions imposed on us "for the benefit of all," but also the very society in all its aspects which sees itself represented and served by sports and of which sports is only the most glamorous, propagandistic function.

The Church: The State: Military Authority: Capitalist Exploitation: these American institutions stand accused of encouraging and upholding the systematic repression of the natural urge for affectionate homosexual relations. They have perverted the impulse for cooperation into aggressive competition for use for profit; they prevent socialization into homosexualism to the end of personality fragmentation and fear to maintain their "authority" and control, and they so thoroughly separate the Ideal of Macho Masculinity from the actual phenomenon of maleness as it exists in society thereby imposing their self-serving cycle of anxiety, frustration and guilt on men.

And, were we to rid our society of this soul-blight of the Macho Straightist Sports Obsession and all it fronts for, males would have to come to terms with this happy fact:

With such pleasure and ease can all men become faggots!

Charley Shively

PETER DOYLE: WALT WHITMAN'S WORKING CLASS CAMERADO

This essay was originally published as part of the book Calamus Lovers: Walt Whitman's Working Class Camerados *(edited by Charley Shively, Gay Sunshine Press, 1987)—the first in-depth study of the homosexuality of our greatest national poet, Walt Whitman (1819–1892).*

▽

AMONG WHITMAN'S working-class lovers, Peter George Doyle left more trace than any other. Dr. Richard Maurice Bucke published an introduction, interview and Whitman's letters to Doyle in *Calamus, A Series of Letters Written during the Years 1868–1880 by Walt Whitman to a Young Friend (Peter Doyle)* (Boston, 1897). Whitman didn't meet Doyle until 1865 (five years after first publication of the Calamus poems); nonetheless, by filling so many of the poet's fantasies, Doyle is commonly remembered as Whitman's Calamus lover. Prefigurations of Doyle appear in Whitman's notes and correspondence. In February, 1863, Whitman cruised a cute, streetcar number, a passenger on the same line where he later met Doyle: "beautiful yesterday, I stood on the platform, rode down to the Capitol and back[.] I rode with yesterday, and felt I loved that boy, from the first, and saw he returned it" (*Notebooks*, 561). In a letter, March, 1863, to "my darlings, my gossips," the poet described his love for a Confederate soldier: "a young Mississippi captain (about 19) that we took prisoner . . . poor boy, he has suffered a great deal, and still suffers—has eyes bright as hawk, but face pale—our affection is quite an affair, quite romantic—sometimes when I lean over to say I am going, he puts his arm round my neck, draws my face down, &c. quite a scene for the New Bowery" (*Correspondence*, 1:81–2). Doyle himself had worn the Confederate grey.

Two characteristics of Doyle appealed to Whitman's sensibilities: the blarney and the suffering—common elements in much gay culture. Doyle had many stories of his past, which varied according to circumstances. Thus biographers will probably never know when he was born; 1845, 1847 and 1848 are years given by Doyle; "in or near Limerick, Ireland," the probable birthplace. He suggested several dates for his arrival to the United States. Doyle always retained some of his boyish playfulness, an impishness, which can be noted in the fragments of the letter of January 20, 1878, when he promises, "If the Spirit moves me, I will give you my opinion of the book . . ." Like many gay men, Doyle liked firemen and uniforms (two of his brothers were Washington policemen). In 1868, he asked Whitman to bring him a New York Fire Brigade badge.

Although Doyle was often whimsical and light-hearted, his adversities moved Whitman deeply. During the 1857 depression, his father Peter, a blacksmith, took the family to Richmond, where several Doyles were employed by Tredegar Iron Works. Young Doyle himself became a Confederate soldier, but how he passed from the rebel army into Whitman's arms remains obscure, as does the date of their meeting. Whitman suggested that Doyle had been captured, imprisoned and/or injured, escaped and came to Washington, D.C. He was listed in the 1864 Washington Directory as a "laborer"; therefore, Doyle would have been in the city in 1863 when the directory was being compiled. Whitman autographed a photograph of himself and Doyle sitting on a love seat: "Washington, D.C., 1865—Walt Whitman & his rebel soldier friend Pete Doyle."

Pete Doyle's love-at-first sight account of their meeting rings true to any gay ear. Forty years later, Doyle recalled the night they first met:

> It is a curious story. We felt to each other at once. I was a conductor. The night was very stormy,—he had been to see Burroughs before he came down to take the car— the storm was awful. Walt had his blanket—it was thrown round his shoulders—he seemed like an old sea-captain. He was the only passenger, it was a lonely night, so I thought I would go in and talk to him. Something in me made me do it and something in him drew me that way. He used to say there was something in me had the same effect on him. Anyway, I went into the car. We were familiar at once—I put my hand on his knee—we understood. He did not get out at the end of the trip—in fact went all the way back with me.

The shifting confusion of dates in the young man's life combined with another element to appeal to Whitman: Doyle's sorrows. As much a Calamity as a Calamus character, Doyle always had a sorrow to relate to Whitman. He told the poet that the ship carrying him from Ireland nearly brought him to the bottom of the sea: Whitman wrote in his notebook: "The heavy storm & danger, Good Friday night—1853—almost a wreck." Doyle provided a first-hand account of Lincoln's assassination, which Whitman included in his lectures on Lincoln. Their surviving correspondence begins in 1868 and continues until they were parted by Whitman's death in 1892; the poet's running motif is encouragement for Doyle in his misfortunes. Whitman gathered stories of trains which wrecked and mailed them to Doyle; evidently melodrama and catastrophe appealed to both their sensibilities.

They were openly affectionate and in continuous contact during the early years of their relationship. John Burroughs described the two men together: "I give here a glimpse of him in Washington on a Navy Yard horse car, toward the close of the war, one summer day at sundown. The car is crowded and suffocatingly hot, with many passengers on the rear platform, and among them a bearded, florid-faced man, elderly, but agile, resting against the dash, by the side of the young conductor, and evidently his intimate friend." Whitman helped a mother whose screaming baby he held until it fell asleep, "utterly fagged out." And then when Pete needed a break, Whitman (carrying the fagged baby) conducted the car.

Another account from 1867 by William Douglas O'Connor describes the remarkable transformation which came over Whitman in his relationship with Doyle. "A change had come upon him," according to O'Connor, "The rosy color had died from his face in a clear splendor, and his form, regnant and masculine, was clothed with inspiration, as with a dazzling aureole." Whitman—"lifting his clear face, bright with deathless smiling, and wet with the sweet waters of immortal tears"—explained what had made the difference: "Love, love, love! That includes all. There is nothing in the world but that—nothing in all the world. Better than all is love. Love is better than all." In an autographed presentation copy of *Specimen Days*, Whitman in 1883 reminded Doyle of their good times together:

> Pete do you remember—(of course you do—I do well)—those great long jovial walks we had at times for years (1866–'72) out of Washington City—often moonlight nights, 'way to "Good Hope";' or, Sundays, up and down the Potomac shores, one side or the other, sometimes ten miles at a stretch? Or when you work'd on the horse-cars, and I waited for you, coming home late together—or resting chatting at the Market, corner 7th Street and the Avenue, and eating those nice musk or watermelons?

Inscribed in Whitman's hand: "Washington, D.C. 1865—Walt Whitman & his rebel soldier friend Pete Doyle." Courtesy of the Library of Congress.

That Walt Whitman and Peter Doyle were a couple within a gay community in Washington can be glimpsed in the letter from Ned Stewart, who was convalescing in Nova Scotia during 1870. In the letter Stewart used the word "gay" three times and used the pronoun "Her" with quotation marks. He writes about two theaters which contained drag artists in the chorus shows, "I suppose there is gay times at Met[ropolita]n & Canterbury halls, *Moses* but I wish I was there with you old Covies for awhile." Covey, coven or covenant suggests a gay circle among Whitman and his friends. Doyle had a witty sense of humor, and Ned quotes a Doyle limerick about a farmer who couldn't build his chimney high enough to prevent Tom cat's pissing on his fire. And he begs Walt Whitman to send a picture of the two lovers together.

As with all couples, when things are going smooth, there is no record; but during crises, records accumulate. The first emergency came in 1868, when Whitman went to New York on September 15th and Doyle remained in Washington. Whitman wrote Doyle regularly: September 18, 22, 25, 29; October 2, 6, 9, 14, 17, 18, 23. Among the very few Doyle letters to survive, seven of them come from 1868 (September 18, 23, 27; October 1, 5/6, 9, and 14). Why Whitman needed to spend so many weeks in New York is not entirely clear. I suspect he wanted to get away from Doyle. On October 26, Whitman was back in Washington and the correspondence temporarily ceases. Again home visiting his mother in Brooklyn in 1869, Whitman wrote Doyle, warning him against suicide: "Dear Pete, dear son, my darling boy, my young & loving brother, don't let the devil put such thoughts in your mind again—wickedness unspeakable—murder, death & disgrace here & hell's agonies hereafter—Then what would be afterward to the mother? What to *me*?—Pete, I send you some money, by Adam's Express—you use it, dearest son, & when it is gone, you shall have some more."

Everything seemed cheerful when Ned Stewart wrote in February, 1870: "I suppose by Pete's letters that he was as gay as usual, but guess the boy is coming to his senses and thinking about settling down in life and is going to benefit by the numerous oportunities which he has. How does he & the widow [Doyle's mother] pull together now, I suppose I [will] find you & Pete in the same box when I return to Washington." However, by the summer, the relationship had heated up as Whitman made his famous diary entry of July 15, 1870, in which he resolved to suppress his "adhesiveness" or love of men. But again visiting his mother, Whitman wrote Doyle affectionately on July 30th: "I never dreamed that you made so much of having me with you, nor that you could feel so downcast at losing me. I foolishly thought it was all on the other side. But all I will say further on the subject is, I now see clearly, that was all wrong."

Two unresolvable changes in their lives were brought on by time. Most gay couples undergo changes sometime between three and six years after they meet—a time when their sexual passion either cools or is transformed. When the age range is great between the couple, even more difficulties arise. Pete had been a teenager when he met Walt, who was nearing fifty. As Pete grew older, he was no longer a boy; and as Walt grew older, he began to suffer the infirmities of age. The strains of his relationship with Peter interwove with his own deteriorating health and his mother's death. Whitman suffered a stroke on January 23, 1873, in Washington. In 1889 the poet recalled Doyle and told Horace Traubel, "I wonder where he is now? He must have got another lay [sic!]. How faithful he was in those sick times—coming every day in his spare hours to my room—doing chores—going for medicine, making the bed, something like that and never growling!" Convalescing from his stroke and the shock of his mother's death in May, 1873, Whitman retired to his brother's house in Camden, New Jersey. He never rejoined Peter.

Unlike several of Whitman's lovers (Vaughan, Brown, Stafford, Rogers and others), Doyle never married, lived a bachelor life, and became something of a quean. Walt Whitman told an English friend (J. W. Wallace) that Doyle hardly represented the average American because, "For years past Pete has been whirled among the sophistications." "Sophisticate" here could be a synonym for "homosexual," since as a baggage clerk Doyle hardly led the life of an esthete. Doyle thus ceased to be straight trade, but Whitman always remembered him kindly. The two remained in correspondence and made occasional visits; for instance, in 1880 Doyle traveled to Niagara Falls to accompany Whitman on his return from Ontario to New Jersey. In 1891 Whitman told one of his visitors, who asked about Doyle, "I should like to know where Pete is as I am rather uneasy about him. The cars used to come to Philadelphia, and he came here every week."

Whitman sent Doyle many letters and cards (the bulk of which Doyle preserved), but Whitman saved virtually none of Doyle's letters. One theory suggests that Whitman destroyed all of the letters; another suggests that the letters survive squirreled away. But my own suspicion is that Whitman thought Doyle's writings so worthless that he simply never saved them. Two letters (November 7, 1875, and January 20, 1878) were cut into pieces and used as scrap paper. Pete's declining favor in his lover's eyes can be traced in Whitman's wills. In 1873, Whitman left his gold watch to his brother and the silver one to Pete: "I wish it given to him, with my love." After the brother died and Whitman had met young Harry Stafford, Harry was to get the gold watch; Doyle, silver (1888); in the final codicil (1892), Horace Traubel, gold; Stafford, silver; Doyle, nothing.

Doyle was almost not admitted to Whitman's funeral in 1892, but Whitman admirers like Traubel, Bucke and others kept track of him; they published an 1895 interview with his letters from Whitman. Doyle died in Philadelphia in 1907 and was buried in Washington, D.C., in the Congressional Cemetery, at 18th & E Streets (S.E.). On March 20, 1981 the *Washington Blade* printed a picture of Doyle's tombstone with an article by Haviland Ferris, "Portrait of the Young Man as Friend of the Poet."

Peter George Doyle like so many gay boys had many stories, but among them all runs one consistent strain. He suffered greatly and found happiness only in his love with Walt Whitman. In the 1895 interview, Doyle brought out a raglan of Whitman's and explained, "I now and then put it on, lay down, think I am in the old times. Then he is with me again. . . . When I get it on and stretched out on the old sofa I am very well contented. It is like Aladdin's lamp. I do not ever for a minute lose the old man. He is always near by." Doyle subtly echoed the Calamus conclusion: "I that was visible am become invisible,/. . . Fancying how happy you were if I could be with you and become your comrade;/Be it as if I were with you. (Be not too certain but I am now with you.)"

Walt Whitman

WE TWO BOYS TOGETHER CLINGING

We two boys together clinging,
One the other never leaving,
Up and down the roads going, North and South excursions making,
Power enjoying, elbows stretching, fingers clutching,
Armed and fearless, eating, drinking, sleeping, loving,
No law less than myself owning, sailing, soldiering, thieving, threatening,
Misers, menials, priests alarming, air breathing, water drinking, on the turf
    or the sea-beach dancing,
Cities wrenching, ease scorning, statutes mocking, feebleness chasing,
Fulfilling my foray.

SPAN OF YOUTH! EVER-PUSHED ELASTICITY!

Span of youth! Ever-pushed elasticity!
Manhood balanced and florid and full!

My lovers suffocate me!
Crowding my lips, and thick in the pores of my skin,
Jostling me through streets and public halls—coming naked to me at night,
Crying by day Ahoy from the rocks of the river—swinging and chirping
    over my head
Calling my name from flowerbeds or vines or tangled underbrush,
Or while I swim in the bath—or drink from the pump at the corner—
    or the curtain is down at the opera—or I glimpse a man's face in
    the railroad car;
Lighting on every moment of my life,
Bussing my body with soft balsamic busses,
Noiselessly passing handfuls out of their hearts and giving them to be mine.

[*from "Song of Myself," Section 45*]

III

GAY LITERARY ESSAYS

Michelangelo's statue Genius of Victory, *ca 1532. The face is modelled on that of the young Tommaso de' Cavalieri, with whom Michelangelo was in love and by whom he desired to be subjugated.*

Rictor Norton

THE PASSIONS OF MICHELANGELO

The following essay appeared originally in Gay News *(London, England) No. 65 (1975).*

▽

FIVE HUNDRED and some odd years ago, on March 6, 1475, a colossus was born: Michelagniolo di Lodovico Buonarroti-Simoni. The lofty plinth of his genius was a magnificent block of marble, but throughout his life he was steadily broken down: by the demands of corrupt popes, the petty thievery of workshop assistants, by the tempest of his times, by the fury of his ideals, and by his passionate love for young men.

However one approaches this rough-hewn titan, it is a story of *power*. In the turbulent background are the financial empire of Florence and the Papal Throne in Rome—dominated mostly by tyrants. It was an age that demanded giants. Public buildings were monumental, private homes were solid, city-walls were massive. It was an Age of Accomplishment: Pico della Mirandola at the age of eighteen spoke twenty-two languages. It was an Age of Magnificence: Lorenzo the Magnificent died drinking a medicine of powdered pearls, and Pope Julius II died drinking molten gold. It was an Age of Grandeur: in 1501 fifty courtesans danced naked in the Vatican in honour of Lucrezia Borgia.

Yet the power of the age—like all power—was pre-eminently masculine. It was a phallic culture, with columns, columns everywhere; every available niche in every building was stuffed with an erect statue; every tomb was an assertion of virility. Pope Paul III dreamed of re-erecting the ancient obelisk of Heliopolis—though the pontiffs finally settled for Michelangelo's pagan temple of Saint Peter's.

Michelangelo towered far above his contemporary athletes of the imagination. He brought a supremely masculine passion to his sculpture to animate the stone with orgasmic thunder and lightning. He was a heroic masculinist in all things. He defined Art as that which has tumescent substance: "The closer you see painting approach good sculpture, the better it will be." Yet his figures, however cyclopean, are nevertheless fully human rather than divine or demonic: for the most part they are naked, with neither halo nor horns, neither wings nor cloven hooves.

And most of them are men, young men. He regularly employed male models even for his female figures, including the famous statue of *Night* on the Medici Tombs. In many of his drawings, the women are distinguishable from the men only by their longer hair. His twenty nude youths—or *ignudi*—in the Sistine Chapel outraged several pontiffs, for they were clearly more Greek than Christian. Most of these marvelous lads are weaving a huge garland of oak leaves, and clustered about them are thousands of acorns resembling the *glans penis*.

Michelangelo was probably anti-feminist; certainly he was sexist, and he believed wholeheartedly in male superiority. In one sonnet he declares that the highest form of love cannot be for a woman, because a woman "is not worthy of a wise and virile heart."

Broken-nosed, lean, with bushy black hair and piercing eyes, arrogantly confident yet hypersensitive, striving towards the perfection of an unbreakable column, producing a corpus of magnificent monuments for at least the base of that column, Michelangelo forever remains the epitome of a particularly masculine genius, which today we call *machismo*.

Michelangelo had a reputation for homosexuality. In a letter to Niccolo Quaratesi he humourously recalls how a father described his son to him in the hopes of the boy becoming the artist's apprentice: "Once you saw him, you'd chase him into bed the minute you got home!" Rumours about the master were already spreading by the early 1530s, and he bitterly denounced "the throng, malign and brutish, scoffing at what the few possess."

In November 1545 Pietro Aretino—himself a known homosexual—viciously attacked Michelangelo's "godlessness" displayed in the naked youths of the Sistine and said quite explicitly: "Even if you are divine, you don't disdain male consorts." He went on to identify two of these paramours, Gherardo Perini and Tommaso Cavalieri, nicknamed 'Tomai'.

The handsome model Gherardo Perini came to work for Michelangelo around 1520; their love flourished between 1522–25, and lasted until the mid-1530s. Whenever Perini failed to show up at the studios, Michelangelo's nights were wracked by dreadful anxiety. In such an anguish of loneliness he addressed his own daimon: "I beg you not to make me draw this evening since Perino's not here." This note was scrawled on a page bearing a drawing of a naked cherub urinating into a vase.

Again he wrote: "Only I remain burning in the dusk / After the sun has stripped the world of its rays: / Whereas other men take their pleasure, I do but mourn, / Prostrate on the ground, lamenting and weeping." This fragment is on a page containing a rear-view study of a nude man, two *putti* or cherubs, and a study of a leg; dated 1520–25, the drawings and verse almost certainly refer to his tormented love for Perini. The drawing of *Venus, Mars and Cupid* (1524) was presented as a gift to Perini, and well renders the onslaughts of the deities of desire that Michelangelo was experiencing.

The finest Michelangelo scholar—Robert Clements (see postscript)—believes this affair was overtly homosexual, and he pinpoints some of the verse of 1520–30 probably written to Perini, including Michelangelo's confession of conflict: "I had always thought I could come to terms with love, / Now I suffer, and you see how I burn."

In the early 1530s Michelangelo was also sustaining a relationship with his much younger model Febo di Poggio. He calls Febo "that little blackmailer," because Febo adopted Michelangelo as "my honorary father" and steadily demanded money, clothes, and love-gifts from him. On a page containing financial calculations, Michelangelo wrote: "Here with his beautiful eyes he promised me solace, / And with those very eyes he tried to take it away from me."

Their passion raged through 1533–34, but ended when Michelangelo discovered that the mignon had "betrayed" him—perhaps by actually stealing money or drawings from his sugar-daddy. The artist felt humiliated by his subservience to the model.

Several poems pun upon the boy's name—"Febo" equals Phoebus, and *poggio* is the Italian word for "hill"—and suggest physical consummation: "Blithe bird, excelling us by fortune's sway, / Of Phoebus' [*Febo*] thine the prize of lucent notion, / Sweeter yet the boon of winged promotion / To the hill [*poggio*] whence I topple and decay!" But such a topple was sweet: "Easily could I soar, with such a happy fate, / When Phoebus [*Febo*] brightened up the heights [*poggio*]. / His feathers were wings and the hill [*poggio*] the stair. / Phoebus [*Febo*] was a lantern to my feet.

Other of Michelangelo's lovers—not to mention unknown models and stone-masons—may have included his servant and constant companion Francesco Urbino;

Michelangelo's portrait drawing of his 18-year-old boyfriend, Andrea Quaratesi.

Bartolommeo Bettini, to whom he gave a drawing of *Venus and Cupid*; and Andrea Quaratesi, the eighteen-year-old boy with whose family he lived for several years. Surviving letters prove that Andrea was infatuated with Michelangelo, and he even expressed a desire to "crawl on all fours" to see the artist one night in 1532. On the back of a letter to Andrea, Michelangelo writes of himself being shot at by Cupid's arrows. His drawing of Andrea is his only finished portrait sketch.

In spite of numerous concurrent affairs—at least two, with Perini and Febo—Michelangelo in 1532 began wooing Tommaso Cavalieri, and even wrote to him: "May I burn if I do not love thee with all my heart, / And lose my soul, if I feel for any other"! Cavalieri was a Roman nobleman, forty years younger than Michelangelo, and a bit fearful of this barbarous sculptor who slept in his boots and rode a mule. Cavalieri was planning on a decent home and family life—he married in 1548—and he was frightened by the amorous insistence of the older man and the gossip concerning him.

They almost certainly never slept together, not that Michelangelo didn't want to, however: "What from thee I long for and learn to know deep within me / Can scarcely be understood by the minds of men." One poem clarifies his intense desire (perhaps the actuality?) to be the erotic prey of the aristocrat: "Why should I seek to ease intense desire / With still more tears and windy words of grief? / If only chains and bands can make me blest, / No marvel if alone and nude I go / An armed Cavaliere's captive and slave confessed" ('Cavaliere' or 'cavalry man' is a pun on *Cavalieri*).

The frankly erotic statue of *Victory* is a similar revelation of his desire for total subjugation: the standing figure is modelled on Cavalieri, and the kneeling figure is Michelangelo. But Cavalieri cancelled appointments and rejected the older man's advances. Their love probably remained 'pure and unsullied', and Michelangelo sublimated his desires into some of the finest 'Platonic friendship' poetry ever written. It contains a strong mystical streak, in which Michelangelo transformed Cavalieri into the Saviour and himself into the "bride" (*sposa*) of Christ. It is believed that the face of *Christ the Judge* in the Sistine is Cavalieri's, and his upraised arm represents his rejection of his wooer.

Other lads did not similarly reject Michelangelo. There is little doubt that by 1542, at the age of sixty-six, he was sleeping with a thirteen-year-old boy named Francesco (Cecchino) de Zanobi Bracci. But in 1544 Cecchino died, cause unknown, and for a full year Michelangelo composed fifty four-line epitaphs for the boy's tomb, which he designed: "Buried here is that Braccio with whose face / God wished to correct Nature."

In a letter to the boy's uncle, Luigi del Riccio, Michelangelo speaks of the youth as "the flame who consumes me" and he relates a dream in which the boy "mocked my senile love," but alludes to a consummation: "My love has ratified the agreement which I made of myself to him." The most explicit proof is a quatrain to which Michelangelo appended a variant: "The earthy flesh, and here my bones deprived / Of their charming face and beautiful eyes, / Do yet attest that grace and delight was I, / In what a prison here the soul doth live." OR—"Do yet attest for him how gracious I was in bed / When he embraced, and in what the soul doth live." Whether these lines are meant to be spoken by Michelangelo or by Cecchino (as a tomb-inscription), the allusion to their common bed is clear. This is accompanied by a note advising Riccio to burn the variant "in the fire without witness." When Michelangelo learned that Riccio planned to publish all of the epitaphs unaltered, he begged him to destroy the prints, for "You certainly have the power to disgrace me." Riccio relented, but their friendship ceased.

Riccio had sent foodstuffs as 'bribes' for more and more quatrains, and Michelangelo returned each epitaph with an acknowledgment of receiving such delicacies as mushrooms, turtle or figbread: "This piece is said by the trout, and not by me; so, if you don't like the verses, don't marinate them any more with pepper." Such morbid jocularity diminishes the fervour of the epitaphs, but we should remember that the notes were written several months after each verse, and in response to Riccio's obnoxious behaviour. Many of the epitaphs are as genuinely heartfelt as the following: "I was only alive; but dead, I grew / Dearer to him who lost me when I died. / He loves me more that when I lay beside him; / Then good is death if love, for it, grows too."

Late in life—a life of eighty-nine years!—Michelangelo was deeply affected by the sober puritanism of the Counter Reformation. He genuinely feared for his soul and repented his past sins. The only way he could quench his raging desires was to transfer them to the saintly Vittoria Colonna, Marchioness of Pescara, a woman whose reputation for chastity was no threat to his natural instincts.

He met Vittoria around 1538 when he was sixty-three and she was forty-seven or forty-eight—and had been married for sixteen years and a chaste widow for thirteen. She had lived in a convent, wrote sad poetry, was a hard-thinking intellectual, and was politically active in the Counter Reformation movement. A contemporary called her "a looming column that stands firm amid the raging of a storm." How ironic that Michelangelo's own 'broken column' now sought serene anchor in Vittoria *Colonna*, whose last name means "column." He placed her on a pedestal, but his love for her can hardly be called 'heterosexual': he called her "a man in a woman" (*un uoma in una donna*).

Vittoria's unique combination of piety, beauty, goodness, and keen mind admirably cleared away Michelangelo's tendency towards excessive emotion. His poems to her are superb testimonials of Platonic affection, and fine reworkings of Dante's poems for the ideal Beatrice. They are difficult to distinguish from poems to Cavalieri, however, for it has been discovered that Michelangelo himself changed the word *Signor* to *Signora* before circulating his verse.

The incredible rigour of Michelangelo's art—the Herculean tasks of the Sistine paintings and the Julian and Medici tombs—demanded too much time and energy to leave room for the 'ordinariness' of love: too much intensity was packed into each relationship. Instead of building a firm ground for love, he boldly rushed into the ambushes he set for himself. His *furia* and *terribilita* could never be matched by his merely-mortal partners. Instead of appreciating their individual personalities, he regarded them as mere rays of a titanic Apollo towards which his Dionysian energy contorted himself in the twisted spirals (technically: *contraposto*) and mammoth pyramids of his sculpture. He may never have possessed the social graces of a Leonardo da Vinci, yet the commonplace view of him as a man of frigid temperament who habitually philosophised his emotions is one of the great myths of art history.

▽

POSTSCRIPT

I apologise for the *chronique scandaleuse* nature of the preceding essay, but it seemed best to right the balance of five-hundred years of expurgation. His grandnephew Michelangelo il Giovane in 1623 published an edition of the poetry in which all the masculine pronouns were changed to feminine pronouns, which remained the standard edition for nearly two hundred and fifty years. Poems and letters concerning Febo and Cecchino are still suppressed in modern editions of the *Letters* (including that by Irving Stone). The Cavalieri poems weren't identified until 1897, and the entire fifty epitaphs on Cecchino weren't translated into English until 1960. Virtually all of the biographies are still untrustworthy and downright dishonest. Articles celebrating the 500th Birthday (1975) in various newspapers were silent about such things as I've discussed. The only exception to such all-round scholarly bigotry is Robert J. Clements, whose three works I have found most useful for this study: *Michelangelo's Theory of Art* (1961), *Michelangelo: A Self-Portrait* (1963), and *The Poetry of Michelangelo* (1966). Joseph Tusiani's *Complete Poems* (1960) is valuable, though he insists that the punning poems on *Febo/poggio* are addressed to Vittoria Colonna (!) and other identifications are equally inaccurate.

"Ignudo"—Vault of the Sistine Chapel, Rome.

John Mitzel

WIT VS THE WARD-HEELERS

This essay first appeared in Boston's Fag Rag *(newspaper) #20, 1977.*

▽

HY ARE STRAIGHT people so dull?
And why is it that so many faggots are witty, sharp, free, fluid and verbally dexterous?

These related questions have fascinated me ever since I became aware of this distinction—sometime around my 15th year.

"Camp culture"—or whatever name you prefer—seems to me to be largely characterized by wit. Dull themselves, straights *love* traditional faggot camp humor; they love it when faggot dishes faggot. But when they become the targets of wit, straights often stop laughing and turn nasty—unless the homosexual can present himself as too much of a joke personally to be regarded seriously—the mattachine.

Yet, as with everything foreign and tantalizing to them, the straights resent it too, in an equal amount. I think they know they are barred from understanding wit—as they are barred from expressing themselves through it—by the psychological blinders they have put upon themselves. Wit acts as a sneaky and deadly threat to the equilibrium of their social roles. By accepting the vision of the world behind the "commodity" of this wit, their social supports would be drained of meaning. Whereas straight people have a vested interest in being dull, literalist, and unimaginative to keep their world going, gay people are, I've learned, in the truest and fullest sense of the word *fabulous*. We lie, tell incredible stories about ourselves (that we expect to be believed), we pretend we're all kinds of people we're not. More than any other people in the macroscopic society, we've broken down the rules that are used for validating the difference between real/true and unreal/false. The control agents of the status quo may know the *power* of lies; dissident sub-cultures, however, are closer to knowing their *value*.

Nothing is more despised by straights than gay wit expressed at and/or during their Rituals of Solemn Occasions. Oscar Wilde, at one of his trials, was on the stand and had upset the judge. The judge inquired: "Are you trying to show contempt for this court, Mr. Wilde?" Oscar replied: "On the contrary, my Lord. I'm trying my best to conceal it." This truth came across as superciliousness and was surely held against Wilde at verdict and sentencing time. I can recall that after my brother swapped marriage vows with his wife at a judge's home, I burst into applause, assuming such was acceptable behavior at heterosexual "joyous occasions" (remembering so well how people in New York City had clapped and screamed at His Holiness when he visited the World's Fair there in 1964—escorted by the decrepit Fanny Spellman—and their demonstrative carryings-on scandalized my protestant-puritan sense of propriety, even though I didn't give beans about the Pope; people screaming, "Yea, Pope!"). So I applauded their nuptials, and my family (and the judge) gave me looks that could kill. The marriage has since dissolved.

In exploring wit's pervasiveness among faggots, I see it as both an expression and technique of self-defense. Evidence of wit gives quick glimpses into the world of gay energies (originating in the fundamentally different attitudes and orientation of choosing to be part of an outlawed and potentially revolutionary sub-culture—and growing up with no beliefs in and, at last, no fear of, the social institutions of conventional support and control). Were they not still obstructed by the tyranny of the monopoly of heterosexual "education," "conditioning," and "behavior control," these energies would bring entirely new ways of reacting and reshaping our worlds. The gay sensibility freed would completely destroy the arts and culture as they exist for contemporary taste-makers and culture-eaters.

My own situation is a case in point. For at least the last 10 years, many people have regarded me as "a wit." I can recall quite clearly when I made my first "witticism"— at age 8—and how it was received, and what pleasant encouragement it gave me. I guess I was impressed then that I possessed something for which there appeared to be a market.

Early in my life I decided that I did not want to think or express myself as I was being instructed to do in the myriad of schools I attended. I relied at first on gladhand and easy sarcasm; I later developed a reliance on ironical expression. And since about 1970—that time in my life when I opted to associate almost exclusively with faggots and lesbians—I have expressed myself, as much and as often as I can, through epigrams and wit. I have come to view wit as an integral and *essential* part of gay male living. Wit and irony provide the only reasonable *modus operandi* in the Amerikan Literalist Terror of Straight Reality.

Faggots are more adept with irony and wit than straight people generally, and much, much more so than straight men. Irony is the patois of the gay male sub-world; I think Oscar Wilde's specific *brand* of wit—playing the contrary to expectations—set the idiom of this kind of expression. Something is expressed in its established opposite, and then, having presented things as contrary, one then tries to cap it off by transforming it into a paradox. This makes for an uneven reality, the faggot's response to the monolithic presence of straight culture. And it makes for the kind of whirligig verbal maneuvering which amazes, titillates and annoys the straights.

I have come to reject *totally* the straight ways of registering and reacting to phenomena. When I find myself in the company of straights, I have to translate my thoughts not only from gay-talk to straight-ese, but I have to switch *modes* of responding. (When a trade trick tells you his daughter is getting married, big wedding, etc., you can't scream and talk of your own sequence of "husbands"; he'll get angry. When with straights, talking of Joan Crawford's death, one must be serious and respectful and not launch into movie-queen faggot jabber, else they'll look at you as though you were a heretic.) When you talk in your own lingo at your own speed, straights become perplexed, tune out, shut you off and become hostile. Hence one must translate and self-censor to communicate with straights; this is a form of unseen but real social oppression which leads to the most unpleasant and harmful forms of rerouting of energies into conventional and acceptable molds for expression.

In an earlier piece (published in the now defunct Philadelphia *Gay Alternative*), I wrote that faggots and lesbians who are part of their subculture (they implicitly accept the idea that *how* they have organized their sexuality *affects* every aspect of their intelligence and imagination) express themselves through their gay sensibility.

This gay sensibility, itself, is just a further refinement of a materialist philosophy, and I think it is essential for the evolution of gay liberation organizing and politics to keep the one firmly rooted in the other. The self-awareness of the homosexual existence/experience superimposed on a materialist political philosophy is the mix that gives us the gay sensibility; it is that which gives us the space we need to attack, with wit, the bloated mystification and solemnity into which the straights imprison our imagination and energy.

All that we are and do stems from sensation processed and qualified by intelligence. Sexual energy is *the* keystone from which we build our supports and networks of determining our specific structures determining pleasure and pain—our social selves. The gay sensibility rejects, on a fundamental level, the *sine qua non* of the Heterosexist Tyranny: the pleasure/duty/virtue/necessity of focusing one's life's energies into heterosexual bonds.

But we live under a tyranny which demands such an organization, and since one is never able to eliminate totally the parameters of the givens (the tyranny's language, customs, rituals, superstructure, its totems of art), the homosexualist develops a forked-tongue, duplicitous manner in reaction. One's rejection of this heterosexist tyranny is defined by the fact of one having come *through it to the edge of it*, trying to get out. All actions, as with all thoughts, are rooted in the existing imprints of social experience. The is/isn't, accept/reject, cherish/mock dichotomy so characteristic of *this stage* of the gay sensibility is defined by still *reacting* and not really struggling for new ways and forms of expressing our experiences. I accept the gay sensibility as *the* mode of perceiving and expressing all sensations; I cultivate the new tracks left for routing sensation through my intelligence; I warm myself at the new fires kindled by a released imagination.

Fortunately for us, the phenomenon of humor and wit is one aspect of psychological behavior which totally eludes the ambitions and capacities of head doctors and their social science colleagues. Our wit belongs to us completely, free of "normalizing" influences. "Scientific literature" on the subject is luckily slim.

Freud's *Wit and Its Relation to the Unconscious* classifies wit as "tendentious humor." It involves, he says, a mental process of intentionally or unintentionally reassigning sounds to alter meaning to affect understanding which *makes* or transforms something ordinary and unamusing into the ridiculous. When done intentionally, this is done to make a point.

One could move on from this simple description and hypothesize that a person or sub-group which has been ostracized from the center of social life would be less inclined to accept the established meanings for words and phrases and would be more intentionally and/or accidentally playful in assigning words to their referents. (The word "she"—and its objective case counterpart—when used among faggots is one of the greatest free-floating items in the language. It carries such baggage around with it—for such a tiny, three-lettered word—that when affixed to a person or thing, warps all received western culture). One of the solemn figures of this century, Freud was lucky to get as far as he did in exploring jokes, though his book reads more like a neurologist (which he was) dabbling into the new field of psycho/linguistics.

I should note that Dr. Bergler, our constant diagnostician, has also written on the phenomenon of wit. As one of the great generals of the shock troops disciplining social deviation, Bergler knows something threatening when he sees it. And he goes right after it. Having diagnosed homosexual behavior as *ipso facto* pathological, he reveals that expressions of wit are also symptoms of a mentally-diseased personality for which therapy is recommended. His Ideal Patient is someone quite along my line: a witty homosexual who likes to drink a lot; there could be a lifetime of therapy in "curing" me.

As twisted and reactionary as Bergler is, he alone from among Freud, Max East-
man, Bergson and the others who have explored laughter/humor/wit does not hesitate to call wit subversive of order. Wit *is* subversive. It is the skill of breaking down
the automatic and conventional domino set up of sensation-impression-association-
concept-thought-word which is aligned with the values of straight society and demands
we keep on a literalist and two-dimensional plane (as we were instructed). Wit pulls
a fast one and replaces one segment of this link-up (usually the last)—this is Oscar's
forte—with its opposite and thereby explodes it of its conventional meaning. I think
subtler varieties of wit back up the chain of causality that takes us from impression to
expression and do the switching somewhere along the nervous system routing of the
transformation from information-digestion and evaluation to vocalization.

To learn *what* to laugh at is socialized behavior—as is hungering for meat, eating
junk foods, praying, smoking cigarettes, getting sick, feeling hurt, etc.—and there has
been, traditionally, a very distinct line between those things acceptable as objects for
laughter and those that were not. When comedians in the late 1950s and early '60s dared
challenge this mind set with a new kind of humor, they were called "sick"—Bergler's
diagnosis. The subjectivity in the expression of wit is obvious by the fact that a witticism may be a howler to one part of an audience and a deep insult to another part (viz.
the Wilde quote above).

▽

The movement called Aestheticism in the last part of the 19th Century gave an organized
expression to the gay sensibility. The Dandies conscientiously opposed the majority culture, yet to some degree they depended upon approval of elements within it, thereby
exploiting antagonisms within the tight class structure of their time. As a movement—
and that's really too heavy a word to identify them; they were, rather, an association
of like-minded artistic individuals—they were top-heavy with male homosexuals. Oscar
Wilde was, obviously, the most flamboyant, successful and, well, fabulous among them.
Wearing a green carnation in the buttonhole became a symbol of the aesthetes/dandies.
(A novel was written with fictionalized, but obvious, depictions of Oscar, Bosie and
Ada Leverson. It was titled *The Green Carnation*.) How odd and resoundingly ironic
that the Irish-Americans in Boston—who, as a community, stand for everything anti-
thetical to gay liberation and the gay sensibility—proudly wear green carnations on St.
Patrick's Day, transforming them all, for me, into followers of Oscar and his boys.
(This is not to belittle Oscar's Irish ancestry. His mother, Speranza, was a fiery Irish
nationalist and poet. In fact, I'd love to see someone write a biography on that whole
family: Oscar's mother and father, Oscar and his sons, and Oscar's brother Willie, every
bit the gab-about and raconteur that his brother was, and Willie's daughter, Dolly
Wilde, a wit in her own right and part of the famous circle of international lesbians
in Paris in the first decades of this century.)

The 1890s can be viewed as a decade of homosexual activism of one sort or another.
Certainly so in the arts. And the gay sensibility as it was embryonically displayed by
the aesthetes played a large part in this.

After Wilde was tried and convicted, the movement, such as it was, collapsed, and
the history of the culture of homosexuals moves to Paris and becomes the story of the
aforementioned lesbian circle there from 1900 to 1940 when it moves to the U.S. (New

York City mostly) and once again centers on faggots. The "decadents," the Dandies, etc., had been crushed by virile English law and its enforcers. In this perspective, Wilde's trial is every bit as much a political act comparable to the Palmer Raids or the HUAC-McCarthy witch-hunt, that is, it was a signal event which was undertaken by those in power to retard or eliminate a divergent development in social affairs. The collapse of the briefly-flowering Aesthetes was achieved easily enough. In their time, they lacked an understanding of the importance of their psychology as it was intertwined with sexuality and how this affects an overall world view of things. They were the Wits— loosely attached to the structure of things—against the Literalists of their day who proclaimed to be defending the letter of the law, the spirit of the scriptures, etc. None of the dandies gave any indication of connecting attitudes of social contrariness to a philosophical (much less political) materialism. They seemed too busy searching Above for the Muse to get a grasp on the history of their social experiences and the direction of their somatic energies. Their movement focused on the very superficial cultivation of the *artificial*, of anything which was against nature. Male homosexuality became an asset to them (or so it was rationalized) precisely because it was taboo and non-procreative. Hence, they developed a kind of neo-Platonic apologia (in, say, Pater and J. A. Symonds), the idealization of same-sex friendships, filled with passion though, ostensibly, without sexual contact.

By contrast Edward Carpenter attempted to meld a crude (and in many ways romantic) materialism with his "homogenic love"; he thereby came up with a new synthesis even more difficult for the upholders of conventionality to stomach. The Dandies, meanwhile, cherishing the citified-civilized corruptions to the core, proceeded in the opposite direction and wound up in the cul-de-sac of "spirituality." They idealized Love (see Bosie's poem "Two Loves"). Poetry and Art were their totems. Platonic same-sexed Love, Great Beauty and Soul were their Holy Trinity. And so, when their bubble was burst after Oscar's conviction, it was no surprise to find many of them becoming converts to the Roman Church (that haven for Camp Queans who don't really understand why they're camp).

One interesting aspect of the Dandies was their relationship to social manners, art and culture itself; it consisted of *posing*. The Dandies struck attitudes—quintessentially queanly—kept their distance and made *objects* of *everything*. Posing is the classic gay ruse used to avoid having to deal with content and/or, if such is your aim, subverting the importance of content. Since all art serves the purpose of propaganda for the Heterosexist Tyranny, what could be the only reasonable response for a member of an oppressed class but to trash it! I would suggest that a subtle form of trashing the content of art is striking an attitude vis-a-vis it. Doing so, the Dandies started a tradition by their example which is alive today: disentangling emotional, intellectual and ideological commitment from the established order's shibboleths. By separating themselves from any need to support current mores, artistic propaganda, or social institutions, they put these matters into their own aesthetic perspective, which usually made such objects diminutive (or grotesquely changing conventional dimensions—especially in some of Beardsley's overblown or dwarfed figures). In Art Nouveau we get a real challenge from style to content—an essential ingredient of Camp, and the beginning of the political aspect of the gay sensibility—cutting off the content's significance from connecting with its audience, and then, one hopes, changing it or removing it all together.

Too, the Decadents put their stamp on another great gay tradition. By constantly assuming *poses*, they changed the focus and even the terms of any discussion. The subject was no longer the content of a work of art but rather it became the attitude the Dandy assumed *to* the piece. The Dandy becomes The Star of the show even though he's not on stage! (It was not that Oscar was first charged with being a pedophile or ass-fucker that got him into libel court. The Marquess of Queensberry, Bosie's father, left his card at Oscar's club; it read: "To Oscar Wilde, *posing* as a somdomite [sic].")

This kind of objectification of what the anticipated subject should be is a distinctive part of the male homosexual sub-culture. Straight men always assume they are to be the subjects in any situation; the gay male world reverses this and turns us into objects. What are we at the bottom line of existence when meat-meets-meat? Well, if you walk into a traditional gay male milieu, you're just "Miss Thing," or, as our French brothers have learned to call you, "Mademoiselle Chose."

That it was the Aesthete's pose which became the center of attention (rather than the artifact) is what gave wit its power. And no one who isn't capable of viewing his/her culture dispassionately and *as though* from the outside will be, I think, able to be witty. Let the profiteers and apologists of a culture construct their ponderous monuments of their civilization; let the wits dart from church to palace to museum to funeral pyre undermining the seriousness of the content and the ritual of all. All it takes to begin to demystify a high Catholic church processional is to throw Tallulah's famous line at the officiating priest: "Your drag is *divine*, darling, but your *purse* is on fire!"

It appears to me that witticisms, and the epigram in particular, have been *the* distinctive expressive form of the homosexual sub-culture. As to homosexual writers, development of a pose is what makes their art distinctive. Brigid Brophy has written (with reference to the work of Firbank, Proust and Henry James), "The pose is good for the prose." Being epigrammatic ("witty") is certainly the most noticeable characteristic of homosexual artists by their straight critics. These latter misapprehend and, consequently, misrepresent the phenomenon of wit. They assume it is like decorations on the icing of a cake, frivolous, unnecessary and, consumed in too great a quantity, probably unhealthy. Yet wit—and its vehicle, the epigram—are at the very center of the gay sensibility. Wit is deflationary; it luxuriates in paradoxicalness; it thrives in a nest of irony. In its standard form, it invests the artificial with high seriousness (another requisite of Camp) and trivializes what is otherwise accorded great social value by straights. Wit is the outsiders' way of telling truth within the limits of the only vocabulary he/she possesses—that of the enemy. The expression of wit as *the* idiom of the homosexual sub-culture is the first step to understanding that social structures and mores need not be regarded as their upholders say they should be. By its very nature, wit draws attention away from the subject of the epigram to the *person* of the wit. This is an essential part of the ambition inherent in the gay sensibility which is, to reshape eventually and totally, how we conceive ideas, perceive social phenomena and express the art in/of our lives.

Straight people by and large fit neatly into existing social categories ("role models") —mommies, daddies, businessperson, team member, beauty queen, expert, professional, etc. Gay people are more socially fluid; the only real social identity even the sorriest quean has is that of Being A Star. What's so wonderful about homosexuals is that, ever so much more than straights, we are *constantly* in the process of inventing *ourselves*! The homosexual sub-culture is the tabernacle of the imagination. It is where *all things imaginable are possible*. In oneself and the "roles" one assumes—just like with the great Stars— all acts are possible.

▽

The important aspects of communications are: content, audience, and media. The owners of straight networks (I'm thinking at this moment of newspapers and slick newsweeklies) have established themselves as the channel through which most of our citizenry absorb ideas, information and attitudes. At their best, these media are active and persistent agents for maintaining the status quo. Many outstanding media brokers use their vehicles to advocate social reaction; their specialty is fueling divisive issues with emotion (Hearst Press, Scripps-Howard, this is the "Checkers Speech" ploy).

The "arts & ideas establishment"—trade book publishers, university idea-setters, high-brow entertainment packagers, and the culture-makers for the masses—are only a tonier, dressed-up edition of the seedy and vicious daily press writers, editors and owners. From the vast majority of the total of the products of the arts & information conglomerate, the "talent" the processors are most at ease with is that which churns out familiar and comfortable lies, casual distortions of truth and the soothing idiocies which flatter the owners and directors of USA, Inc. Ideas and issues are reduced to a level of emotions and personalities. The journalists share with the culture bosses a common ward-heeler imagination. No matter their tone, their topic, or their politics, *they are all on the same payroll.* The arts racket in America displays a poverty of imagination. And even worse, an actual fear of imagination. (I don't regard the consistent lies of the daily journalists and commentators as evidences of imagination. These merely reveal the corruptions inherent in the kind of "talents" that are capable of deadline-writing, though I do endorse, at times, the notion that peoples' lies, in whatever context, are more interesting than their *truths*.)

The artistic expressions of a subculture can either remain static parts of their communities, or they can become universalized. I think what makes the gay sub-culture so important (and so threatening to the straights) is that, because we are not strictly a language, ethnic or racial sub-group, what we *are* and *can offer* can be easily universalized (hence, in a way, "proselytizing" is very much what we are all about). I'm enough a subscriber to rudimentary behaviorist theory to accept that what kind of behavior you get out of people will pretty much be the result of the information/disinformation, rewards/punishments, easy choices/closed options you put into them with a given set of operating instructions. Since our fellow citizens are conditioned to respond primarily to cycles of buying and selling, they have been reduced to a reified condition themselves. Gay "lifestyles," as the ward-heelers are promoting them these days, can plug right into this condition. Gay liberation, at least as it boils down to its marketplace version, can be auctioned and sold just like any other commodity. But, we must ask, on what terms? And to whose advantage?

The earlier consumption of gay wit—as provided by the likes of Noel Coward, Cole Porter, Carl van Vechten, and Thorne Smith—was strictly on terms of the straights. Things are looser and more two-way now, and yet, more perverse, at least as far as radical gay liberationist critics of America are concerned. I think we are at a very important cross-road. We are fast coming upon a time when, as more and more men and women break away from their straight-imposed "role models" (that vile phrase so vogueish with respectability-obsessed faggots and lesbians which is a ruse that plays into the hands of the agents of social control), and enter gay life, the time is right for a mas-

sive dislocation of our growing subculture from the dominant ways of conceptualiz-
ing our lives and our art. Not only to acknowledge but to *act on* the irrelevance of the
culture of the majority! If nine out of ten profit-making book publishers vanished overnight, if all grand opera were never performed again, if all TV studios blew up, if never
another symphony filled a music hall, if all universities collapsed tomorrow, are we im-
poverished? No! Such would be the best situation to begin anew in a void and create
our own culture out of our gay sensibility, rid of the detritus and deadwood of "art"
and "culture" (both high and pop) which is the "heritage" of centuries of religious persecutions, economic exploitation and heterosexist tyranny. Alas, these monoliths of
straight culture will not disappear overnight; we must operate in a world where the
junk of this culture is pushed at us from every direction as The Ideal by the ward-heelers
on orders from their cultural commissars. Amazingly, we do have a history of actually finding out and sharing those few items which make it through the hostility, cen-
sorship and persecution of the gendarmes of the heterosexist tyranny. What is important
finds its way to many of us through the gayvine in spite of the machinery of oppression. As Roger Austen writes in his book, *Playing The Game, The Homosexual Novel
In America*: "Forty years ago, about the only way one had of discovering what it meant
to be a homosexual—especially if one were in the closet—was to somehow find a copy
of an underground gay novel. One man recalls that in those years 'the classic Gay Novel
was passed around like the Eucharist, with moist eyes and a warm endorsement . . .'
But now, with no one having to rely on gay fiction for information, amusement, or
encouragement, nearly everyone agrees that the 'moist eyes' era is over." New channels of communication are springing up everywhere for gay people, and the ward-heelers
are busy trying to establish themselves (and the power of their bosses) as brokers for
these channels.

   Within the gay community, things right now are in a state of flux. Straight cultural commissars and their gay ward-heeling lackies would harness our vitality into their
familiar ways and to their ends. They would control the direction of our imaginations—
such has been their traditional domain—and, ultimately, when convenient, they will
snuff out our independent way of viewing things, or at least so successfully blend us
in with the majority culture of dead-heads that we'll forget we ever once were separate,
distinct and *alive*.* The brokers of art & expression will once again have usurped the
function of *mediating* everything that touches our lives (and, of course, thereby distort-
ing, censoring, perverting as suits their needs). The viciousness, the corruption, and
the monolithic banality of straight culture is a given unchangeable, and chiseling away
at it with reforms is tactically secondary. What is of paramount interest to me right
now are the shapes, forms and the directions of the increasing expressions of our imagination, intelligence, and energy.

   Will we demand that our gay sensibilities be free of all impositions to have the space
they need for liberated expression? Or will we gradually deny the importance of our
gay sensibility, distrust its wild, anarchic explosions and settle down for a slice of the
pie proffered by the ward-heelers in exchange for our toeing the line?

   As the gay liberationist movement has developed over the past eight years, I have

---

*Readers are also referred to Winston Leyland's comments on this same syndrome of gay oppression whereby some
gay writers rush to the straight establishment to have their work published, ignoring or being condescending to
the independent gay media. See *Gay Roots* (Vol. 1), p. 336 (Gay Sunshine Press, 1991).

observed with interest the growth of the accommodationist faction within our ranks—
Berglerites in their own fashion, ones for whom wit and displays of gay sensibility are
now Out-Of-Place, for whom radical strategies are "embarrassing" and infantile," etc.
What began as a movement almost entirely inclined toward collective and grass-roots
organizing—a movement, after all, which literally *began* in the streets—and virtually
unfathomable to inquisitive straight interlopers (police spies at gay meetings are iden-
tifiable as much by their *dullness* as by their evil manipulations and divisiveness) is seeing this daring and anarchic energy being *squeezed out* and attacked by the new gay
ward-heelers. Our anger, "madness," "dizziness" is being denied support by those who
believe that the validity of *our* organizations, publications and structures can only be
measured by the degree to which these resemble their counterparts in the straight world.
It's the imagination of the ward-heelers rudely elbowing their way to the helm, moving
into our community, making us ever-conscious of the power of the bosses, and warning us not to "offend" the powers that be. It is this encroachment we must resist, this
new muzzling of ourselves in the name of *real-politik*, forcing us to become "positive
role models," gaining respectability, achieving acceptance with the help of our powerful
"friends" in Washington, New York or wherever.

I recall remarking to Shively back in 1971, in a somewhat and totally atypically cynical mood: "What will happen to gay liberation? Well, what the Mafia can buy up,
they will. Everything else will boil down to some safe and respectable social service-
counseling racket." The ward-heelers are everywhere present among us today, putting
on the squeeze and talking "common sense" at us: religion flunkies, "respectable" academics, group therapy quacks, money-hustlers, power-groupies, etc. Media-mad organizations have sprung up out of nowhere which claim to represent the gay
community, even though they patently do not. Toadies to those in power, whether
they be in activist groups or writing for gay publications, would give credence to one
of Anita Bryant's wisdoms: "Homosexuals already have the best jobs and the best
houses."

I define the homo ward-heelers by their most striking characteristic; they are all absolutely obsessed with the *image* we project to the straight world. They want nothing to exist in our lives which would embarrass, upset or offend the people in power.
What this comes down to in our community is that the homo ward-heelers are always
attacking drag queens, radical faggots, lesbian feminists, the sexually promiscuous, the
drop-outs, the counter-culturists, the freaks, the poor, the shabby, the queer-looking—
all those who don't fit in conveniently with the literalist demands of the Heterosexist
Tyrants. This bulk of our community commits what one homo ward-heeler recently
wrote was "the ultimate crime—being in poor taste in public"!

The ward-heelers know how it is done. They organize *from above*, ignore the masses,
suck up the money and talent from the community, challenge it to please the bosses
they seek to get in with and thereby achieve their personal ambitions of becoming the
established brokers between the seats of money/power/straight authority from on top
and you and me on the bottom—where they intend for us to stay. Their establishment
and legitimization of this role for themselves is built on a lie. We must expose them.

As an instance locally, some ward-heelers were busy in the planning for Boston's
Gay Day Parade, 1977. I had a grotesque vision of how the march would turn out if
the ward-heelers had their way unopposed: a line of clerical-collared divinity drags leading off this year's march, carrying a street-wide banner proclaiming "Gay Liberation

Through Jesus Christ." They would be followed by the straight local dignitaries who like to march in every parade. Behind them would be the gaudy floats plugging bars and discos. And from there on to the end would be a procession of Cadillac convertibles filled with bouquet-carrying, gaily-waving drag queans.

In other words, no march for *people* in our community, only space for those who have been created out of straight concepts about how our lives are to be organized. Sell-out time.

The ward-heelers achieve their power by making sure we stay in line. They discipline us, silence us, and package us as to be indistinguishable from other interest groups in this society. It seems to me that if we ignore or deny the importance of the gay sensibility, we are fated to become just *that*—another Special Interest Group, Legislative Lobby, Marketing Area. Our particular threat to the established straight tyranny will be radically diminished if the ward-heelers can set us up all neat and tidy with carefully delineated boundaries, with anticipatible interests and demands which can be serviced in exchange for deals with our brokers.

It seems to me that gay people are "special." We are all special to the degree that we are committed to the vitality of our gay sensibility and to the extent that we reject all straight-promoted forms of understanding and expressing experience. We must let the culture and institutions of the superstructure collapse through sheer top-heaviness—and hope the collapse takes a good number of their apologists and missionaries with it. Once crumbled, I think we'd skip merrily through the ruins and busy ourselves immediately with repainting the horizons in *our colors and through our perspectives*.

Wit is the cutting edge of the gay sensibility. It's what is on hand right now to constantly deflate the much-advertised importance of the culture-pattern-setters. We must subvert, destabilize, unnerve, and harass the enforcers of the Het Tyranny with whatever means we possess. An upfront demonstration of who and what we are—our "madness," our imagination, our mercurialness—are constant and frightening challenges to the upholders of the straight life and its culture. If we constantly expose them *in* and *through* ridicule, the ward-heelers within the gay community will, one hopes, be kept at bay and revealed for the fraudulent self-seekers they are.

Again, it is important to remember that most "high culture" and virtually all pop culture communicates the established values of the society that contains it. It is propaganda. (Who, after all, *pays* for symphonies, opera houses, educational TV, tidy reviews of literature, university presses and unending Wagner festivals?) The artifacts of high culture are, by and large, ads and apologias for a system of superstition and exploitation of a slave class/women/& faggots. Where apologists for high culture see "talent," "beauty," and "educational opportunity," I see only the rivers of blood and mountains of corpses on which rest the thrones and pulpits which created and filled the British Museum, The Louvre, the Hermitage, Paris Opera, the Vatican, Harvard University, Lincoln Center (more aptly called Rockefeller Center West), and the list goes on and on with monuments to the jealousy and greed of power-mad Christians and capitalists whose symbols must flatteringly reflect and celebrate their twisted condition. And this they call the "world of art and ideas."

Anyone electing to express (through the conventional genres) attitudes &/or ideas not acceptable to the Het Tyrants will have a difficult time gaining access to an audience. Someone daring to explore new genres, inventing or rediscovering different structures for perceptions, evidence and information will likely be benignly ignored or actively prosecuted. Such has been the theme through the history of artists to date who attempt to operate on their gay sensibilities and who optimistically hope they can slip through the censors/editors/heresy-hounds to reach an audience.

The social supports for straight culture, and the hostility to any direct challenge to its propagandistic function, make the "fact" of this culture so seemingly impenetrable that those trapped within it were always frustrated in their attempts to break out of it. The branding-iron Rules of The Game was impressed onto every gay imagination, to the injury and detriment of gay sensibility. Wiggle, twist, explode: do what it might, gay imaginative energies, to get through to an audience at all, had to clean up their acts and had to get screened through the taboos of the time. The squirming around of the gay imagination within these tight confines connect with the *outrage* of being entrapped to create the energy for what's called "camp"—the gay sensibility howling out for independence from the shackles of heterosexist imagery, referents, trappings, apologies, and "role models" (*those* again!).

I think it hasn't been until this decade, really, that homosexuals have had all the right equipment—corrected social analysis, strong support from the like-minded, a proper contempt for the enemy, and a recognition of the vulnerability of the established culture—to take the next step: to actively clear away the old cob-webbed maze of taboos, hypocrisies and intolerance of the Heterosexist Tyranny. Now is the time; we will either successfully create the intellectual and imaginative revolution against the strictures of current agencies of social control or we will fail. To succeed, we must ridicule, shout down, and discredit the new variety of apologists for the given order of things, i.e., the homo ward-heelers in our midsts and their payrollers. If we do succeed in this intellectual and imaginative revolution, it will be like having well-oiled skids to slide into place everything else that will follow. We will fail only if we lack the courage to invest full confidence and authority in re-inventing our world based on impulse, daring and visions that come out of our gay sensibility. If we do fail, and if we crumble beneath the firm-jawed, money-hungry, power-obsessed class of homosexual ward-heelers in the current machine, we will not have another chance, such as we now have, in our lifetime. I think the worst thing that could develop is that we'd retreat from the front edge of our expanding consciousness of our imaginative powers and settle down with the lot that the ward-heelers dispense: being content with being dull. Ward-heelers are happy to service our liberation from the waist down (tastefully, of course); what they want is for us to be dead from the belly-button up.

Everything will be done by the lackies of the Het Tyranny to bring us back into line and secure us there. Money, publicity, fame and rewards are (and will continue to be) presented to the malleable gay ward-heelers and their minions. Homosexual authors who can write novels with romantic and/or guilt-ridden characters and themes for the mass market will be published, feted and promoted as The New Gay Talent of Today; they will be made into Stars. (Natalie Barney once remarked—and this should be beat into every wordy journalist, academic writer, and pop-trash scribbler—"How lazy it is to write a lot. If you can put a whole novel into a few sentences, why not?")

Musical queans who can tinkle out pretty tunes with clever lyrics that do not offend the powerful consumers among the straights will be offered Broadway/Hollywood opportunities. Balladeers who croon of heterosexual commitment (or, as lately, a sort of neuter love—no names and no pronouns) will make it to The Top Of The Pops. The emphasis on the values of the existing Market Place Structure will be the magnet to get us into the groove. Faggots & dykes (less so the dykes, it seems, than the queans) who keep their talent within established mores—more new grand operas, more brilliant but conventional, dull, inoffensive literary studies about dead straights or closet cases, safe poetry characterized by Heavy Syntax or Deep, Obscure Meaning, and always, *always* in all work propagating the superiority of business men with money—will trigger a cascade of prizes, dinners, awards, cash grants, lecture dollars, interviews, etc. (One of our Good Gay Poets remarked that he had great respect for a local writing homo ward-heeler because "he is a professional journalist"—as though *that* were something a gay person should aspire to or be proud of!)

The control agents of the Het Tyranny are *right now* deciding who within our community (or better for them, who it will be that they can *implant* into our community) are to be acceptable "role models" for us to imitate to also try to gain acceptance, win cash prizes, fabulous jobs, wealth and fame and the Respectability Reward from the tyrants.

Homosexual cultural myopics will be singled out and acclaimed "visionaries," gay accommodationists will be lauded as "realists" who can "get things done for their people," gay hack writers and editors working for (probably straight owned) publications which imitate dull straight journals will be rewarded with fat ads, eager distribution, helpful printers. And those who engage in rear-guard divisiveness—red-baiting, woman-hating, blacklisting, distortion, sexual exploitation—will be particular favorites of the control agents of the Het Tyranny, and they will be lavished with the most serious attention of the Het Rulers of anything within our community.

The homosexual ward-heelers busily sew up their minions into an increasingly closed world; all new information must pass through them in their role of brokers. If they succeed, we will once again be robbed not only of our voices and our inventiveness, but what will also be taken from us is our means to create a world in which we are no longer trapped in a million gigantic and trivial ways.

Since the Days of Stonewall, I have often heard or read laments about gay wit. Usually the criticism follows this line: homosexuals have for too long made each the "victims" of their own wit. I hope I have contributed to burying this chestnut once and for all time. Let me say that wit has been for gay people a double-edged sword. It can cut either way. Mostly it has been a rearguard instrument fighting off attacks that threaten our survival. But we can use it best in the other direction. We must sharpen our wit on each other—like knives against whetstones—so that when we must strike, our edges will be their sharpest to cut our enemies to the quick.

▽

POSTSCRIPT, 1993

This essay was written back in 1977, but as B. Holiday sings in "God Bless The Child," it still is news today. Why? Why do so many gay men perceive and act on the world so differently from the straight culture? Is it our gay genes? Something in our gay brains? Or can we rely on good old concepts like political theory and strategies for social struggle to explain these differences?

This essay, now a bit prolix for my tastes, would be trimmed down and made more punchy if done today. But what's important about it is its historicalness, that it is part of an emerging literature in our time, from Sontag's "Notes on Camp," to Michael

Bronski's *Culture Clash*, all of which attempt to probe the differentness of gay men to culture. That is, I think, the refracting point, and we go off in a useful oblique direction.

There is a vast network of gay men who have always taken culture, all culture, very seriously, and I mean seriously in the sense that they give cultural expressions great time and attention and look for the fun in it, for enjoyment, rather than merely "instruction," (that hangover from the religioso-uplift movement in the arts) is central to the way gay men use culture. At the other end of the spectrum, the New York *Times* also takes culture very seriously, but with such a leaden foot and such a narrow vision, that those events which they don't see (many) they could well crush with their ponderousness or misreadings. As they used to say on the Benson & Hedges cigarette ads, back when weeds were still advertised on the TV: "Oh, the disadvantages!"

As the late columnist Arthur Bell used to note, there is a chasm in our community between the Politikos and the Culture Queans, and when Arthur, an old gay radical, got exhausted with the dullness of the gay ward-heelers, he always joyfully retreated to gay cultural life, always a solace. In my life, I have found very little cross-over between the Politikos and the gay culture mavens. Back in the mid-70s, times were very different. The gay political radicals were also usually the gay cultural radicals. A brilliant and dramatic demo at the State House in day-light hours, and then rush back to put on some utterly mad drag troupe revue that night in a church basement. This doesn't happen much anymore.

With the growth in our movement's numbers, roles are more clearly demarcated. Fundraising and big salaries had something to do with it. The past dozen years of conservative political regimes, and the terrible toll of death in our community, have been a great blow. Before he committed suicide, the great artist Ethyl Eichelburger was asked if he had ever received any government grants. Ethyl replied: "I'm a drag quean, honey. They don't fund us." There is much work to be done. I recently asked an important gay political leader in my town (he's a teacher in his mid-30s) if he was going to the Nina Simone concert that night at Symphony Hall, a concert which had had the culture queans all adizzy for weeks. He looked at me and asked: "Who's Nina Simone?" So there you are.

It seems to me that the essential thrust of the gay cultural movement has been, as with similar efforts by other traditionally excluded minorities, one of reclamation: finding our history, our voices, and documenting fully those who have gone before. The growth of this body of cultural understanding in the past 20 + years has been revolutionary. And it really is the growth of community and culture which drives the politics, something, sadly, the politikos have yet to come to realize.

In early 1992, *The Ghosts of Versailles* premiered at The Met in New York, a commissioned piece put together by three gay men of enormous talents. It was an instant hit, particularly popular with the gay legions who support the opera. But one scribe for the heavy-footed NY *Times* was clearly upset; he wrote that what had happened at The Met was "nothing less than an act of cultural terrorism." Months earlier, in the very same cultural pages, old sad-sack Hilton Kramer weighed in against the work of R. Mapplethorpe, calling it "pornography," that inevitable moniker they have stuck on us in all times.

I recently asked a dear friend if he was planning to teach his Gay Lit. course this fall at a local university. He said no. I asked why. He said: "The last bunch of young gay men we had in the course was disappointing. They had absolutely no idea what literature was all about. When we read Isherwood's *A Single Man*, they couldn't understand why the man should be so unhappy. Some suggested he should see a therapist or join a support group or maybe try a 12-step program. It completely discouraged me."

That's pretty much the sad analysis of the war between the wits and the ward-heelers, in their many new incarnations. I actually don't mind so much that some of the Top-Cat Politikos don't know who Nina Simone is; they actually know all the names of this crop of state legislators, their phone numbers, and their voting records. We wouldn't want to over-tax the delicate gay brains of our comrades. But the therapists and the normalizers within our community are the biggest threat. They are out to denude our thriving culture, determined to erase all the contradictions, cover over the dark spaces, iron out the crazy poetics, and tailor our prose into works of self-affirmation and personal esteem-building. Theirs is a juggernaut of single-vision. And we must forgive them for they know not what they are doing. If they win—and I am working every day to prevent it—each and every one of our daring artifacts in the future, if made public at all, will come with an approved rating and a barf bag. As Bette Davis, playing the gay young bride in *Dark Victory*, saw while flipping through her personal file on her Doctor-husband's desk, the grim news read: PROGNOSIS: NEGATIVE.

John Mitzel

Robin Maugham

DIETER

Robin Maugham (1916–1981), nephew of the famous Somerset, was a prolific writer of books, including the novel The Servant *(later made into a movie with Dirk Bogarde),* The Wrong People, Enemy *(the last published by Gay Sunshine Press), and the short story collection,* The Boy from Beirut *(also published by Gay Sunshine Press, 1981, and now out of print). The autobiographical story "Dieter" is taken from this last mentioned collection. It had previously appeared in Maugham's* Search for Nirvana *(1975).*

The following Preface to "Dieter" was provided to Gay Sunshine Press by Robin Maugham in 1981:

After my autobiography *Escape from the Shadows* had been published, some of my friends were so enthusiastic about the book that they regretted that for obvious reasons of length I had omitted many events and journeys in my life which must have had considerable importance to me. It was then suggested that I should write a book entitled *Search for Nirvana* in which I would tell of my quests and adventures when I had escaped from my strict middle-class family. Where did I go to find release and happiness?

The idea of writing about my searches for nirvana appealed to my publishers, W. H. Allen, and they commissioned the book.

I spent a whole year travelling once again to Ceylon and preparing notes for the work. I then began to write. Now, it is evident that scenes or incidents which are part of larger events that have changed the shape of the world—such as the war against fascism—may affect one individual for the rest of his or her life, whilst to another person the war seems to have had no impact on the formation of his character and have had no emotional impact whatsoever. So I have come to the conclusion that what affects us in our hearts and souls may have no more importance to world history than does a leaf falling down from a tree. But the author is naturally tempted to lend importance to what are obviously world-important events and to dismiss the falling of a leaf in one brief sentence. While I have been writing *Search for Nirvana* I have tried to resist this temptation. And I have several reasons for having tried to do so. After all, I am not writing a history of social events in the world from 1930 to the present, I am writing about myself. Secondly, during the year when I was making notes of the journeys and adventures in my life I discovered to my surprise that a year's travel to the Southern Hemisphere might have left little impression on my character, while an event which occurred only a day's travel from England and lasted only one night might somehow have pierced into my subconscious so deeply that now, as I sat at my desk patiently bringing the event to the surface, the memory of the episode was so poignant to me that I could hardly bear to set it down on paper. Thirdly, I am convinced that I personally can only hope to hold the interest of my readers if I write with complete honesty—however many people I may shock by so doing.

I am not what is known as "a natural writer"; each sentence is an effort for me to write. Such success as I have had, I am certain, has been due—as many reviewers have pointed out—to the fact that I am ruthlessly sincere in my work, and somehow that sincerity manages to communicate itself from the printed page to the reader.

The story of my meeting with Dieter in Salzburg had on the world no more importance than the falling of a leaf. Moreover, it became partly obscured in my mind by the excitement and hard work of being at university and by the war which came soon after I left Cambridge. It was only when I recalled the whole of that evening that I realised how much it had meant to me and how deeply I still cared.

When I had finished writing about the encounter with Dieter, my assistant Peter Burton discovered that I had in effect written a complete short story.

In memory of Dieter, here it is.

▽

for Peter

*I*N THE SUMMER VACATION from Cambridge, in 1936, soon after my twentieth birthday, I went to Salzburg with my sister Honor. Though we both had little money we managed to see *Don Giovanni, Orfeo* and *Tristan and Isolde*. Then Willie Maugham's companion, Gerald Haxton, appeared in a Voisin coupé, and our existence changed abruptly. In his early forties, well-dressed, attractive and slim, very European though he was an American by nationality, Gerald exuded vitality and charm and money. Two years earlier he had tried to seduce me in Vienna; he now tried—without the slightest success—to persuade Honor to sleep with him. Unabashed, Gerald took us both to *The Meistersingers*. Wagner and schnapps went to his head. After supper, he insisted he had left his camera in Honor's bedroom and made one last attempt to get her to bed. Then he said goodnight to her affectionately, and swept me off to a *Bier-Stube*.

The beer hall seemed packed with fat middle-aged men in ample *Lederhosen* and boys in scanty ones. Gerald spoke to a waiter who evidently knew him. We were shown to one of the wooden tables and given mugs of lager.

"You look surprised, duckie," Gerald said. "Don't tell me you've been here a fortnight and haven't visited *this* place?"

"But it's true," I replied.

"Gaze around, and just see what you've been missing," Gerald proclaimed with a drunken wave of his hand, as if he were a magician who had produced the whole scene for my benefit. "Let *that* teach you to travel with an elder sister."

"But she understands," I protested.

"But I also rather fancy she still disapproves."

I was silent. I loved my three sisters. Indeed, we were an unusually united family. But I was aware that my sisters hoped that what they considered to be only a slight homosexual streak in my nature would disappear as I grew older. I tried to find something to say; I need not have bothered. Gerald's eyes were now staring at a boy. At first glance, he did not appear to be very different from the others who were posed attractively at the barcounter, waiting to be picked up. He was blond with pale, corn-coloured hair which flopped over his gentle, slightly fleshy face.

"That's Dieter," Gerald told me. "He's a Viennese. He must be nearly seventeen by now. He's a good romp—if you're firm enough with him."

Gerald raised his hand as he caught Dieter's attention. He beckoned to him. Obediently, Dieter left the bar, came over to our table, and gave Gerald a curt little bow of his head.

"*Servus*," he said, smiling.

"Sit down," Gerald told him. "Sit down and have a drink with us." Then he turned to me. "Robin," he said, "this is Dieter. Dieter—this is Robin."

It was when I shook hands with Dieter that I noticed his expression. Though he was smiling pleasantly, his eyes did not link with his appearance. His face showed subservience and a keen look of anticipation; his eyes, which were dark yet blue, proclaimed—or so it seemed to me—mistrust and doubt that amounted almost to fear, yet in their expression there appeared an odd look which I tried to understand: it was the look of someone lost, someone who was yearning. Or had I transferred my own feelings to his gentle, soft, blonde features? Dieter sat down next to Gerald.

"How long have you been here, Dieter?" Gerald asked him, as the waiter produced a tankard of lager for him.

"*Zwei Wochen*," Dieter answered. "Two weeks."

"I only arrived in Salzburg yesterday," Gerald explained. "Or I'd have been down here sooner."

As Gerald spoke, he moved his chair close to Dieter. Then he slid his hand under the table. Dieter did not move. He was still smiling. Suddenly he winced.

"Not in here," he said to Gerald. "*Später vielleicht*."

"I just wanted to make sure it was as good as ever," Gerald laughed. "And it *will* be later—don't you worry!"

Dieter gave a slight nod of his head. Gerald glanced at me, then turned back to Dieter and spoke in German—which he spoke badly, yet better than I did.

"My friend Robin is all of twenty years old," he told Dieter. "But he's shocked because he's pathetically romantic. He still can't understand what our lives are all about."

Suddenly Dieter looked at me. This time I could not mistake the expression. It was one of complete sympathy. Then, abruptly, he turned towards Gerald. But Gerald had seen the look between us. Laughingly he waved his unsteady hand in my face, and leaned close towards me with his back to Dieter.

"Surely you've learned by now." he said. "Am I mistaken? Or do I not remember a previous episode of this kind? When, oh when, will you learn? A boy like Dieter doesn't want your love or your sympathy or your adoration. All he wants is to be thoroughly fucked and given the sum of money he's used to—or more, if he's been particularly amenable—and then to be sent home with the cash for his poor, starving mother. For never doubt. Dieter has got a starving mother. They all have."

Gerald swung away from me and faced Dieter.

"Have you got a starving mother?" he asked.

Dieter stared at him. For an instant his face trembled. Then he smiled as pleasantly as usual.

"Yes," Dieter answered.

"You see!" Gerald cried in triumph. Then, as if to exclude me deliberately from their conversation, he began to talk to Dieter about well-known queers in Vienna. But although Dieter spoke brightly with his delightful smile, I could see that he was growing bored as Gerald's slurred words began to grow more confused. Gerald turned more frequently towards the bar.

"When are you going back to Vienna?" he asked Dieter.

"Soon," Dieter answered, pushing the floppy blonde hair from his forehead. "My holiday is finished. I must go back to my work."

"With a good sum of money for your poor mother," Gerald said as he lurched round towards me. "Dieter works in a factory." Gerald explained. "But what he earns for the whole year is less than he makes during his holidays. Isn't that true, Dieter?"

"*Jawohl*," Dieter answered. "What Gerald says is true."

"Then why don't you find yourself some rich protector?" Gerald enquired. "There must be plenty of them about."

"Not now," Dieter answered. "Since they killed Dolfuss there is no one rich except the Fascists."

"Fascists in bed can't be any worse than Communists," said Gerald.

"Yes," Dieter replied. "*Das ist wahr*. But if I go with a Fascist, I can be made to work for the Fascists. And in Austria that can be dangerous for me."

"See?" Gerald said to me. "Dieter is a realist."

Dieter stared at him with solemn eyes, while the waiter brought more drinks.

"My mother is *ein wenig krank*—a little ill. She can only do light laundry to make money," Dieter said. "My father has left us. I am the only one who can bring in the bread for us to eat."

"So there you are!" Gerald exclaimed to me. "Just like all the rest of them, he's playing for an extra tip. What's more, he'll get it—if he's good enough to deserve it. And I can tell you from experience—he knows the whole bag of tricks. The trouble is . . ."

But at that moment Gerald stopped. He had raised his head. He was staring at a young boy who had just come in and was standing at the bar. The boy was very young, perhaps fourteen, and he was less obviously dressed as "rent" or "trade" than Dieter. Probably to disguise his age he wore long trousers rather than the short *Lederhosen* of the other boys at the bar which could reveal as much of their sexual charm as they cared to show. But this boy's black gaberdine trousers were elegantly cut and contrasted with a fawn silk shirt. He was slender, with a pert little face and large brown eyes.

"Well, I never," Gerald murmured to Dieter. "That's little Felix. His old friend Rombach would never let him come out to a bar like this. Felix must have done something really naughty and been turned out."

Gerald gulped down his schnapps and beckoned to the amiable waiter. "Tell Felix to come over to our table and join us for a drink," he said pointing out Felix to the waiter. "And bring us four beers and four more schnapps."

"*Jawohl*," said the waiter with a sly look and crossed the crowded room towards Felix.

I watched little Felix as the waiter spoke to him. At first he looked glum. Then as the waiter pointed to our table he recognized Gerald, and as if he had put on a different mask, his face was suddenly transformed: he became an eager yet innocent schoolboy, smiling in acquiescence at the master who was about to punish him. Immediately he moved with light steps towards us, and as he walked the gaberdine trousers displayed his trained, sinuous control of his muscles as well as did a stallion in the *Spanische Reitschule*.

Gerald rose from the table and kissed him.

"*Mein Schatz*," Gerald muttered. "*Mein lieber Felix*. Are you free? Are you free for me tonight?"

Felix smiled. His teeth were uneven but very white. He took a quick look around the room. Customers were beginning to leave the *Bier-Stube*.

"*Aber natürlich*," he said. "As you know, I am always free for my *Onkle Gerald*."

Gerald finished the schnapps which the waiter had brought him.

"Now?" he asked. It might have been a command.

Little Felix glanced at me and then at Dieter. He gave a smirk. "Do you want to leave such good company?" Felix asked coyly.

Gerald stood up. He was drunk. "Why not?" he demanded.

Then he threw a bundle of banknotes towards me.

"Enjoy yourselves, children," he said. "Pay the bill, Robin. This party has been on me." Gerald paused, and his bleary eyes looked for an instant at Dieter whose face was once again stiff and solemn. "And one more thing, Robin," he added, "Give your new boy-friend what he's accustomed to—financially, I mean. He'll tell you his tariff. The rest I leave to you."

Unsteadily Gerald moved towards the door. But I noticed that he turned to make sure that little Felix was following him. He need not have worried. Felix, with his trousers now seemingly plastered to his body, was following him, just as Gerald wanted, with a smile on his face and a look of utter subservience.

I was left alone with Dieter.

For a while we drank our lager in silence. Gerald's remark about paying Dieter his usual tariff had managed to subdue my sexual excitement. For it saddened and revolted me to think that if I were the grossly obese Austrian with warts on his flabby face who was sitting at the next table to us I could still lie with Dieter's slender body clasped against mine—provided I paid the tariff. I realised that I was perhaps stupidly romantic and prudish. But I was twenty years old; I had formed my own ideals, and I wanted to try to follow them.

"You look *traurig*," Dieter said. "Why are you sad?"

I smiled. "I'm not sad," I said. "But this place is terribly hot and smoky."

"Shall we go?"

"Let's have one more drink. I'm not feeling tired. Are you?"

Dieter stared at me. He was frowning with concentration as if he were trying to solve a complicated problem. Then the wrinkles vanished from his forehead and he smiled.

"Listen to me," he said. "I have an idea. We cannot go to my room for a last drink, because I share it with two friends, and the *Wirtin* will not let me bring back friends. *Ausserdem*, we cannot go to your hotel because they will not let you take me in at this time of night. But I know a path that leads up the hillside. If we buy a bottle of *Kirschwasser* when we pay the bill, we can take the bottle with us and drink it and talk and stay there until the dawn breaks if we want to."

Though I did not want to sleep with Dieter, I was already fond of him. I wanted to find out more about him and more about the life he led. I also liked Kirsch, the liqueur made from wild cherries.

"Right," I said and beckoned to the waiter.

We paid the bill with the money Gerald had given me, bought the Kirsch and left the tavern. The night was pleasantly warm. There were no clouds in the sky; there was a full moon. Dieter found the path and led the way up the hillside. He was silent, but now and then he would turn round and give me a smile. The sadness I had felt in the tavern had gone. I was glad to be young and strong; I was happy to be with such an attractive companion.

Presently the path led to a gate beyond which lay a field with a hut in the lower corner of it. Dieter opened the gate. "They use that hut to put the sheep in during the winter," he explained. Then Dieter pointed to a flat stretch of grass. "If you like, we can sit there," he said. "We should be able to get a good view of the city at sunrise."

Together we sat down. Dieter opened the bottle of Kirsch and handed it to me. Not only his well-made limbs, but his personality and soft smile attracted me.

"You drink first," he said.

I took a swig. I could feel the liquid burning its way to my stomach. "*Wunderschön*," I gasped. "It's delicious. *Wunderbar*."

Dieter grinned as I handed him the bottle.

"*Prost*," he murmured and drank. Then he put a hand on my shoulder. "Promise you won't leave till we have finished the bottle," he said.

"I promise," I answered solemnly.

"Where did you learn your German?" Dieter asked.

"I didn't," I replied. "As you can hear, it's *sehr schlecht*. Rotten. *Ich kann garnicht Deutsch*."

"But you speak with the accent of Wien!" Dieter exclaimed.

"That's because I was staying in Vienna when I learned the little German I know," I told him.

"When were you in Vienna?"

"Just over two years ago."

"Think of it!" Dieter cried. "We might have met. If fact, you may have seen me without knowing it. My two beats were the Kärtner Strasse and the main Bahnhof—railway stations are always a good place to get picked up."

I stared at him. "How old are you, Dieter?" I asked.

"Seventeen."

"And you were getting picked up at the age of fifteen?"

"*Sicher*," he answered. "*Warum nicht?* I was only thirteen when I was first broken in."

"How did that happen?"

"It just came about," Dieter answered. "Perhaps I was lucky. Perhaps I was unlucky. It's too late to worry about it now."

"But *how* did it happen?"

"Why do you want to know?"

"Because I like you," I replied. "Because I'm interested in you."

Dieter gazed at me for an instant in silence. With a quick movement he pushed the blonde hair back from his forehead.

"When you've only known me for a few hours?" he murmured.

"Yes."

Dieter nodded his head as if in agreement. He took a gulp from the bottle and handed it to me.

"*Na also*. If you want the truth, here it is," he said. "Very well. During the school holidays I used to make pocket-money by working as a ball-boy at some tennis courts in the town. I realised now that I was paid very little—but then to me it was a fortune. Almost every afternoon towards five there was an Englishman, perhaps forty years old, who used to come and play tennis with an Austrian of his own age. At that time, all I knew about the Englishman was what I had overheard at the tennis club. I knew that he was unmarried and a businessman. He was strong and well-built, and he played quite good tennis. But though the Austrian sometimes gave me a smile, this Englishman never even glanced at me. It was always the Austrian who threw me a tip at the end of the game."

All the time he was talking, Dieter was watching me.

"One afternoon at five o'clock," Dieter continued, "I was waiting on the court as usual for the two of them. Soon the Englishman appeared, but not the Austrian. 'Have you seen Herr Dirksen?' he called out to me. He spoke almost perfect German. 'No,' I answered. At that moment a servant came out from the club-house to announce that Herr Dirksen had telephoned to say he had been delayed at a meeting and regretted that he could not come. 'Right,' said the Englishman and began to walk away. Suddenly he stopped and turned round towards me.

" 'Come here,' he said. I moved quickly towards him.

" 'You'd better have your tip as usual,' he said. He put his hand in his pocket and then tossed me a coin.

"Well, I was so surprised he should even think of me—let alone give me a tip— that I missed the catch. The coin fell on the ground. I stooped down to pick it up. When I stood up again, I saw the tip was the largest I'd ever been given.

" 'Thank you, sir,' I said to him. And I really meant it. Then for the first time— for the very first time, the Englishman really looked at me. He looked at me from my untidy hair down to my broken gym shoes.

" 'What's your name?' he asked in a cold voice.

" 'Dieter,' I told him.

" 'How old are you?'

" 'Thirteen,' I answered.

"When I spoke he scowled as if I'd said something to annoy him. 'You can't be only thirteen,' he exclaimed.

" '*Aber wirklich*,' I said. 'Honestly, sir. I'm thirteen.'

" 'Then you're tall for your age,' he said.

"I was silent. He was staring at me with such anger in his face that for a moment I was afraid he would strike me. Then I noticed that his gaze was no longer fixed on my face. The shorts I was wearing were too small for me. I had begged for a new pair, but my mother had said that there was no money. She couldn't afford such useless purchases, she said. It was summer. My skin is very fair, but it goes quite brown in the sun. The Englishman was staring at my thighs which were completely exposed by my small shorts. He turned away, and I thought he was leaving. But his gaze stayed fixed. He couldn't control his eyes. His expression was now so strained that I was afraid of him. I wanted to run away. I had a feeling that something terrible was about to happen. I longed to go, but I couldn't move. His hands had begun to tremble. By now I was really frightened. Suddenly he took in a long, deep breath and then let it out. Then he spoke. His voice was very hoarse.

" 'Dieter,' he said, 'Would you like a present of money? A present twenty times as much as the tip I gave you?'

"I did not reply. I remained silent, for I had suddenly understood what it was all about. I had overheard boys talking about it at school, but I didn't quite know what happened.

" 'Answer me,' the Englishman said. 'Think of it. Twenty times the amount of the tip I gave you. At least twenty times. You understand what I mean? I can see from your face that you do. So answer me, Dieter. I promise I won't hurt you.'

"At that moment I realised that he was more frightened than I was. And it was this fact—in addition to the sum of money he was offering—which made up my mind for me.

" 'Yes,' I muttered.

"The Englishman sighed. His hands were now trembling horribly.

" 'And you'll never tell anyone?' he said hoarsely.

" 'No,' I muttered.

" 'You swear it?'

" 'I swear it.'

"He turned his head nervously to make sure that no one was observing our conversation. But there was no one about.

" 'I don't want anyone to see us leaving in my car. *Verstehst Du?* So you'll have to make your own way to my flat. Do you think you can do that?'

" '*Natürlich*,' I said. 'Of course I can.'

"Then he repeated his address several times, and made me repeat it back to him. It wasn't far away from the tennis club. 'My flat's on the top floor,' he explained to me. 'So you ring the top bell outside the front door. I'll come down to let you in. Do you understand? The top bell. I'll be waiting for you. There's no concierge to worry about.'

" 'I understand,' I answered.

" 'Then I'll see you in about a half an hour's time,' he said and walked quickly away from me.

"I found my way to the address easily," Dieter continued. "I pressed the top bell as instructed, and a few moments later the man opened the door and let me in. Hurriedly he closed the door behind me. He said no word of greeting. In silence he led me up the stairs and showed me into his flat—or as we'd call it, *Wohnung*. Carefully he bolted the door behind us. We crossed a small hall and entered a large living-room. Immediately I noticed that the curtains were half-drawn. The room was comfortably furnished with some *fabelhaft* paintings on the walls and a thick carpet on the floor. He pointed to a sofa. 'Sit down,' he said—and those were the first words he had spoken to me since I entered the building. 'The maid who looks after me always leaves at five in the afternoon, so we've got the place to ourselves. We shan't be disturbed. By the way, would you care for a glass of lemonade?'

" 'Please, sir,' I said.

"He went to the sideboard and poured me a glass, brought it to me, and sat down on the sofa, close beside me. 'When we're alone together, you don't have to call me "sir," ' he muttered.

"I could see that his hands were now shaking with nerves, and while he'd been waiting for me he must have had several drinks from the decanter on the sideboard because his breath reeked of liquor. He stared at me in silence while I drank my lemonade.

" 'Do you live with your parents?' he asked me after a while.

" 'Yes,' I told him.

" 'Do you get on with them?'

" 'I get on with my mother,' I answered truthfully. 'But not with my father.'

" 'Why not?'

" 'Because when he drinks he becomes *ein Teufel*. A devil.'

" 'Does he beat you?'

" 'Sometimes.'

" 'Have you any brothers or sisters?'

" 'No. I'm the only child.'

"The man was silent. He was breathing heavily. I'd finished my drink, but I was still thirsty. 'Some more lemonade?' he asked. I nodded my head. His nervousness had infected me. I found it hard not to shiver. The man leaned across me and put my glass on a side-table. Then he began to stroke my head. I didn't move. 'You've got a fine mop of hair and it's a glorious colour,' he mumbled. His trembling hand now touched my cheek and pressed against it. 'And very soft skin,' he said, speaking almost to himself. He drew away from me. 'Dieter,' he said in his hoarse voice, 'you're sure you're not going to mind this? Because we can stop at any moment you like, and I'll still give you a present. Would you like to leave?' I shook my head. Suddenly he gave a long sigh and bent down and kissed my forehead. 'Oh Dieter,' he whispered. 'You're wonderfully sweet, and I'm mad for you.' Then he began to kiss my mouth and my neck. As he kissed me, his hand began to stroke my thigh nearest him, running his fingers up and down my skin, then clenching my thigh so hard I winced. 'I'm sorry,' he muttered. 'I must remember how soft your skin is.' Presently, he began to undo the buttons of my shorts. I did not move. Nor did I try to stop him when his hand slid between my legs. Presently he led me to his bedroom and stripped me naked. Then he took off his own clothes."

Until that moment Dieter had been gazing at me constantly, as if to assess the effect that his story was having on me. But now he turned away and began to pluck at the blades of grass beside him.

"For a man so strong, he was very gentle," Dieter continued, staring down at the grass. "He tried not to hurt me. And eventually he managed to get me excited too. When it was all over he held me in his arms. Soon he went to sleep, and so did I. When I awoke, I saw from the clock on his bedside table that is was after eight o'clock. I would get scolded for missing supper. I turned to wake the Englishman, but he was already awake. And for the first time he smiled. 'When I awoke I couldn't imagine for a moment what a beautiful person could be lying in my arms. Then I remembered.' He leaned forward and kissed me. 'Oh Dieter,' he said, 'you've given me such happiness. Promise me you'll come here again.' He looked at me so earnestly that I didn't like to disappoint him. 'All right,' I replied. 'I promise.' Again he smiled, and his face now looked quite different. He seemed far younger. 'Dieter,' he said, 'what about some cold food? There's masses laid out for me.'

" 'I must go home,' I told him. 'I'll get scolded for being so late as it is.'

" 'I tell you what,' he said, 'in addition to your present, I'll give you some extra money for a taxi. You can take the taxi to a few streets away from where you live. That will save you time. Please stay and have some food with me.'

"So I stayed a while longer with him," Dieter continued.

"And over supper—strangely enough, considering the difference of age between us—we became friends. He was no longer at all nervous. Nor was I. And I began to like him—perhaps because he never talked down to me. He treated me as an equal. For instance, he insisted that when we were alone together I should call him by his christian name—Tony. He told me stories about his life in England, where he'd worked for a big insurance company. He made me eat far more than I'd ever done. He gave me double the money I'd expected, together with careful instructions for hiding it from my parents. His instructions were so expert that I smiled.

"'What are you smiling at, young Dieter?' he enquired.

"'I'm smiling because your instructions for hiding cash are so expert that I realise I'm not the first boy you've taken to bed with you.'

"Suddenly he looked sad. 'No. You're not,' he answered. 'But there has only been one other.'

"'Here in Wien?'

"'No. In England,' he replied. 'But he was several years older than you are. He was seventeen when I first met him. He had red hair, and his name was Alec.'

"'Where is he now?'

"'I don't know,' Tony answered. 'He left me to get married. Alec and his wife decided to go and live in Australia. Perhaps he's still there.'

"'Have you ever been married?' I asked.

"Tony smiled. 'Never,' he replied. 'And I don't suppose I ever will.'"

Dieter lay back on the grass and gazed up at the stars. His *Lederhosen* had rucked up, and I noticed that the skin of his lean thighs was still very brown and very smooth.

"That very evening," Dieter continued, "Tony and I arranged that if it was safe for me to visit the apartment he'd give me a sign at the end of his game of tennis by casually putting his right hand to the back of his head. For a whole year I used to visit Tony, the Englishman, in his apartment—at least three or four times a week. After a while, I came to look forward to the visits. You see, I'd grown fond of him. Apart from my mother, he was the only person who had ever shown any interest in me. Besides, by now, Tony was in love with me. And I soon found I enjoyed going to bed with him as much as he did going to bed with me. I no longer liked accepting his presents of money. But I needed the cash. Because in the terrible poverty and unemployment that had now spread over Austria, with little businesses going broke and factories closing down, my father was sacked from his job. One morning he left the house without a word to my mother. He never returned. We suspected that he had joined one of the secret Fascist organisations who would take on any tough—so long as he was ruthless. Anyhow, we haven't seen him since. As I told you, my mother is crippled from arthritis, and she cannot go out to work. Soon we had not enough to eat. So I lifted the floorboard in my room where I had hidden part of the cash Tony had given me and gave her most of it for the household—on the condition that she would never question me about where it came from. I only assured her that I had not stolen it. My mother took the money and said nothing, but I think that even then she must have suspected.

"When I began to give my mother money for the housekeeping every week, she must have known that I hadn't earned it on the tennis court. But since then I've talked with dozens of boys like me. They've all told me that their mothers *must* know for certain that they're on the game. But a mother may be virtually sure that her son goes with men, these boys have told me. But so long as she doesn't know completely and utterly *for certain*, she will manage somehow not to be concerned about it.

"For another six months all went well," Dieter continued. "Tony had started giving me English lessons, and it gave me pleasure to see the pride he took in my progress. Now that my father had left the house, it didn't matter so much if I came home late.

We were both of us happy. Then trouble began. Neither Tony nor his Austrian friend appeared at the tennis club for three days running. I was worried because they used to play tennis almost every day. Tony didn't have a telephone in the apartment, and I didn't know his office number. Even if I had, I wouldn't have wanted to disturb him at his work. I didn't want to go round to his apartment in case he was entertaining guests and my appearance might give away our secret. I suppose I could have written, but Tony had warned me against putting anything on paper that might be compromising. However, on the sixth day, I decided I must see Tony—whatever the risk. If there were people with him when he opened the door, I'd say I'd come to the wrong address and run off.

"My heart was thumping when I rang the top bell. I waited on the doorstep for so long that I was beginning to think he must be out. Then the door opened and Tony appeared. But I could hardly recognise him. His hair was untidy, his face was haggard and mottled; I could see that he'd been drinking heavily.

" 'You can't come in,' he said hurriedly. 'Go quickly. I'll meet you at the Café Hirt. It's a small café in the third street on the right going towards the Ring. There's a back room. Wait for me there.' Then he shut the door.

"I still couldn't imagine what had gone wrong. Half an hour later Tony appeared in the back room of the café. He was carrying a despatch case which he put under the table as he sat down opposite me. I was drinking lemonade as usual. Tony ordered himself a double brandy.

" 'I daren't stay long,' he said. 'So I'll make it as short as I can. A week ago I had a visit from the police. They told me that they had been given information that I'd been entertaining a very young boy in my flat. He'd stay there for several hours, they stated, and he'd been seen going there over a long period of time. I'd been denounced, in fact. And I think I know by whom. It must have been someone in the building—because the police knew the exact time you'd arrive and the exact time you'd leave. I believe I was denounced by that fat woman with dyed hair in the flat below mine. She's always complaining about something—I play my radio far too loud or my bath-water leaks into her kitchen. Anyhow the harm has been done. The police asked for your name and address. That gave me some hope—because it meant they couldn't have got hold of you to question you. I told them that I refused to answer any questions whatsoever—except in the presence of my lawyer. I ignored their threats, and presently they left.

"Tony stared down at the table-cloth. 'When I told you that you were the second boy I'd loved in my life, it wasn't a lie,' he continued. 'But there was one thing I didn't tell you because I thought it was better you shouldn't know. When Alec left me to marry his girl, I was terribly upset. I felt desperately lonely. I began drinking. One night in London I went out drunk and picked up a boy. He was about sixteen and obviously a prostitute, but I didn't care. I took him back to my flat. But the police were after the boy because he was not only a tart but a thief. He was arrested. He had made a note of my address. The police found this on him. They questioned him about me. He claimed I had got him drunk and seduced him. My flat was searched. They found evidence. I was prosecuted. It was thanks to a good lawyer that I was only given a suspended sentence which meant I didn't have to go to prison. But the episode was reported in the newspapers. It was to escape the scandal I eventually came to Austria. If the Vienna police find out about the case, then all the denials that you and I could make wouldn't help us. Besides, I know a bit about police methods in this town. If you don't talk they'll beat you up until you *do* confess. And I'm afraid that somehow they may trace you.'

"Tony took a gulp of his brandy. His hand was shaking. 'There's only one solution,' he said. 'I must leave the country. If I leave, they won't worry about you. So I've settled my business affairs. I've packed. I'm leaving tomorrow. I've brought a farewell present for you. I have only one question to ask you. It is this, Dieter. If I found a safe place for us to live together, would you join me?'

"I couldn't speak. I just nodded my head.

" 'Thank you,' he mumbled. 'I hoped you'd say that. I've got your address. From what you've told me I don't suppose there's any danger of your mother opening a letter addressed to you?'

" 'No danger,' I said.

" 'Then I'll write.'

"Tony opened his despatch case and he handed me a thick envelope. 'Put that in your pocket,' he said, and he couldn't control the trembling of his voice. 'By the time you've spent it, I hope I'll be able to send you a train ticket so you can join me, and we'll live together for good.'

"Tony gave some money to the old waiter. 'Stay here for a few minutes after I've gone, and then go straight home,' he told me. 'I won't say goodbye. I'll say *Aufwiedersehen*.'

"Then Tony got up from the table and walked quickly from the room."

Dieter sat up and clasped his knees with his hands. For a while he was silent.

"At the end of a month there was still no letter from him," he said. "At the end of two months the money he'd given me had been spent. After a time I gave up all hope.

"It was then that I started my search. I wanted to find another man like Tony—not only because I was short of money, but because I was lonely. I'd never been able to get on well with boys of my own age. Their jokes and conversation bored me. A man as kind and as intelligent as Tony was what I needed. And at last I thought I'd found one. I was strolling down the Kärtner Strasse and had stopped outside a shop that sold leather-ware. From the reflection in the window I saw a man standing near to me. He was well-dressed and powerfully built. For a wonderful moment I thought it was Tony. Then as I turned to look at him, I saw the difference. His face was more pale and a little fatter, and perhaps he was a few inches taller. He had noticed my glance. He smiled at me. By then I was fourteen, and, as Tony had remarked, tall for my age. When I smiled back at him, I could see that the man fancied me from the way he was examining me. I felt that in his mind he was stripping me naked. He gave a little laugh.

" 'Shall we go and have a coffee somewhere?' he asked. He spoke with a slight German accent.

" 'All right,' I replied. '*Ist gut*.'

"The German smirked. 'I think an invitation to coffee is the appropriate opening,' he said as if he had not heard my answer. 'I would invite you to my hotel, but at seven o'clock in the evening it might upset their sense of what is correct.'

"I thought quickly. I had heard of a cheap lodging-house where men could take under-age girls or boys.

" 'I know of a place,' I said.

" 'With a clean bed, I hope,' the German answered.

" '*Bestimmt*,' I replied. 'And we can walk there.'

" 'Splendid,' he answered. 'You walk ahead, and I will follow you. I think we might become close friends.'

"Getting into the place was easier than I had supposed. As soon as we had reached our room, the German locked the door and took me in his arms. 'How long can you stay?' he asked. 'Till midnight if you like,' I replied.

" 'We'll see,' he grunted and began taking off his clothes. He was bigger than Tony, but I wasn't afraid. I stripped quickly and lay down on the bed.

" '*Fabelhaft*,' he muttered. 'Now we can really enjoy ourselves.' "

Dieter glanced at me and then turned away.

"He was very rough with me," Dieter said. "But I hadn't made love since Tony left. Only by myself. So I was excited, and I let him do what he pleased. We made love several times. Then he got up from the bed and began to dress. He had already paid for the room. He now took out his wallet again and handed me some money.

" 'Thanks for the fun,' he said.

" 'When can we meet again?' I asked.

"He smiled at me. But I could see that it was now a smile of contempt. 'We can't meet again,' he announced. 'I leave for Berlin tomorrow.' Somehow I felt he was lying.

" 'But you said you wanted us to be close friends,' I blurted out.

"He laughed. 'And haven't we been close?' he demanded. 'We could hardly have been any closer. And now I've given you the appropriate present, *aren't* we friends?'

" 'But you never want to see me again?' I asked. After what I'd done for him, I still couldn't believe it.

"Perhaps there must have been bitterness in my voice, for suddenly he looked at me with open dislike. 'I can't speak for other men,' he said. 'But so far as I am concerned I believe in the Chinese proverb. *No man bathes in the same river twice*. But I've adapted it to boys. And as far as I'm concerned no man should go up the same arse twice. *Gute Nacht*.' And with that, he left the room."

Dieter took out a crumpled packet of cigarettes from his pocket, lit two, and handed me one.

"You'd have thought I'd have given up after that. But I didn't. I still was determined to find another Tony. Besides, I needed the cash. But I never found a man who was interested in me as a person. They just wanted to lie with me, have me for one or two nights—and that was the end of it. Gradually I became more or less resigned to the treatment I'd get. Soon I came to expect it. If they were especially brutal or unpleasant—and you can have no idea how vicious and brutal and dirty men can be in their tastes—I'd object. Otherwise I'd let them do as they pleased.

"My mother's illness was worse, and she was sent to hospital. I was worried. I went to see her whenever I could. But her illness had this advantage. I now had the house to myself. So at night when the neighbours were asleep I could bring back a client. I'd grown careless in my choice by now. Any man of any age—provided he looked as if he'd got money to spare—could pick me up for the night. But every morning when I'd open the letter-box I'd hope to find a letter from Tony. But I never did. In fact, I've never heard from him. Perhaps he had an accident. Perhaps in despair he picked up another boy prostitute in London and was arrested. I don't suppose I'll ever know. So I just carried on with my whoring.

"However, as you're aware, in the heat of summer men like our friend Gerald don't go to Vienna. The opera is closed, and there's nothing to do, so they come to places like Salzburg. By this time I'd left school and found work in a radio factory. At least it gave me a rest from endless patrols up and down the streets. So in the summer holidays I become a *Wandervögel*—'a bird of passage,' I suppose you could call it. And my wandering would generally take me to Salzburg."

Dieter swung round and looked at me.

"Are you shocked?" he asked.

"Heavens, no," I said. "I expect I'd have done the same if I'd been in your place and had got your looks."

"But you have got my looks."

I laughed. "What nonsense!" I said.

"What's more, you always did have."

I stared at him. "What on earth makes you say so?" I asked.

Dieter gave me a mysterious look and smiled.

"Tell me, Dieter. How can you possibly tell? And it's not true anyhow."

"I know about you," Dieter announced.

"How?"

"Can't you guess? From Gerald."

"But you only met Gerald tonight."

"Correct," Dieter said. "But how do you think he knew my name? Can't you see? I met Gerald in Salzburg two years ago. That first night before he took me off to a lodging-house of a kind, we had several drinks together. As usual, Gerald was drunk, and he began telling me secrets."

Dieter took a gulp of kirsch and handed me the bottle. "Can't you remember what happened two years ago?" he asked.

"No," I answered.

"But you must remember. You've just told me you were staying in Vienna. It was in Vienna you first met Gerald. *Nicht wahr?* He fell for you. And a few weeks later he sent you a railway ticket to Venice so you could both meet there. True or not?"

"True," I replied.

"In Venice, Gerald tried to have you," Dieter continued. "But you told him you could only go to bed with boys of your own age. *Nicht wahr?* So a few days later Gerald drove you back to Vienna, and left you there. From Vienna Gerald came to Salzburg. It was that very night I first met him."

I gaped at Dieter. "Gerald told you?" I exclaimed.

"Remember Gerald had by then become very drunk," Dieter said. "And I think he was still a bit in love with you. He even showed me a photograph of you. You'd been swimming, and you were naked. As soon as I saw the photo I was excited by it. I found it very attractive. I wanted to keep it. But Gerald wouldn't let me."

Dieter was silent, and I began to wonder. Why had he wanted to keep the photograph? Why had he told me the story of his life in such detail? Was it possible? Could Dieter possibly be attracted to me? Perhaps . . . But at that instant Dieter spoke, and for the first time the tone of his voice was bitter.

"You probably just pity me," he said. "And there's reason enough for pity. You've never done as I have. You wouldn't even go to bed with Gerald. But I've been to bed with anyone who wanted—old men who needed special fondling to get a hard on, men who wanted dirty sex as a change from their wives, and boys who were just bursting for a fuck. And at the end of the whole performance, it just meant nothing to them—no more than their nightly piss before turning in. I loathe the lot of them. Sometimes I dream that I'll win a lottery and become rich. And then, I'd never let anyone touch my body again. Never."

Dieter put a hand on my shoulder. "I shouldn't have told you all that," he muttered. "*Aber ich bin besoffen.* I'm drunk."

I took out of my pocket the money that Gerald had left behind—together with all the money of my own I was carrying. I gave it to Dieter.

"Thanks," he said. Then he examined the notes and looked up at me suspiciously. "There's more here than Gerald left behind," he announced.

"I don't think so," I said.

Dieter's eyes peered at my face. Then he grinned. "You're lying," he laughed. "Take some of it back. I won't take your money."

"Yes, you will," I said and tried to put the money in his pocket. But he was too quick for me. His hand grasped my wrist, but I was three years older than Dieter. Though I was laughing I managed to pull away his wrist. Then we began to wrestle. But he too was laughing and I managed to press the money into his shirt pocket. But while we had wrestled I had felt the softness of his body, and the strength of him. We lay back exhausted on the grass.

"You know you're the only person I've ever told about Tony," Dieter said suddenly. "So I might as well explain the rest. I don't want a lover to go to bed with. I want a friend. If I found a friend, I'm sure the rest would follow. I'm certain of it. But I'm lonely. You can have no idea how lonely I feel."

Dieter took a sip of the kirsch.

"When Gerald talked about you," Dieter continued, "he said that deep down you were a lonely person. Perhaps that's why I've thought about you so much. Perhaps that's why I always hoped to meet you—because I felt sure we could be friends."

"Do you think I'm *ganz verrückt?*" he asked. "Quite mad?"

"No."

"Then listen to me, Robin," Dieter said. "I promise you I'm not saying this because I'm drunk. Come with me to Vienna. Come and live in my little *Wohnung*. I'd do my best to make you comfortable. I'm certain we'd be happy together. You would be the only person I'd go with, I promise it. We could live so wonderfully together. I'd do all the housework. I'm used to it. And while I was working at the factory, you could find a job—translating or giving English lessons. Please, Robin. Come to Vienna with me."

I looked at this young boy lying beside me. He was the most attractive person I had ever seen, and there was a sweetness and gentleness about him I have found hard to describe—together with an almost heart-breaking wistfulness. Lying next to me was my nirvana. In all of my life I would probably never have a chance like this again. I could love Dieter; I loved him already. To live with him would be to attain nirvana. Even if the bliss was only transitory it would have been worthwhile. My spirit rose with the exaltation of the existence I contemplated.

Then came the misty clouds of my conscience and of my eternal guilt. If I left with this lovely boy I would always be fretted by worries when I thought of my mother and my sisters who would be concerned about me. I would fail to get a degree; I would not pass my law exams. I would be living in an alien country without any qualifications, and already war seemed inevitable. Moreover, I had the sense to understand that if I left with Dieter for even a fortnight of happiness in Vienna—which in my elated drunken condition I was sure I could do by making excuses to my sister Honor and by borrowing money from Gerald if he had not yet left to join Willie in Bad Gastein—it would only make things worse. For to leave Dieter after only two weeks would cause both of us more unhappiness than the pleasure we had gained.

Gently I tried to explain this to Dieter. I could see his eyes give a little flinch of pain with each argument I produced. When I had finished he was silent. Suddenly he shivered. "It's cold," he said. "Let's go into the hut."

The stars were now pale in the sky. Dawn was approaching. For a while we watched the golden light spread over the domes and spires of the city.

"You've given me more money than Gerald," Dieter said. "Let's go into the hut. I wouldn't mind making love to you. I'm sure I wouldn't. In fact, I'm certain. And then . . . then perhaps you'd change your mind about coming with me to Vienna."

I began to wonder if the hut was not a place he had used to take some of his clients when he needed money.

"Listen, Dieter," I said quietly. "You see from my eyes that I feel the same about you as you say that you feel about me. But we've drunk too much. I understand all you've told me about having to go to bed with anyone who will pay you. I've given you money. Let's meet at the *Bier-Stube* this evening. Then we can try to make some plan. And if you still want to maybe we can take a room somewhere."

Dieter gaped at me.

"But I thought you knew," he blurted out. "I thought I'd told you. I have to catch the first train. I have to report to my factory."

Dieter was shaking with nerves. It was as if he had withdrawn from a deep dream to find himself in a waking nightmare of reality. He clutched at my wrist and looked at my watch.

"It's late," he said. "We must go straight to the station."

"What about your clothes?"

"Clothes!" he cried. "But I'm a *Landstreicher*. I've got no clothes here. If my shirt gets dirty I wash it—or some man buys me a new one. Come. We must go."

Dieter scrambled to his feet and pulled me up. Together we hurried down the hill.

As we approached the *Bahnhof* he turned to me. "I have my ticket," he said. "Come on to the platform. But don't watch the train leaving the station. *Das bringt Unglück.* It brings bad luck."

The train was already waiting. It was crowded. Dieter held my shoulders, leaned forward, and kissed my lips. There were tears in his dark blue eyes.

"*Ach* Robin, *mein Schatz*, my dear Robin," he said in a choked voice, "if only you'd understood why I climbed the hill with you to the hut."

The train gave a jolt as if preparing to move. Dieter sprang on to the steps of the carriage. At that moment, despite my drunkenness, I remembered.

"I haven't got your address," I cried.

"But Gerald gave me yours," Dieter said.

He had let his floppy corn-coloured hair fall over his forehead—perhaps on purpose —so that it veiled his eyes.

"Dieter," I said, "promise me that you'll write to me."

"Yes, Robin. *Mein Leiber*. Yes, I'll write."

I could see that his cheeks were now wet with tears.

"Perhaps one day you'll understand," he said. Then he began to sob. Abruptly he turned and disappeared into the over-crowded carriage.

He never wrote to me—or if he did, the letter never reached me. I never heard of Dieter or saw him again.

But I did understand. Even before I had walked up the hill and gone into the hut where, in a corner, I found an old blanket—and a soiled towel. I had understood it already.

I understand it now all the more. In fact, with each month and year that I live, I understand that perhaps I had irretrievably lost a chance of finding the nirvana I sought.

Richard Hall

IN QUEST OF KLAUS MANN

This article by New York writer Richard Hall, author of The Butterscotch Prince, *first appeared in* Gay Sunshine Journal *38/39 (Winter 1978). Richard Hall died of AIDS in New York City, November 1992.*

▽

KLAUS MANN, who was the eldest son of Thomas Mann (there were six children, three sons), and a source of much grief and pride to his father, is the subject of intense scholarly and literary interest in Germany today. In 1963, the re-publication of his collected works began, with a projected goal of 13 volumes. In 1973, the Klaus Mann archives in Munich were launched, with some generous funding from the Mann family foundation. From this archival source will emerge the previously unpublished letters and papers of Klaus Mann—a posthumous feast, of which only the first two volumes of letters have so far appeared. The outpouring of related works by people who knew Klaus Mann, or had opinions on his work, is enormous. A recent article by Prof. Ilsedore B. Jonas, a Mann expert at Carnegie-Mellon University in Pittsburgh, contained five densely-packed pages of bibliographic data. It appears not unlikely that the hoard of Klaus Mann-related artifacts will eventually rival the 7,000 items that now constitute the mother-lode for Thomas Mann himself, indexed by two university presses. The complete Klaus Mann bibliography is available from Edition Klaus Blahak, Wiesbaden (1976). There has also been talk about founding a Klaus Mann Society in Germany, although I have not been able to trace its exact whereabouts, if any.

While Klaus Mann has been taken up with a vengeance by the literary industry in Europe, he has also been granted additional, if minor, status as a gay saint by German homosexuals. They recognize in him one of the few literary figures of the previous generation who was widely if unofficially acknowledged as gay, alluded to it with varying degrees of frankness in his writings, and used his gay experiences as a source in his creative output. While France had Gide and Cocteau, and England had Isherwood and Auden (to say nothing of Oscar Wilde), Germany had no literary figure of comparable distinction to match the achievements of Magnus Hirschfeld and Kurt Hiller in the medical and political field. Klaus Mann fills this need. He is on the verge of becoming a cult-figure, or totem, for German gays in need of literary ancestors.

It has been a different story in America, Klaus Mann's adopted homeland from 1938 until his death by suicide in 1949, aged 42. Although he was once popular here, he seems to have suffered a literary eclipse. All but one of his novels are out of print, and that one—*Mephisto*, republished by Random House in 1977—has aroused almost no interest in the general or gay press. *Mephisto* is a fine work (more about it later) and deserves a better fate. But it is symptomatic of the general disinterest in Klaus Mann here—a disinterest which I think springs from three causes, adding up to an unfortunate combination of circumstances.

First, there is the overwhelming fact of Klaus Mann's paternity. Thomas Mann is still widely read and studied in America. He is a figure who straddles the generations, towers above the political events of his day without being isolated from them, and still echoes themes of universal concern. Compared to this titan, Klaus suffers. Alongside his father's dense and complex output, spanning 60 years, Klaus' work seems glib and superficial. The elder Mann recognized this, writing to Hermann Hesse six weeks after his son's suicide, ". . . he worked with such facility and speed that there is a scattering of flaws and oversights in his books." While Klaus was initially given extra attention because of his father's fame, he later paid double for the privilege. One American reviewer, commenting on a youthful novel by Klaus about Alexander the Great, couldn't resist gibing, "It is extremely doubtful if Klaus Mann, though he is still very young, will succeed to his father's throne." (*The Nation*, Dec. 24, 1930). These odious comparisons have persisted, as the shadow of his father's fame has lengthened over Klaus' output.

A second problem is that Klaus Mann was caught up in the cauldron of Hitler's rise to power and forced into exile when he was just 27 years old. This uprooting, which occurred when he was beginning to expand his

KLAUS MANN (1906–1949)
Photo by Erika Mann

powers as a novelist, reinforced his sense of alienation, his apartness, not only as the neurasthenic son of a famous father but as a homosexual offspring of a Jewish mother. The mental energy required to compensate for these various oppressions must have been enormous; when exile was thrown in as well, the burden became even greater. Klaus' dependency on drugs—a dependency he was unable to shake despite repeated cures throughout his life—possibly dates from this period. Two themes that were to sound throughout his work—an interest in suicide and the isolation of a man who is without a country—emerged at this time. Perhaps because of all these pressures, Klaus Mann never quite fulfilled his original promise. The talent was there, but largely unredeemed. For Americans, with limited interest in the cultural matrix of central Europe during the pre-Hitler years, Klaus Mann seems a peripheral figure. He does not travel well. He has not transcended the particularities of his time and place.

A third reason for the neglect of Klaus Mann in America derives from his homosexuality. His writings cannot be assessed without clear and unambiguous reference to his sexual tastes, which were central to his psychology, his sensibility and the subjects he chose to treat. As we all know, mainstream critics tend to shy away from this kind of writer because of the challenges he presents to their homophobic assumptions. To evaluate Klaus Mann dispassionately would require them to re-appraise many of these assumptions—an unpleasant undertaking for most of them. Another problem is the Mann family. Three of the six Mann children, repositories of vital information, are still alive. It is safe to say that they want their brother's reputation refurbished, and a frank treatment of his homosexuality is not likely to do so—or so they believe.

In hopes of righting this balance and providing a starting place for longer and more exhaustive studies, I have taken on myself the job of reading all his books published in English and available at the 42nd Street Research Library in New York. What follows is a brief annotation of these books, with an attempt to tie them into some kind of psychohistory that will illuminate not only the texts but the man who produced them. Before beginning, let me admit that my chief purpose is to reclaim Klaus Mann as a *gay* writer—not as a political thinker, anti-fascist or aesthete. Although the evidence is sometimes scanty or camouflaged, I will try to trace those aspects of his life and work which are of historic and ideological interest to gay people. While this represents a narrowing of focus and would be undesirable in a full-length biography or critical analysis (and lay me open to a charge of psychosexual determinism as well), I think it needs doing now.

THE TURNING POINT

The best place to begin is with Klaus Mann's autobiography, *The Turning Point*, written in English, while he was living in New York and published in New York by L.B. Fischer (1942) and in London by Victor Gollancz (1944). Later, Klaus wrote an expanded version, with new material, for publication in Germany. Called *Der Wendepunkt; ein Lebensbericht*, it was brought out posthumously by Gottfried Bermann Fischer at the insistence of Thomas Mann. (Bermann Fischer was the son-in-law of Samuel Fischer, Thomas Mann's lifelong publisher, who had first taken a chance on *Buddenbrooks*). *The Turning Point* was actually Klaus Mann's second autobiography, the first being *Kind dieser Zeit*, or *Child of My Time*, written when he was 19 and never translated into English.

Klaus Mann, born in 1906, was 36 when *The Turning Point* appeared. That may seem precocious for a first, let alone second, autobiography, but by that time he had lived several lives.

First there had been a pampered, spoiled life as the oldest son of a patrician family in Munich—a family that combined artistic and business success. There was a stately villa on the banks of the Isar, belonging to his parents. There was a sumptuous renaissance palazzo belonging to his mother's parents. There was a country house in Tölz in the Bavarian Alps. There was also Mother and Father—Mother nicknamed Mielein, Father known as *Der Zauberer*, the Magician, because of his ability to tell tales and exorcise illness and demons. Mother is close, Father remote. Mother is soft, untidy, caressing; Father is dreamy, neat, absent-minded. He disappears into his studio each morning at nine and takes the children for a walk at four.

There are governesses, games, pets. But most of all there is his sister Erika, one year older. Until Klaus was twelve he had no friends but Erika, his spiritual double. "Erika and I belonged together," he writes, "our solidarity was absolute and indisputable. We acted twin-like in an almost provocative way: the grown-ups as well as the kids had to accept us as an entity." (It was this brother-sister twinship that inspired their father to write his notorious *Wälsungenblut*, or *Blood of the Walsungs*, published in 1921, about a brother and sister who consummate their closeness with incest; the family went to great lengths to explain that this fiction was not based on fact.)

With neighbor children, Erika and Klaus formed a gang, then a theatrical club. They played practical jokes, made friends with a local matinee idol. By the time they were 15 or 16, they were patrolling the deserted streets of Munich after midnight. Once, when their parents were away, they gave a party with refreshments consisting entirely of stolen items, from sausages to vermouth. Even World War I brought no real hardship to the children, although at times their parents found it difficult to find food. The upshot of all their prankishness was that Klaus was sent away to school in 1922. He went to an experimental community based on the ideals of the Youth Movement—a back-to-nature, religious, nationalistic cult that flourished in Germany between the wars.

It was here, at the Odenwaldschule, that he met his first love, an athletic school-mate named Uto. "There was one lad . . . whom I liked to watch in particular," he writes. "His name was Uto. He was sturdy and deft, but by far not the strongest or most dexterous one of the lot. Nor was he especially handsome. But I loved his face. He had the face I love. You may be smitten with many faces when you live long enough and possess a responsive heart. But there is only one face you love. It is always the same. You recognize it among thousands. And Uto had that face."

He goes on to describe Uto as looking "like a little Swede with a drop of Mongolian blood." Klaus wrote poetry to him, called him by the names of Hellenic champions and demi-gods. He showed Uto a scrap of paper on which he had written, "I love you." Uto read it and gravely replied, "But of course you do. Friends must love each other."

After a few months of this, one of those curious reversals, so typical of Klaus Mann throughout his life, took place. Suddenly he couldn't bear being close to Uto. "Uto was so much stronger and lighter than I was, and I envied him so," he writes. "He was all vigor and serenity; no problems existed for him." Klaus decides to leave school, giving various excuses. In a final apostrophe, he asks, "What sorrow drove me away? What disorder awaited me?"

The following year, 1923, he journeyed alone to Berlin for the first time, noting the sights: the Russian emigrés, the drag queens, the hermaphrodites, the whores. One of the latter, a fierce amazon in green leather, brandished a cane at him and whispered, "Want to be my slave? Costs only six billion and a cigarette. A bargain. Come along, honey!"

The Berlin scene fascinated him. "I was magnetized by the scum," he writes. But lack of money sent him home again, where there was at least one consolation—his friend Ricki Hallgarten, perhaps the one person he loved without ambivalence or reservation. He describes Ricki as "a neurotic gipsy, with a tangled mass of dark hair falling on to a low forehead; black, bushy eyebrows over a pair of violent eyes set very close to each other. He was witty and naive and quivering with that attractive nervousness typical of certain hyper-aristocratic dogs and horses. His face was all softness and sensual innocence, but his hands seemed appallingly old . . ." Ricki came from a cultivated bourgeois family but grew up full of doubts about his homosexuality, his Jewishness and his talent as a painter. He was one of many in Klaus' intimate circle who committed suicide—in May, 1932, shortly before Hitler came to power.

In 1924, when he was just 18, Klaus began his literary career. He became second-string theater critic for one of the Berlin papers, and published a collection of short stories, *Vor Dem Leben* (*Before Life*). He also wrote and published a play about a brother and sister and their friends, which had not only incestuous but distinctly lesbian overtones. It was called *Anja und Esther*. Klaus reports that he read the play to an intimate family party the very evening he finished writing it. It was greeted with "a dismal stillness," until his father mercifully murmured, "Strange. Very strange indeed." His Aunt Lula voiced strong disapproval of the fondness the two young ladies in the play displayed toward each other, but the elder Mann saved the day by telling her it was only "a sentimental friendship."

The play, prophetically, was dedicated to a young actor whom Klaus had seen in Berlin—"an unusually gifted chap with the features of a transfigured pugilist and a striking, metallic voice." This was Gustaf Gründgens and he was the star of the Hamburger Kammerspiele, a literary theater. Klaus would embark on a passionate love affair with Gründgens, who would later marry Erika as a "cover" and who would inspire the savage *à clef* novel *Mephisto* ten years later.

Gründgens loved *Anja und Esther* and wanted to produce and act in it. With a superb instinct for publicity, he realized that if the author and his sister, who were not only the children of a famous writer but the models for the brother and sister in the play, were to star in it, it would create a huge sensation. He persuaded the pair to act in the play—it didn't require much effort—and the scandal was as juicy as predicted. All the newspapers ran stories, creating "a hullabaloo from the Baltic Sea down to the Danube." Erika and Klaus became instantly famous and remained so all their lives. It was a fame not without liability, however, especially for Klaus. For one thing, it probably came too soon. For another, it stemmed not from a solid achievement of his own but from gossip and media flackery. And third, he really became the object of public attention because of his father's status. This led to constant sniping in the press, which dogged him all his life with complaints about his exhibitionism and "decadence" and his exploitation of the family name. Klaus could never, ultimately, be sure how much of his notoriety was due to his own work or to his father's renown.

Although the play was an enormous success and could have gone on touring for years, Klaus, in a typical turnabout, quit after two months. The madcap project lost its charm for him. "It was my mania," he writes, "or a kind of fear of anti-climactic developments, to break up situations before they might become stale. I ruined (and sometimes saved) human relations, professional opportunities, studies and pleasures, by rushing away, just in order to move, to change, to remain alive."

He went to Paris, Vienna, Nice. He started another novel (it would eventually turn into *The Fifth Child*). He floated between classes and nations, between literary camps and cults. He wrote another play, called *Four in a Revue*, which starred the same actors (the fourth being Pamela Wedekind, daughter of playwright Frank Wedekind). The newspapers ballyhooed it up again, this time because *The Magic Mountain* had just been published.

Referring to this event, Klaus writes, "It is against this background of solid glory that one should conceive the tawdry glamor surrounding my own start. The truth is that, at the age of twenty, I was unduly well-known and unduly disparaged. Incessantly flattered and teased, I amused and revenged myself by behaving the way I was apparently expected to. What I failed to realize was the amount of embarrassment my eccentricities caused my father."

His difficulties were echoed by his mother, Katia Mann, in her memoirs, *Unwritten Memories*: "Klaus was a writer; he was certainly born for that, but it wasn't a very fortunate choice for him as his father's son. It made it very hard for him; in the beginning, it made it easy, but then it made it hard." Interestingly, the recently-published volume of Klaus Mann letters dealing with this period bears the subtitle, *Unordnung and früher Ruhm* (Disorder and Early Fame), an obvious play on the senior Mann's novella, *Disorder and Early Sorrow*.

In 1927 and 1928, the careers of Klaus and Erika, always intertwined, reached some sort of climax. They toured America, where *The Fifth Child* had just been published, going as far as Hollywood. They were feted, admired, publicized. They met Dorothy Thompson, Sinclair Lewis, Otto Kahn, H.L. Mencken, Emil Jannings, Greta Garbo, Upton Sinclair, Conrad Veidt. They were the literary Mann Twins, darlings of the journalists and hostesses. It was a triumphal procession and they wound up on a ship crossing the Pacific to Japan, and thence via Siberia back to Munich. When asked by their younger brother what they had seen on their trip around the world, Klaus replied with a casual and grandiose gesture, "Nothing much . . . *rien que la terre.*" Together they wrote an account of their travels, *Runderhum, ein heiteres Reisebuch.*

Back in Europe, Klaus moved in the best intellectual circles. His literary friendships in 1928 and 1929 sound like a gay pantheon: Jean Cocteau, the Duchess of Clermont-Tonerre, André Gide, Paul Morand, Maurice Rostand, Julien Green, René Crevel, Magnus Hirschfeld. He meets "dynamic dandies" in the great salons of Paris and describes these young men as being "childlike yet depraved . . . Some of them had the grace of bewitched infants when they dallied with narcotics or the risky anomalies of sex." With Erika and her lover, Annemarie von Schwarzenbach, daughter of a Swiss industrialist, he traveled to Spain, Italy, Morocco, writing up his travels for the leading journals.

The Nazis were coming to popularity in these years, but Klaus like many other intellectuals, ridiculed them. He was, in his words, "still isolated, irresponsible, erratic; dallying with subtle jokes and wistful reveries. I failed to join any liberal anti-fascist organization. I refused to have anything to do with the whole sordid mess." But his days in Germany were numbered. His notoriety was too great to be ignored by the Nazis, and in March 1933, just two months after Hitler came to power, he and Erika were forced to flee the country. They had been warned in time by the family chauffeur who for years had been acting as a Nazi spy in the Mann house. Their exile took them to Paris, Zurich (where their parents later joined them) and then to Amsterdam.

The years in Amsterdam (1933 to 1938) were good years for Klaus, according to his brother Golo. He produced three novels and founded a literary monthly called *Die Sammlung (The Collection)*, which channelled the voices of the exiled intelligentsia into print. Besides the German exiles, *Die Sammlung* published Stephen Spender, Ignazio Silone, André Gide, André Maurois, Jean Cocteau, Benedetto Croce, Ernest Hemingway, Ilya Ehrenburg and Boris Pasternak. Klaus also did a great deal of journalism, traveling to Czechoslovakia, Hungary, Russia and Spain.

In 1938, Princeton University offered Thomas Mann the post of lecturer in the humanities and Klaus emigrated to America with his parents. He spent much time travelling the country, giving lectures on the Nazi menace. With Erika, he wrote a book about the political exiles, *Escape to Life.*

The Turning Point ends with a series of staccato diary entries covering the years 1940 to 1942. During this time, Klaus founded a literary magazine in New York, *Decision*, which collapsed in its second year due to poor management and lack of funds. He started writing *The Turning Point* to stave off the depression caused by the liquidation of the journal. The last entry, June 6, 1942, speaks of his readiness to be drafted into the U.S. Army.

Of all Klaus Mann's books published in America, *The Turning Point* earned the best press. It was lauded by *The New Republic, The New Yorker* and *The Saturday Review of Literature*, with the early chapters dealing with his childhood and family life coming in for the most praise. The book still makes good reading, full of vitality, fascinating people and great events. The episode in which Klaus eavesdrops on Hitler while watching him stuff himself with strawberry tartlets in a Munich tea-room for example, is brilliant. Also exciting are the vignettes of Gide, Bruno Walter, Emil Jannings, Greta Garbo, André Breton. The high spirits of Mann's youth, his endless quest for novelty, his intellectual adventures—all these are rendered with a natural flair for self-dramatization. The allusions to his gay affections are tantalizingly discreet, but the careful reader can infer a great deal. In effect, this discretion about his sexual activities comprises an additional subtext—by what is not said we can gain new insight into the social and literary inhibitions of the day. It was Klaus Mann's peculiar destiny that he was almost, but not quite, able to come out in his major writings.

By the time *The Turning Point* appeared, the Mann parents had left Princeton and built themselves a house at Pacific Palisades near Los Angeles. It was from here that Thomas Mann wrote to his son to congratulate him on the *The Turning Point*: "Was it," he inquires, "as autobiography, a slightly premature undertaking? Some may say so, but if you had waited until you were fifty, the early memories, which are always the best in confessions, might not show the freshness and bounce they have here. We parents certainly can be content with the figures we cut . . . It is a tremendously European book, and perhaps will discourage the American reader because of its somewhat bizarre picture of pre-Hitler Europe, especially of the many bizarre chums it was your fate to encounter . . ."

The last seven years of Klaus Mann's life took him back to Europe. Like many emigrés, he had been eager to be drafted. At the end of 1942, he went into the U.S. Army and after training at several camps, went overseas, taking part in the Italian campaign. He earned several medals for bravery in action, to his father's delight. In May, 1945, Klaus was able to revisit the old Mann home in Munich as part of the liberating army. It was a return full of nostalgia for the wanderer: "Yes, our poor, mutilated, polluted house!" he wrote to his father. "Most of the inside is altogether destroyed, but the outside structure has remained fairly intact . . . We could reconstruct the place if we cared to do so . . . I discovered that the balcony in front of my room was occupied by a girl—a bombed-out stenotypist who had no other place to stay. It was all very curious and romantic."

The Army years were happy for Klaus, but the post-war period was not. His dream of a united world, without political problems, didn't come true. He wasn't really at home in Germany after Hitler, and America had become increasingly alien to him. His addiction to drugs became stronger and more destructive. Although he was working as a staff reporter for *The Stars and Stripes*, touring Europe on assignment, his letters reflect increasing loneliness and longing for death. In the summer of 1948 he made his first suicide attempt. Upton Sinclair, hearing the news, wired him, "Don't do it, you've written fine books and you can do a most important job in helping interpret Europe to America and vice versa." His father's birthday letter the following November contained further encouragement: "We are very thankful we can celebrate this day together even though you are far from us at the moment . . . you have remained dear to us and you have kept your special, rather sad, inwardly nervous but indomitable and active charm."

But death was not to be put off. On May 21, 1949, when he was not yet 43, Klaus

Mann committed suicide with an overdose of sleeping pills. On the day previous he had written to Erika, his spiritual double, calling himself "a sick hermit and a neurotic mouse." He also wrote, "I am angry and disgusted and cannot make myself do any major work." This was probably the last letter he wrote. The final words he committed to paper were: "And it is raining in Cannes."

Among the papers found after his death and now in the Munich archives were notes for several works. One was a synopsis of a World War II novel titled *The Last Days*. There was a script of a drama, *The Seventh Angel*, another play, *The Dead Don't Care* (available at the NY Public Library), plus outlines for several novels. One of them, *Windy Night, Rainy Night*, was intended to come to grips with the problems of several homosexual characters. There are also synopses for films never made, including one on Mozart to be done in collaboration with Bruno Walter.

THE NOVELS

Klaus Mann's first novel was *Der Fromme Tanz* (*The Devout Dance*), which appeared in 1925 and has not been translated into English. His second, *The Fifth Child*, was published in Germany with the title *Kindernovelle*, and brought out in America by Boni and Liveright in 1927.

It's the story of a youngish widow named Christiane, who lives in an enchanted wood with her four children. She had been married to a noted philosopher and writer, an ex-priest, who has died. The two older children, a boy and girl not unlike Erika and Klaus, play whimsical games and run wild. They tease and confuse their elders. Enter Till, a young man who is savagely attractive, unfettered and original. He is, in fact, the new intellectual, and was admittedly modeled on the young gay French novelist René Crevel, whom Klaus met in Paris in the early '20s and who committed suicide in 1935. Till brings post-war Europe to Christiane's cottage in the timeless wood— not only the new radical politics but the new sexual freedoms: "He spoke with gay non-chalance of erotic abnormalities that she thought reprehensible. He could not control his laughter because she did not know what a transvestite was. He was often very much irritated because she called homosexual love 'abnormal' compared to heterosexual."

Till, despite his championship of sexual non-conformity, does what is expected of him. He makes love to the older woman. His disrobing is described from Christiane's point of view: "She could have wept because he had such shoulders, such thin arms, which he folded shivering over his breast, such adorable knees, such a forehead, over which his short hair hung moist . . . Nothing in the wide, sad world seemed to her sadder than to be in this condition. This sorrow of the body was beyond the petty intellect, inescapable and great . . ."

A daughter is born of this union, the fifth child of the title, who will presumably share in both Christiane's traditional values and the new freedoms of her father. Till departs as mysteriously as he came, leaving Christiane bemused but content.

The Fifth Child, which is really a novella, is not very good. One wonders if it would have been published had the author not been the son of Thomas Mann. It is literary in a bad sense—inert and pretentious, full of false mystification. The themes fall all over one another, none of them adequately dramatized: oedipal replacement, the radicalizing of post-war society, an end to German complacency, the insemination of the older generation by the younger, etc. It is all very obvious. The book suffers from the fatal facility that mars much of Klaus Mann's work. Maeterlinck had created the enchanted wood in more rich and allusive ways with *Pelleas et Melisande*, as far back as 1892; Thomas Mann found the perfect metaphor for ailing Europe in *The Magic Mountain*, published in 1924. This novella, despite its symbolic trappings, is probably closer to the Brothers Grimm than to any of the modernist works that Klaus so much admired.

However, the tale is notable for a portrait of Christiane's older boy, Heiner, who bears a remarkable resemblance to Klaus himself. Rather forebodingly, the author writes of the boy's mouth, "Did it not have dangerous softness? This mouth did not deny itself nor the others anything. It was a woman's mouth under the manly brow, so completely did it yield itself to life. But was it not probable that it would soon be old and corrupt, if it offered itself so ardently to life's kisses? A certain carelessness and abandon in Heiner's bearing had a disquieting effect and gave one a presentiment of bad things. . . ."

While this is partly adolescent angst, it also provides a clue to Klaus' perception of himself at the time.

In 1928 and 1929, Klaus worked on a new novel, *Alexander, a Novel of Utopia*. He wrote it in hundreds of hotel rooms as he roamed around Europe, hauling with him a reference library dealing with the Macedonian hero.

Alexander is a moony and over-embellished fantasy about a young Greek who could conquer the world but could not give himself completely to a male lover. There are three boyhood friends—Alexander, Clitus and Hephaestion. Alexander seeks love from both. When he is 13, he goes into Clitus' bedroom, thinking, "I must have him, this is to be my first really important victory." But Clitus humiliates him and rejects him. Later, when Alexander is 20 and crowned, he is overcome with loneliness. Aboard ship, he kisses Hephaestion and beseeches him for love. But Hephaestion rejects him too: "You, Alexander, are strongest by yourself. You know you do not need my help." Alexander grows rigid with pain and hatred. "Now I will offer myself no more, he thought, at peace after his exuberance."

Years later, at a victory banquet, Clitus recounts the epic Babylonian story of Gilgamesh and his lover Enicdu. Alexander's pain and loneliness return. To the assembled company he says of Clitus, "If he knew how he has disturbed me ever since I can remember, ever since I have been alive." Clitus gloats at this, saying, "You have not even disturbed me. I do not know you at all . . . I only felt compassion for you. Did you not lie at my feet?" Alexander, in a drunken rage, drives a spear into Clitus' back. Alexander eventually marries but rejects his wife on their wedding night, mourning, "Oh, him whom I would have liked to touch the most, him I killed . . ." The novel ends in a colloquy with the Angel of Death, by whom the dying king is comforted with the promise that he will return to find love in some future life.

The Alexander novel is one of many dealing with the Hellenic Eros, although Antinoüs, Hadrian's paramour, seems to have been more popular with gay German romancers. Klaus Mann commented on the appeal of this sort of subject to certain members of the reading public, without actually naming them as gay: "It was this strange community of an idiom and an emotional climate to which Jean Cocteau referred when he addressed me, in a preface he contributed to the French edition of my Alexander novel, as one of his 'compatriots,': *'je veux dire, d'un jeune homme qui habite mal sur la terre et qui parle sans niaiserie le dialecte du coeur.'* " In the coded parlance of the time, this accolade could be taken as a statement of literary gay brotherhood.

Not surprisingly, *Alexander* fared badly with the New York critics, who in 1930 were not prepared to accept the notion that Alexander conquered the world because of a thwarted boyhood passion for a disdainful friend. ". . . reflects an unfortunate mixture of timidity and resentment," said the critic for *The Nation*. *The New York Times*, moralizing as usual, faulted the book not on aesthetic but on ethical grounds: "The atmosphere of the book is decadent, full of that 'sweetly stale odor' described as penetrating all the nooks and alleys of the Babylon which Alexander conquered." The book certainly deserved panning, but for literary rather than moralistic reasons. It would be a quarter-century before another novelist, Mary Renault, would manage to combine literary worth with Hellenic subject-matter, enabling the critics to overlook the homosexual content of her tales in a chorus of praise for her style.

After leaving Germany in 1933 and settling down in Amsterdam, Klaus Mann wrote three novels. They were *Journey into Freedom* (1934), *Pathetic Symphony—A Tchaikowsky Novel* (1935) and *Mephisto, The Story of a Career* (1936). The first two, he tells us, "deal with the drama of uprooting which, in a sense, always was and now admittedly became, the crux of my own experience." The exile in Holland thus became a metaphor for his permanent sense of not belonging and his status as an outsider, which also kept him out of such trendy intellectual homelands as Marxism, Eastern mysticism, nationalism or a passive absorption in Christianity. All these he dismissed as simplifications that were tempting but dangerous.

The first novel was published in Amsterdam as *Flucht in Den Norden*. It appeared in America as a Borzoi Book (Knopf) in 1936, titled *Journey into Freedom*, thus missing the symbolic value of the original, which means "flight to the north."

Because flight is what the novel is about—specifically, flight from Europe and its looming tragedy. A young German woman, Joan, who is modeled closely on Erika Mann, arrives in Finland, after having just escaped arrest in her native country. She makes the trip at the invitation of a lesbian friend who lives there on her family estate. Although Joan is boyish in appearance and dresses daringly in pants and sailor outfits, she does not respond to her hostess' advances. She rejects her in favor of her handsome brother Ragnar, a powerfully-built man of 30 with slanty, gold-brown eyes, high cheekbones and honey-colored hair. He is moody and impractical—he reads all Klaus' favorite authors—but irresistible. They begin an affair. Their first love-making, a gem of sensuality, is told from Joan's point of view: "Nameless, recumbent, he has become a symbol, a god, and she his votary. As she bends over him, her lips leave his mouth to glide over his throat, over his breast, while her hands retrace the silhouette of his body. She tastes the moist hair on his chest; her lips caress its sensitive mounds. With humility her bowed face descends, her lips tracing a path across the breathing expanse, lingering a moment at the tiny well whose cord united him longest to his mother; drawn even further till they are lost in a deep and curling growth of hair and come at length to the goal toward which her eyes have preceded them . . ."

It is with a shock that we realize that in Ragnar, with his oriental face and strawy hair, we are face-to-face with Uto of boyhood memory. But it is Uto removed from the playing fields of the Odenwaldschule and transmuted into the dream-stud of fantasy, the reborn Adonis whose image has haunted the author across the boundaries of Europe. The affair with Ragnar focusses Joan's dilemma: can she indulge her sensuality, her fierce need to take root again, or must she return to the continent and continue the fight against fascism? The conflict is heightened when her former fiancé is killed on a secret mission.

Unable to reach a decision, she sets out on a car trip with Ragnar, to the northern reaches of his country, desolate and windswept, peopled by Lapps living outside the burdens of time and history. It is this flight, a nightmare journey into the most fearful parts of herself, that gives the book its original title and reminds one of the best of Conrad or Prokosch. At the end, having explored her affair with Ragnar to the last degree of love and lust, she returns to Europe, aware that she is tied to it by bonds she cannot break.

The novel holds up well, due largely to the combination of objectivity and drugged sensuality with which the love-affair is handled. The character of Ragnar is a fine creation—graceful, selfish, neurotic, virile. The final hundred pages of the book are incandescent. Although Klaus maintained that he wrote the novel to illustrate the conflict between love and duty, his words belie that intention. The love is rendered in vital and intense strokes; the return to duty is rhetorical and perfunctory.

Journey into Freedom received a mixed press. The critic for *The New Statesman and Nation* called it "amateurish and high-falutin'." However, Alfred Kazin, writing in *The New York Times* called it "not extraordinary but well-made and moving." It seems to me one of Mann's better works . . . which is more than I can say about the next one.

Pathetic Symphony, the novel about Tchaikowsky, was published in Amsterdam in 1935, but did not appear in America until 1948. It was dedicated to Christopher Isherwood (whom Klaus' father referred to as "the starry eyed one"). Klaus gives this motive for writing about Tchaikowsky: "I wrote his story because I know all about him. Only too intimately versed in his neurasthenic fixations, I could describe his aimless wanderings, the transient bliss of his elations, the unending anguish of his solitude . . . He died the lonely and furtive death of a man who feels he can't bear life any more, but is ashamed of his weakness. I love his music for the sake of his lonely death, to which it is the sweet and powerful prelude."

Since the novel clearly states that homosexuality is Tchaikowsky's major fixation, this declaration in *The Turning Point* virtually amounts to coming out. However, the novel's frankness about Tchaikowsky's sexuality is almost the only thing to be said in its favor.

Peter Ilyich's first infatuation is with a school comrade named Apukhtin, who introduces him to sex, and with whom he spends countless thrilling nights from age 17 to 25. He knows these activities are naughty but can't resist his friend's "gently mocking laugh" and "thin, supple, always slightly dirty hands." " 'Do you like that?' Apukhtin whispered to him, 'Do you find it pleasant? . . . We will never fall in love with women—promise me that, Petrushka! It's silly to love women—it's wrong for people like us.' "

It is the anguish brought by all this which Peter Ilyich decides to transmute into rhythm and melody, changing in the process from a lazy young man into an obsessive artist. In fact, whenever his inspiration flags, he need only recall his homosexual urges, coded in his mind as "THIS"—to return to his music. An episode with a hustler, for instance, leads directly to the Fifth Symphony; his frustrated love for his nephew Vladimir takes him directly to the Sixth.

The relation between art and neurosis, one of the older Mann's persistent themes, is here simplified into a neat, sentimental package. As I followed Peter Ilyich around Russia and Europe, I was reminded not so much of a musical genius suffering real torment as of Cornel Wilde impersonating Chopin in *A Song to Remember*. Even the agonies of artistic creation, so complexly rendered by Thomas Mann in *Tonio Kroger* and *Doctor Faustus*, are here reduced to remarks like, "Don't you think, Modest, it would be a good idea for me to drop the piano sonata for the time being and concentrate on the violin concerto?" The novel is almost entirely misconceived both as history and fiction, a fact noted by *The Saturday Review of Literature*, whose critic condemned it as "a book which has neither the reality of a creation of character nor the reality of an honest biography." *The New Yorker* called it "hackneyed" and *The Library Journal*, with admirable succinctness, classified it as "a not very desirable acquisition."

The third Amsterdam novel, *Mephisto*, is more successful. It probably deserves the acclaim it has recently had in Europe. It has appeared in Austria, Switzerland and Yugoslavia. It was hugely successful in France. Although it was published in Berlin in 1956, it was met by the longest lawsuit in the history of German publishing. The suit was brought by the adopted son and last lover of the actor Gustaf Gründgens, who was the model for the protagonist in the book. After a trial lasting ten years, the Supreme Court of Germany banned the book in a 5-to-4 decision. The *clef* could be too easily turned and the book was considered slanderous. It is safe to say, however, that the text had been read widely in Germany, in smuggled or samizdat editions.

It was this success in Europe that probably led Random House to bring out *Mephisto* here in October 1977. Whatever the reason, the book badly needs a critical preface to set it in context and examine the models for many of the characters—not only Gustaf Gründgens but Pamela Wedekind, Elisabeth Bergner and Max Reinhardt—and relate it to events in Klaus Mann's life as well. This wasn't done and one result has been complete neglect of the book by critics and public.

Mephisto is sub-titled, "*Roman einer Karriere*," or novel about a career. Mann wrote it, he said, in order to "analyze the abject type of treacherous intellectual who prostitutes his talent for the sake of some tawdry fame and transitory wealth." It was to be a polemical chronicle of corruption. The object of this polemic is Hendrik Höfgen, a thinly disguised fictional portrait of Gründgens, who made peace with the Nazis in order to be able to continue his career as an actor. It was Gründgens, as noted earlier, who took up Klaus Mann's first play, *Anja und Esther*, and launched it and the Mann twins on their first success.

The novel traces the rise of the Höfgen/Gründgens character, whose career begins at a small theater in Hamburg 1923. He is distinguished from the other actors in several ways: his huge talent, his cynical opportunism and his bizarre sexual tastes. He can act and direct brilliantly. He can do Wilde, Strindberg, Büchner, Wedekind, Schiller, Shakespeare. He can play juveniles or old men, princes or villains. He can be "generous or base, haughty or tender, scornful or overwhelmed, exactly as the part required." There is only one hitch. He requires heavy S&M sex offstage with a black prostitute in order to keep going.

These scenes consist of the following: first the prostitute, whose name is Juliette Martens, or Princess Tebab, whips Höfgen's palms until red welts form. Then she makes him dance, lashing him if he starts to tire. When he is worn out, she lets him stop. After that, they make love while she murmurs endearments like, "You really are the weirdest little shit I've ever seen."

The scenes with the Princess have a bizarre believability to them. The interplay between art and neurosis, so crudely handled in the Tchaikowsky novel, is here dramatized with much more skill. Marcel Reich-Ranitzki, in his study of the German emigrés, *Die Ungeliebten Sieben Emigranten* (1968), expressed surprise that Klaus Mann didn't saddle the Höfgen/Gründgens figure with homosexual motives. This was certainly to be expected. Instead, he points out, the author settled for the sexual tastes which would expose him to blackmail or retaliation from the Nazis.

By 1930, the protagonist has made a huge success in Berlin. He has also married a respectable girl—a marriage he cannot consummate—and continues his private sessions with Princess Tebab. However, the accession of Hitler, whom he has hardly noticed until now, brings new problems. But playing Mephisto in Goethe's *Faust* in the 1932/33 season enables him to score a personal hit with a Nazi figure obviously based on Hermann Goering. Goering takes Höfgen under his wing (just as he did Gustaf Gründgens), promoting him to director of the German State Theater (as he did Gründgens). The novel ends with a hallucinatory scene in which Höfgen/Gründgens, alone in his mother's house, wonders why the anti-fascists hate him so, since he is no more than "a perfectly ordinary actor."

Despite its flaws, *Mephisto* is probably Klaus Mann's finest work. The closeness of the story to his own experience, its passionate and ironic tone, the mixture of love and contempt with which the main figure is treated, combine to create a work of some depth. The central figure, especially, is magnetic and iridescent—even though some critics maintain that it does an injustice to the actor Gründgens, who was cleared by Allied tribunals after the war and allowed to perform again. The novel makes a good introduction to the work of Klaus Mann.

THE ATTRACTION FOR GIDE

If *The Turning Point* is the best guide to Klaus Mann's emotional and psychological development, then the book on Gide—*André Gide and the Crisis of Modern Thought* (1943)—traces his intellectual development most fully. It was published in New York by Creative Age Press.

"Gide's work," Klaus had written earlier, "accompanied me throughout the years as an older brother, a beloved friend . . . Gide anticipated, echoed and infinitely deepened our questioning. We recognized our own certainties in the continual monologue of his writings."

The parallels between the two lives are instructive. First, Gide helped the younger man accept his homosexuality. "The great self-analyst helped me to discover myself," Klaus wrote in *The Turning Point*. "He guided me through the labyrinth of my own nature and sanctioned whatever I found, the desires, the qualms, the oppressed impulses . . . he gave me self-assurance and the fortitude to endure life and to accept my own being with all its potentialities, dangers and dilemmas." Gide, after all, had been writing on homosexuality as early as *L' Immoraliste* (1902), *Corydon* (1925), and *Si le grain ne meurt* (1926). Another early Gide work, *Le retour de l'enfant prodigue*, had great resonance for Klaus. In it, the returned prodigal son of the title recounts to his younger brother stories about the wonders he has seen on his travels. He offers his brother not wisdom and peace but restlessness and an invitation to the voyage. It was an offering with strong appeal to Klaus, Gide's "younger brother." His own itineraries seem to parallel those of Gide. As Gide had done in the 1890s, Klaus embarked in Marseilles for Tunis and Algeria, where Gide had met Wilde and Douglas. He made pilgrimages to Cairouan and Biskra. Similarly, he returned to Europe via Sicily and Naples. At the time of these trips, Klaus was 18 years old—a prodigal and precocious son.

From Gide, Klaus also learned the value of sexual frankness in literature. Gide admired Montaigne for his audacious personal revelations. He also disapproved Proust's policy of disguising boys as girls. Klaus, though never quite attaining the openness of Gide, came close. He used autobiography freely in the creation of his best fictional works. (Interestingly, one of Klaus' least favorite works by Gide was *Corydon*, whose purportedly "scientific" method he thought did not do justice to the complexity of Gide's thought and experience of homosexuality).

In the mid-1920s, Gide became politicized for the first time in his life—a process that Klaus was to repeat a decade later. The immediate cause of Gide's new social conscience was a trip to Africa which showed him the true face of French colonialism, racism and imperialism. His outrage was expressed in *Voyage Au Congo* (1927). This political awakening, the change from aesthete to genteel activist, marked an important development in Gide's thinking. It would lead him in 1932 toward a conversion to Communism, a trip to Russia (and subsequent disenchantment). The same shifts marked Klaus' intellectual development. The dandy and sensualist of the 1920s became, with the advent of fascism, committed to politics. Klaus too flirted with Marxism and made a trip to Russia in 1934, ultimately rejecting it as authoritarian and puritanical.

The war brought somewhat similar experiences to both men. Klaus fled Europe; Gide was forced out of Paris, his intellectual center, to the south of France—which, under the Nazis was no longer France as he knew it. This experience of uprooting was shared by both men, who corresponded regularly. Gide also contributed to the journals which Klaus edited.

Viewing the two lives, one is struck by the similarities of temperament which led both men into constant reappraisals of their intellectual positions. Both were skeptic by nature but determined to arrange their lives in accordance with rules acceptable to "the candid mind." Both veered from hedonism to asceticism and back again; both were torn between the demands of art and social conscience, order and aesthetic anarchy, classicism and romanticism.

In *Si le grain ne meurt*, Gide asked, "In the name of what God, of what ideal, do you forbid me to live according to my nature?" The crucial words here are "God" and "ideal". Gide, like Mann, would abandon his homosexuality only if a superior set of rules and ideals could be found. Mere sensuality, the sway of appetite, had not enough force to make him accept his homosexuality; he also had to be convinced that repression was against God's wishes. "I will not live without rules," he said, "and the demands of my flesh require the assent of my spirit."

It was the articulation of this moral world that appealed to Klaus Mann. Although he indulged his senses liberally, he sought spiritual approval for his activities. It was the alternation between forgiveness and self-punishment, between rational knowledge and unconscious impulse, that runs through the life and work of both men. Both were protean, of strong contradictory tendencies, with consolidating and disintegrating impulses. Whereas Gide managed to resolve these warring urges through a deep commitment to his writing, and thus make it to the end of a long and eventful life, Klaus Mann could not. In his book of Gide, Mann quotes from Baudelaire's *Journal intime* on the urge toward chaos rather than order: "Prodded by this demoniac impulse, the individual is always inclined to jeopardize his own logic, run risks, gamble, split, go to pieces, lose his poise, or transcend his limitations." It is a quote that pertains more to Klaus Mann than to Andre Gide, whose art ultimately saved him.

Whether the emotional and physical displacement that is at the core of Klaus Mann's experience and writing is relevant to American readers today is a basic question. Certainly his experience of the years around World War II does not parallel ours. We did not wrestle with issues of Pan-Europeanism, the seduction of leading intellectuals by the Right, nor institutionalized anti-Semitism—at least not to the same degree. Nor did Americans suffer the trauma of invasion or exile. Our experience of those years is more accurately rendered in the naive and pastoral landscapes of Willa Cather and Sherwood Anderson. Even when war came, it was James Jones, Norman Mailer and Irwin Shaw who spoke to us about men who were in some ways replicas of Henry James' young men of a generation earlier—journeying to Europe and fighting battles there without philosophical angst.

It is instructive that Thomas Mann called *The Turning Point* a "tremendously European book." This explains its popularity in Germany today, as well as the unflagging interest in all of Klaus Mann's work there. Nor is it surprising that *Mephisto* was a big seller in other European countries. Despite his mastery of English, his protracted stay in America and his service in the U.S. army, Klaus Mann remained profoundly European. His birth in 1906 made him witness during his youth to the events that created today's Europe. He was on the spot, encapsulating in his person the major social movements of the day. He stood at the crossroad where the intellectual and political forces of his day collided. With his talent for self-dramatization he was able to create a public persona that engaged his contemporaries and continues as a useful metaphor for Europeans today. However, it does not mirror the American preoccupations of those years.

The question then arises, for gay readers, whether the homosexual content of his books makes them of special interest. Can we read him as the record of a man who tried hard but didn't quite come out? Here the answer is more positive. Although Klaus Mann wasn't indiscreet enough to write openly gay books, they are still full of the special sensibility, the doomed gracefulness of the sexually displaced artist. They are full of overtones, allusions, secret clues—the whole repertory of a writer sending out signals as he struggles to be free. For these clues the books are valuable as history, as psychology and as art—further necessary evidence of our aborted literary past.

While it is a mistake to attribute an event like suicide to any single cause, especially in the case of someone as complex as Klaus Mann, it is tempting to speculate on the writer's block he alluded to in his last letter to his sister. Was "the major work" he had in mind the novel in which homosexuality would be treated directly? Was he unable to work on it because of the demons of sexual repression and self-hatred that had pursued him all his life? Was he unable to make a last heroic breakthrough into the kind of freedom and frankness for which he so admired Gide? Intriguing speculations only—and must remain so.

▽

The author wishes to acknowledge the assistance of Richard Plant, without whose encouragement, research assistance and translation skills this article could not have been written.

Rictor Norton

HARD GEMLIKE FLAME:
WALTER PATER AND HIS CIRCLE

Walter Horatio Pater (1839–1894), English critic and essayist, celebrated for the fastidious delicacy of his style, was born in London. Educated at Queen's College, Oxford, he settled in Oxford and tutored with private pupils. In 1864 he was elected to a fellowship at Brasenose College. Pater then began to write for the reviews, and his essays on Leonardo da Vinci, Botticelli, Pico della Mirandola, and Michelangelo, with others of the same kind, were collected in 1873 as Studies in the History of the Renaissance *(later called simply* The Renaissance*). The volume had a Conclusion which promulgated a sort of aesthetic gospel. The Conclusion reads (in part):*

"The service of philosophy, of speculative culture towards the human spirit is to rouse, to startle it into sharp and eager observation. Every moment some form grows perfect in hand or face; some tone on the hills or the sea is choicer than the rest; some mood of passion or insight or intellectual excitement is irresistibly real and attractive to us,—for that moment only. Not the fruit of experience, but experience itself, is the end. A counted number of pulses only is given to us of a variegated, dramatic, life. How may we see in them all that is to be seen in them by the finest senses? How shall we pass most swiftly from point to point, and be present always at the focus here the greatest number of vital forces unite in their purest energy?

"To burn always with this hard, gemlike flame, to maintain this ecstasy, is success in life. . . . While all melts under our feet, we may well catch at any exquisite passion, or any contribution to knowledge that seems by a lifted horizon to set the spirit free for a moment, or any stirring of the senses, strange dyes, strange colours, and curious odours, or work of the artist's hands, or the face of one's friend. . . .

"Well! We are all condamnés, *as Victor Hugo says: we are all under sentence of death but with a sort of indefinite reprieve*—les hommes sont tous condamnés à mort avec des sursis indéfinis: *we have an interval, and then our place knows us no more. Some spend this interval in listlessness, some in high passions, the wisest, at least among "the children of this world," in art and song. For our one chance lies in expanding that interval, in getting as many pulsations as possible into the given time. Great passions may give us this quickened sense of life, ecstasy and sorrows of love, the various forms of enthusiastic activity, disinterested or otherwise, which come naturally to many of us. Only be sure it is passion—that it does yield you this fruit of a quickened, multiplied consciousness. Of this wisdom, the poetic passion, the desire of beauty, the love of art for art's sake, has most; for art comes to you professing frankly to give nothing but the highest quality to your moments as they pass, and simply for those moments' sake."*

The publication of this volume made Pater the center of a small group in Oxford. He had relations with the Pre-Raphaelites, of whom he was to some extent the heir, and he began to insinuate something of their spirit into his academic world. By the time Marius the Epicurean *appeared in 1885 he had a following of disciples.* Marius *is his most substantial work. It is a romance of ideas in which Pater's ideal of an aesthetic and religious life is elaborately set forth.*

His life was almost all spent in Oxford, and he died there in 1894. Patter wrote with difficulty, correcting and recorrecting with infinite care. There is a reserve and reticence about his writing, maintained also in his personal life. The primary influence on his mind was his classical study, colored by a highly individual kind of Christianity, pursued largely as a source of refined artistic sensations. Oscar Wilde, George Moore, and the aesthetes of the 1890s were among his followers.

The following essay, written especially for Gay Sunshine *by Rictor Norton, deals with Pater's personal life, specifically with his homosexuality. It appeared in* Gay Sunshine Journal *21 (Spring 1974).*

▽

*I*N A REMARKABLE ANECDOTE, Frank Harris records that during a visit with Walter Pater at Brasenose College, Pater "seemed at times half to realize his own deficiency: 'Had I so-and-so's courage and hardihood,' he cried once, 'I'd have—.' Suddenly the mood changed, the light in his eyes died out, the head dropped forward again, and with a half-smile he added, 'I must have been a criminal—heh, heh,' and he moved with little careful steps across the room to his chair, and sat down."

Could Walter Pater—one of the most influential art critics in English history—have been a criminal? His more conventional contemporaries regarded his aesthetic vision as the product of an immoral imagination, and in this respect he was certainly a criminal in the field of art. One wonders about his life as well, though, of course, like Jean Genet, Pater would have been a saintly criminal, an archetypal high priest—dressed in robes of saffron, with purple grapes pressing against his pale temples—officiating at a sacred ritual of, say, castration. He would no doubt have admired the delicate crescent blade wielded by the transvestite priests of Cybele, the Phrygian goddess of frenzy and voluptuous languor. An orgiastic dream may well lie beneath the hard surface of Pater's gemlike flame.

If we look at Pater outside the context of the schoolbooks—look at him squarely in the eyes as a man, a poet, an aesthete, a treasurer of things foreign to English soil, rather than as the "father" of a school of thought—we cannot, in all honesty, be quite certain that his sensibility would have blanched at perusing the Marquis de Sade's *120 Days of Sodom*. And we must bear in mind that in one of his *Greek Studies*, Pater appreciates, however coyly, not only the Divine Marquis, but also Gilles de Rais, that notorious ravisher of boys.

It is, in fact, quite probable that Walter Pater was in reality a criminal in Victorian England: i.e., a practicing homosexual.

Mark Pattison, in his diary for May 5, 1878, records that he went "to Pater's to tea, where [I saw] Oscar Browning, who was more like Socrates than ever. He conversed in one corner with 4 feminine looking youths 'paw-dandling' there in one fivesome, while the Miss Paters & I sat looking on in another corner—Presently Walter Pater, who, I had been told, was 'upstairs' appeared, attended by 2 more youths of similar appearances." Query: was the threesome upstairs *also* "paw-dandling"?

Surely we know what the fivesome in the corner was contemplating, for Oscar Browning three years earlier had been dismissed from his mastership at Eton under grave suspicions of pederasty. Concerning this dismissal, Pater had written to Browning in October 1875, that he was "very glad to hear, not for your own sake only, but on public grounds, that you had decided not to leave Eton without a struggle." Struggle he did, but dismissed he was nevertheless—only to become a Fellow of King's College, Cambridge. The visit that Pattison described had occurred in the tenth year of the close friendship between Pater and Browning—to whom Pater had been introduced in 1868 by John Burnell Payne. It was Payne, a close friend of the homosexual artist Simeon Solomon, who drew some fine charcoal portraits of both Pater and Payne.

Walter Pater is not known to have had more than a passing acquaintance with any women except his sisters Hester and Clara (with whom he lived all his life) and Violet Paget, lesbian poetess (alias "Vernon Lee"). Most of Pater's friends were young and handsome men and boys, many of whom, like himself, died bachelors, and many of whom were practicing homosexuals. The closest friend of his adolescence was J. R. McQueen. Unfortunately, we know little about the specific nature of their friendship other than it was "very close," for the numerous letters that Walter wrote to Mark from 1858 to 1862 were suppressed by the Miss Paters when Thomas Wright was preparing the first biography in 1907. Wright was allowed to examine some of the letters, but forbidden to quote directly or to paraphrase too closely their contents. But the half-words that remain in his biography suggest an intimacy that it would have been impolite to have delved into in 1907. The letters have since been destroyed.

Walter Pater

The closest friend of Pater's adult life was Charles Lancelot Shadwell (born in 1840, one year Pater's junior), who became Pater's private pupil at Christ Church College in 1863. In 1874 Pater published *Diaphaneite*, modeled upon Shadwell's rare spirit, a portrait of an ethereal youth. In the summer of 1865, Pater and Shadwell, master and pupil, together toured Italy—Ravenna, Pisa, Florence—without the company of Clara and Hester. Shadwell spent nearly his entire life studiously engaged in painstaking research into the history of Oriel College, Oxford, of which he was a fellow and later became Provost. He is the "C.L.S." to whom Pater dedicated his *Studies in the History of the Renaissance* in 1873. Shadwell died in 1919, a bachelor.

Rupert Croft-Cooke, in his book *Feasting with Panthers*, tells of two close male friendships which Pater had in the later part of his life.

"In 1877, when Pater was a year or two short of forty, that dangerous age at which Wilde met Alfred Douglas, Pater met a man twelve years younger than he named Richard Jackson. Jackson believed himself a poet; he was also rich. He became devoted to Pater in a sentimental if not a passionate way and this devotion lasted for many years. [Pater's biographer] Wright believed that he was the original of Marius and in old age Jackson seemed to have claimed this quite seriously. If it is true it is shocking to know what the writings of Marius would have been like, for this is a quatrain which Jackson wrote at Pater's request as a song for his birthday—

> *Your darling soul I say is inflamed with love for me;*
> *Your very eyes do move I cry with sympathy:*
> *Your darling feet and hands are blessings ruled by love,*
> *As forth was sent from out the Ark a turtle dove.*

'I am glad to write about you,' he added, 'for owing to you my life has been enriched, its minstrelsy swelled . . .'

"Jackson introduced his young friends to Pater . . . [One of these] was Walter Blackburn Harte whom Pater first saw as an acolyte wearing a scarlet cassock in the chapel of St. Austin's. He seems to have been irresistible to all who met him, having literary ambitions and a cockney sense of humour. Pater said he had 'a darling personality' and asked him down to Oxford, but most of Harte's time was spent at Jackson's Camberwell home, for he found Pater's dull dreary rooms at Oxford 'a great disappointment. . . .' A portrait shows a beautiful youth with curling lips, deep expressive eyes and a fine profile." Harte later emigrated to America and became in the 1890s a successful journalist.

We really don't know for sure that Charles Algernon Swinburne, with whom Pater became friendly in 1858, was homosexual. Swinburne is notorious for his desires to be whipped by prostitutes, but his biographers insist he hired only female prostitutes for such purposes. On one occasion, however, Swinburne asked Solomon to draw for him a set of pictures showing schoolmasters flogging boys. (These are contained in Swinburne's unpublished *Whippingham Papers*, which are locked up in the British Museum. The Trustees of the Museum will allow only Solomon's descendants to view them— but since Solomon doesn't have any descendants, one supposes they will be locked up forever.) Pater, Swinburne, and Solomon were members of the Old Mortality Club, a society for budding literati and a haven for homosexuals.

In 1861 Swinburne became acquainted with Lord Houghton, whose own collected poems contain passages not entirely heteroerotic. Swinburne borrowed from this gentleman's extensive library of erotica the complete works of the Marquis de Sade. Simeon Solomon, who at the time was residing as a guest at Fryston, Lord Houghton's country house in Yorkshire, was there introduced by Swinburne to Oscar Browning. Simeon and Oscar struck up a match, and together toured Italy in the summers of 1867, 1868 and 1869—without the company of Swinburne.

In the early 1860s Solomon had been friends with the homosexual artist Edward Poynter, and had specially designed for him a series of homoerotic allegorical drawings. One of the better ones is a pen and ink drawing of "Love Talking to Boys," dated 1865, showing several lovely lads embracing while Eros—i.e., Cupid in an Edwardian silk waistcoat with wings—encourages them. Most of the drawings have been lost—or locked up.

In 1865, the date of "Love Talking to Boys," Swinburne went up to Oxford and introduced his friend Pater to his friend Solomon. Solomon then and there drew a very good portrait of Pater, gave it to him, and decided to stay the night, and the next night, and the next. For the next several years he would return frequently to share Pater's rooms "upstairs" at Brasenose, and then at London. As a measure of what Solomon's company may have been like: in 1866 he and Swinburne visited Dante Gabriel Rossetti in Cheyne Walk, and for a time disturbed Rossetti's work by chasing each other naked up and down the staircase.

Simeon Solomon (1841–1905) is often regarded as the central tragic hero-victim of the Age of Decadence. At the age of eighteen he had already exhibited a painting at the Royal Academy. This, however, was the height of his career, and his fall was slow and painful. In a letter dated August 20, 1917, Edmund Gosse (who incidentally was a repressed if not practicing homosexual; he contributed the essay on Pater for the *Dictionary of National Biography*, as well as the biography of the homosexual Renaissance poet Richard Barnfield) reminisced to Robert Ross (a close friend of Oscar Wilde) that Solomon "sometime during 1870" was threatened with legal proceedings for certain unspecified sexual activities, and that he had been forced to fly to Italy. Gosse's recollection is probably a bit faulty, for this likely refers to Solomon and Browning's hurried departure for Italy in 1869.

In 1873 Solomon was arrested for "indecently molesting" a man named Roberts in a public urinal north of Oxford Street. He was sentenced to eighteen months' imprisonment in Clerkenwell House of Correction, but the sentence was suspended and he was placed under the supervision of the police. In a letter dated June 6, 1873, Swinburne wrote to the Welsh squire George Powell that "I saw and spoke with a great friend of Simeon, Pater of Brasenose. Do you—I do not—know any detail of the matter at first hand? Pater, I imagine, did." In Gosse's recollection to Ross, Swinburne had dashed off to Oxford "to discuss Solomon with his [i.e., Solomon's] friend Walter Pater." We don't quite know what the discussions were, but in any event Pater was certainly informed of the facts (if he didn't know them before), and he nevertheless remained friends with Solomon for several more years, even welcoming him "upstairs." There is no hint in his correspondence or elsewhere that he was startled by Solomon's behavior. There is only a discreet silence.

Over the period of the next twenty-five years, Solomon got into more trouble because of sexual escapades, was imprisoned, and was incarcerated in an insane asylum by his concerned relatives. They relented and tried to arrange for him to escape, but he knew the doors had been unlocked for this purpose. So he went and locked them rather than play their game. He wasn't insane, and upon his official release he became a professional vagabond and hack artist. He sold Swinburne's erotic correspondence with him in order to make money. Every so often he returned home to get a new set of clothing, which he promptly sold and returned to his rags. For most of the remainder of his life he literally lived in the gutter, became a drunken pavement artist in Brompton Road and Bayswater, and selling matches and shoe laces in Mile End Road.

Pater's masterwork, *The Renaissance*, was published in March 1873, several months after the scandal of Solomon's arrest. A number of people quietly murmured that there was an affinity between the hedonism advocated by Pater in his "Conclusion" of the study, and the pleasure-seeking of his "degenerate friend." Pater responded by suppressing the "Conclusion" in the 1877 edition, and in the 1888 edition he stated that the "Conclusion" was omitted because "it might possibly mislead some of those into whose hands it might fall."

Mark André Raffalovich records that the art critic Sidney Colvin warned Raffalovich "to avoid making the acquaintance of men such as Walter Pater and John Addington Symonds." Symonds was generally recognized by his contemporaries as a homosexual— and this warning implies that Pater was similarly recognized. Raffalovich, himself homosexual [his lover, poet John Gray, is said to have been the original model for Oscar Wilde's Dorian Gray —ED.], ignored Colvin's advice and became friends not only with Symonds and Pater, but with Oscar Wilde and Simeon Solomon as well.

Pater may well have been regarded by his contemporaries as a dangerous influence upon young men in the same way that Socrates was so regarded. In W. H. Mallock's *The New Republic* (1877) Pater is satirized as "Mr. Rose," who plays a role similar to that of the pederastic Pausanius in Plato's *Symposium*. The most damaging part of Mallock's satire was not his portrayal of Pater/Rose as a languid espouser of Pre-Raphaelite aestheticism, but his portrayal of Pater/Rose as a passionate apologist for *paiderastia*. Mr. Rose delivers a eulogy, for example, upon "life as a chamber, which we decorate as we would decorate the chamber of the woman *or the youth* [italics mine] that we love, tinting the walls of it in symphonies of subdued colour." Mr. Rose refers in passing to "the boyhood of Bathyllus" (the boyfriend of Anacreon), to "Narcissus, that soft boy," to "lean Aquinas in his cell," and to "a boy of eighteen whose education I may myself claim to have had some share in directing." Mr. Rose rises to sublime eloquence

when it comes to a defense of "passionate friendship" in a passage quoted almost verbatim from Pater's own essay on the friendships of the homosexual art critic Winckelmann: "Think of the immortal dramas which history sets before us; of the keener and
profounder passions which it reveals to us, of nobler mould than ours—Harmodius and
Aristogeiton, Achilles and Patroclus, David and Jonathan, our English Edward [sc. King
Edward II] and the fair Piers Gaveston, or, above all, those two [i.e., Socrates and Phae-
drus] by the agnus castus and the plane-tree where Ilyssus flowed."

All these pairs of men are mentioned in Pater's own essays, and Mallock properly
recognized them as homosexual pairs. Mallock's work was one of the most popular
books of the day, and part of its popularity lay in people's recognition therein of the
pederastic Mr. Pater. It seems more than likely that at least a hint of this suspicion lay
behind a general ill-will towards Pater. His "decent" contemporaries simply refused to
grant him his just rewards. In 1874, the year following Solomon's arrest, Pater was
passed over for the Junior Proctorship, a post which should normally have been his by
right of seniority. In 1876 he was forced to withdraw his candidacy for Professorship
of Poetry, because of the "immorality" of *The Renaissance* and for other reasons still
unclear. In 1877 he was satirized by Mallock and almost physically shrank away in pain
and hurt. In 1885 he was defeated in his candidacy for Professorship of Fine Arts, even
though he was now regarded by many as the foremost critic of fine art in his time. In
fact, Pater met everywhere with a series of rebuffs and frustrations to such an extent
that in the late 1870s he had noticeably developed, in the view of Laurence Evans, the
recent editor of his letters, "a guarded, evasive manner, a style or strategy of polite accommodation, a strategy of studied blandness."

Pater's blandness is really the perfectly composed lassitude of a fallen maenad. Nearly
all of his criticism and fiction moves with the ritual frenzy of a Dionysian ceremony
at whose center is the death of a beautiful boy. It is a theme with a "dark message"
that doesn't quite fit into the Gay Liberation (or even humanistic) scheme of things;
but it nevertheless happens to be the central image of what might almost be called *the*
homosexual aesthetics. The theme is found not only in Pater's *Marius the Epicurean*, but
in a great deal of modern homosexual literature as well, with variations: Thomas Mann's
Death in Venice, Tennessee Williams' *Desire and the Black Masseur*, James Baldwin's
Another Country and *Giovanni's Room*, William Burroughs' *Naked Lunch*, particularly
Jean Genet's *Funeral Rites*, even Edward Albee's *Who's Afraid of Virginia Woolf?* (Sunny
Jim), and Yukio Mishima's *Forbidden Colors*—in which there is a passage referring ex-
plicitly to Walter Pater. Not to mention a host of homosexual poems on the dying
Adonis or Narcissus or St. Sebastian, in *Manroot* and *Gay Sunshine* as well as the early
Greek Anthology.

In *A Study of Dionysus*, published posthumously and edited by Shadwell, Walter
Pater leads us by careful insinuation and subtle seduction, from the sunny groves of
Arcady to a dark glade in Thessaly where we may feast upon a fair youth. The *raison
d'être* for this study is to apprehend the fullest possible meaning of a primordial fact:
"That the sacred women of Dionysus [the maenads] ate, in mystical ceremony, raw flesh
and drank blood, to commemorate the actual sacrifice of a fair boy deliberately torn to
pieces." Pater repeatedly glances the edges of the rite that he dare not name too directly.
He refers, for example, to "the delicate, fresh, farm-lad we may still actually see sometimes, like a graceful field-flower among the corn," without quite acknowledging that
Triptolemus, to whom this farm-lad is compared, was a corn-spirit of homosexual can-

nibalistic rites nearly identical with the Centipede Rites in William Burroughs' *Naked Lunch*. He refers to Neptune devouring the ivory-white shoulder of his boyfriend Pelops. He lusciously hints at "the dark and shameful secret society described by Livy, in which Dionysus' worship ended at Rome, afterwards abolished by solemn act of the Senate"— without explicitly mentioning that this was a homosexual secret society. Nowhere does Pater actually *come out* and tell us that his favorite deity Dionysus, whom he acknowledges was "somewhat womanly" and appealing to "feminine souls," was (and is) the most homosexual of all the gods.

Pater's praise of "virile youth" and "passionate friendship" in his studies of *The Golden Youth of Laceademon, The Age of Athletic Prizemen*, and *Winckelmann* is a bit guarded, but nevertheless clearly homosexual. And the content of two short stories is almost explicitly homosexual—"Denys L' Aurroix," in which a Dionysus figure is literally torn to pieces, and "Apollo in Picardy," in which a boy is accidentally killed by his lover just as Apollo killed Narcissus. These two stories are, in fact, quite bold when we realize that Genet and Burroughs had not yet taken up the theme.

We would never dare call Walter Pater a humorist, but whenever he approaches the sensuousness of beautiful boyhood with less indirection than usual, we can clearly see him camping it up, as in this description of an engraving of satyr-lads by Robetta: "Their puck noses have grown delicate, so that, with Plato's infatuated lover, you may call them winsome, if you please; and no one would wish those hairy little shanks away." It is not insignificant that Plato's "infatuated lover," as Pater very well knew from frequent perusal of his favorite work the Phaedrus, was not a *paederast*, but a *pederast* pure and simple. And from a perusal of John Payne Knight's *Worship of the Generative Powers* Pater equally knew that the thyrsus symbolized an erect penis and the pine cone atop it symbolized the glans. So he coyly warns us that "our fingers must beware of the thyrsus, tossed about so wantonly by Dionysus and his chorus, and that button of a pine-cone." Walter Pater, in his own way, created the camp style as much as did Oscar Wilde in *The Importance of Being Earnest*. We need to keep this in mind as we read him, to note that there is usually a sub-narrative of homoerotic reference based upon assumptions not shared by the "decent" reader. Pater, of course, is quite serious in his art, but he's never solemn, and the word unsaid keeps echoing between the lines.

Pater's studied blandness, his seemingly ethereal rather than earthly demeanor, has put his biographers off their guard, and they quite unreasonably assume that Pater was therefore chaste, cloistered, cold, and nearly a loner. But, in fact, a peripheral biography of Pater could be expanded with quite warm-blooded speculations concerning his close friendships with Arthur William Symons, bisexual poet and critical theorist of decadence; with Francis Fortescue Urquhart, bachelor don nicknamed "Sligger" because of his sleek looks, model for Pater's short story "Emerald Uthwart," and a man who was so thoroughly a faithful friend to many young men that he should have been homosexual if he wasn't; with poet Gerard Manley Hopkins, one of Pater's private pupils, author of a number of fine ballads on boys bathing; with Thomas Humphrey Ward, whom he tutored in Plato for a month in 1867 in Sidmouth in a secluded cottage near the sea; with A. J. Butler, tutor to the son of the Khedive of Egypt and author of a translation of the homoerotic *Greek Anthology* that Pater recommended to Gosse because the latter "delights also in Greek things"; and others, especially his long friendship with Oscar Wilde from 1877 to at least the early 1890s. All the circumstantial evidence points to only one conclusion; that Walter Pater was a practicing homosexual, though after the scandal of 1873 he began to carefully guard his emotions. He may have even begun to recoil from himself because of the realization that such love can be crudely celebrated in public urinals as well as at symposiums of British schoolmasters and their pupils.

IV

GAY FICTION

Frits Bernard

Costa Brava: a Novella

TRANSLATED FROM DUTCH BY A. RONALDSON
ILLUSTRATIONS BY ALOYSIUS HEYLAERTS

▽

Part One

Many are the ways . . .

I

The sea looked like a grey oil-slick alongside the golden yellow sand. The water was as smooth as a mirror, and the rays of the setting sun tinted the white houses of the village orange. The little church stood serene and peaceful on its rock beside the sea, like a stake arising from the water. It was one of the very warm summer days, and the siesta of the inhabitants was prolonged somewhat beyond the customary duration. The few small beach cafés beneath the slender palm trees were still deserted, with the curtains drawn in their windows. In the village itself, people were occupied in pushing aside the canvas awnings that had been hung between the roofs across the narrow streets in order to keep out the sunshine, and others were sprinkling water on the sandy and irregular pavements.

In the distance, the melancholy song of a flamenco-singer accompanied by the plaintive chords of a guitar softly recalled his dear Andalusia . . . *en Córdoba la sultana y en Sevilla la giralda*. . . . A cart supported by two high wheels and drawn by two mules, one behind the other and both wearing straw hats with their ears poking through, carried locally-picked grapes to one of the houses. After unloading, they would be trampled underfoot and in due course become the local wine. A farmer drove three donkeys heavily-laden with fruit and vegetables before him in the direction of the little market. On the beach, the fishermen began to get their boats ready for the night. At ten o'clock—as usual—they would make sail for the part of the Mediterranean that was their fishing ground, and at seven o'clock the next morning they would be back with their catch, part of which would then be sold on the beach there.

In the meanwhile, the sun had set. I crossed over the path beside the beach and looked into the calm water, which was changing colour at that moment. The village had now become busy; the time for the evening promenade had arrived. People sauntered along the footpath and the beach cafés were quite crowded. Voices rang clearly through the evening air, which had become appreciably cooler. I went and sat down on a stone bench in order to let the atmosphere and the peace have their effect on me. A beggar came up to me with dignity and asked me for alms. He expressed his gratitude with the words: "may the good Lord repay you" and disappeared among the crowd.

A book about Catalonia lay open on my knees, but I could not be bothered to read it. There was much so much to see, so much to observe. I had scarcely been in Spain for two weeks, and before going to the south of the country I intended to spend a few more weeks at the Catalan coast. This was the plan I had made before leaving Venezuela, my homeland. How much had I looked forward to seeing something of the land of my ancestors—Spain! A dream-wish of many Venezuelans: one which is seldom fulfilled, however. And now it was being fulfilled so far for me. My grandfather had emigrated from this Catalan coast to South America, like so many others from the Iberian peninsula had done at that time. There were innumerable links, in fact, between the two territories: Spain the motherland and her South American offspring. Here I sat and looked out over the sea just like my forefathers had once done.

A sea-breeze arose. In the meanwhile, it had become completely dark and the stars twinkled in the sky above: the Great Bear, the Milky Way and Orion. Moonlight bathed the landscape, the hills, the flat roofs of the village and the apparently boundless Mare Nostrum. The voices of the fishermen made a monotonous sound as they strained with their shoulders against the hulls of their boats to propel them across the beach—on short rollers thrust beneath the keel—and into the water. One, two . . . one, two. . . . One after another the boats slid into the sea. This was not always achieved without difficulty; sometimes they got stuck in shallow water, and then it was a big job to get them afloat again. The purr of the rhythmically drumming motors could be heard for a long time. Later on a cluster of small lights appeared on the horizon; the fishing operation had begun.

My thoughts then turned to my own small motor-boat, which lay on the little beach about a hundred miles to the north, surrounded by steep rocks. It had been lying there a week before, after a visit I had made to a fellow-countryman who had a country-house there on the Costa Brava and spent his summer there. I had bought the boat cheaply, second-hand, through a relative when I arrived in the country, in order to be able to make short trips along the coast during my stay—mainly so that I could take photographs and shoot some scenes. It was my intention to go and fetch it in the near future.

After walking some more and drinking a glass of vermouth with sodawater, I made my way to a small restaurant under the palm-trees behind the fishermen's beach and ordered a *paella*, one of the local specialties, made of rice with chopped fish, meat, poultry, vegetables and spices. It was brought to the table steaming, and its delicious fragrance mingled with that of the sea. The house wine that was served with it was not bad. Everything was so restful and peaceful; nobody was in a hurry—people didn't eat before ten or eleven o'clock in the evening.

At midnight I went to the open-air cinema, which was situated in the back-garden of a café somewhere in the middle of the village. A canvas sheet was suspended above the simple wooden seats, to keep out the moonlight. The main film had not yet begun and it did not last long or there was an interval. A couple of peanut vendors appeared, calling out *cacahuetes, cacahuetes* . . .

Beside the rows of seats there was an oblong pond surrounded entirely by blue tiles, with a fountain at one end spraying fine jets of water round about. It had a cooling effect, and reminded me of a Moorish garden. The influence of the southern neighbours was unmistakable.

The Spanish main film interested me—as the manager of a Venezuelan film company—very much. Although most Spanish films are also screened in South America, I had not seen this one. It was about the life of a priest and the secrets of the confessional.

All of a sudden the projector stopped, a great sigh came from the audience, and the noise of shelling peanuts ceased, only to begin again at once, unlike the show, because there was a power-cut and the village lay in darkness, apart from where it was relatively light thanks to the bright moon. The cinema show thus ended early.

I strolled for some time through the narrow streets that ran up and down between the many neat white houses with their mostly blue doors and windows. It had become silent in the village. The passers-by seemed unreal in the moonlight, especially because you didn't hear them coming nearer on their *alpargatas*—linen shoes with rope soles and straps.

This was my first really long holiday for many years and I discovered that here in these surroundings I was at peace and new ideas could come to me. There were two films to be made during the coming year, one of which dealt with the links between Spain and Venezuela. The script was almost ready, but not yet fully worked out in all detail. I had made up my mind to shoot some of the outdoor scenes right here.

With a candle which I had got from the night-porter in my hotel in my hand, I made my way to my bedroom, where I undressed and put on my swimming-costume and a short dressing-gown. I left the hotel again, crossed the beach-side path and ran across the beach. A few moments later I was swimming in the dark sea, still unaware that this was one of the last restful days that I would enjoy in this part of the world.

II

It was 20th July 1936. In a few days' time everything was changed: the civil war was raging in Spain. The tension was unbearable, with one rumor circulating after another. Connections were broken, everything seemed to be disorganized. Nobody was able to predict how it would all turn out. Men wearing overalls with guns over their shoulders peopled the streets. The church on the rock was burnt down. . . . The country was divided into two camps; the Republicans on one side and Franco's supporters on the other. Catalonia belonged to the former, the "red" side.

The land-owning class and the clergy were hit hard. People went into hiding, or disappeared to safer places if that seemed to be possible. There were murders, buildings were set on fire . . .

A British cruiser appeared off the coast, in order to carry the British subjects away to safety. That was a bad sign.

These developments prevented me from putting my plans into effect; there was now no question of a journey further south. What should I do? Could my Ford—with its Caracas number-plate—take me back to France via Barcelona and Port Bou, or La Junquera? Normal railway services no longer existed, only troop trains. As a foreigner I had nothing to fear directly, I belonged to the privileged few. My car was also not requisitioned. I had painted "Venezuela" in large white letters on the sides of the bodywork, and a Venezuelan flag fluttered above the left-hand mudguard.

My suitcases were packed, and already lying in the boot of the car. Only a few necessities remained in a bag in my room at the hotel. I was prepared for all possibilities.

The next few days brought no improvement in the general situation, indeed everything was more confused. Groups of whispering people were all over the streets. . . . Shots were heard in and around the little square, and from the distance came the sound of a machine-gun. Food became scarcer and more expensive.

I sat once again on the stone bench and stared at the deep blue sea, which sparkled in the bright sunlight as if nothing was the matter. The beach that had once been so jolly lay abandoned, and the pretty white and coloured sails were no longer to be seen. The British cruiser had disappeared along with the British subjects.

Slowly, with his head bowed forward, a boy came towards me. He was alone. A few yards in front of my bench he stood still and looked around, as if he were afraid of something. He then made his way to the bench and sat down. To judge by the cloth of his *fresco*—very thin summer-wear—he was not poor. There was something proud about his bearing, despite his sombre expression. His dark brown eyes looked into mine. They troubled me. He smiled, and in the smile there was something so intimate that I had the feeling that I had known him a long time. What a remarkable encounter. We looked at each other several times, and the same feelings occurred again . . .

"Señor, can you help me?" he asked and looked in front of him.

Whether I wanted to help him. What was the matter then with this boy? He related his story, his tragedy, to a stranger in this dangerous time. His father had been killed a few days before, he was left all alone. . . . His mother was no longer alive. His father had told him that—if anything should happen—he must try to escape to France. . . . He had eaten nothing since the previous day, his money had run out . . . could I give him something to eat, bread would be enough . . .

He carried himself bravely, like a proud Spaniard. I seized his hand and shook it. "What's your name, *amigo*?"

"Juan José."

"How old are you?"

"Twelve."

Twelve years old, in such tragic circumstances. As I took Juan José to the hotel, I thought how trivial were my own difficulties in comparison with this boy's. I felt sorry for Juan José, who sat still facing me across the table, looking very attractive. His slim boyish hands handled the knife and fork, and he even seemed to forget his misery. His almost black hair, which he wore combed straight back, his slightly thick— but beautifully curved—lips gave him a somewhat sensual appearance. His shoulders were broad for his age, and his muscles well-developed. You could see that he enjoyed sports. The colour of his skin was too dark for that of a Catalan, but typical of that of a person from Andalusia. I did not ask him for any more details; that seemed to me to be indiscreet during a civil war. I really knew nothing about him—not even his surname—it was just as if he was a close friend with whom I felt at home. We looked at each other understandingly.

The waiter brought us *arroz a la cubana*: white rice with tomato sauce, eggs, pieces of ham and fried banana. Considering the circumstances, the food was remarkably good, indeed exceptionally good. The ordinary holiday-makers had disappeared from the hotel and now only various *milicianos* sat in the dining-room with their weapons leaning against the tables and chairs. Some of them had not shaved for days, they spoke a lot and noisily, mainly about the situation and the new times that were to come.

There were some more shots in the distance. Juan José stared straight in front, his fork fell from his right hand and he toyed with a lump of bread with his other hand. He wanted to say something, but his lips remained cramped together. I got the feeling that he was no longer there, that his thoughts were somewhere else . . .

The waiter brought fresh coffee, and looked with surprise at the boy. I got up from my seat and seized Juan José by the arm. I turned to the waiter and said "He's not feeling well, it must be the stomach-ache again. I'll take him upstairs and drink my coffee later." Juan José climbed the stairs vacantly with me. Once in the bedroom I laid him on the bed, took off his alpargatas and served some brandy in the water-glass. Even before I had time to give him a little to drink, he burst into tears and hid his face in the white cushions. The reaction to all he had gone through—and had borne so bravely—came, and he wept and wept. . . . From time to time he stammered a few words . . . *papá . . . no puedo más.*

No, he could take no more, it was too much. I sat on the end of the bed and leant over. "I will help you, Juanjo."

I ran my fingers through his thick black hair. He was more restful. He had completely stopped crying. He drank a tot of brandy.

"Try and get some sleep."

His eyes had returned to their normal expression, and he looked understandingly in my direction.

"Yes—I'll try."

Sitting at the table in front of the window, I looked out through a chink in the shutters. It was getting on for four o'clock, the sun's rays illuminated the path differently from the sea. Not far away stood two open lorries with armed men in rolled-up shirt-sleeves. Some of them were still very young, almost children. One of them was rolling a cigarette, others were busy loading their guns. Each lorry had a big red flag beside the driving-cab. On the sides of the load compartment stood the letters F.A.I. The scene did not last long, as both lorries moved off and disappeared down the road. A small group of people remained on the pavement talking. They did not appear to be agreed about something, but I could not hear exactly what it was all about.

I glanced towards the bed. The young features lay relaxed, one hand over the edge of the mattress hung down, his head was turned slightly to the right and his breath came regularly. Juan José was asleep. His first sleep, since when? What was going on inside him? He was not safe here; his father had been killed for political reasons, he was afraid. Afraid of what? What would anyone do to him? Put him in a camp, as he was afraid they might? Or . . .

He wanted to go to France, to an uncle who was living in Perpignan. That was his late father's last wish . . .

I reviewed the possibilities. How could he cross the frontier? Under the prevailing circumstances this did not seem to be feasible. There must be another solution. But what? I began to apply myself intensively to his problem; I had promised to help him. But how?

Sounds from outside put an abrupt end to my meditation. I peered through the shutters, a small crowd was shouting in the street there. Two people—middle-aged men—were being taken away. It was a dispiriting sight. What a dreadful thing was this war between brothers. And it could be so beautiful here on the coast. . . . Juan José remained fast asleep, he heard nothing. His face had something so noble, something of an angel. He must be a good person.

There was a knock at the door. Footsteps sounded in the passage. I opened it gently.

"Identity-card, comrade!"

The Venezuelan passport was passed from hand to hand. Finally it reached someone who could read.

"Foreigner—from Venezuela! A good country."

There were no more questions. They went on to the next door.

"Salud, camarada."

I shut the door. Juan José had woken up, he was bathed in sweat, drops of which ran off his forehead onto the cushion.

"*Señor*," he began nervously, "you got rid of them that time! Had they come for me?"

I pushed a cane chair to beside the bed and sat down next to the boy.

"No, don't worry, it wasn't important," and after a short pause I added "don't call me 'señor'; my friends call me Santiago."

He put out his hand and shook mine.

"Thank God I met you," he continued emotionally. "Friendship is the most wonderful thing in the world and it helps us come through everything; I never appreciated that more than I do right now. You didn't know me at all, and yet you do everything for me. I feel myself to be so safe beside you. Despite all the misery, despite this revolution, the last moments have been wonderful and incomprehensible."

He took the words out of my mouth. He spoke like a man.

"Listen to me for a moment, Juanjo; while you were asleep I was thinking about the possibilities for getting you out of here. I didn't get very far, but perhaps we can do better if we go over it together. As far north as Tamariú, I have a small motorboat on the Costa Brava. With the car—it has foreign licence plates—we could try to get to Tamariú, and then make an attempt to sail to France in my boat. All this is clearly not a simple business in war-time, but it is worth having a try. Of course we must think about food and above all about fuel, but that, too, can be arranged . . . "

He interrupted—"You are a good friend—and that's why I don't want you to run a risk for me. If they catch you, you'll be in real trouble, even if you are a foreigner. And I don't want anything to happen to you."

He sat up straight and looked at me trustingly. His eyes had a special brightness. I felt uncertain; a strange feeling came over me. Despite the tragedy, I felt quite happy. What kind of boy was this, who spoke in this way? He made me feel small and insignificant.

"I have no choice, Juanjo, just because I too feel this friendship, I can't leave you in the lurch. I could never forgive myself. I must. It will all be all right . . . "

There was another knock at the door. The waiter stood in the doorway and asked if the young man was feeling any better. He had brought the coffee with him.

I filled the time with one thing and another. I went downstairs and sat down to drink a soda in the small hall leading to the way out. It was getting on for six o'clock, and the heat still hung heavily over the street onto which I looked out. The door stood open, and a bead curtain with a maritime scene hung in the opening. It showed a little fishing-boat under sail, such as are often seen in this part of the Mediterranean Sea. It was made up of numerous colours with a bright blue background. In no sense could it be called artistic—an artist would have had a fit—but it gave a cheerful effect, and so achieved its purpose. A young girl carrying a wicker-work basket full of melons and water-melons came in, and the beads rattled merrily as she went by. She came past me, modestly averting her eyes from me, as is customary in the Latin countries, and walked elegantly through a door marked *servicio* into the kitchen. A few moments later she came back through the same door with the same charm, walked past me again and went out through the bead curtain. I could still perceive her slim silhouette faintly between the beads until she disappeared behind a high cart.

The evening paper lay open on a table; it consisted of only a single sheet with big black headlines giving the news about the progress of the front. In order to keep abreast of what was being written in the press I began to read it. The revolt had grown into a full-scale civil war, and everything suggested that it would not be a minor affair. Poor country; as a Venezuelan I had sympathy with the territory that once was the *tierra madre*—the motherland—for the South American states.

Some people had come into the adjoining dining-room without my noticing. The radio was switched on; they were waiting for the news-bulletin from Barcelona. Marching music could be heard. The announcer introduced his colleague from the news department. He read the news nervously. The whole of Spain appeared to be in rebellion, from the Canaries to the Pyrenees. Then followed a series of announcements for the civil population. It was alarming. The military music that followed raised the enthusiasm of the listeners to a peak. It seemed to be a winning battle. . . . More or less unnoticed, twilight had fallen. The sun had become a fireball, the air was red and orange. A plume of smoke appeared on the horizon. The villagers stood looking at it in groups; they were afraid of being bombarded from the sea. The air was again buzzing with rumours.

I then went out for a walk beside the beach, which had become my habit at that time as it was for the villagers. A light breeze from the sea refreshed me, and produced little white-horses in the bay. During the walk I would take a decision. Had I really considered everything fully? Was it not an unnecessarily risky adventure? Would it really help Juan José? Anyway, it was necessary to act quickly; what the next few days would bring could not be foreseen.

At the window of a watchmaker's I halted. A collection of Swiss wristwatches was displayed in it, and I went inside, without really knowing why. An old woman sat behind the counter; she stood up as I came in. She looked at me in a friendly manner and asked:

"What can I do for you?"

While I examined the watches that interested me, the old woman complained about the situation. She was older than I thought; she said she was over seventy. She was not afraid—what could happen to her now—but some of her children and grandchildren were on one side and some on the other, and they were drawn into fighting each other. . . . She paused, and sighed.

The woman looked at the gold wristwatch that I was wearing and was somewhat surprised when my final choice fell on a similar one. It was still wrapped up in an elegant little box with pretty paper and a multi-coloured cloth wrapping, as was the custom in feudal times. Her old fingers were still nimble and she knew her business; she knew human character too. By sticking on a label bearing a picture of St. George and the dragon, she completed the whole.

As she handed over the package, she said with a smile: "I hope the wearers of both watches will be very happy . . ."

I thanked her, and left the shop. When I was in the street, I looked back and saw a large picture of St. George and the dragon, Catalonia's patron saint, above the door. The shop bore the name *San Jorge*.

After a quick drink at one of the open-air cafés, I went straight back to my hotel. I had made up my mind; we would leave that night. And there was no time to lose.

III

Juan José sat on the cane chair in the bedroom. He had had a shower and looked refreshed. The shutters were open and the night air was flowing in.

"We're leaving this evening, Juanjo."

He looked at me with eyes that glowed with gratitude. I had the evening meal served in the bedroom, with the excuse that the boy was not wholly restored to health. We did not eat much; the excitement was playing tricks on us. We sat opposite each other as we ate, each with his own thoughts.

After paying the bill, and giving a good tip to the waiter—who accepted this capitalistic gesture without scruples—we got into the car. At eleven o'clock we drove off in the darkness. There were no problems in the village; everything was quiet, with only a few people to be seen in the streets. Once we had reached the main road, which twisted its way through the mountainous countryside beside the sea, we were accompanied by the moon and the stars. One bend followed another, we climbed, and on the right the sea glittered below us. The petrol tank was full and in the boot were two jerry-cans with five gallons in each. I had also to think of the boat. Its tank was also almost full, but that was certainly not enough to get us to the French frontier. Similarly, we would have to take care of drinking water and food too, as there was only a tin of biscuits on board. A small compass, a chart and a few other things that were required for navigation had been left in the small cabin. The boat was many years old, but despite that she was still in a good seaworthy condition. At this time of year, storms were very rare, so that there was no great danger on that account. We could make sail under the cover of darkness, with our lights doused . . .

After a severe hairpin bend our progress was interrupted by a large barricade erected across the road; only a small passage remained open on the left, just broad enough to allow a car to pass. A *miliciano* waved a lamp backward and forward and ordered us to stop. On the verge and at the barricade gun barrels could be seen.

"*Alto!*" said a voice.

I dimmed the lights and brought the car to a halt. A few moments later we were surrounded by a group of men.

"Your papers, comrade!"

The passport was passed from hand to hand; provoking praise for my country.

"And the boy?" I was asked.

The lamp was held high in front of the car, revealing the externally calm face of Juan José.

"He is my nephew," I said; "his papers are in Barcelona. We are on our way to get them now." I tried to keep my voice as ordinary as possible.

These circumstances did not appear to be for the best. The group considered what to do.

"You can go on, Señor, but the boy must get out."

"I can't leave my nephew behind on his own; I'm staying here too."

This appeared to complicate matters. They would have to go and speak to the Commandant. The group disappeared, leaving only two men beside the car.

Juan José had grasped my hand, and he held it tightly in his own. We said nothing and sat next to each other. We understood without words. Five hundred feet beneath us little wavelets were breaking against the steep rock wall. In the distance a dog was barking monotonously. It seemed like a century before the reply came. Finally it did.

"The Commandant is at the next barricade, about a mile and half down the road. You can drive as far as there, but we don't give much chance for the boy. Even if the Commandant lets him pass, he will still be stopped at the following barricade. Bon voyage."

I started the motor quickly and drove through the small opening. There was only one thought that crossed my mind, the only possible solution. A couple of hundred yards down the road was another bend. I switched off the lights and stopped. Then I walked to the back of the car and took the luggage out of the boot and put it on the rear seat.

"Quick, Juan José, get into the boot; there's a travelling rug in it, lie down on it!"

The boy disappeared in the cramped boot, and I shut the lid on him. A few minutes later I drove slowly up to the next barricade. Here, too, a lamp was waved to and fro.

"Good evening, comrade."

My passport was taken to the Commandant. If only he had not been warned! I got out of the car and walked up and down beside it. My eyes were on the road that we had just come along. If a messenger should happen to come along it. . . . These thoughts made me nervous. If they had sent somebody to follow us?

The commandant sent for me. I followed the half-uniformed *miliciano*. A young man wearing a beret was sitting on a crate in an improvised hut. He received me in a friendly manner and asked what the purpose of my journey was.

"I am on the way to my consulate, *Señor comandante*." I wondered whether I should still use the word *señor*, or if it was no longer acceptable in the present circumstances. I had no idea.

"What are you doing in Spain?"

"I am a tourist."

He expressed regret that my visit had been spoilt.

Ten minutes later I was back in my Ford. Then I froze: two small lights were coming towards us down the road. A car was approaching us, slowly but surely. Would everything now be lost?

The engine wouldn't start, too . . . at last it did . . .

"Bon voyage!"

Before the other car had arrived, I had left the barricade behind me. I put my foot down, but not for long, as a new barricade soon appeared, and the same routine began again.

"Your papers!"

No difficulties arose. I kept my eye on the road behind by means of the rearview mirror. You never can tell. And if they were to telephone a post on the way in to Barcelona, telling it to stop the car with the Venezuelan licence-plates. What then?

I stopped on an isolated part of the road, ran to the back, opened the boot and leaned over to ask: "Have you enough air?"

"Yes, Santiago."

"Everything is all right, my boy."

The boot was shut again, and we were off once more through the mountains. It was already long after midnight. The moon was hidden behind a hazy cloud, the sea was less bright. A couple of mules crossed the road, accompanied by a farm-worker.

They took fright at just the noise of the motor, and looked about in fear. Farther away a farm lay in darkness. Maize was hanging along a wall. Then came slopes covered with vineyards, a few palm-trees and grape-vines again. A hamlet, a small street, a few rows of houses, all in deep slumber. The countryside changed; it became flatter and the road straighter. A few lorries passed in the opposite direction, heading southwards. On a crag on the left-hand side stood the Casteldefels—the castle of the faithful—surrounded by agaves and cactus. And suddenly another barricade. Valuable minutes of delay. Then off again. And there were more of them.

The Ford was doing a good job. When I had decided to bring the car with me to Spain, I did not realize what a role the vehicle would play in these surroundings. My thoughts also went back to Caracas, on the other side of the ocean. How were the film studios doing? What a long way away all that was now, in another world. Did this all not seem like a film?

Ahead of me, the lights of the Catalonian capital, the metropolis Barcelona, were becoming brighter. The city with a million inhabitants and broad boulevards, tall buildings, the crowded Ramblas, the twin hills of Tibidabo and Montjuich, the Paralelo with its amusements and the statue of Columbus beside the harbour, pointing in the direction of America, the new world. We have a Barcelona in Venezuela, too . . .

A lamp, a pair of armed men, and another check-point.

"Get out of the car."

I stood beside the car.

"We have to search your car for weapons; orders of the commandant."

That was just what we needed! If only Juanjo would keep quiet! The bonnet was opened and a glance thrown to make sure that there was nothing hidden in it.

"What have you got in the boot? Will you open it?"

It was as if someone had given me a cold douche.

"There's nothing in it, only a spare tire. Unfortunately I have lost the key and can't open it any more. It's a great nuisance."

And the man tried the handle, but was unable to force it open. I had locked it. He looked inside the suit-cases. Suddenly he asked:

"Whisky?"

An idea shot through my mind. Perhaps this could save our lives.

"Yes, here you are—you can keep it, I'll get some more in town."

This struck home; the key to the boot was forgotten and we were off again towards the city. I drove through one of the suburbs, at some points the signs of past fighting were clearly visible: burnt-out trams and motor-cars, dead horses and broken-up streets. A few churches were still smouldering. A desolate sight. Occasional shots could be heard. The magnificent city lay like a wounded animal in the countryside; its injuries were many.

Gradually it got brighter, the stars grew pale and the air took on a grey tint. We had put the town and the working-class district of Badalona behind us, and the second part of the journey had begun. After we had passed the last houses—and left them a safe distance behind—I stopped the Ford beside the road, got out and took a deep breath. So far, all was well. The sun was just beginning to rise and the temperature to increase. After opening the boot I let Juan José get out. The boy was completely stiff as a result of having lain bent, and he needed a few minutes to recover. He walked back and forth and filled his lungs with fresh air, stretched himself several times and blinked in order to become reaccustomed to the light. We sat down on the running-board and gazed at the awakening countryside before us; the hills, the olive-trees and an abandoned broken-down house on which the letters P.O.U.M. had recently been painted. On one of the neighbouring hills stood an old tower, about ten feet high, which had been originally built by the Moors.

"I am a great nuisance for you, Santiago; without me you would already be at the border."

I felt that he was getting anxious.

"No nuisance at all, Juanjo, it's my pleasure, as you know." I paused, then continued, "I'm awfully thirsty, and perhaps you would like to eat something."

I took a thermos flask of coffee from the car and a few sandwiches that I had had made at the hotel.

Only when we began to eat, did we realise how far we had come. It did us good, and we continued our way refreshed, the boy in the back and I behind the wheel.

The traffic began to get thicker in both directions. The stream of refugees of the first days of the civil war had dried up, it now consisted of light vehicles and old trucks, as well as private cars with armed men in them. There were also all sorts of vehicles carrying food stuffs on the road. Beside it were various written messages. In some villages banners and portraits of the leaders were displayed. The form of greeting with raised left fist and the words *salud camarada* appeared to be the fashion. The number of red flags increased. By means of a screw driver jammed in between the lid of the baggage-compartment and the bodywork, a small opening was provided, almost invisibly, to let air and a small amount of light into the boot. In this way Juanjo could to some extent orient himself in the small space.

The road became worse, and holes in it more frequent. I had to reduce my speed significantly in order to avoid injuring the boy. Ultimately we were moving at barely walking-speed. There was a lot of dust on the road; after passing anything going the other way you could see little or nothing for a few seconds, until the cloud had settled.

In a small farming village, lying peacefully in a valley, I was able to obtain some more food: a bag of potatoes, some bread and maize. The little settlement lay so peacefully between the lovely hills that one could really not be aware here that a civil war was raging. There was not a single political slogan to be seen, nor any flags or weapons.

IV

It was the hottest hour of the day, and the sun was almost directly overhead the country home of my friend Esteban Muñoz, on the Costa Brava. It stood on its own here on a crag beside the sea and could only be reached by means of a small private road. A few fruit-trees stood in the garden, as did some plane-trees and agaves. A series of irregular steps led down to the little beach, which was completely surrounded by sheer cliffs, and could only be reached by these steps from the land. It was shaded by pine trees and a few stunted olive-trees. The house was coated with white lime, and the brown shutters were closed at this hour of the day. On the north side stood a pergola with a view along the coast, the hinterground and the bright sea.

Because the house was situated on a rise, the panorama was indescribably beautiful. Our host was an artist, and he had picked out this site many years before. There was no electric light; the pergola was lit by candles in colourful Chinese lanterns.

On the great iron garden gate a piece of paper had been attached, bearing the words *"propiedad extranjera"*—foreign property. The Venezuelan flag was flying from the mast in this enclosed piece of ground . . .

Esteban was amazed at my return after so short a time. He had not thought it to be possible. There were so many tales to tell about it, but when I opened the luggage-compartment, he had to laugh heartily.

"Welcome, my boy"—he said in a friendly voice.

We sat in the shade beneath the pergola. A row of red geraniums contrasted strongly with the white. Jaime, the butler, brought drinks. I lay down on a comfortable chaise-longue and let the ambiance have its effect on me; here everything was suddenly so completely different. Juan José stretched his limbs and walked up and down a little. Esteban, seated in a rocking-chair, described the neighbourhood. His wife Elvira sat beside him, occupied with her handwork; she was a native of Catalonia.

I was too tired to talk much and I preferred to listen. At times events of the past twenty-four hours came into my mind, then my thoughts turned to what was yet to come. Jaime appeared and announced that the meal was ready to be served. We went indoors; it was more sheltered there, which gave a pleasant feeling of coolness and equilibrium. Esteban gave a toast to our friendship. In days gone by we had been at school together in Caracas, and he had later come to live here, mainly for the sake of his wife who had found it difficult to settle down anywhere else. In the course of time he had come to love the country like his own, so that it was more than a second homeland to him. His forté was painting landscapes and sea; only a few weeks before there had been an exhibition of his most recent works in a small gallery off the *Paseo de Gracia* in Barcelona. How that was doing now he did not know, nor did he care. Esteban was a born optimist; it had been just the same when he was at the primary school in Venezuela. Now Muñoz belonged among the leading figures in the world of art, and his paintings had an international market.

The meal was served. Jaime waited at the table, wearing white gloves. The revolution had not yet penetrated here.

After the meal, coffee was served in an adjoining room. Esteban asked about my plans.

"I need your help, Esteban."

"Whatever you want. I have never forgotten how, when we were still both children and I was younger and weaker than you, you came to my rescue when our school-fellows wanted to throw me into the swimming-pool despite the fact that I was unable to swim. I was really scared to death and was almost in despair. I screamed, and you were the only one who appreciated my distress, who stepped into the breach and finally got me out of the hands of the boys. And thus ran the risk of reprisals. You have helped me more than once when I have been in need, you appreciated me so much." He paused a moment, then continued: "I don't think you have changed, for that matter." He looked across at Juan José. . . . "I have never been able to do something for you, and I have been waiting for this opportunity."

Jaime came in:

"Don Esteban, it is almost time for the news-bulletin."

"Thank you, Jaime."

The radio was switched on, and the newsreader related the progress that had been made at the fronts.

Elvira and Juan José had retired for their siestas. The boy needed to sleep after the exertion of the drive. In the meanwhile, I discussed with Esteban the possibility of reaching France in the motorboat.

"A very risky experiment, dear Santiago; if they catch you, your foreign passport won't do you much good, and the distance is very great for such a little old boat. All the same, if . . . " After a short pause, he continued, "What do you need? My reserves of fuel and food are at your disposal, you know I look on you as a friend." A little later he added: "Now I am sure that you are still the same as you used to be." Esteban smiled and rang the bell which stood on the table beside the cups. Jaime appeared.

"My guest needs one or two things. Will you give him a hand this evening after the sun has set?"

"Yes, Don Esteban, I'll take care of him."

When the butler had disappeared, Esteban remarked, "A good and trusty servant, one of the old school, who considers it an honour to be of service."

We then recalled a few memories of days long ago when we had been together. In conclusion we drank a glass of sherry under the pergola, and watched the sun disappear beneath the horizon. The gramophone played saetas, fandanguillos and fandangos from the southern provinces and sardanas from the neighbouring district softly in the background. It had been an unforgettable afternoon. Darkness fell swiftly, and it was time to act. I put Juan José on watch from the flat roof—armed with a telescope—for *carabineros* or other unwelcome visitors. At his age this was something important, and I was convinced that he would do his best more than an adult would have done. With Jaime, I descended to the cellar and looked for what would be essential for the sea-journey; first of all we filled several containers with fuel, which we three—Esteban, Jaime and I—carried down to the beach, where I began by filling the fuel tank to the brim. Then we stored the containers as well as possible within the ship. I had just put the last one on board when Juan José came up to us panting.

"Stop everything, at once!"

We hid ourselves in a cave as quickly as possible. Just afterwards we heard the faint noise of a motorboat and the beam of a searchlight swept over the rocks. . . . We had got out of the way just in time, less than three seconds later the light shone onto the beach. . . . The voices aboard the motor-boat could be heard through the still air: "Nothing unusual, a deserted beach with a little boat. . . . That must surely belong to the artist."

They were obviously searching for something else. The light went out and the boat continued towards the south. Juan José stood close beside me; I could feel and hear his heart beating, his head resting on my shoulder.

The danger had receded. Still frightened, we climbed up the irregular steps. The boy disappeared to his look-out post again, and we carried down tins filled with drinking-water. An hour later we had completed loading the stores. If only the boat did not seem to be too heavily laden. Well, in that case we could put something or other over the side. I felt my muscles; they were not accustomed to taking me up and down so many irregular steps, nor to carrying such loads.

Elvira had prepared hot coffee in thermos flasks, and she came again with a couple of bars of chocolate.

Everything was ready for the departure. I checked that nothing had been forgotten: compass, chart. . . . Oh, yes, the flag that I had flown on my car, that might well come in handy. I left the Ford in Esteban's hands.

The moment of departure approached. Esteban squeezed my hand. Elvira kissed Juan José on the forehead and said: "may God protect you." Esteban put his hand on his shoulder: "you are in very good hands."

We made a final round to see if everything was safe. Esteban and Jaime came down to the beach with us in order to help with pushing the boat into the water. We had some difficulty in getting it to move. I had put on my swimming-costume and stowed my clothes in the cabin, so that I could push the boat the first hundred yards—to outside the little bay—without starting the motor. Everything was settled. Esteban and Jaime would return to the house as soon as the boat was launched, for any contingencies. Juan José was shown how to start the motor and how to use the oars. Elvira kept watch from above. The boat slipped into the water. The sea was very calm. The cold water did me good. Prudently I pushed the boat out of the bay, and a few minutes later I climbed on board. Juan José tried to start the motor; after a few misfires it caught and the boat began to move under its own power. Seconds later two shots sounded and a voice from the cliffs shouted:

"Halt!"

I pulled Juan José into the cabin and went to take the helm. The motor was doing its duty and the distance from the coast was increasing steadily. We heard a few more shots and a bullet struck the deck right beside my feet. Then it was quiet.

We were now well away from the coast. I thought anxiously about Esteban, Elvira and Jaime. If they were to get into any trouble . . .

On the ship's bow, the previous owner had had the word *Salvador*—Saviour—painted. I hoped it would be appropriate . . .

After setting the helm I went down into the cabin to get the compass. Juan José took one look at me and blurted out: "You're bleeding, Santi!"

A trickle of blood was running down my left arm. I looked at the wound; the bullet that had struck the deck had also grazed my arm, fortunately, it had caused only superficial damage. In the excitement I had not noticed it.

Juan José washed the wound and wrapped a bandage around it. I sat down on the edge of the small bunk. The boy was putting so much care and devotion into his work!

"You have done this sort of thing before, Juanjo."

"No, but if you like somebody, you know just what to do, it comes naturally . . ."

We looked at each other and laughed.

V

The water lapped gently against the wooden hull of the fragile vessel, which rocked slightly on the calm sea. The motor made the only mechanical noise with its monotonous purring at that time of night, beneath the starry sky which now seemed to be brighter than the land. We had first sailed a few miles out to sea, and now we were heading northwards. The coast was no longer in sight. Sometimes a fish would come into view, then it would disappear with a flick of its tail into the depth. The *Salvador* bore herself according to all the rules of the art; we had indeed to put part of the stores overboard, as she lay too deep and was thus unable to make full speed ahead. We doused the lamp on board, as it was not needed and might also reveal our position. During the voyage, a weak wind got up. It was indeed beneficial. Juan José sat on the fore-deck—a triangular space adjoining the cabin—and peered silently over the water. What was he thinking about, the past or the future?

I lay comfortably on a pair of red cushions beside the helm, my head did not protrude above the gunwale and my left hand resting on the tiller. My feet were wedged against the sill of the low cabin door, which stood ajar. The green superstructure of the cabin contrasted with the yellow planks of the fore and afterdecks. The previous owner had kept her in good repair, you could tell by the paint. A sail could be hoisted on the short mast, and in favourable wind that could be important. Although the distance that had to be covered was not very great, it was doubtful whether the fuel would be sufficient. There was a bench on the left of the cabin, which could also serve as a bed. A mattress and other bedding were available. On the right was a folding-table—on which the chart of the coastal area lay open, with a few books—and a folding-chair with a collapsible back-rest. The associated cushions were hanging on the wall beside a picture of the holy Saviour. A small blue tile with a portrait of the black 'Virgin of Montserrat' was inlaid on the right side of the front bulkhead. Swinging gently next to it on a little chain was a small wrought-iron candle-holder. The slender, finely-made candle had already been used. Nothing in the interior had been altered since I had owned it, apart from the new oil-lamp at the ceiling.

The outer walls were partly white and green. A small anchor hung from the bow. The motor was located at the stern and was of British make.

We had been travelling for several hours, and it was after midnight. It was cooler, even fresh. The dark, slim—though sturdy—boy's figure stood up and came astern, past the mast above the cabin. A little later he sat down on the cushions beside me, put on a poncho, and pressed his head against my chest. I had put on a woolen jersey shortly before, and lit my pipe. The aroma of the tobacco mingled with the sea air. Beside me was a thermos flask that Elvira had filled before our departure. I unscrewed the top and discovered a piece of paper inside. By the light of a match I read the following message in Catalan: *Deu vos guard*—"may God protect you." I read it out aloud and poured out the coffee. We drank it turn and turn about.

"You have good friends, Santi," said Juan José looking up at me. "I had already seen the little bay where the *Salvador* was kept, you know," he added.

"How was that?"

"In a painting at home. It was by Esteban Muñoz; I looked at the signature on the canvasses yesterday afternoon and compared them with that of the painting at my home."

The boat began to roll; a light south-west wind had arisen. Juan José snuggled a bit closer to me and put his arm around my shoulder.

"Santi, there is such a lot I want to tell you." He paused, then continued: "You don't even know my last name."

It was a very well-known name. His father apparently had become a prominent figure in political life, on the far right. A few hours before he had been taken away he had had a talk with his son on whom he had impressed the need to try to reach France if anything went wrong. His father intended to leave that day, to stay with acquaintances and remain in hiding there, but was too late. Juan José recounted all this with difficulty, at times the words appeared to stick in his throat.

"Then they came to take him away . . . several men pushed him out of the house . . . I stood beside the stairs . . . when they came past me, my father again said . . . do what I told you . . . " He burst into tears. I hugged the boy to me and let him continue his story.

"A few hours later he was found by the roadside . . . shot dead . . . finally I made up my mind to run away, without knowing exactly what I was doing . . . "

I poured out some more coffee and let him drink. It restored him somewhat.

"For a couple of days I wandered about . . . nothing could make any more difference to me . . . "

He took another swallow of coffee, put his head close beside mine, and said softly: "and then came my salvation. I felt that something must happen, anyway when I was walking along the beach path I saw a stone bench with you sitting on it. I wavered. You looked at me in such a friendly way that I was quite at ease . . . I felt something very special inside me . . . something that was new to me . . . and can't be expressed in words . . . it really came down to feeling safe and secure. I did not know that anything so sudden could exist, merely as soon as our eyes first met, before we had exchanged a single word. I had the feeling I would be helped . . . and I was not mistaken."

He kissed me lightly on the forehead, got up quickly and disappeared into the cabin.

I understood his sudden reaction; he was feeling ashamed. A few moments later, when I had checked the course and set the helm, I descended the few steps down to the cabin too.

"I could not have put it better myself, Juanjo; indeed I could not. I, too, had the same feelings, and I too had never felt them so strongly before; if you had not suffered so much misery—and if the country was not at war—those hours would have been the happiest of my life," I added, with a smile. "You speak the language of Cervantes like an adult, you have a gift for it."

"I am one year older today: today is my thirteenth birthday."

I stood up and looked out to see if there were any ships in the neighbourhood. I then lighted the candle beside the tile with the picture of the Virgin of Montserrat. The cabin became somewhat sombre, yet festive. Out of a box I took a small elegantly wrapped package with a multi-coloured ribbon around it and a label from San Jorge on the side. I presented it to my young friend.

"Happy birthday, Juanjo!"

His dark eyes sparkled and widened in the candle-light. He eagerly opened the package with his fine dark fingers. The golden watch glittered . . .

"Santi, you shouldn't have! You are really too kind . . . "

I took the watch, and fastened it around his small boyish wrist. It was a bit loose, but he pushed it enthusiastically up his arm and then it fitted. I was reminded of the words spoken by the old woman in the shop, which now made sense: that the wearers of both watches would be very happy.

We drank a glass of red wine from the forecastle. It gave Juanjo a touch of colour. I suggested that he should get a couple of hours' sleep, so that he could then take the helm while I took a rest.

"Telling you about myself has done me so much good that now I feel quite relieved, almost a new person."

A few minutes later he was asleep. The night gave way to the first glimmerings of dawn. I took a small telescope to scan the horizon. The coastline was faintly visible in the West, probably a prominent rock. In any case, we were on the right course, that was the most important thing. A tunny kept pace with the *Salvador*, swimming back and forth or diving and then surfacing again. It was as if the fish enjoyed looking at the boat from all angles. It was a large specimen, and sometimes it swam so close to the boat that its wake sprinkled the deck.

The sail was hoisted in order to take advantage of the south-western wind, and so to save fuel. Juanjo had already been asleep for five hours; I couldn't bring myself to waken him as he lay there so peacefully and confidently.

The new day was not so bright as the previous one had been.

We were already further north, which showed itself in the climate. The sea was somewhat rougher. At about eight o'clock a plume of smoke could be seen on the eastern horizon. I quickly took down the sail and altered course slightly. Just as it appeared that things were going to turn out badly, the vessel, which looked like a warship, suddenly stopped coming towards us and steamed off into the distance.

I prepared coffee and toast in the small galley. Juan José awoke in the meanwhile and looked proudly at his watch.

"Why didn't you wake me earlier?"

The toast and coffee tasted good. I explained how to hold the right course and hung the spyglass around the boy's neck.

"Sleep tight" he told me in his clear voice. A few moments later I dropped like a log onto the bunk, having had no sleep for the past two nights.

My dreams were confused to begin with, later I saw attractive landscapes with lush vegetation, where it was good to be alive . . . peace on earth, said the people . . . a golden gondola lay on a beach with a handsome boy standing upright on it, calling to me in a friendly voice . . . graceful birds flying in the clear blue sky . . . Caracas, my street and my flat . . . a friendly boy on the doorstep. . . .

It was midday when I awoke. Through the door I saw Juan José sitting with the tiller in his hand, keeping a lookout in all directions. Everything had been cleared away, plates and glasses washed and put away. My arm hurt. The boat rolled and through one of the portholes I saw a threatening sky in the east. I stood up and put the water on to cook a couple of pounds of potatoes that had not been thrown overboard. I opened a tin of meat.

Juan José had maintained a good course and was proud of it.

"Did you know that you spoke in your sleep, Santi?"

"What did I say then, I wonder."

He did not answer, but began to talk about other things. We ate our meal on the rear deck. The tunny had deserted us, and the *Salvador* sailed on alone towards the French coast.

VI

Dark threatening clouds hung over the sea. It was already several hours since it had been blue, and now it consisted of a great moving mass with white tops. The freshening wind made the waves rise higher, and in the distance summer lightning flickered from time to time. The thunderstorm came steadily nearer and we could hear the thunder roll above the noise of the sea. The *Salvador* rolled on the storm-tossed water; the bow dipped sharply and then rose again with a jerk from time to time, the propeller coming right out of the water occasionally and causing the motor to scream as the speed rose when the load was removed. The sail had been taken down, and the cushions and other loose items on deck put in the cabin. Below decks, the table and chair had been stowed away and everything fastened down as far as possible, the oil-lamp and candle-holder put into a box, the tins of fuel and food tied down, portholes and cabin-door shut tight. Occasionally the top of a wave broke over the foredeck. The wind was from the north and the boat had difficulty in making any way against the storm.

At about noon there was a heavy rain-shower. The water streamed down, as was often the case in that part of the world. You could not see for more than a few hundred yards, which represented a danger for a vessel sailing close to the rocky coast of the Costa Brava. Flashes of lightning lit up the sea again and again, and the thunder was deafening.

There was no question of cooking now. The boat began to rock heavily from side to side and the joints creaked as one wave after another came over the deck. It was with difficulty that we kept her heading into the waves. We ate some old bread and drank milk from a tin.

The anchor had worked loose, and was hanging a few feet under water. With difficulty we hauled it aboard the fore-deck and lashed it fast. The motor, which had kept going well so far, began to run warm and its exhaust note became irregular.

The storm drove fiercely over the boiling water. Suddenly, the rain stopped and it started to get brighter, but the force of the wind did not diminish, however. The waves were like hills which rolled threateningly down onto us. Fortunately neither of us had more than a touch of sea-sickness, which would have made our situation considerably worse. I had attached the boy to a cord so that he was free to move about but could not fall overboard. Although he could swim, it would have been very difficult to fish him out of the water again.

Then came the moment that I will never forget: the motor stopped and we ceased moving through the water, which made the boat difficult to steer. She drifted round to lie parallel to the direction of the waves, and the danger that she might overturn was not imaginary. Like a toy ball she had become the plaything of the waves, completely off her course. With the greatest difficulty I managed to bring her head round to face into the waves again. It began to look very black for us and I reproached myself. Had I not been stupid and gambled with Juan José's life and my own? Had I not been too rash? The boy appeared to read my thoughts and took my hand in his own. "Don't reproach yourself, Santiago," he said.

How remarkable all this was. We only had known each other for such a short time, and yet it was as if we had been together for our whole lives. Chance had brought us together, on a stone bench, one summer's day beside the blue Mediterranean Sea. We were created for each other; I was increasingly conscious how great my affection for this boy was. Despite the dangers we had encountered, we remained completely calm and unworried—we were above all together. Could anything more beautiful exist?

At about four o'clock the storm had reached its peak. A few planks of the deck had worked loose and the water began to leak into the cabin. We took turns at bailing; the water was about four or six inches deep and if it were not stopped the worst could be expected.

The storm abated quite suddenly at sunset. The rough sea was transformed quickly into calm water, the wind dropped and the clouds disappeared. Standing on the after-deck, we had just the time to see the sun go down like a ball of fire, then darkness fell rapidly and the stars came out. The helm was back in its former place, but it was too dark to repair the motor without a lamp. We therefore sat in the dim light cast by the oil lamp. Fortunately the motor was of a simple design, so that anyone with a little technical knowledge could see how it worked. Nonetheless it took us several hours to get it running again. With less than half power the *Salvador* set off again; various pipes leaked and the fuel consumption had increased alarmingly, so that we would soon run short. But we were not worried about that then, we were so happy that we had come through the storm intact. With the help of the compass we took up the correct course again, although we did not know our position.

We took turns to sleep, four hours at a time. The motor was running irregularly, but the *Salvador* crept forward. The next morning the weather was superb: the clothes dried in the sun, as did the cushions that had been soaked. We repaired the deck as well as possible and fixed the loose planks in place again. The vessel had really suffered in the storm.

My thoughts were occupied with the boy's future. What would he become—a refugee? Where would he ultimately go? He had not spoken much about his uncle, whom he knew only slightly as he had met him only once, many years before in Barcelona. Could I not take him with me back to Venezuela? He could complete his *bachillerato*—secondary school—studies there. One thing seemed to be likely: that the civil war would continue for quite a long time, especially now that foreign intervention was being talked about, according to the latest bulletins. Was it not the case that the boy wanted to stay with me? He was intelligent, adroit, and above all balanced. Was he not turning the cruel blow that fate had struck him into something positive? How had I come to do all this so suddenly for some other person? It remained evenly balanced until I took a decision. Yes, I would let him be educated in Caracas in a direction that he himself would choose, and in an environment of peace he could work in future. Was this boy's future not in my hands . . . Was I not responsible? But how to make all this into practical reality. Could the official agencies supply the necessary papers? It would not succeed. . . . Yes, it must succeed; as soon as we arrive in France I will go and arrange everything with the French officials—and at my consulate. But I needed his family's authorization. As his parents were no longer alive, his uncle would have to provide it . . .

Without my noticing it, Juan José had come and sat down close beside me on the after-deck. Suddenly I heard his tender voice:

"Santi, I scarcely dare to ask you, you have already done so much for me, even putting yourself into danger. Can I come with you to South America?"

Were we so close to each other than our thoughts passed between us? I bent over, looked him straight in the eyes and whispered in his ear:

"I shall do everything to make it possible."

"Thank you—*querido* Santiago."

With a tranquil and contented expression he gazed over the water towards the north, where a new life would begin at the invisible coast. His hand remained in mine.

"Have you ever thought about the distant future? What do you want to be when you grow up?"

He did not reply at once.

"I don't want to be a burden to you, Santi, I will find work as quickly as possible so that I can earn money and . . ."

"That's not what I meant, *querido* Juanjo; you are no burden, on the contrary I will help you willingly as I feel myself linked with you in such a special way. My only wish is that all will go well with you and that you become whatever you can be happy at being."

"Nobody has ever appreciated and understood me so well before. I didn't know that any such thing really existed, but thought that it was possible only in fantasy."

"Yes, Juanjo, despite the present circumstances we are enjoying something that is very beautiful and sublime."

After a hot meal which consisted of an omelette, rice and tinned vegetables, I made my way to the cabin for my siesta. Through the doorway I saw my young friend sitting proudly at the helm, with his slim muscular left arm on the tiller and his right arm on a cushion. With complete confidence, I fell asleep a few minutes later.

VII

Another night drew on. The fuel was nearly exhausted . . . and still the French coast did not come into sight. We had peered with great hopes to the north through the telescope, but in vain. The *Salvador* must have been driven some distance east by the storm. We didn't even approximately know our position. As the wind had dropped, the sail hung limply from the mast, and due to a weak current we drifted southwards. The worst thing was the decrease in the stock of drinking-water, so that this was rationed. By my reckoning we might end up somewhere to the south of Port Vendres— just past the Spanish frontier . . .

Juan José sat on the fore-deck in order to keep a look-out, with a white towel over his shoulders contrasting with the brown colour of his young limbs. He had made himself a hat out of an old newspaper in order to protect his head from the sunshine. I could watch him like that for hours without becoming bored, there was always something new. Sometimes he would look around with a smile, so his pearly-white teeth gleamed in the sunlight, and in a boyish way he would raise his right hand in a sign of greeting. On his left wrist glittered the gold watch at which he glanced from time to time like a child. Later on he went and lay on his back on the cabin roof, clad only in a brief coloured loincloth; his well-built youthful body had something fascinating about it. His right hand played with a piece of cord that had come loose from the sail. His thick black hair was matted, and hung in clumps over his forehead; his dark brown eyes scanned the skies, his long black eyelashes stood out clearly from the skin, like fine whiskers, his just visible ribs rose and fell with his breathing; his long slim bones and well-shaped muscles were continually in motion. He made me think of a noble thoroughbred. . . . From time to time he turned his head, without raising it, towards me and asked questions like:

"What did you do when you were thirteen?"

I had to think about my answer.

"I had already been living in Caracas for several years, and I was going to school there. I was born in Mérida, in the interior. We moved to Caracas because my father got a government job there. He had become a minister some time before. We lived in a large house in the suburbs."

Juan José began to recount his own life in detail. It was a pleasure to listen to his beautiful Spanish; his lips moving quickly and his elegant hands gesticulating gracefully. At the end of his story he became aware of his situation again, and the so fatal early

days of the civil war came back into his mind. He stood up slowly and came towards me, sat down and leant his head against my shoulder. He said, falteringly:

"My poor father—I will never forget him . . . I said so many things against him that I shouldn't have . . . and had rows with him sometimes . . . now I can do nothing about it, never put things right . . . I feel so ashamed . . . Oh, Santi, how miserable can anyone feel."

"Yes, Juanjo, we all do things like that. Later we are sorry but we cannot change things afterwards, no matter how much we would like to. It's always the same story. You aren't the only one. You probably don't see things in proportion now; time will change that, and heal a lot. By seeing things in proportion I mean that you put too much emphasis on particular events, as if you saw them through a magnifying glass. Just tell me what is on your mind."

Still leaning against me, he continued talking. It had to come out, he had to tell somebody. I listened attentively, without saying a word. When he had finished he looked at me and said gently:

"Santi, your eyes are wet, you're crying."

He went down into the cabin and got a handkerchief which he held lovingly against my eyes. I took his head in both hands and kissed his luxuriant hair . . .

"You are an angel, Juanjo."

A gentle breeze began to blow, and the sail caught it so that the *Salvador* got slowly under way. The water gurgled softly again against the bow, and from time to time small fish would leap out of the water not far away. Despite the so-peaceful scene, I began to get more and more anxious; no land had yet come into sight, just water and still more water. Where were we? Could the *Salvador* really have drifted so far? I had now set course in a westerly direction instead of heading north. My plan was to sail as far north as necessary once the coast was in sight. We could keep going for a couple of meals more, then our drinking water would run out . . . The food appeared to be sufficient for several more days. We kept the daily ration of drinking water in a bottle hanging overboard at the end of a cord, so that it was pulled through the seawater. The day wore on without incident.

In the evening, Juan José toasted some old bread over the open flame of the little cookstove and opened a tin of butter. I put him on watch; in that way he could be usefully occupied and express his devotion.

Afterwards, he brought the cooled water back on board and filled two glasses with it. We then sat on the deck to eat while the day drew to its close. That was a particularly delightful evening; at sunset the sky continually changed colour. I lit a cigarette, inhaled deeply, and blew the smoke out in front of me with a sigh.

"Can I have one too, Santi?"

I had pleasure in his smoking. He exhaled the smoke in short puffs . . .

"Did you ever do something you shouldn't have done in the past?" He looked at me in a special way as he asked me this question.

"All boys do that, indeed that is normal . . . "

We drank our glasses dry as if it were the most precious wine. In fact, that was the case. Juan José cleared the things away and hung another bottle in the sea, softly humming a tune which resounded with a subtly arabian effect over the surrounding water. Suddenly he was silent and pointed to the west. In an excited voice he said:

"Santi, I can see land, a rock!"

With emotion I took the telescope and looked. Yes indeed! There was something that seemed like a rock, sticking out of the water. The *Salvador* drew slowly nearer to it. In the meanwhile, it had become quite dark. The little speck got bigger and appeared to move . . . there was something floating on the water . . . it looked like a little boat. We looked at each other in astonishment. No reply came to our shouts . . .

When we came alongside, we could see by the light of the oil-lamp that there was nobody aboard her; the little boat had deliberately had holes shot in her and was drifting in an unseaworthy state. What drama had been played aboard her? The name *Margarita* was painted on her transom in small letters. Soon afterwards we left the wreck behind.

The next morning found the *Salvador* among low-lying white clouds that seemed to float upon the water and almost completely obstructed all sight. It was as if we were gliding; everything seemed unreal, even our voices sounded strange. . . . It was humid, and everything was damp. The wind had dropped again, and the sail hung limp and useless from the mast.

The mist remained unchanged, as if it wanted never to go away. Suddenly, a silver bird flew over our heads, and we looked up in surprise. In the distance a fog-horn sounded. . . . We held our breath and listened attentively, eagerly trying to identify the direction of the sound.

Without any warning, a threatening black shadow loomed out of the mist and headed rapidly in our direction. I grasped the boy by the arm, ready to jump. A collision seemed to be inevitable . . .

▽

PART TWO

VIII

It was ten years later, August 1946. The din of heavy traffic flowed in through the open windows of my office in one of the main arteries of Caracas, an office arranged on modern lines on the fifth floor of a tall new building. The town had been growing rapidly; oil and everything connected with it had made that possible. There were extensive plans for whole new residential areas on the site of old ones . . . Modern schools and hospitals were springing up. The North American influence was increasingly apparent on the architecture.

In the avenues beneath my windows the cars were following each other in files; sometimes traffic jams were unavoidable. A large insurance company had established its headquarters on the other side of the road. The evenings were animated by the neon signs flashing on and off.

The office was bright and cool. On the grey steel desk lay the day's correspondence. Some photographs and a painting of Rio de Janeiro decorated its walls. There was a knock on the door and my secretary came in.

"Señor Capmany, will you sign this letter too, please; it's about our Mexican contract."

Her very well-looked-after fingers with painted nails placed the paper to be signed on the blotter in front of me with a familiar gesture. She remained—as always—waiting while my eyes ran over the text. In the meanwhile she arranged some curls of her hair with her right hand. She was an accurate worker who took pleasure in her duties and who, without doubt had a certain affection for her boss, without however ever thinking about it . . .

"Señorita Jimenez, everything is as it should be; you can send the letter."

I signed it and leaned back in my chair. With satisfaction she took up the letter with her supple hands and in a voice that indicated agreement, she said:

"Yes, Señor Capmany, I will have it posted at once; it will still catch the evening plane."

She disappeared with careful steps on her high heels through the leather-panelled door, which she closed quietly behind her. Señorita Jimenez had been my secretary for several years, and was now an indispensable asset. The telephone rang and I picked up the handset. It was apparently a long-distance call, from Maracaibo. A business contact wanted some information about a film.

In my usual way I drove home that evening to my flat on the outskirts of the town. Sitting on the balcony there I read the evening paper and looked at a few pages dealing with the cinema. As I lived on the top floor the view included an unobstructed sight of the sea of rooftops, and after sunset there were tens of thousands of little lamps twinkling around me. It was just the right kind of place for meditating and philosophising . . .

The maid, Enriqueta, brought me the whisky and a soda syphon at about ten o'clock. I switched the radio on and listened to Argentinean tangos, sung by Carlos Gardel. The melancholy, but also stimulating music gave a very definite frame to the whole. Deep in thought, I looked out before me towards the Venezuelan capital and the starry firmament.

The years slipped away, the scene changed. The Catalonian adventure . . . Dear me, how long ago all that was. The Spanish civil war came to an end in 1939; the last communiqué was issued on the first of April that year. After almost three years of turmoil. Who would have thought so in the days of July 1936 . . .

General Franco's troops had ultimately won, the country had taken a right turn. Slowly it recovered from its deep wounds. A quite considerable number of refugees remained abroad, in South France, North Africa and Mexico. A government in exile was formed.

Shortly afterwards, still in 1939, the second world war broke out, in which a whole series of countries were involved. The atomic age began. Now everything was peaceful again, humanity breathed again.

With a certain melancholy my thoughts went back—after all those years—to the Costa Brava.

What a wonderfully delightful experience that had been. A photograph of a small boy stood on my writing-table, a smiling Juan José. He still occupied a large place in my now somewhat older heart. From time to time I saw the events again—as in a film—our first meeting, our sea-voyage, the *Salvador*, our so-extraordinary rescue . . . our jumping into the water after the collision . . . the helpful crew . . . the friendly face of the captain of the *Ville d'Oran*, the steamship making its way from Algiers to Marseille . . . our great delight on arriving in France.

The attempts to be able to take the boy with me . . . my return journey to South America . . . and then the letter from Juan José's uncle in Perpignan, with the terrible contents which made me despair . . . the boy had unexpectedly died after a short illness . . . I could not accept it, it was too bad . . .

Time heals all wounds, at least partially. The memory remains.

My whisky-glass was dry and the radio programme had come to an end. I stood up and switched off the set. It was already late at night and the town was asleep. I took a couple of deep breaths and went to bed.

The next week I was fully occupied by business; it was one thing after another, and scarcely any day went by without a business lunch or dinner. Señorita Jimenez, who was never unwell, had to stay in bed for a fortnight because of an ear inflammation. One of the typists, Señorita Vargas, did her work for better or for worse. She was of a completely different type, somewhat on the stout side, who did not have such an elegant way of putting letters on my desk for signature. However, she possessed a number of positive qualities.

Somewhat later in the month a cousin of mine and her husband came from Mérida to spend a few days in the capital, where they stayed at the Hotel Imperial. We spent the last weekend in August together at a small resort on the Caribbean coast, where we went water-skiing with her friends. I took the opportunity, however, to go and see Esteban, who had left Spain with Elvira during the civil war after his country retreat near Tamariú had been completely looted by the mobs. They had now been living here for several years, although Elvira was occasionally nostalgic for her homeland.

Esteban sat on the terrace with his easel, working on a painting of some fishing-boats. He was glad to see me.

"Welcome—Santiago, it's already six months since you were last here. How's everything doing, old chap?"

Elvira came outside. She still looked quite young for her age, although she had indeed changed considerably since when she was at Tamariú.

"*Deu vos guard*," she said in Catalan.

Sitting there we quickly got into animated conversation. Her nine-year-old daughter, Pepita, was playing with some friends in the garden.

"How are the sales of your paintings going, Esteban?"

"I can't complain; this week I received a commission to do a seascape for the new town hall. It must be going in the entrance-hall."

Elvira took up her needlework, just as she had on the Costa Brava . . .

The same evening I returned to the city with my relations from Mérida.

The fresh air and the water-sports had given me a healthy feeling of tiredness. When I got home, I relaxed, took a shower, and went to bed. On the bedside table, beside the latest issue of *Time* magazine, was a volume of poems by Ramirez which I had bought at a kiosk a few days before. I took the book, and began to read. The poems expressed so great a sensitivity, and I was taken by them to such an extent, that I had not switched the light off several hours later. A short poem entitled *to a dead friend* was the best that I had ever read. It was certainly as good as anything by Walt Whitman.

IX

It was October and the *fiesta de la raza*, the day on which the whole Spanish-speaking world commemorates its collective heritage. Although the former extensive Spanish colonial territory had split up into a series of independent states in Central and South America during the nineteenth century, the Spanish stamp remained on the region, in particular through the language and the religion. Brazil is the exception here, because of its Portuguese origins.

This day fell during my holidays; I had decided to take a week's rest at home, rather than travel as I usually did. Enriqueta had already set breakfast in the *comedor*—dining-room. A little later I got up, and after a refreshing shower I sat down at the table with the morning newspaper. I was principally interested in the list of the day's events; it appeared that there were plenty of things to do. The fan hummed above my head in its usual way, doing its best to provide some cooling. After a visit to the hairdresser's, I lunched with some friends in the club. The conversation, and the subsequent discussion, was in the domain of philosophy, and about Ortega y Gasset and his book *The Revolt of the Masses* in particular. The ladies present preferred to talk about the latest fashions.

Afterwards, I drank a cup of black coffee with a dash of cognac beneath a sunshade. Not very far away the traffic held my attention, especially the latest models of cars from the United States. How their bodywork design had changed during the past few years. It was good to be sitting and relaxing here, on the terrace, which was occupied by only a few small tables and surrounded by plants in tubs. It was that afternoon that I had the most remarkable—both surprising and at the same time delightful—experience of my life.

The waiter had just brought me a second cup of coffee when my eyes fell on a young man sitting reading at a table to my right, I don't know why . . . he reminded me of somebody . . . no, that was impossible . . . ! Suddenly he pushed the sleeve of his left arm up a little way with his right hand and looked at his watch . . . my heart began to pound . . . I was no longer puzzled . . . it was the golden watch from the shop with San Jorge over the door . . . and that gesture, which I had seen so many times before, could only mean that it was . . .

The young man suddenly glanced in my direction, as if he also felt my anxiety, doubt, fear and hope. His dark eyes looked straight at me . . . I felt as if I could sink through the floor . . .

He stood up slowly and walked hesitantly towards my table. Without warning he greeted me:

"Santiago . . . "

"But this is crazy . . . Juanjo . . . how on earth . . . no . . . "

I stood up automatically and we shook hands, as we had done more than ten years before and many thousand miles away somewhere on the Mediterranean sea . . .

We both had difficulty in controlling our emotions, tears filled our eyes. We didn't understand . . .

Juan José was the first to speak.

"Why did my uncle get a letter in 1936 that you . . . were dead? I . . . "

"Oh, dear Juanjo, I received a letter like that too, telling me that you had died unexpectedly . . . and for ten long years I have been living with the belief that you were no longer alive . . . "

"I think I am beginning to understand a bit better."

He looked straight in front of him and reflected. A great bitterness came into his face, similar to hate. I had never seen him look like that before.

"I suspect my uncle did it. Yes, I'm virtually sure it was him. That was really something for him. Look, Santiago, he disliked the link between us, he couldn't stand you and so he thought of this . . . How could anybody be so rotten. I never want to see him again, never again!"

"In other words, you think he staged the whole business? That he really murdered both of us somewhere, Juan José?"

His uncle had thus given Juan José false news and had written me a false letter. That was how the link had been broken; there could have been no more effective method.

We sat down again; he joined me at my table. We needed to get accustomed to the situation, it was too unexpected, too sudden. We felt a certain tension. So there he sat, my Juanjo, ten years older, a grown man. His features were still handsome, his eyes even darker and deeper, but they lacked the sparkle of childhood. His hands, although elegant and supple, had become more robust. His hair was not tidily parted. The . . .

He interrupted my meditations.

"Yes, Santi, fate struck us a cruel blow. I can read your thoughts." He added, with a smile, "I used to do that before, do you still remember? But we are not now sitting holding hands like we did then . . . "

"Ah, yes, Juanjo, how different everything could have been!"

We were silent for a few minutes. The traffic and people continued to pass by. We did not see them.

"Yes, Santiago, when my uncle told me the dreadful news I didn't eat for days, and I couldn't sleep at night. Why was that man so cruel as to do such a thing to a child—as I still was at the time? Your name was continually on my lips . . . Santi . . . Santi . . . I felt so lonely and abandoned. I relived the days we spent on board our faithful *Salvador*, our saviour, again and again. I dreamed about it at night until it became a nightmare. I missed you dreadfully. I knew that that was love, really deep love . . . I must tell you something, Santiago, my heart really ached . . . "

The waiter brought the sherry we had ordered and put the glasses down in front of us. Juan José continued:

"I had set all my hopes on South America."

After a short pause he suddenly said:

"And I have never even been able to thank you properly for all that you did for me. Your love must have been deep too."

We told each other how life had treated us. Juan José had got married not long before, to a Chilean girl he had met in Barcelona. He had a bookshop on the Diagonal, and also wrote poems. The Spanish Government had awarded him a money-prize for one of his collections of poems, and he and his wife were making this journey to Venezuela on the strength of it.

"I don't need to tell you why we chose this country . . . "

I interrupted him:

"Are you Ramirez?"

"Yes, that is my pen-name. How did you guess?"

"A couple of months ago I bought a copy of your prize-winning collection in a kiosk. One evening I read some of it and enjoyed it, particularly the poem entitled *to a dead friend* . . . "

A little later, I continued: "Do you remember, Juanjo, that I once complimented you on your beautiful Spanish? I said then that you were talented . . . "

"Quite right, I still remember it clearly. I gave you a kiss on the forehead that evening, and was embarrassed . . . "

We had so much, so very much, to tell each other and we didn't know where to begin. Our love had developed into friendship, true friendship. If it had not been for the separation of over ten years, this transformation would have occurred gradually and harmoniously; it would have run its natural course. Now we had to speed up the process, to compress it into a few hours.

Suddenly Juan José looked at me questioningly, waited a moment and said:
"Do you still feel the same way as you used to do?"
"Yes, Juanjo, exactly the same; some people are the same throughout life . . . "
In his case, things were different; he had just got married.
"That's the way it has to be, Juan José; we few are there to offer support and help to boys of a certain age, to boys to whom we are attracted. That is how we perform the task that is given to us by nature. That is our mission, our so delightful and responsible duty."

It was already the evening when we got up. Juan José looked at his watch and said with a laugh: "How the time has gone by, Santi . . . "

We ran through the town. The lights had gone on and the neon signs gave the streets a gay appearance with their many colours and shapes. In the hotel, Juan José presented me to his wife, to whom he first explained the extraordinary event that had occurred only a few hours before. He had previously told her a lot about me. She was a particularly charming and attractive young woman, the daughter of a manufacturer.

In the main hall of the hotel she offered me her hand. I bowed and kissed it. Her first words were:
"Thank you for all that you have done for Juan José. If it was not for you, we would probably not be here now. Two of his cousins were sent to Russia at that time, and they never came back. We know nothing about what happened to them. You had such a lot of influence on Juan José that he has you to thank for the successes in his life. I am so happy that you are alive and well."

We dined together in one of the restaurants in the city center. The band played boleros, rumbas and tangos. Our table was beside the window, and we looked out onto a public garden.

I felt very happy. My Juan José was on the right road and had found his place in life. He had the makings of a great poet, and he was on the way to becoming a famous man. It had not all been in vain . . .

It was late when we returned to the hotel. Juan José accompanied me to the car-park. He walked round my Chevrolet and stopped beside the baggage-compartment . . .

"This is a bit more comfortable than the one we had ten years ago . . . it is remarkable what fate can bring . . . "

Lost in thought, he gazed into the distance, just as he had done long ago . . . I felt that he wanted to say something to me, but was unable to.

"What is it, Juanjo?"

We were standing near a lamp-post, and the light shone obliquely onto his face. There was something melancholy about his eyes.

"Santi, please don't consider what I am going to tell you as a reproach. But it is something that I wanted to say ten years ago, yet never dared to. Now, as an adult who has had rather more insight and experience of life, I can choose my standpoint better."

He fell silent and looked again like he had done when, as a thirteen-year-old boy, he had peered across the water towards the French coast, hoping for rescue . . .

"Santiago, at that time with me, you could have . . . Do you understand what I mean? I have always felt it to be lacking, as something that should have happened in order to achieve complete harmony. I am a little poorer, not as rich as I could have been. If we had only experienced it once, then we would have had the memory of it . . . It was an unnecessary obstacle—for a few years—while I was growing up. You might say that I had missed part of my adolescence. I believe that our tragedy—if I may call it that—lies in the fact that it is now too late and we cannot turn the hands of the clock back . . . Therefore the gold watch that you gave me is also a splendid symbol; the noblest metal, and the time factor that plays such an important role . . . In other words, the most noble sentiments, but don't let the right moment go by . . . "

He had put his hand on my shoulder. My eyes were damp.

Twenty minutes later I was at my front door. On my writing-table stood a photograph of a small boy: a laughing Juan José.

The cars drove past one after the other below my window.

There was a knock at the door. Señorita Jimenez came in.

"Good morning, Mr. Capmany—Here is the post."

The carefully looked-after hands laid the letters on the writing-pad. While I ran my eyes over their contents, she fiddled with a few curls of her hair, as usual.

After dictating a few replies to her, she disappeared on her high heels through the leather-clad door, which she closed almost noiselessly behind her.

The film studios were working at their full capacity. We had a bright future ahead of us.

Costa Brava was written in the summer of 1958. At that time, the theme of this novel—boylove—had scarcely become the subject of public discussion. *Costa Brava* was published in Rotterdam by the Enclave International Press, and right from the beginning it was a much demanded book. The monthly magazine of the Netherlands Association for Sexual Reform (N.V.S.H.) *Rational Parenthood* said, in the issue for December 1960, it is: "a well-written and straightforward story about people whom you might meet any day. (. . .) Specially recommendable because the attempt to give the reader an insight into socially unacceptable feelings is decidedly a complete success." Part of the book appeared as a short story under the title "The storm" in *Der Weg* (February–March 1963).

The daily and weekly press in the Netherlands also reviewed the book, notably *De Haagse Courant* and *Elsevier*.

Costa Brava lives on. This is emphasized regularly. The periodical *N.I.K.S.* (the integration of child-sexuality, published by the N.V.S.H.) mentioned my book, as follows: One can really only come to the conclusion that human love is experienced in all possible variations. There are no deviant forms of behavior. *Costa Brava* confirms this conclusion . . . It is well worth while . . . to read *Costa Brava*."

More recently, *Costa Brava* was mentioned in the English-language magazine *Pan* in June 1979, and the chapter "The storm" was reprinted in Joachim S. Hohmann's historico-literary survey entitled *"Der heimliche Sexus" (The Secret Sex)*, presented by the editor in the section on "homosexual fiction from 1900 to 1970" and mentioned in a detailed essay illustrated with photographs.

My story has even found its way into the scientific literature. Thus, it is mentioned in the *Lexikon der Sexualität* by Willhart S. Schlegel, volume 1 of the series "Mensch und Sexualität" published in Munich in 1969.

The historian E. O. Born mentions the publication of *Costa Brava* in his *Pedofiele Intgratie na 1959* (Utrecht 1973).

Furthermore, the story is quoted as an example of a happy depiction of boylove relationship in specialist publications such as *Sexualmedizin, Betrifft: Erziehung* and *Arcadie, Revue littéraire et scientifique*.

The Dutch-language edition, which was published twenty years ago, has brought me into contact with a large number of readers at home and abroad, both in person and by correspondence. From them I have learnt that the book is a moral support to numerous people. It is therefore opportune that an illustrated English edition is now being published by *Gay Sunshine*.

Frits Bernard

V

GAY POETRY

For Gay Roots Volume 1 *(1991) I chose work by fifty-four different poets—all of them published by Gay Sunshine in the past. For the present volume I have decided to concentrate on the work of four poets whose work has, I believe, been catalytic in the evolving Gay Cultural Renaissance of the past two decades.*

ALLEN GINSBERG (b. 1926) is one of the most prominent poets of his generation. The poem "Many Loves" (Part 1) is presented here for the first time, joined with his earlier "Part 2." And the marvelous "Old Love Story" is a paean to boylove.

EDWARD A. LACEY (b. 1938) has lived outside his native Canada for most of the past twenty-five years: in Mexico, South America, Greece, the Middle East, India, Thailand and Indonesia. The best of his work (his travel poems) often engender in me a Cavafyesque poignancy, or a Proustian remembrance. His work has not received the recognition it deserves—due in part to the author's disinclination to self-promotion. The generous sampling of his poetry in Gay Roots *Volumes 1 and 2 will hopefully introduce new generations of readers to his work. Gay Sunshine Press has also published four books of superb prose translations by Edward A. Lacey (from Spanish, Portuguese and French):* Adonis Garcia, *novel by Luis Zapata;* Bom-Crioulo, *novel by Adolfo Caminha;* My Deep Dark Pain is Love: A Collection of Latin American Gay Fiction; *and* The Delight of Hearts *by Ahmad al-Tifashi. The poems printed in the present anthology have the following provenance: "Poeme des amour fugitifs," "Being," "Two Poems for Leobardo," and "Kite Boys" were written in the 1960s and early 70s and appeared in* Path of Snow Poems 1951–1973 *by E.A. Lacey, 1974; "The Double," "Desencuentro," "Desire and Chefchaouene," "Rejean," "L'envoi," are taken from* Later: Poems 1973–1978 *by E.A. Lacey, Catalyst Press, Toronto, 1978. "Afghani Love Song," "The Two Macaws," "Flawed Archetypes," "Barrio Chino," "The Man in the Village" and "Cafe 'To Neon'" were written in the 1980s and were chosen by editor Winston Leyland from unpublished manuscripts of the author.*

J.L.S.E. (JIM EGGELING) (b. 1934) has lived and worked in southern Texas for most of his life. His poems celebrate the joys of boylove.

JIM EVERHARD (1946–1986) is perhaps the most brilliant of the younger poets writing in the post-Stonewall era. His life was cut short by AIDS. Many of his poems were collected in the Gay Sunshine Press book Cute *(1982). For the present anthology I have chosen from his now out-of-print book* Cute and other poems *(Gay Sunshine Press, 1982) and from his unpublished manuscripts presently in my care.*

—Winston Leyland

Allen Ginsberg
1926–

MANY LOVES

I

"Resolved to sing no songs henceforth but those of Manly Attachment"
     —In the manner of Whitman

Now I will speak out boldly, nay sing, not argue, dispute or justify, dainty,
But preach by example the image of love known between men,
And number my lovers among men, their names and stations, carnal days
     together,
Providing by life what was not known in books, nor morals, nor Bibles—

And there was Paul my first friend, but I lusted & dreamed & didn't know
     him because of high school timidity . . .

And there was Eric Law a handsome youth and drunkard angel, rich and
     brilliant and I didn't know him through timidity
Tho he stripped himself naked in his room and sat crosslegged on the bed
     mocking in pride of youth
and smiled & beguiled me: but I wouldn't, out of shame & distrust,
—so slept all the night in his chair, and regretted my stiffnecked fear
But occasion was gone, he woke in the morning impatient and pissed off his
     hard-on.

Later we knew each other, made it, I his first, and he my first love, he lay on
     my couch, I climbed on him, lay with my cock at his back,
and he groaned, and moved with me—I came, he caressed me, we were sweet
     together,
And after that many times in disguise, then no more. But we loved each
     other, so went our ways: he to marriage, I to search out other loves—

Met Dom whom I loved a blonde prince of college, athlete with starry
     forehead, an Indian head and mind,
piercing eyes & hooked nose, wiry pale body, had known the snows of
     Denver, exhaustion, and bodies of girls in cabins, read Nietzsche
We were acquainted room mates, slept together months, and moved close to
     each other friends on the same mattress clasping silent, but never open.
Stripped naked one day he lay on the bed for prosaic massage, face down his
     limbs pale muscular hairless: I felt them, moved them,
ran my hand down his back from nape of neck to the bone of his ankle,
touched palm to his buttock, and moved it, gripped under arm round his
     biceps, spread out his hands, caressed his shoulders, my knuckle went
     down his backbone, almost an hour in his half sleep

turned him over, his arm lay over closed eyes; yellow hair on his loins,
put my palms on his muscles on his breasts, lay my hands down his abdomen
    played with light finger on his nipples which were red.
And I bent down and put my lips to his breast, and passed over down to his
    belly: and his belly shuddered.
And I saw the beautiful works of his body naked, the man's body, muscles
    and loins, at ease, in a bed, golden hair on the pillow,
the lines of the wall of his stomach, and lines of the hips to the thigh, the
    hollow in the muscle of the thigh,
and the breastplate of the man who has strength and affections, the sensibility
    of the inside of the thigh
the slow rising of the cock, its throbbing, the dew of heart on its head, pale
    semen of offering and the nest of yellow hair in which man held his
    beauty.
And I blew him, after long play with my lips to his body, his buttocks, his
    hole and the backs of his ears, the sensitive eyelid, fine cheek, and inside
    hollow of armpit—
in all his beauty I blew him: he rose up with his buttocks & pushed up
    toward me as I knelt, he groaned
and said, "Make me come, Allen, take it in and swallow it"—
and shuddered all over and came, I swallowed his come and tasted his
    manhood & knew him
And blew further, he pushed himself up again, and arched his back & lifted
    his buttocks, straining,
and came; I blew him more, and my head was attached to his body and
    swallowed his cock
and his come flowed into me for an hour; then lay with his eyes closed and
    rested.
Dom why reject me years thereafter? I was ever your lover, that was my
    great pleasure, remember me then and bless me again
For ecstasy's rare among men; and liberation of ecstasy's a blessing.
And god'll speak for me and plead my case when we come to him, and so
    will the beautiful angels, such is my hope for Mercy.
And I lusted to get my asshole fucked, these are the words of my bowels.
To feel the goring of cock in my belly coming from behind,
humiliation before the pride of man: and ecstasy in the humiliation:
the adoration of the living body of pride; for the proud cock will suffer and
    perish, shrivelled into dust
And the perishing cock in its pathos I redeem with my honor
and make it eternal with love; and cherish its pride for a year
For the cock that fucks me remembering Change is meek to its maker
to take its orgasms in a day, and dig its delight for an hour—
and I'm beholden to it for a lesson of love, a mastery humble and soon to
    perish, I take on the suffering & pleasure,
My manhood and godhead nailed together at the root.

Jack Kerouac who heard my first confession when I was virgin to men
groaned & ran down to the village and got drunk; he was on a ship
Phoned later, in Macdougal's Bar scrivened poems together & rewrote Eric's
    parable
"Human-kindness versus Humankind-ness" on the enamel top of the narrow
    urinal.

II

Neal Cassady was my animal; he brought me to my knees
and taught me the love of his cock & the secrets of his mind
And we met and conversed, went walking in the evening by the park
Up to Harlem, recollecting Denver, and Dan Budd, a hero
And we made shift to sack out in Harlem, after a long evening,
Jack and host in a large double bed, I volunteered for the cot, and Neal
Volunteered for the cot with me, we stripped and lay down.
I wore my underwear, my shorts, and he his briefs—
lights out on the narrow bed I turned to my side, with my back to his Irish
    boy's torso,
and huddled and balanced on the edge, and kept distance—
and hung my head over and kept my arm over the side, withdrawn
And he seeing my fear stretched out his arm, and put it around my breast
Saying "Draw near me" and gathered me in upon him:
I lay there trembling, and felt his great arm like a king's
And his breasts, his heart slow thudding against my back,
and his middle torso, narrow and made of iron, soft at my back,
his fiery firm belly warming me while I trembled—
His belly of fists and starvation, his belly a thousand girls kissed in Colorado
his belly of rocks thrown over Denver roofs, prowess of jumping and fists,
    his stomach of solitudes,
His belly of burning iron and jails affectionate to my side:
I began to tremble, he pulled me in closer with his arm, and hugged me long
    and close
my soul melted, secrecy departed, I became
Thenceforth open to his nature as a flower in the shining sun.
And below his belly, in white underwear, tight between my buttocks,
His own loins against me soft, nestling in comradeship, put forth & pressed
    into me, open to my awareness,
slowly began to grow, signal me further and deeper affection, sexual tenderness.
So gentle the man, so sweet the moment, so kind the thighs that nuzzled
    against me smooth-skinned powerful, warm by my legs
That my body shudders and trembles with happiness, remembering—
His hand opened up on my belly, his palms and fingers flat against my skin
I fell to him, and turned, shifting, put my face on his arm resting,
my chest against his, he helped me to turn, and held me closer
his arm at my back beneath my head, and arm at my buttocks tender holding me in,
our bellies together nestling, loins touched together, pressing and knowl-
    edgeable each other's hardness, and mine stuck out of my underwear.

Then I pressed in closer and drew my leg up between his, and he lay half
    on me with his thighs and bedded me down close, caressing
and moved together pressing his cock to my thigh and mine to his
slowly, and slowly began a love match that continues in my imagination to
    this day a full decade.
Thus I met Neal & thus we felt each other's flesh and owned each other
    bodies and souls.
So then as I lay on his breast with my arms clasped around his neck and his
    cheek against mine,
I put my hand down to feel his great back for the first time, jaws and pectorals
    of steel at my fingers,
closer and stiller, down the silken iron back to his waist, the whole of his
    torso now open
my hand at his waist trembling, waited delaying and under the elastic of his briefs,
I first touched the smooth mount of his rock buttocks, silken in power,
    rounded in animal fucking and bodily nights over nurses and schoolgirls,
O ass of long solitudes in stolen cars, and solitudes on curbs, musing fist in cheek,
Ass of a thousand farewells, ass of youth, youth's lovers,
Ass of a thousand lonely craps in gas stations ass of great painful secrecies
    of the years
O ass of mystery and night! ass of gymnasiums and muscular pants
ass of high schools and masturbation ass of lone delight, ass of mankind, so
    beautiful and hollow, dowry of Mind and Angels,
Ass of hero, Neal Cassady, I had at my hand: my fingers traced the curve
    to the bottom of his thighs.
I raised my thighs and stripped down my shorts to my knees, and bent to
    push them off
and he raised me up from his chest, and pulled down his pants the same,
humble and meek and obedient to his mood our silence,
and naked at long last with angel & greek & athlete & hero and brother and
    boy of my dreams
I lay with my hair intermixed with his, he asking me "What shall we do now?"
—And confessed, years later, he thinking I was not a queer at first to please
    me & serve me, to blow me and make me come, maybe or if I were
    queer, that's what I'd likely want of a dumb bastard like him.
But I made my first mistake, and made him then and there my master, and
    bowed my head, and holding his buttock
Took up his hard-on and held it, feeling it throb and pressing my own at
    his knee & breathing showed him I needed him, cock, for my dreams
    of insatiety & lone love.

—And I lie here naked in the dark, dreaming

Arctic, August 10, 1956

Part 1 of this poem was also published in Allen Ginsberg's mid 1950's Journals *(Harper &*
Row, 1993); Part 2 appeared originally in As Ever: Collected Correspondence Allen Gins-

berg & Neal Cassady *(1977) and was later reprinted in* Straight Hearts' Delight *(Poems and letters by Allen Ginsberg and Peter Orlovsky—Gay Sunshine Press 1980) and* Allen Ginsberg Collected Poems 1947–1980 *(Harper & Row, 1984). Both parts are printed here together for the first time with Allen Ginsberg's permission.*

OLD LOVE STORY

Some think the love of boys is wicked in the world, forlorn,
Character corrupting, worthy mankind's scorn
Or eyes that weep and breasts that ache for lovely youth
Have no mouth to speak for mankind's general truth
Nor hands to work manhood's fullest delight
Nor hearts to make old women smile day and night
Nor arms to warm young girls to dream of love
Nor thighs to satisfy thighs, nor breath men can approve—
Yet think back to the time our epic world was new
When Gilgamesh followed the shade of his friend Enkidu
Into Limbo's dust to talk love man to man
So younger David enamored of young Jonathan
Wrote songs that women and men still chant for calm
Century after century under evergreen or palm
A love writ so sacred on our Bible leaf
That heart-fire warms millennial cold grief.
Sametime Akhileos won the war at Troy
Grieving Patroklus' body, his dead warrior boy
(One nation won the world by reading Greek for this
And fell when Wilde was gaoled for his Bellboy's kiss)
Marvelous Zeus himself took lightning eagle shape
Down-cheeked Ganymede enjoyed God's thick-winged rape
And lived a youth forever, forever as can be,
Serving his nectar to the bearded deity
The whole world knew the story, the world laughed in awe
That such Love could be the Thunder of immortal Law.
When Socrates climbed his ladder of love's degrees
He put his foot in silence on rough Alcibiades
Wise men still read Plato, wherever they are,
Plato whose love-lad Aster was his morning star
Plato whose love-lad was in death his star of Night
Which Shelley once witnessed as Eternal Light.
Catullus and tough Horace were slaves to glad young men
Loved them cursed them, always fell in love again
Caesar conquered the world, Top Emperor Power
Lay soft on the breast of his soldier of the hour
Even Jesus Christ loved his young John most
Later he showed him the whole Heavenly Host
Old Rome approved a beautiful bodied youth

Antinöus Hadrian worshipped with Imperial Truth
Told in the calm gaze of his thousand stone
Statues standing naked in the Vatican.
Michelangelo lifted his young hand to smooth
The belly of his Bacchus a sixteen-year youth
Whose prick stands up he's drunk, his eyes gaze side-
Ways to his right hand held up shoulder high
Waving a cup of grape, smart kid, his nose is sharp,
His lips are new, slightly opened as if part-
Ed to take a sip of purple nakedness,
Taste Michelangelo's mortal-bearded kiss,
Or if a hair-hooved horny Satyr happens to pass
Fall to the ground on his strong little marble ass.
Michelangelo loved him!   What young stud
Stood without trousers or shirt, maybe even did
What the creator wanted him to in bed
Lay still with the sculptor's hand cupped on his head
Feeling up his muscles, feeling down his bones
Palm down his back and thighs, touching his soft stones—
What kind of men were the Slaves he tied to his bed?
And who stood still for David naked foot to head?
But men love the muscles of David's abdomen
And come with their women to see him again and again.
Enough, I've stayed up all night with these boys
And all my life enjoyed their handsome joys
I came with many companions to this Dawn
Now I'm tired and must set my pen down
Reader, Hearer, this time Understand
How kind it is for man to love a man,
Old love and Present, future love the same
Hear and Read what love is without shame.

I want people to understand! They can! They can! They can!
So open your ears and hear the voice of the classical Band.

October 26, 1981

The preceding poem was originally published in a limited edition (150 copies) by LoSpecchio Press, New York, 1986.

Edward A. Lacey

1938–

POÈME DES AMOURS FUGITIFS

Young Inca boy with a guitar:
the dark waterfall of your hair
splashed over me as we made love;
your body, slim and arched, above
me darted in and out
of my well-trained and willing mouth
until the salt sweet sperm came; then
at peace, accomplices and men,
we licked each other's sweaty skin,
confessed our prides and told our sins,
—a poet growing old, a young
confusion with a life-style—song—
and then sleep came and brought us dreams
of childhood, in each other's arms.

The gold of bodies does not melt;
preserves itself in what was felt.

Moroccan boys in mountain towns:
djellabas, snow-white or leaf-brown,
hid slim white cocks that like sharp knives
cut my ass; then the cool kif pipes;
Mexican boys, met on the road,
in jails, cantinas, briefly had
and disremembered; dusty faces,
small cocks, tight balls, great eagernesses;
Argentines, Uruguayans, complex
city boys needing simple sex;
treacherous, delicate Indian lads
from beautiful, deadly Trinidad;
—all of you are dimly with me yet;
I keep the faith; I do not forget.

The gold of bodies does not melt;
preserves itself in what was felt.

Brazilian boys with laughing cocks
earnest with need to get your rocks
off in some way, and set your seal
on woman, man or animal;

247

Dário, Fabrício, Adonai
—you will not age, you will not die;
my mind will keep you always young,
brown-skinned and eager and well-hung;
kisses you did not have to give,
and gave, I, while I live,
will recall, and how you would lie
beside me afterwards, till the sky
went white, and the bem-te-vi at dawn
woke us with his three-note song.

The gold of bodies does not melt;
preserves itself in what was felt.

This is not boasting, for who cares
these days? I have made love in cars,
especially taxis (always prefer
cabbies and shine-boys; they're quick and sure),
on beds and hillsides, in ruined churches,
on beaches, mountain-tops, under bridges;
and though I happen to dote on boys,
like Jews who've nothing against goys
I hold no brief against the man
who lies with girl, sow, ewe, or ram;
and, growing older, only enthuse
for money, to keep on buying youths
to warm my age with their hot hands:
the best loves are one-night stands!

The gold of bodies does not melt;
preserves itself in what was felt.

The bem-te-vi *(stanza 3) is the Brazilian version of the kiskidee flycatcher; the name means* "I saw you, I did".

TWO POEMS FOR LEOBARDO

1. Your body here beside me, warm and still
    this morning, as so many mornings now;
    still webbed in sleep the dusty face; the smooth
    boy's arms are crossed upon the hairless chest;
    only the heart beats the stomach's tender drum;
    the genitals at peace; the strong legs curl
    hunched against mine.
    Surrendered to the other violence of sleep,
    you make no protest as my roaming fingers
    explore you, alien continent. I know
    your body in the act, not in repose; I do not
    know you at all.
    The furrow of a dream now cuts your forehead,
    for you are travelling in distant places;
    the future for you has the shape of dreams,
    for me, the shape of time.

2. Far away now I sleep, my little one.
    I do not have the smooth silk of your skin
    to wrap me in
    but huddle curled up in a dense cocoon
    of memories and wishes and regrets.
    I am getting older fast; my hair is falling;
    though in myself I feel I cannot age;
    I drink too much, and there are clinical signs
    of some sort of malaise in the whole organism.
    Also the tropical climate does not agree with me.
    Do I bore you with details? There are many palm trees here.
    The dark people are kind. The nights are warm.
    But you were warmer.

KITE-BOYS

Hawks and eagles!
Red and black ones!
Gold and white ones!
Yellow and green ones!
Captive, for sale on the beach at Copacabana!
Three feet from wing-tip to cloth wing-tip they measure,
poised sharp bodies, cruel hieratic faces,
outspread wings of cloth ready for flight.
Three thousand cruzeiros a kite, and the man who makes them
sits cross-legged, fat, unaquiline, feet rooted in sand,
on the beach in front of the tourist hotel,
old-womanishly sewing and stitching, answering the tourists' questions.
Around him the blue-and-gold afternoon, cliff-shadows of buildings advancing
    now across the white sands of Copacabana,
and a scurry of brown young half-naked helpers who, when they aren't
    assisting him,
jump in and out of the surf, scuffle at soccer, ogle the girls,
or run along the beach to the other hotels
hawking their wares.

These fly too, these eagles, mocking their cloth,
fly briefly, touched with sun, arched over beach and bathers,
fly high in the afternoon wind that comes in from the open sea,
in a wind that too soon dies away, draws them to earth again;
but if you're young and agile and a kite-maker's helper
you can keep them up in the air in their blaze of colour for almost
    an afternoon,
running along the beach, snaring the wind.

You fly too,
young hawk boys of Copacabana,
your brown rapacious bodies circling sunlit over mine,
hungry, hunting for sex, for money, for experience,
in afternoons of sun and sea and wind that are all one afternoon;
but the long shadow crawls indelible across the sand,
and there is a secret no one will ever tell you, but you will learn it,
    kite-boys,
seeking the sun and not reaching it,
wanting the world and not getting it,
nor knowing why your flight must be as brief as your cloth birds' flying:
one eagle moment bright in the sun, and then the slow going-down
    to the end of all flight,
to sticks and rags and tattered colours fading,
and darkness and old age.

RÉJEAN

On his chest he had tattooed "*vivre*,"
and I knew *just* what it meant
the night he sat down uninvited
at the table where I was drinking
in the dear, dead Altesse Tavern.
He spoke absolutely no English,
but we got along well enough.
Son of a poor farming family
from the country near Trois Rivières,
he had come to the city,
like all boys, trying his luck.
His long black hair was lustrous.
His smile was young and mocking.
His cock was pale and urgent.
"Je suis aux hommes," he told me.

He stayed with me for one winter,
a season of discontent
(like all seasons in Canada),
and at night his pale candle consoled me
for my sun-skinned South Americans.
He cost me a lot of money,
for he liked to wear fine clothing;
he liked steak and seafood dinners;
he frequented PJ's nightclub,
where he joked with the transvestites
and drank *crème de cacao*
avec du lait (I paid,
but I got my *lait* for free.)
He smoked a lot of dope,
and he dropped a little acid,
and he caused me all sorts of problems,
for all his friends were hoodlums
who belonged to *la petite pègre*.
He was a good boy, basically,
but eighteen years old, and crazy.

He stayed with me all winter,
and in the spring I left him.
because he cost me money,
and he caused me many problems,
and his feet stank most disgracefully,
and I grew tired of his penis
—as I grow tired of everything;

so in the end I left him
—as I leave everybody—
to go on with my searching.
And God knows what's become of him.

Réjean. His motto, "*vivre*".
And he lived for a while off me.

BEING—*for Paulinho*

a translation of "Ser" by Brazilian poet Carlos Drummond de Andrade

he would be growing up now,
the son I never had;
now he blows in the wind,
no body with no name.

from time to time I meet him
in a brushing of clouds
he rests upon my shoulder
his shoulder of nothing.

and then I ask my son,
that being made of air:
in what sea-shell or cave
are you hiding, abstraction?

and the breath answers me:
where I was always waiting;
you never listened to me
although I called to you

just as I keep on calling
(beyond, beyond all love)
where everything and nothing
aspires to come to being.

the son I never made
is making himself.

Edward A. Lacey

DESENCUENTRO

A boy is waiting for me tonight in Santiago.
He does not know he has seen me for the last time.

At nine, under the university clock, I told him:
I'll take you to dinner, and then we'll find a hotel-room.

He walks back and forth under the clock, smokes a cigarette,
stares after the passing buttocks, wonders where the *maricón* is.

But *maricones* are always late, like women,
and, anyhow, where else could I find a man like him?

He has brown eyes, brown skin, He's—let's say—a mechanic.
He was passionate in bed. I think I liked him.

At nine-thirty he decides he'll give me fifteen minutes.
At ten he definitely decides to go, but yet . . .

I gave him food, I gave him money, I gave him my body.
I even gave—I guess—affection. But I could not give him my time.

He's tired. It's getting cold. He's out fifty pesos.
But he should have known. A *maricón* is a *maricón*.

He stands under the clock in Santiago.
He knows now he will never see me again.

BARRIO CHINO

Mohammed, from Meknes, slept with me for money,
but he loved Elizabeth, out of Perpignan,
who was a prostitute, and also a lesbian,
and loved Alma, old whore born in Uruguay,
who loved me, because I knew her obscure country,
and I loved Abdelkader, from Algeria,
who lived with a Spaniard (who loved him), also slept with me for money
and loved—perhaps—someone, or no one at all.

(The Barrio Chino is the low-life district of Barcelona—don't ask me to explain the name, because no Chinese at all live there or apparently ever did. This is based on a rather similar poem by the Brazilian poet Carlos Drummond de Andrade, but is not a translation or imitation of it; rather, his poem provided me with the structure on which to stretch my own experiences.)

THE DOUBLE

I loved you doubly for years, doubly nescient:
the perfect bow of the lips; smooth cupped jaw-bone;
cheeks rounded as ripe peaches whose stone one senses
within; nacre-shell of ears; deep pools of eyes
with their reed fringe of lash; fine flair of animal
nostrils scenting; flat brow, hair not blond,
nor dark, not curled, nor straight, blown by some invisible
wind; imperceptibly Indian cast of the features;
and every time I kissed you, each time I fingered
your tranquil sleeping statue, paused and wondered:
where had I seen your face before, where was I seeing
your double?

      And then the trip to the interior
to visit the cities of gold with their baroque churches,
and the day—where? São João del Rei?—we stood together,
admiring that lost harmony of God, man, nature,
and saw a stone angel in an archway niche
who was you; and in that moment you knew, I knew
you were the baroque, faintly Indian angel gamboling
—grave though gay, sexless yet sexed, cherub but human—
in reredo and retable, gilt wood or gray stone,
of every church from México to Prague. Now
your stone face grows more perfect to my vision
daily, while, ah, the other, the human features
alter, decay.

L'ENVOI

for Cavafy

Now you are leaving, but you will not leave, stranger.
Goodbye, Godspeed, bon voyage, but you will not go.
You will never depart from Rio de Janeiro.
Wherever you travel, you will take Rio with you;
in a thousand distant places you will walk her dark streets,
sit to rest for a moment in the shade of her almond trees,
hear the wind along the avenue rustle her palms.
Whenever you smell the sea-smell, you will remember Rio.
Whenever you sit in a sidewalk café and watch people passing, you
    will be here.
Whenever you kiss a boy, he will turn in your arms and will be
    Paulinho.
You will not escape, traveller, though now you try to leave us:
Now we are part of you.

I chose to print this poem about Rio, the city where I live and love for part of each year, for its Cavafyesque/Proustian poignancy. —Winston Leyland

DESIRE AND CHEFCHAOUENE

That winter night on the hillside in the moonlight
by the brook whose waters were colder than the night wind
I'd already had three boys, and my mouth was aching,
when you and your friend, with your snow-flecked djellabas,
drifted in like mist (how long you had been watching
I don't know) and asked if I wanted more.
But there was a local problem with traveller's cheques,
which the tourist hotel would exchange only when it had money
in the till, and that was not always, and I lacked dirhams
to make the token payment I felt was demanded
by the rules of the game. So I said "No. I'm tired. Tomorrow."
I'd already met you down in the village that evening
at the café, while drinking mint tea and sizing
and being sized up. Your friend was—well—not my type, say,
but you were a bold, brown-cheeked seventeen-year-old,
and you'd singled me out from the first moment with your stare.

The next day, at the café again, you and your buddy,
threading your way through the throng of brown djellabas
and the kif smoke and dancing boys in that upstairs room,
approached me, suggested I go with you both to your house now:
you lived with your brother, and he was away working,
and we could be alone, the three of us
("translating each other's languages," you said).
But I, the compleat paranoid, of course
suspected a trap. Morocco's a tricky country,
and too much kif had jangled, I guess, my nerves.
So I said "Thank you. Not today. Perhaps tomorrow,"
and I beat a retreat to the Spanish bar, to drink.

The third day was the market, and you were everywhere
in the press of buyers and sellers, of brown-clad hill men
and bean soup and *méchoui* and mint and honeycomb,
slyly smiling at me across the olives and tangerines,
your eyes blacker than olives, your cheeks brighter
than tangerines, your body more desirable
than honeycomb. But you and I spoke nothing.

The last day, in the souk, we met for the last time,
in that warren of curving streets and pale blue houses;
you were alone this time, and you repeated
softly "Come to my house with me. We'll be together."
The invitation, staring me down with your laughing
bright éyes; and only then I realised
what at my age had simply not occurred to me
—you wanted *me*, not money. Perhaps the cachet
of having a foreigner, perhaps, too, the challenge

of my reluctance, maybe merely desire,
which is indiscriminate at seventeen.
But my bus was due to leave in half-an-hour,
bearing me and my silly American travel companion
forever from Chefchaouene, and I so informed you,
and you laughed and said "What a joke. Forget the bus.
There'll be other buses, but the time you'll have
with me you'll never find again." I'd have taken
your advice, I suppose, let the bus and my silly
friend (for whom I acted as nursemaid, guide, translator)
go, and followed you to the bed and its delights.
But I've always been a conscientious bloke
who believes in timetables and hates to waste
tickets already paid for, so I said "No.
Some other time." And you urged "You've half an hour.
In half an hour we could still do something
that would be fun." But I dislike running for buses
at the last moment. I'm tachycardiac and
such exertions do the heart no good at all.
So I said "It just can't be. Goodbye. I'll be back."
And you answered "No, you won't," and shook my hand
and stared after me with your bright laughing eyes,
as I walked downhill to the bus stop where my friend
was waiting for me with ten bags full of trinkets
and twenty complaints and fifty demands and questions.
And the bus left for the south, and that was that.

Now and then I think of you and resolve to go back
in time to Chefchaouene and find and have you.
But it's unlikely I'll ever return, and you'd surely
be married now, with a family, perhaps living elsewhere
—I never learned your name—and, anyhow,
I'd be an old man to you now, at forty
(I still had remnants of youth at thirty-three),
and you of course are no longer seventeen.
So be it. I never scented the hidden garden
of your body, never searched out its secret waters,
never climbed and descended its pinnacles and caverns.
And the *bel ragazzo* André Gide kissed but had not
in a stagecoach in Italy is dust.
As is André Gide: I have completely forgotten
the other boys, size of their cocks, taste of their semen,
even their names, but of you I retain
—more durable, fragrant and haunting than any remembered
experience—a regret.

Chefchaouene—a small "holy city" in the Rif mountains of northern Morocco. The people are of Jibali Berber stock, and very sexually approachable.

THE TWO MACAWS

There was a shop
—a pet shop ¿te acordás, hombre José?—
on Athenai Street, just below Ommonia:
a shop full of parakeets, guppies, small macaques,
beside the vegetable market that sold kiwi fruit's
emerald antipodal testicles,
apples grown by centaurs, bananas from Crete,
rouged pomegranates, Morean tangerines. . . .
Catcorners across from that subterranean porno theatre
where you could hear
the metro rumbling off, down to Piraeus
—the ships, the salt air and the foreign sailors—
and where young men sat all day, gently caressing
bulbous appendages deviated sideways into pockets, noiselessly squirting
the magic liquid
into sheets of kleenex or handkerchiefs embroidered
by adoring maiden aunts.
Around the corner from the sidewalk café
—the one shaded by a great scaly plane tree
the one that sold cheap ouzo and had such good hors d'oeuvres
of octopus and potato mayonnaise—
don't you remember, José?
And that shop, you will recall, had two macaws.
A blue-and-gold one, and a red-and blue one.
They sat outside, taking the fruit-scented air,
dreaming of distant jungles,
chained by one foot to horizontal perches,
huge squawking sylvan birds,
balanced and swung, ate fruit and sunflower seeds,
with those murderous curved black beaks, gentle as a child's touch,
and endlessly shrieked "Arara! Dry crackers!"
Transported from the deeps of who knows what shimmering
South American fantasy
by some sailor, they were the only memory
each had of each. Of their lost green world.
And they had us, too. We used to go by
and joke with them, feed them pieces of fruit.
The two *araras*. The two *guacamayas*.
After all, the two of us were just as exotic
in that city as they were. Just as colourful.
And just as alien, tropical, just as lost. . . .

And then, one day, the blue-and-gold macaw
was gone.
Sold, the shopkeeper informed me, to a rich client

who'd paid ten thousand drachmae and transported *his* bird
on his yacht, to Rhodes. The red-and-blue *guacamaya*
stayed on outside the shop, chained to its rod,
balanced and swung, ate fruit and sunflower seeds,
but there was no longer any sun or flower
in *that* life. It turned vicious and pecked
and only rarely cried "Arara! Dry crackers!"
Its world had gone. Its other had gone.
It was a slave now, waiting to be sold
in the market square.

And the young Greeks kept on watching cocks and cunts
and squirting into pocket handkerchiefs.
An I kept on drinking ouzo and eating hors d'oeuvres.

And one wet afternoon in February,
with the wind blowing from Russia, you, José
—who'd drunk with me in a hundred small tavernas
and slept with me in reeling, drunken beds
and sailed with me to islands with magic names:
Mykonos, Naxos, Thira—
visited me. Your shoes were sodden sponges;
your face had lost its mestizo brown, paled to yellow.
You'd been laid off from your boatbuilding job and you knew now
you'd never get a ship here. You were going
to Barcelona. We drank hot sage tea
and planned to meet again in—who knows where?
And I got you a ticket for an evening bus
to Marseille, and you left that city.

                              The red-and-blue macaw
lingered and lunged from its horizontal bar
—but never shrieked "Dry crackers!"—
through that particularly raw and dreary winter
till spring came, and the plane and mulberry trees
sprouted small leaves,
and the market fruits were no longer tangerines
and apples from Mount Pelion, but young figs.
Tart heart-shaped strawberries. Black Sea cherries.
And one day when I passed by the pet shop
on my way to pursue the latest urgent researches
in my favourite theatre of investigation, I happened to notice
that the red-and-blue macaw no longer swung from
its horizontal bar. It had died, the owner told me,
of some tropical disease or other no veterinarian
could diagnose. Psittacosis, no doubt.

I too left that city shortly after. You, José,
are (I guess) on some ship or (I hope) back home
in San Pedro Sula, tending bar,
downing your *guaro* and curing hangovers
with tamarind juice. But sometimes when I drink
and remember that city, Piraeus, Ommonia, I think
of the two macaws, José. ¿Vos comprendés? My last word
on the matter is to repeat Ford Madox Ford: "This is the saddest story
I have ever heard."

—Blue-and-gold, red-and-blue tropical bird!

(José was an unemployed Honduran sailor from San Pedro Sula, the second city of that country, whom I met in the sailor bars of Piraeus while I lived in Athens, and who became my close friend. Arara is the Brazilian Portuguese name for the macaw, guacamaya the Latin-American name in Spanish. Guaro is sugarcane brandy, that is, cheap rotgut white rum, in Central America. The form of Spanish employed, using "vos" instead of "tu" and accenting the last syllable of the verb, is current in most of Spanish America except Mexico. The quotation from Ford Madox Ford, which I have used elsewhere, is the opening line of The Good Soldier.*)*

FLAWED ARCHETYPES

Now that these things are over
and the countdown had begun
I perceive all relationships
were really only one.
Under the glittering surface
variety of form
a single theme unfolded
the same pattern was spun.
The archetypes of absence:
lost father, searching son;
the teacher, fount of wisdom,
the pupil, yearning, come.

From some I sought protection;
I gave harbour to some;
from some I sucked experience;
some came to me to learn.
But we each tried, unknowing,
to play both roles in one:
at the same time teacher-father
and questing pupil-son.
The teachers were not teachers;
the pupils could not learn;
My fathers did not protect me;
I abandoned each son.

THE MAN IN THE VILLAGE

The man with the sparse hair and the white moustache,
in that village where the asphodels were blooming
and the winter wind howled through the rainy night,
when I asked in the square what time the bus passed through,
informed me, shook hands, then took me by the arm
and led me to the thirteenth-century church
(he had the key; he must have been the sexton),
where blackened, crumbling murals display the Baptist
regarding his own head, the death of the Virgin,
then invited me to his house for a cup of coffee.
A strange, low, rambling structure he must have inherited
from his family; rooms full of beds and couches,
yet: "I live alone. I have no family."
He hobbled out painfully to get coffee and sugar,
mixed and heated them in a little pewter kettle,
poured the thick black drink into a small white cup
to cool, and asked me questions. I answered,
but I was waiting, watchful, for the question
that might or might not come, until it slipped out,
painfully, slowly, as I knew it had to do
with no encouragement or help from me.
The Swedish porno mags, one after another,
with their repellent ice blondes, their nude coupling crudeness,
their ultimate hard Nordic commercial coldness.
And the old man turned the pages, talked of summer
when the hippies come, and the young Italians—so hot!—
and I knew why so many beds. Then he brought out
the pornographic playing cards, flipped through them for me
and muttered "sex" with a question intonation,
tenderly placed his hand on my knee, groped himself,
murmuring pleadingly, tentatively, "sex" again.
While I stayed cold as Canada. No arousal.
I was tired. I was in the region for isolation
and writing, not for games or even friendship.
And he was *so* old and creepy. I assumed
my air of embarrassment, of mild annoyance,
of religious rectitude, perhaps, or straightness,
left the coffee untouched, put on my coat, got up,
left him behind his door. But karma was working,
as it always does, for at night, when I'm alone
with my fears and sadness, in my bleak hotel rooms,
I have begun to become the man in the village.
(His winter nights, waiting behind his door.
His Onliness.) The One. The Village Queer.

Edward A. Lacey

CAFÉ "TO NEON"

Try to recapture
them as they once were
when they were yóungmen.

(Same green baize table
where mottled hands shuffle
greased, battered card-pack.)

Pass time's sponge lightly
over those age-marks.
Tighten the pouched skin.

Dye the sparse hair black.
Straighten the bent necks.
Still the hands' trembling

(clutching their shot-glasses
—cold fire of old men—
clutching their memories).

Pull up the corners
of smiles that turned earthward
with knowledge of gravity.

Banish, vanish those wrinkles,
plastic surgeon of transience,
brighten the dull eyes

(staring so sadly
into a distance that
no longer is distance).

Give me four young blades sitting
at life's café table,
joking, planning their long day.

Stiff cocks sharp as knife-blades,
girls, money, fame waiting,
the card-game just starting.

All time before them,
cutting, shuffling the card-pack,
sure players, born winners.

Contemning the old men
just like all the young bloods
who now sit around them

watching bright-eyed through doorways
the girls; planning, plotting;
beginning their card-game.

(Now *these* watch musing
the passage of everything
—girls, time, yóungmen, card-games.)

And above all, remember,
this is where they are headed,
to this table at game's end
(and the sad thing, they know it)
—all, all the yóungmen.

(Most Greek towns have a Café called "To Neon"—"the new"—which is on some central square or corner, and is patronised by everyone, as a sort of town meeting-place, but especially by old men playing the card games Greeks love. "Yóungmen" is [intentionally] a reminiscence of John Rechy's City of Night. This is of course another version of the poem called "Vanitus." I spent a lot of time in cafés in Greece: they are the centre of life there.)

Edward A. Lacey

AFGHANI LOVE SONG

There's a boy across the river with a bottom like a peach,
And I have to get to him!
There's a boy lives there that loves me, and he's *almost* in my reach,
But I don't know how to swim!

His bottom hides a precious pouch that's lined with Persian silk
with gold threads on the rim.
I want to pour within it pearls and opals white as milk;
I have to get to him!

The glaucous mountain water is as cold and quick as death,
but love is not a whim;
I love that boy, I need that boy, I dive, I hold my breath:
I have to get to him!

Our almond trees are soft pink snow; each love-bird calls to each,
But my eyes are growing dim;
there are lessons life can set you that a life alone can teach:
I don't know how to swim!

There's a boy across the river with a bottom like a peach,
but I don't know how to swim!

Author's Note: Lines 1 and 4, i.e., the refrain, of this famous and traditional Afghani folk song are quoted by innumerable writers on India and the Pashtuns of the Northwest Frontier. Nobody ever quotes the entire song though, so I have decided to complete it, à ma manière.

J.L.S.E. (Jim Eggeling)

1934–

LIFE-ODOR *for Alejandro*

> black
> Hair, red rose
>   th
> Piquant
>   smell of
> Wine in clay,
>   and
> Something more ancient:
>
> Show me your sperm.
>
>   I want to
> Stroke you—this
>   way,
> That. Let
>   me be your
> Hand inside yr tangas'
> Elastic band.
>   Es de
> Huevo stroking huevos.
> Never / ending
> Sperm. . . my friend—
>   don't
> Despise it. It's th symbol
>   and
> Product of man's joy.
> What man won't sell pearls
>   to
> Buy it? It is, if not children,
>   then their
> Seed, and its ejaculation,
>   an
> Experiment in boundless ecstasy.
>
>   It's no idle
> Fantasy to which I now urge
>   you then—to
> Sow with me th few wild seed
>   you need
>
>   to
> Spend to know
>   yourself in,

> Alejandro, and to let me worship
>   at th red-hot
> Tip of your active volcano.
>
>   This in not just
> Love my friend, it's more.
> Love is promised
>   by
> Wives and paid
>   for by
> Whores. For me to sex
>   you's the act of a
> Friend.
>
>   And when it's
> Alive, it's alive,
>   and when it's
> Over, it ends.
>
> Pay me, then, th price of friendship.
> Pay me what you owe—
>   not
> Money—pay your body.
>
>   I
> Tell you—Love
>   is
> Love,
>
>   and your
> Body is mine, for free!
>
>   and
> Only for a moment's pleasure;
> Eternity's a nightmare.
>   Th
> God has power
> Only for th duration of th hardon—
>   at the
> Most, for maybe
>   a single
> Hour.

The following six poems are translated/adapted by J.L.S.E. from the Mousa Paidike, *edited by Strato in the reign of the Emperor Hadrian (117–138), lover of the boy Antinous.*

by Stratonos

Passing by th florist's
    just
Now
    I noticed a
Boy wreathing his berries
    around
    a pink
Rosebud
    nor did I
Leave there unpricked.

    shopping
Near him I queried
    him sotto
Voce
    HOW
MUCH FOR A LEI?

    blushing
Rosier than th rose
    my little
Rosebuddy hissed SHHHHH!
Beat it before my father
    catches
On

    so I bought some
Altarflowers to cover my play
    and bringing them
Home
Laid them on my idols
Praying to th gods

    LAY
THAT ONE ON ME!

by Automedon

An
Athlete had me to dinner
    with his
Team.
they
Hovered all over his couch.

One of them fed
    him;
    a
Second one poured him big drinks.
    a
Third draped over his shoulders,
    while th
Fourth one filled his neighborly
lap.

Observing all this teamwork
    I
Fumbled,

    "And
Tell me, dear Couch ---
    at
Night ---
    do you
Coach
    them?"

by Glykos

Once upon a time
Boys could be won with a ball
    a
Pet
     a set of
Dice. but nowadays
     they're
Hungry for more than a dime
(Maybe th family silver)

     their
     Former toys exert no power
     so keep on
Searching
    you
Lovers of boys!

by Stratonos

Boys from the upper
Classes are too high
     for us merely
Honorable men to catch

     and
So,
     like
Mis-prized fruits,
     they
Grow on such heights
     that
Only th crows
     or th
Vultures can possibly snatch
     them.

by Stratonos

     With
Menedemos, don't be shy
     or
Bother to flirt
     with him.
     Just
Cock yr eyebrow
     and he'll say "Let's
Go; I'm with
     you all th
Way". Nor have
     you any banal
Delay—He may
     even
"Start without
     you"—more a
Canyon than yr average canal.

by Stratonos

Rejection bothers
     me, th
Screams and th yells . . .
     those
Slaps from trembling palms

     but
Hairtrigger capitulation
     is even
Worse ––– th boy who leaps
     into your
Arms and submits
     with lascivious
Whoops ––– I'm looking
     for a
Boy more appropriate –––
     whose
Surrender . . . means
     something.

CHRIS' NEW TOY

        would you like to handle my
Penis
Chris

NO

        I really would be
Pleased to have you handle
        it
Chris

WELL . . .
        I DON'T
WANT TO / JIM.

        how 'bout for a
Quarter?

HEY! THAT'S
        O.
K.!

That's th way
        just
Jiggle it up 'n down

        (I
Think I'm going to CUUU ∗ OH!   THIS
uuuuuuuuuuuuuuuuuuuuuu ∗ STICKY–STUFF
uuuuuuuuuuuuuuuuuuuuuu ∗
uuu   ∗
Don't stop yeuuuuuuuut   ∗ (JIGGLE/JIGGLE)
   Keep yr
Fingeuuuuuurs mmmmmmmmmmmoving . . . ah! . .

JIM, DID THAT FEEL GOOD?

Yes

        DO YOU
WANT ME TO DO IT AGAIN?

        I
Don't have another quarter
Chris

    WELL YOU CAN
PAY ME LATER
JIM

Chris . . . I don't know . . .

PLEASE JIM PLEASE!
   I'LL
DO IT FOR FREE!

WHAT THE AMERICAN SAID
TO THE MANCEAR IN EL PARQUE

I am 54
   I am
Malleable.
Someday a male of great beauty
   is going to
Entice me. for him,
   I shall become
Corrupted; I will do anything,
Just like anyone else.
   I will
Sink into th slime of depravity
   and
Wallow in the pit.

   in th
Meantime, I remain innocent.

   (Mere
Sex doesn't count)
   but I shall count th
Days as a tourist
Counts his money
   and
Continue wasting my youth.

   (I am
Very malleable.
   I am
Also quite expensive.)

THE INVITATION

          after a
Long and hard day
Emilio in green gymshorts
          had his
Puberty smeared all over
          him—

Just like vaseline—
          and he seemed
Ripe to have a little more manhood
          rammed

Deep inside
          of him—
          so when he
Eyed

          me with
Sparks th spunk
Burned
          in me

          like
Chicago
          and how could I
Depart from him—seeing
          that he was so
Eager to get started

MARKETING

          this
Muchacho, perhaps fourteen, stands waiting, young and generic among nationally
advertised and garishly labeled old brands.

Waiting with his apparently oblivious mama at th grocery check-out, young brand
X advertises himself in other

          if somewhat
Makeshift ways. Wisely or not, th boy just catches my eye, smiles, and,
pressing his crotch against the top of th counter, displays

          a
Sausage in his jeans, remarkable for an hombre of any age.

J.L.S.E. (Jim Eggeling)

"ABANDON SWEET CARE, YE POETS"

-i-

Abandon sweet care:
    th
Picture's not all black.
    th
Boymuse
Takes up Her slack,
      as
Eros always did
      for
Aphrodite. And not only
    is His little ass more
Tidy, but its tight.

    but on th
Other side of His goldpiece
"Knock, knock

    who's
There?" is th gentle tapping
    of his
Enormous Pointed Penis
Always willing,
    from a
Boy's Point of view
    (a head
Shorter on th top—
    and on

    th
Bottom, one harder
    than anyone

Else's! —), to come in
    and
Gossip away yr night
    (or if you have to
Pray,

Then all
    yr next
Day).
    And its
All

for
Free.
       for

   He
Knows
      He

      has no
Market/among
      such
Magazines
         as the
Immortal
Ladies Home Journal,

      and
Besides, he says, "There's plenty
      more where
That came from," as he whips
      down a broken
Zipper.

-ii-

"Knock-knock"

      "Who's
There?" "Dragon."
"Dragon

Who?" "Dragon
      yuh
Ass." Alas,

      from l'heure
Bleu to th crack of dawn
      he's all
Over you, planting poems
      in
Every place
      he
Can/ and,

      when yr
Pot grows raw,
      the little

Cock wants to take
        you in His
Craw

    or else He
Flips up His black flowerbed
        and
Begs you to plant yr seeds
        in His
Own smooth crack.

    if
Hope is such sweet care
        as
Dreams are made
        of

This Boy's blows
        have unraveled my
Sleep's naked elbows.

    sweet
Jesus! what a couple!
He flays you alive
        with what

    you thought you
Wanted
        while
She minds yr and His little poems
        with the
Undaunted

    ferocity of an
Angel. Th clear
        mark of
Abel is on Her brow,
        but over His rear

Portal He
        has had tattooed:

    "y'all
Come inside,
'Yhear? an' just abandon
        sweet
Care."

for Ricky

He won't
Kiss me, but he will
　　　suck my
Cock; I like
　　　that in a
Boy—

　　　he
Makes

　　　the
Important

Distinctions.

PASSING EROTIKS

　　　as th
Fiesta Parade passes
By me, so do two twelve-year
Male asses,
Staring at me. With my eyes,

　　　I
Drop their pants.
　　　and with
Their eyes, they let
　　　me drop them,
Too, right gladly.

Right there on South Alamo
　　　Street we
Squirt each other with lascivious squints.

Suddenly I wake up
　　　and quit playing
Publicly with their bloodshot vents.
　　　and their
Eyes pull up their innocence
Across their skins
　　　again, as if opalescent
Concupisence had never been
　　　all
Over
　　　them instead of
Raspberry jam.

APOLLO TOUGH LOVE:
SUCH AS TENNYSON ONLY HINTED

to Osvaldo

–i–

Grandfather's generation trained
its boys with rods.
Nowadays such disciplinary art
Seldom is permitted.

Boys, however, are smart—
Streetboys teach schoolboys
Just where to find such training.

"Out on th streets"
Bedding down with strangers,
Today's guys complete their education.

–ii–

Men: beware . . .
Some such boys will talk – – –
Go for their asses!

Teachers by default:
Learn this lesson well—
Lead with a big red hardon.

Boys who've been fucked
Know how to keep secrets—
That one, anyway.

–iii–

Some boys are fully trustworthy.
Look for them everywhere.
Obedience shines in their eyes.

Trustworthy boys, every one,
Offer you their asses.
Pledging them for their silence.

      Yr
Reputation will be safe

with
"Me, sir, please. Try
    me. To
Know me is to fuck
    me."

        Conocerme
    es
Cogerme

–iv–

Streetboys, however, can play hard to get.
"Roll on your side, buddy."
Slip in some grease,

Pop in the "Silencer of Tongues".
Teach 'em a little respect.
Mutter you're giving 'em (grease for
the soul) two dollars.

Next time, let 'em ask.
Bask in their hot embarrassment.
Train 'em not to be whores.

–v–

You, th boys know, can gossip too—
Back they will come each week,
Blackmailing themselves on your rigid . . .
discipline.

(Rods up their asses,   Teach
young men to be straight,
Finishing their sexual objectification—

Now they can do "anything"!—
    husbands and
Fathers are initiated
Only by courting th thrusting rod.)

Jim Everhard

1946–1986

JIM EVERHARD (1946–1986)
at Rehoboth Beach, Delaware, Summer 1984.
Photo by Orry Kelly

This section of Gay Roots Vol. 2 *has been prepared by me as a tribute to the late Jim Everhard. It complements and expands on what I have published of his work in* Gay Roots Vol. 1 *(pp. 659–667). I first became aware of Jim's writing when he submitted a manuscript of gay poetry to Gay Sunshine Press in the early 1980s—later published by me under the title* Cute and other gay poems *(1982). It was obvious to me at the time that Jim's work is probably the most brilliant, insightful among that large body of poetry engendered by Stonewall and the subsequent gay liberation movement—a conclusion which has deepened into a certainty as the years have passed.*

Jim died of AIDS in summer 1986, one of that large number of creative artists lost to our community and country over the past decade. Jim left a vast amount of unpublished writing—mostly poetry, but including some prose, too. His literary manuscripts are currently in my care. From them I have chosen the material presented here (with the exception of the poems "Curing Homosexuality" and "Memory of Roanoke" which are taken from his book Cute).

The opening prose pieces are autobiographical fragments, the latter two of which, at least, were apparently intended as sections of a larger, never completed, work. Jim would have polished these prose pieces literarily before publishing them, but I have left them in their rough-hewn state apart from minor punctuation corrections. The last four poems printed in this section are a sensitive interpretation of how one gay man saw death. We have lost many gay brothers to AIDS over the past fifteen years: here is a recovery of part of what one of those brothers left behind.

—Winston Leyland

THIS IS MY LIFE

1.

I WAS BORN ON DECEMBER 2, 1946 in Dayton, Ohio because my father was stationed at Langley Air Force Base after the suicide mission he almost went on to Communist China was shelved; and my mother who has exquisite bone structure was impregnated one night before she started having her head aches drove me to the hospital inside her. The doctor said I looked intelligent. My father was always self conscious about his lack of height though he was tall enough to do the things most men like to do. My mother says she is part Amerindian.

2.

I cried the first day of school in front of our house with Linda and became the victim of morning sickness meaning I couldn't eat breakfast or maybe a little toast and milk which may be why I am a lean person. By now my mother was in her wheel chair looking out the window trying to keep my two brothers from looking out the window at their older brother crying because he had to go to school. Luckily Dad wasn't there or he would have seen me crying but I suppose in bed that night she probably turned to him and said, "Jimmy cried this morning" and he said "I hope he didn't cry real loud" and she said "When he came home he was real excited" and he said "He can't cry every morning he goes to school" before they refused to make me or hire someone to make me the bunny costume I needed for our May Day celebration. My class did the bunny hop and I practiced every day and the teacher asked us every day about our costumes and I nodded my head but I couldn't go to the dance without looking like a bunny so the next day the teacher had to ask me why I wasn't there and I said it was because I wasn't a bunny.

3.

I dressed up in Linda's mother's old clothes with Linda and Karen and Suzanne and we walked up and down the street once thinking it was a good joke. I forget what happened because of that but I tried on my mother's ear rings once in a while on her vanity where the mysterious mirror changed my sex. I sat in her wheel chair and pretended my legs couldn't feel though she told me she only couldn't walk but she could feel even better than before the way nature compensates for our losses. She was a real believer in loss.

4.

In high school I bummed around with a fat guy and a guy with a caved in chest. Their names were Nick and Rod. David, a chess champion, tried to befriend me but he always wore suits to school and even today I picture him in a gray suit or a blue blazer with his skinny face and oily black hair. Terry had a problem with his hand which hung limply by his side and killed him. It was attached to his brain where two small blood vessels were and one large one was supposed to be burst like a hidden bomb. His family moved quietly back to the midwest where they came from. I had one date in high school with a girl named Gay in ninth grade at the homecoming dance. Afterwards I became a famous recluse.

5.

I started smoking when I turned nineteen and dropped out of college after seeing a movie inside the human lung with cancer all over it like breathing shit. This was my self-destructive period though I have never been suicidal: I joined the Navy because my mother had been a WAVE and I didn't know how to swim or fight with a knife which you need to know how to do in jail. So I didn't resist or flee to Canada but spent weekends going home watching double feature foreign films and adopting various subversive attitudes which introduced me to groups of conscientious objectors who led me to the first love of my life, Harry, who loved me until he found out I was gay when I told him (in a letter) years later that I'd always loved him. Where is that letter now? Locked away in crazy brain cells in the cluttered past.

6.

College was neurotic and self-fulfilling prophecy. I became a famous writer in a small circle but was sexually unfulfilled and dated some girls one who had a vision of me in a field in Wales that I was a village shaman who did something evil or upsetting and was in trouble until his old age when I was exonerated and honored above all others. Debbie had a way with words, said she'd suck me but I didn't want to have sex with her after she told me she almost got married once in Florida but the day before the wedding her boyfriend told her he was gay and I am gay so I couldn't tell her since she liked me. She was a white witch and made things levitate when she was a child but couldn't do it any more and had lousy luck with men it seemed.

7.

Finally I came out gay and contracted mononucleosis and fucked up my last semester at college. Four months later I had a job and moved into the city after horrendous scenes with my mother and had my first lover who left me shortly afterwards. Then I had casual affairs and met Michael who was married and saw my first lover again and dropped both of them and fucked around and wrote some of my famous early poems soon to come out in book form. I met Richard and went home with him once and met Tom and he moved back to Roanoke and I visited him in Roanoke and Richard asked me to have dinner with him the night I returned, disillusioned, from Roanoke.

8.

Richard and I became lovers eventually and broke up because I couldn't settle down and wasn't interested in a career like he was. Then Winston called me all the way from California and told me he got a grant and could do my book [*Cute and other gay poems*, Gay Sunshine Press, 1982] which I have dedicated to Richard or that part of my life when we were quite goofily in love but hurt each other and he slept with me a whole month while I had syphilis and afterwards I didn't want to make love very much which he took offense to. He came to my apartment and laid it out. We had a discussion and looked at it for a while and he walked out. I became manicky-depressed meaning I followed him and called and left notes and dumped out a lot of venom until I had to see a shrink who talked it over with me. Now I agree, venom isn't nice. I made an ass out of myself and have almost recovered. I'm kicking out a room mate now who can't write a good check. I feel stronger twelve ways:

9.

1. Spiritually, I am closer to my body
2. Analytically, I see other peoples' lives so much clearer than my own, I should be leading someone else's life
3. Emotionally, I'm on top of what love doesn't mean
4. Historically, I think back what if Harry had been gay
5. Honestly, the truth isn't all there is to see
6. Philosophically, I'll always be a Platonist
7. Physically, I'm a Sagittarius
8. Astronomically, I always wish upon the first star I see
9. Surrealistically, I rarely remember my dreams
10. Dietarily, I love ice cream, pizza and beer
11. Musically, I sing flat
12. Poetically, I thrive in negative capability

10.

I will always be somebody else's other man. I am currently interested in five men, all of whom have lovers. Perhaps this is because I am gun shy or simply because I am tired of jealousy. I just kicked out my room mate and after fifteen years of distance have begun to talk to my father again and think he's not a bad man after all. I am his other man, the man he does not understand inside himself, the man he has cowered away from in shame and fear. And he loves me. Or he wants what a father wants from his son. Love. Everyone wants to be loved. I want to know more about this crazy life I've been led by to this point just before breaking so many times. I've never broken as deeply as I might have since I'm always stronger than I thought which surprises even me. I'm not terribly successful the way the world measures success but I feel very successful on my own terms which are not without their innate value. The only way to get rid of the venom is to bite something real hard like a stone or old bones.

11.

And now for the personal messages without which I would cease to exist:
>   to Harry, you will always be number one
>   to Walt, I am not the man we were
>   to Michael, marriage is not forever
>   to Tom, you go your way and I go mine
>   to Richard, you are no longer an absence
>   to Bill, you were the first all over again
>   to Eric, forever a prologue
>   to Harry, my first friend
>   to Randy, I fell in love with your name

12.

Others not mentioned: Evelyn, Margaret, Debbie, Ed, Peter, Stuart, Frank, Ron, Stanley, Dick, Margaret, Richard, Jim, Don, Janet, Bobby, Paul, Willie, John, Harry, Kathy, Win, Ralph, Mark, Mark, Tim, John, Billy, Faye, Gladys, Nauvlet, Rhonda, Angie, Tim, Mr. Meadows,

[written ca. 1982]

How I Got Mixed Up In This World

IT ALL STARTED IN the basement of a church. I read about it in an underground paper. I was twenty six (1973) and had never had sex with anyone. I suffered through a brief affair in college with a hefty Jewish girl who had a good sense of humor and had previously graduated from a speed-withdrawal center. But because I didn't want to have sex she did everything she could do to get me into bed and finally worked it out. I was a miserable lover but she encouraged me to try it again and I didn't have the courage to tell her I was attracted to men. I remember how, afterwards, we lay back in bed and pretended to sleep. Before I knew it morning birds were singing in the misty trees outside. This was rural Virginia. I don't think I slept a wink.

So I told my mother I was going to a poetry reading. I lived with her at the time. I was one semester away from graduating from George Mason University, major in English literature. I wrote poetry and worked on the school literary magazine. All my friends were the freaky creative type. I knew two brothers who were hung up on Faulkner. One of the teachers was an Adrienne Rich fanatic. Others thought highly of surrealism and horror movies. Their idea of kink was remarkably tame. Yet we were the avante garde of George Mason. Since then the two brothers have published novels. I wrote two novels after that, both failures. Back then, however, I was almost entirely hung up on poetry and sex. Come to think of it, that's pretty much my situation today but I've been through a lot in eight years. I'm older than I ever believed I'd make it.

I had this passion for Keats in high school. I memorised "Ode to a Nightingale" and at different times wrote papers on "Hyperion" and "Lamia." But I never wrote like Keats. I identified with his boat trip to Italy mostly. He thought he was going home he was so fevered. A friend was with him. This is all in Walter Bates Jackson's bio. His father wanted him to be a physician but possibly he was reminded of that old quip, "Physician, heal thyself," and became a poet instead. To be a poet you have to keep your eye glued to another world without ignoring what's in front of you. What's in front of you creates the vocabulary of your embattled tongue. I thought a lot about other boys.

The first boy I thought about was Chuck who lived on my street. I rode my bicycle down behind his house at night one summer and watched his bedroom window hiding behind bushes. His room was in the basement. Occasionally I caught him coming out of the shower with only a towel wrapped around him. Once, before this I saw him in nothing but shorts on top of the hill that rolls down to his back yard. My brother and his younger friends charged up the hill and Chuck turned the hose on them.

I think that was the only time in my entire boyhood that I ever deeply cared about being one of the boys. I wanted to run up that hill with the other guys charging this naked boy with his watery sword and tackle him down to the ground where our lips would fuse and our chests would quiver against each other. It was about this time I read Sherwood Anderson's story, "Hands" about the guy whose hands were unholy or something. As if most of us don't have odd little dream lives for our hands, the kinds of things we never tell anyone else. Our hands are barriers against other people ever entirely knowing us.

Yet they are almost always naked. If you cover your hands people think you are strange. Or they suspect they were tragically burned or deformed at birth. Or you have a shameful tattoo on them. I once knew a guy with the word "love" tattooed on the back of the fingers on his left hand. One letter on each finger in steely dark blue. I always wanted to use peacock blue ink in high school because the teachers made us use regular blue. Perhaps peacock blue was too pre-Raphaelite for the school board's taste.

My hands are long and slender. I played the piano for four years and just last year when I visited my ex-lover one night he had rented a piano and I picked up a piece of music by Scarlatti and played it well enough to recognize the melody. But my hands have lost the resilience of my youth. I played "Für Elise" in a recital one year. Then my teacher died. She always mumbled to herself when she came up the sidewalk. She was under five feet tall with brazen red hair and an opera singer's chest. She died because she was a Christian Scientist and did not trust modern medical science. Since then I have known other people who died.

Before I had sex I never felt really involved in this world. That was why I was so interested in radical politics, even when I was in the Navy. After I had sex my political interest waned though never entirely died. I've never voted. I wrote an article against electoral politics for the college paper with a quote from some French anarchist that went something like this: "The vote is like beating the ass of some sonorous donkey."

Stevie Nicks has just confessed on the radio that she and Lindsay Buckingham were never really good friends. I have always managed to have at least one good friend. Now most of my friends are gay but before they thought I was a sexual vegetable. Like I had a secret relationship with pollen and the wind. The Jewish girl was not the only one who tried to get me into bed. The others were more lovely perhaps but lacked the soul to be found in someone who has suffered from a lack of physical attention.

Physical attention is important developmentally. The famous wire monkeys only proved how damaging it can be at an early, twilight age but I suspect it is of greater harm in later years once we have looked out at the awesome world of lovers and seen what perfectly normal people can do to each other. For a long time I acted like a wire monkey, reaching out to be touched by almost anyone available. And lots of men were available for one reason or another. I doubt Punk is an improvement over Disco but people only want to keep on dancing.

The greatest mistake of my generation has been to mistake dancing for a plausible life style. Isadora Duncan meant something different by it. In the grand confrontation this century between the Dionysians and Apollonians, the Dions have abandoned the political arena to celebrate the apocalyptic vision of medieval saints without any of that old visionary talk. Our vision has no content like a tv that's been left on all evening while the people sit around talking or looking out the window or applying a new shade of lipstick to the mouth or playing Risk. People leave on radios and televisions as if they are part of the Beckettish chorus of monologues that substitute for conversation today. My mind jumps around too much, is uncontrollable and in it I hope to hit upon something stunning, something that will send the chill of a touch of reality up your spine. I care no longer for story or character or symbolic stability.

I believe in Jack Kerouac. I love Jack Kerouac. I admire his belief in unrelievable jiving. Hit on a beat and play in the foam of the waves. Yet my mind can be too staccato at times. And I am too truthful at times. I think I should get back to church.

I was in front of this church afraid to ask anyone what room the gays met in. I wandered around the hallway with its community-minded bulletin board. I was obviously early but I hoped no one would ask me if I was a Unitarian. I didn't look gay then. I had long hair like a student because I was a student and a poet. I always looked nervous, on edge, ready to leave. I walked down some stairs to the basement and found a room which must have been used for a day care center. The Unitarians are caught up in all the modern concerns. Fingerpainted pictures were scotch taped to the wall. Lots of houses in the land of giants. And huge, colorful flowers you could almost wish were real. Kids always want to draw where they live and who they live with. Maybe that's why psychologists use art therapy today. They ask the child, "Who is that?" and the kid says, "The prick I live with." This measures high in hostility. The child is obviously the product of a nuclear family. A nuclear family is composed of a mother and a father and one or more children. Occasionally relatives like grandparents and uncles or aunts drop by with presents. But I was in this church looking at the kids' drawings. I was staring at this purple boy holding a wagon next to an orange dog chewing on something that looked like a cock when a voice broke my concentration.

"You're new here," he said. These were the first words I'd ever heard from a gay man.

"I . . . I thought Angela Davis was speaking here," I replied, nervously. I turned around. He was thick waisted and bald. When he smiled I squirmed uncomfortably.

"The gay awareness group meets here," he said, instantly putting me on the spot.

"Not Angela Davis, then," I mumbled.

"She was here lately but not here," he said, somewhat tongue-tied, nervous, I suppose, because I was nervous. I've found that nervousness is very contagious. I'm sure that if you acted nervous around an unseasoned murderer, he'd probably blow it and let you escape. People do not like nervous people. They think of them as seriously ill. Hiding something. Perhaps a longer knife than the knife under his shirt sleeve. He gulped.

I felt immensely innocent, rapable. I watched his large, hairy hands clutch and miss each other.

"Interesting art work," he said, beginning to move his head back and forth in front of the wall. His eyes settled on the purple boy. "Funny, it looks like that dog's chewing on a . . . penis," he said.

This was not doing at all. I wanted to escape before this infantile giant that had jumped out of the imagination of a six year old should attack me. I didn't even know what he would do to attack me. I didn't understand where a man desired to place his cock. I never dreamed about putting one in my mouth. If he had asked to suck me off right then and there I don't know what I would have done. Suck off? Off on? His lips were tight like the edges of a wallet. His fat tongue wetted his lips and his nervous eyes jutted around the room again. He didn't know what to do with me. I began to feel at ease. A little chaos in a simple situation can go a long way.

Then some other guys arrived. People started standing around. Some of them knew each other. My friend soon found another older man who he began talking to. They each eyed me suspiciously.

"Hello, I'm Herbert."

I didn't want to turn around to that voice but I did, mostly to avoid looking at my first gay friend. My second gay friend had glasses on so thick they magnified his already large eyes. His lips were large, too, and buttery. He carried a briefcase under his arm. The briefcase set me at ease. Perhaps he was lost, too.

"I thought Angela Davis was speaking here," I said, half-smiling.

"This is the gay growth group," he said, straightforwardly.

"Oh," I weakly replied.

"Everyone here is gay and proud or working toward becoming proud of their gayness," Herbert said. "I'd like you to meet my friend, Kimberly," he added.

Kimberly was the same height as Herbert and myself but better built and very clean cut looking with blond hair and a chin chiselled by an angel. It was the way a chin should look, squared off, smoothly fleshed, almost glossy with a cleft. Kimberly was a dancer. When he talked his chin danced under his lips.

"You go to George Mason, don't you," he asked. I was taken completely by surprise. The last thing I expected was to be recognized, even by someone who I didn't recognize. I wasn't sure if he was spying on me or merely being friendly.

"Yes," I replied, my short yes sounding a little more educated than Gary Cooper's "yep" but not much more generous.

"Aren't you glad you aren't alone after all," Herbert said, looking at the wall where the purple child was still, I imagined, standing by the dog with the prick in its mouth. Herbert walked away from us toward the wall with a studious look on his face.

"Herbert's studying psychology," Kimberly said, matter-of-factly.

"Very interesting," Herbert said behind us as if he had just discovered the justification for working diligently at his BA in psychology.

"The dog's got a prick in his mouth," I said, trying to make the word "prick" sound natural as it slithered out of my mouth.

"Yes, I see that," Herbert replied musingly. "I'm always fascinated by the way a child sees himself so . . . so . . . immersed . . . part of the whole . . . seeing without seeing. . . . It amazes me. We were all born such egomaniacs. . . ,"

"We were at an art show the other day," Kimberly added, "where this woman did giant portraits of rats."

"She's disgusted by urban renewal," Herbert said.

"Yet the rats were somehow . . . beautiful. Large, white rats in basically dark interiors with lots of shadows and strange illuminations. They looked more like laboratory rats than city rats. Laboratory rats, you know, are purer than ourselves. They are bred in entirely controlled environments for the purpose of scientific research. We had biology class together but I guess you don't remember." I suddenly realized I was being addressed.

"I'm afraid I don't recall," I said, noticing that the room had become crowded in the last few minutes. Someone was calling us to order. Everyone looked toward the sound of clapping hands. Some older man was clapping his hands over his head.

"Quiet, everybody," he called to us. Everyone turned around.

He wore love beads and long hair with an open collar. A shirt manufactured in Pakistan by simple village women paid in peanuts. Nixon was our president. We were friends with China. It was after Stonewall. But people were a long shot from no more suffering. This was the beginning of the end of feel good therapy. The first thing he had us do was get in small circles and touch each other. Almost everyone was awkward but a few of the guys were overly eager which compensated for the others' misgivings. I'd never felt the reality of another male body before except when I was in the Navy and people in the seat next to mine fell asleep. I got a hard on from just feeling a guy's leg next to mine. How was I ever supposed to avoid this?

It was a relief to end the touching exercise. Everyone joined in one large circle and closed in on everyone else as if someone had sucked the air out of the circle. I remembered childhood games like dodge ball and red rover and how I was always the doctor when the guys played war games. I lost a lot of patients because I was afraid to amputate. I saw a movie once where this guy's leg was amputated and all he could talk about was how he felt like that leg was still there and it hurt. The human mind agrees on certain common hallucinations to create a world in which to operate. But we are always defying that world. We always see what isn't there and don't see what is.

At the moment I was wondering if the world hadn't been created all over again without my knowing.

"We'll break up into discussion groups next," Herbert said to me.

"You can join us," Kimberly said.

"We talk about things like coming out and lovers and how to tell it to your parents. It's quite helpful, I think," Herbert said. He pulled me by the arm and before I knew what to say we were squatting in a circle of about eight men. The discussion tonight would be the bar scene.

The bar scene? Had I stumbled into a group of reforming alcoholics, I wondered. I, who had never haunted bars outside of a few occasions in the Navy. I got so smashed a couple of times once this elderly woman in the Robin's Nest on the Boston Common thought I looked like her son dead in Vietnam and my friend, Harvey, on his knees, proposed to her in front of her husband who was as amused as she was while this platinum blond in a shimmery red dress cut up above her knees was pouring champagne into plastic glasses for everyone. She had come out of the mafia party in the back room long enough to appear in our dreams. So we drank champagne and got lost finding our ship and ended up in a pizza parlour unattended. A thin, young woman sat at a table with a little girl with dirty hair and ate pizza. It must have been four o'clock in the morning. We stole a pizza and caught a free taxi ride back to the base but were lost and reported to the same wrong ship three times before they threatened to get the shore patrol after us. Then we saw the two red lights. Harvey saw the red lights across the channel. So we found our way back to the ship and I broke about a hundred fluorescent light bulbs crawling around in this dark bin while Harvey found ten dollars when he bent over his bunk. It fell out of nowhere. Rose's picture on the back of a cereal box at morning mess and that mess are another similar story but took place in Philadelphia where I was sent to Operation Buttercup.

Operation Buttercup was a simulated sinking ship. I was a hole plugger. I was given several large, rubber corks to plug into holes on the side of the ship. Like the Dutch boy and his finger in the dike. They set it on fire and we rushed in with our hoses turned on, tore through the fire and stopped the water when someone turned it off. We lost the ship but so had ninety per cent of the other classes passed through that ship. That's why I got to Philadelphia with my friend who liked to take pictures of fire plugs. He took a picture of me spread leg straddling a fire plug which, in some minor way, now seems prophetic. I don't know what he did with the photo? Perhaps he sold it to someone in the porno industry. I didn't know anyone gay in the Navy though after my discharge I heard that's all they were; but I didn't find it true about long, restless sea crossings.

That wasn't my first experience with fire fighting. I spent a week in a training school in Norfolk doing the same thing. They set cement block houses on fire and the crazy Canooks were the first to rush in and put it out. Everyone had a chance to be at the head of the hose. You were instructed to wave the nozzle in large circles out in front of you where the fire was. But the water pressure in the hoses was intense and the hose had a life of its own. I was afraid it would knock me over but fear increases your strength. I managed okay until I had fought my way into the very midst of the hellish flames. The instructor was lagging behind me shouting for the others behind me to keep the hose steady. Like a cobra listening to a different drummer it sprayed its hood of water up over my head behind me at the fellows backing me up causing everyone to lurch backwards. I tripped on something and the hose jumped completely out of my control. People behind me couldn't see what was happening because of thick smoke.

The instructor was pissed off at me. He called me a jerk-off and blamed me for the sinking of the Titanic. Like an iceberg, I only showed ten percent of my entire despair. I didn't want to go to Vietnam anyway. I didn't want to remind some old woman about her dead son. It must have been the uniform. That was when bell bottoms were gaining a notorious appeal among the drug addicts.

So this guy opened the discussion about bars. He was good looking in a sixtyish sort of way. Later he would tell me he had one dream, to someday cover his entire body in jewels. But at that moment, before I had met him, he looked like a gypsy who had lost his dancing bear.

"The bars are okay," he began. "You just have to control your use of them. Control is very important because if you lose control you're liable to end up in an awkward situation. When I get stuck in an awkward situation I tell the other person that I just got a call from Public Health. It works every time. But if I'm drunk, I forget my line and often end up going to bed and regretting it."

"I think the bars ruin relationships," another fellow said. He was maybe thirtyish with brown hair and a diamond earring in his left ear. His hands were neatly cupped in his lap and he spoke slowly and clearly as if he were in a public speaking competition. His piercing eyes arrested his listeners long enough for him to add that he had never found a lover in the bars. Only tricks.

What kind of tricks, I wondered. I was becoming increasingly naive about the discussion as it unfolded. Two obviously inseparable men spoke about their commitment and how it had begun in a bar but now took place mostly in the green house they had built behind their lovely home on Capitol Hill. They were obviously very successful and reminded me of how girls used to talk in high school about an outcast's misfortune in dress. It seemed her mother did all the family shopping at Montgomery Wards.

I was reminded about the pain of never owning a hoola hoop while it was in fashion.

The way the one guy held the other guy's hand as if he was afraid to tell him he was terminally ill bothered me.

Or maybe the test results hadn't come back yet.

Marianne Faithful singing "As Tears Go By" on the radio.

The green and red neon sign across the street below my window at Trios advertising "Pizza" and "Submarines."

Soon I must go out. Yes, I am going down to a local gay bar. Will probably drop into three. These are the neighborhood bars. Tomorrow I'll get back to my growth group and how I grew, like five little peppers. Like on the prairie.

Being an impressionistic masterpiece, I can afford this casual approach. I want to reflect my mind. This, unfortunately, is the way it reflects. But it embraces many ways of life, many small miracles and this is only the beginning.

A GHOST STORY

This autobiographical fragment, apparently planned as part of a longer manuscript, was written by Jim Everhard in the early 1980s. It is a portrait sketch of a lover of that period and, as such, complements the love poems written by him and printed in Gay Roots *Volumes 1 and 2.*

BEING A CREATIVE PERSON I have always expected room service. This is one of my worst possible characteristics. I drop clothing off my body like a snake abandoning his skin. I don't look back until laundry time and then I utter, incredulously, my god.

But this is not a story of profanity as of yet. Profanity may enter one's life at any juncture but as of yet John, Jeffrey and myself have not become profane. Jeffrey was not the ordinary variety of spook you get in a ghost story.

Jeffrey was the world's most innocent femme fatale.

Jeffrey had hair not so much red as glowing, phosphorescent, an ember set ablaze by passion. He resembled a flaming clipper ship searching for harbor. He sent out volleys and signals which carelessly hit their target. He was spontaneous and cheerful. He fell in love with me. That's something I would never say if I didn't, in the deepest sanctions of my heart, believe was and is true.

When we met he was in the middle of a tempestuous marriage. Two men, you know, are not allowed to take holy vows of marriage. This leaves them to their own devices and most people don't care that society doesn't sanctify any human relationship. It shows how deeply the terror runs.

But Jeffrey did not look like a faggot. He stood out even if he was so short because he had an open, radiating smile. And he smiled at me, ever so hesitant at first. He was already afraid he might lose me. And when I first looked his way I felt a quick rush of indifference until I realized I wasn't looking away.

I had been playing it up big in the bar that night. I thought I was pretty hot shit but it was only a reflection of my antagonistic nature. I have always thought of myself as reticent, quiet, even demure. Never raucous. But I was feeling arbitrary, like Ruby Fruit Jungle. Or Huck Finn. I was so sick of propriety and custom. We are by nature spontaneous, but culture culls it carefully out of us. We begin to have expectations. And expectations blind us. We become aggressive and competitive. We forget that each of us is absolutely amazed to be here and we should, before anything else, celebrate this amazement. That's why I want to tell you about Jeffrey. Because he amazed me or helped me to amaze myself more than I have been amazed in a long time.

Astonished.

If astonished was something besides a word, it would be what ghosts sound like when they try to explain to the living what it's like to be a ghost.

Jeffrey is like a ghost to me. When we are not together I am submerged in the sensation of his death and I want to mourn for the whole world. I want to write Lycidas. Or something equally as passionate and cosmic.

We spent very little time at the bar where we met. This bar is populated mostly by suburban children who keep everything at a high pitch and the odor of vomit tends to overcome whatever room freshener they use. The music is masochistically loud and leaves the human ear positively bleeding. I know several people who work there, including the door man, and I usually get in for free when they charge two dollars at the door. So we were both glad to leave the bar even though I felt a slight nudge about maybe missing out on some excitement. He was a smaller man than I usually picked out. But he was enthusiastic and smily and when you meet the Pied Piper of Hamlin, you can't help but follow. He could have been Pan piping a song down the streets we walked toward my apartment. Yes, I am in love with Pan, the small man, the compact man. And Jeffrey is wonderfully male.

My room is an eyesore to some people, especially the anally compulsive. I often misplace things, usually books or poems and when I want to find them I have to look through everything. But I don't mind this process actually. I end up finding things I haven't looked at or for in months or years. Cleaning up my room is a matter of deepest heart break and innumerable shy smiles.

So Jeffrey came into my room where I keep my books and writings and my type writer and bed and a radio and not much more. My makeshift desk. It is made out of two bureaus of unfinished wood which I bought originally for five dollars apiece. And the board on top of them I found some place. It has always honorably served its original intention. Perhaps the wooden board was once going to be a door?

And we fell into each other's arms. Maybe even before, on the elevator. I often cornered my men in the elevator. The sensation of rising upward and of kissing at the same time is almost too simultaneous. It drives people crazy because they really want to kiss each other but they don't know when the door is going to pop open. Luckily, my elevator is very slow. And it was late at night. We kissed for a very long and deep time, long enough for an enchanted forest to grow up around us and conceal our nudity. We slipped out of each other's shirts and fell back on the bed. My brain had become my lips and all I wanted to know about Jeffrey at that moment was what my lips would tell me. And they couldn't stop telling me to wander deeper, always deeper, into his furry little body.

Somewhere along the way we managed to pull off each other's pants.

When two men pull off each other's pants, a very dangerous pattern is struck. We are taught from our earliest days that people of the same sex do not become exuberant about a body similar to their own.

I, however, love the male torso. I'm so skinny that one time a sickly looking puny little Spic faggot whispered to his friend as I passed them in the street, "stringbean." The word has haunted me ever since. But not in a bad way. It has been a companion, an ability to accept my petite body for what it is, another pure example of the body electric. Jeffrey is not a string bean. He is, however, a ghost. The kind of ghost that can become your dreams. That was how Jeffrey entered my body and soul. By becoming what I wanted more than anything else in the world. And it strengthened my own magic, my gift for the absurd and genuine benevolence.

I have always striven to be a beatific person. I have always believed that we were the fallen angels and that we need only to know this to return to our original state of grace. When I think of the most horrific stories of our history, such as the Nazi concentration camps, I realize that there was an angel present somewhere to stop that from happening around the world. Men cannot reach around the world. That is their shame, yet a blessing as well.

Anyway, Jeffrey and I made love. It was that simple. He had planned to leave early to get home to his lover but he stayed out until five thirty in the morning making love.

Making love must be done with the hands.

Jeffrey dragged his heavy chain into my arms and together we dissolved it, if only for a moment. He was in my arms, then he was gone. Like a rabbit falling into a hat. I didn't realize that I had been bewitched. And that I was bewitching myself.

Jeffrey was not an ordinary fellow. He was ordinary enough but he had something else going for him. He still has. Because even when you find out that magic is being performed on you, you want more. It becomes a heightened sensation, a catalyst. Heightened sensations are heightened because they heighten every other experience but in a strangely ghostly way. In one sense, someone in love loses all contact with reality. And I may still be at this point. But the world is suddenly lit. I know this much. Love produces light. It becomes a kind of star that people look for when they want to make love. It's what wraps us up in each other in a gooey little bed asleep and enchanted.

I still do not know who Jeffrey is. I know I am telling you this story too early. I have not allowed my mind to sift through the sediment. It is not easy to love a ghost.

When our eyes crossed, something extremely powerful occurred. I barely have words which would satisfactorily convey the sensation so that you could feel it also. Perhaps it was only the old cliché, magnetism. But it was deep magnetism. Yet it was urgent not simply in an animal sense. We were two people in a bar suddenly struck by each other's eyes. After that it was immediately warm and friendly. We talked for a very short time. He told me that he had noticed me earlier. I was leaning against a railing with my back to the dance floor. Everyone else was looking at the dance floor but I was watching them. That was true. I was conducting an experiment. It was the beginning of a crazy phase I went through with Jeffrey. I followed him down the rabbit hole and before I knew it we were standing against each other in my bedroom gently unbuttoning each other's shirt. You didn't even seem to notice all the books and the clutter of papers. But I made you read a poem I'd written called "Cute." Then our pants slipped off as if we were snakes crawling out of old skin. And we thought we were new men.

Jeffrey is handsome. That is the only undisputable fact about him. His beard and longish hair are strawberry blond and his eyes are blue. His puckish lips, partially concealed beneath his moustache, open naturally when he smiles. And he smiles often. I will never forget his blue eyes and his smile. He was five foot seven and weighed one hundred and twenty-six pounds. His skin was pale but not uncontoured. The hairs on his chest were darker than his strawberry blond hair and his pubic hairs glowed like hot wires. He did not seem small so much as compact. His only flaw, perhaps, was the eczema on his hands. He almost always had one or more fingertips bandaged. At night he rubbed cream on his hands and the many nights we were unable to share I fantasized him unscrewing the top of a jar of cream on his chest and rubbing the cream into his hands. He slept with plastic gloves on his hands to help protect the moisture. This, however, did not bother me. My previous lover had had a wide scar around half his chest from an open heart operation when he was four. Rather than upset me, I found out eventually that the scar became very dear to me, as if it was the only way I could be sure I was with Richard. I didn't mind kissing it. I grew to love kissing it as if it were something special, something divine. If you have loved more than one person, you probably have experienced this also. I felt a deep sympathy for Richard. I knew he was probably a very brave person. I knew he had suffered.

Sometimes I wondered what Jeffrey would have looked like if he truly suffered? I have seen tears in his eyes when we had to part with his lover beside him. I saw tears in his eyes when I surprised him on his birthday. First, let me explain that this all happened during a very extraordinary period of my life. And whatever transpired after I met Jeffrey was as largely due to my own magic as it was to his. We were going to create something that possibly neither of us could tame. But at first I started out more like the Captain Kangeroo of Jeffrey's troublesome life.

MEMORY OF ROANOKE

for Tom

I am still haunted
by the memory of that knock
on the door after we had
already undressed and touched,
and of the boy waiting
outside when you opened it.
Later you told me some guys
in the bar sent boys
to knock on your door at night.
These boys would make love to you,
then report something
to these guys who
couldn't seem to learn enough about you.
You are the quiet sort.
Only some of these boys
would return and tell you
not to give them away,
and they would stay the whole night.
To you it meant nothing, you said.
You could hardly see their faces
in the dark,
for they always came after dark
and you could not turn on your porch light.
This was, after all, a Southern town.
They came. You invited them in.
And afterwards you would sleep
in the warm spot on the sheets
like a ghost.
I knew then how easily
your heart could be broken.

CURING HOMOSEXUALITY

for three incurables, Frank, Stu and Richard

"There are no homosexuals, only fallen heterosexuals."
                              —Dr. Reuben Sebastian Wildchild

Of the many known and proven
cures for homosexuality,
the most familiar, perhaps,
is the Catholic Church's version of
"Confession-is-good-for-the-soul."
According to this ritual, every time
you feel an unclean urge to touch yourself, you stop your hand with the
mental image of the Pope staring you
in the face and these words: "if-I-do-this-
I-have-to-tell-the-priest-again."
Then, when you go to confession you
enumerate and fully describe every such
forbidden act leaving out not the
slightest detail and the priest,
who lives anonymously in a dark box,
tells you what you must do to redeem your lost
soul. This usually amounts to kneeling
before a statue of this virgin
who has never allowed the sinful hands
of any man to ever infest her body
with the puerile desires of the flesh and
mutter a prayer that
you won't touch other men hail Mary as you,
in a religious rapture,
fondle your beads.
                    If this doesn't work,
and one wonders about these
good men whose career it is to sit in the dark
and listen to the pornography of everybody
else's life, the next step is psychoanalysis.
The doctor sits solemnly in the dark
behind you, his hands suspiciously folded
in his lap, and doesn't say a word
while you lie down on a long, lumpy sofa
and tell him about your childhood
and how much you hate yourself
for thinking the things you think
so uncontrollably

and you wish your tongue would fall out
and it almost does as you go on and on
wondering what the hell this fellow
is listening for as you start inventing
stories about Uncle's anus and house pets.
You soon find out he is interpreting
the things you tell him. According to
psychoanalytic theory, everything you say
means something else even more sinister
than what you meant. Your unknown desires
live within you and control your outward behavior. For instance, if you say,
"It's such a beautiful day today
I wanted to leave work early,"
the psychiatrist will interpret this to mean
you are dissatisfied with your job
and this in turn means you are sexually frustrated and this goes back to your miserable
childhood which means he'll probably
respond with, "Do you think that this means
you resented your mother when she
wouldn't let you play with yourself?"
If you say you had a dream about flying
he'll interpret it as a dream of sexual
frustration and penis envy meaning
you are really sick since only women
are supposed to have penis envy. He'll
probably ask you, "How did you feel when
you first saw your father's instrument?
Did you notice if it was bigger than yours?
Did he seem ashamed of his?
Did you want to touch it?"
If you tell him you don't recall
what it looked like he'll tell you
you unconsciously wanted it to fall off
so you could flush it down the toilet.
If you tell him you wanted to kill your father
and rape your mother he'll tell you
you had an Oedipus conflict.
He will listen for key words like
umbrella, closet, brother, rooster, shit, nude
and Judy Garland, all of which convey
a large surplus of unconscious homosexual material. For instance, never say:
"I put my umbrella in the closet
and found my brother in the backyard
beating the shit out of a rooster

while looking at nude pictures of
Judy Garland." To a psychiatrist this means:

umbrella = phallic symbol = womb = death = fear that it will rain at
    your funeral and no one will come
closet = phallic symbol = womb = mother = castration = desire to
    work for a fast food chain = prostitution = fear of underwear
brother = phallic symbol = sibling rivalry = castration = desire to
    stick your finger up your ass and smell it
rooster = phallic symbol = cock = flying = fear of Karen Black =
    crashing = fear of impotence = hatred of women = fear of oxygen
shit = phallic symbol = fear of dirt = work = puritan work ethic =
    father's penis = sexual frustration = deviations = fascination with
        dirt = bad toilet training = sexual hostility toward pilgrims
nude = phallic symbol = opposite sex = original sin = truth = fear of
    gardens = self-deception = poor sanitation habits = desire for
        death and return to Earth Mother = return to disco = hatred
            of mother = love of analyst but always waiting for some-
                one to come along and say no = desire to live in a
                    hole in the ground
Judy Garland = phallic symbol = fear of tornadoes = love/hate of
    sucking = confusion of identity = desire to have oral relations with
        a lap dog = necrophilia = fear of Easter bonnets = desire to
            be a woman = fear of bad breath = spiritual destitu-
                tion = desire to be Dr. Kinsey = existential mal-
                    function = fear of tubas = fear of dude ranches
                        and desire to perform unnatural acts with
                            Mickey Rooney = fear of short,
                                pimply people
Like a cancer, one sentence can devour your entire psyche.

If you say you had a hard time coming today
and you don't have anything to say
he'll call that resistance. If you say
it isn't, he'll say that's more resistance.
If you stop resisting, he'll call that
passive-aggressive. If you tell him
you've had it, you're tired of wasting
time and money when you haven't even begun
talking about homosexuality, he'll tell you
your problems run even deeper than he
initially realized and you need hospitalization.

Once you are hospitalized, the doctors
will begin electric shock therapy.
They call it therapy. There is no resistance.
You are not sure who's getting the therapy,

you or the sadistic maniacs who strap you down
and wire you up and turn on the juice
while they flash pictures of naked men
on a screen. The idea is to associate pain
and the fear of death by electrocution
with naked men. Then a comforting female
nurse unstraps you and wheels you, unconscious,
back to your room where she slowly
but surely revives you and stuffs a few pieces of
stale toast and cold eggs down your gullet.
This is supposed to turn you on to women.
                                              If
none of these cures works
you will probably be thrown out of high school
as a bad influence for all those guys who
make you suck them off in the shower,
then beat you up at the bus stop. If you
still wish to remain homosexual, you will probably be arrested in the public library
for browsing too long in the "Sexuality"
section or during one of the periodic raids
of a local gay bar or face charges for soliciting
a cop who arrested you and forced you
to give him a blow job while he played
with his siren. In prison
you will probably be gang raped by
lusty straight men who are only acting out
their healthy but stifled heterosexual impulses
and if you are lucky one of them may even
win you in a knife fight and protect you
from the gang except when he trades you
out for a night for a pack of cigarettes or
a shot of heroin. Once you are released
you will become an expert in American
legal procedures as you face future charges
of child molestation, murder and attempts
to overthrow the common decency, whatever that is.
When you have had it, and decide to hijack
a jet and escape, you will discover the small
but important fact that no nation under god
or red offers asylum, political or otherwise,
to a plane full of pansies.
Your best bet is to fly over
the Bermuda Triangle and click
you little red pumps together whispering,
"There's no place like home, there's no
place like home."

                    In olden days
the main cure for homosexuality (then
often known simply as witchcraft) was
to tie the suspected faggot to a tiny seat
on the end of a long pole suspended
over boiling water. The suspected faggot was then
submerged for half an hour or until
he stopped struggling, whichever happened first.
If he was still alive when they lifted him
from the vat, they spread an oil slick over the water,
resubmerged the suspect and struck a match.
If he went up in smoke,
it meant he was a godless heathen faggot
who deserved to go up in smoke. If a choir
of angels emblazoned the sky and God,
humming the Hallelujah Chorus,
personally pissed out the flames dancing
around the suffocating faggot's body,
he was allowed to return home if he promised
to register four times daily with the local
police and never get his hair cut
in a place called a boutique.

                    So, you see,
liberalism has increased the life expectancy
of fairies. That's because we've evolved
into the world's wittiest, best groomed
ballroom dancers. Everyone's into
the Queen's vernacular, pierced ears, disco
and poppers. So long as you seek your partner
after dark in the mountains of Montana
at least one hundred miles distant
from the nearest living heterosexual
and keep your meeting anonymous and
under fifteen minutes with no visible
body contact or non-contacting foreplay,
you could not conceivably, even by the
most homophobic, be considered
or accused homosexual by anyone but the most
adamantine and intolerant straight person.
Thanks to science it is now well known
that homosexuality is not transmitted by
tiny springing bugs or bats. We are not burned
at the stake (except during ceremonial
occasions of state for example only)
in the larger urban centers today
though we may still face a constant barrage

of misdemeanors (nastier than a case of crabs)
such as littering, (i.e.,
don't drop your hanky in a city park),
jaywalking (i.e., no matter how cute the
cop may be, don't wiggle your ass when
you buzz across Connecticut Avenue
during rush hour in the middle of the block
waving you-whoo, you-whoo to your colorful friends) and loitering (i.e., situated
under the romantic moon in an open
park after dark behind willowy shade trees
on your knees with a look of ecstasy
on your face as he creams into your eager mouth
is considered loitering among other things).
Simple precautions will save you
from a life of humiliation and
all those long blank spots on your résumé
that you have to explain as time
to get your head together or
extended vacation or time spent nursing
your mother back to health
when you were really fired for
turning on a fellow office employee.

In conclusion, there are no known cures
for homosexuality. Faggots have survived
Christianity, psychiatry, social ostracism, jail,
earth, air, wind and fire, as well as the pink
triangle and concentration camps. Nothing
can reckon with you if you can reckon with yourself.
The facts have been available for a long, long time:
where there are human beings, there are faggots.
We were around clubbing each other over the head
just like straight cave men. We were considered magical
by some people. We were considered mysterious.
We were obviously different but not always hated.
Hatred is always self-hatred.
Denial is always fear.
It's easier for THEM when
we hate ourselves,
FEAR OURSELVES.
I don't have to and
I WON'T.
None of us knows how he got here,
for what reason we are here or
why we are who we are.
It is not obvious

and a swish doesn't make me any more obvious
than the lack of one.
I am obvious
because I AM.

THINGS WE DO TO HURT THE ONES WE LOVE

He forgets to call.
He calls but he doesn't
ask you out again.
He asks you out again but
he's an hour late.
He asks you out again but
after you have waited for an hour
he calls and cancels.
He doesn't cancel but he
shows up drunk. He shows up drunk
but you are drunk too because
he's an hour late. He kisses
somebody else. He wants to kiss
somebody else. He forgets
to light your cigarette.
He leaves town without calling.
He calls about leaving town
to tell you you can take the
champagne off chill. He's left
town and he calls to tell you
he's not dead. He forgets your birthday.
He remembers your birthday but
he buys you a sweater two sizes small.
He remembers your birthday and
buys you a sharp sweater but
he forgets it in lay away.
He claims you never told him
when your birthday is.
He forgets you are allergic to roses.
He doesn't buy you roses,
he buys you daffodils
knowing yellow is your least favorite color.
He buys you white daffodils but
breaks your best vase.
He hates your mother.
He acts like he owns the world
and he proves it by crushing you
in his arms until you can't breathe.

He can't get it up one night.
He gets it up but he cums before you do.
He gets it up and comes alright but
flops over and falls asleep.
He goes to sleep on your side of the bed.
He goes to bed on your side but
rolls over in an hour
and now you can't sleep.
You can't sleep for twenty-one days.
He thinks you look used
because you were not resourceful enough
to ignore his bad manners.
You pick up his bad manners.
You lose your best friend.
He wants to marry you.
It's like marrying an octopus
with a mind for each tentacle.
He forgets what color your eyes are.
When you are hit by a car
in front of your dream house
and the children are at school
he forgets to answer his phone.

1 Jan 1981

Simple Angels, Perplexing Minds

If your eyes look up
they will reach no higher
than paradise
          —Reverdy

When you are gone
the angel of your absence
remembers me.
The angel's name is
Once in time, always.
When I open my eyes
the angel sighs this music.
I no longer need.
The angel is my need.
Only imagination
could find the right words.
Together, we are the angel.
This way I do not cease
      to exist.

TOUGHNESS

Cars are tough
little images of immortality,
like the beautiful girls
paid to sell them. The idea
that I can have all of it
is impossible, however,
since I have not learned how to drive.
I have been castrated
by this fact, this inability
to move from state to state
faster than the petty crimes
of an average accumulative life style.
How will I ever arrive at
the state of grace? I don't even possess
the beautiful face that possesses
the nightmare of ephemerality.
I could live forever
I am so pliable and homely
like a maiden aunt
who disapproves of the nuclear family
because it lacks charm
like a lonely picnic.

Once I wanted to look tough
and I smoked enough cigarettes
to kill a laboratory rat.
When I was called a queer
because of the way I held my cigarette,
I learned my first lesson in
the difference between style
and content, without having to read
Robert Creeley. I became
a rebel without a cause but
I was still my grandmother's
favorite grandson. In the Navy
I learned how to look invisible
in the shower stalls. Everybody
had a bigger cock than myself.

I smoked dope
because of peer pressure.
On November 2, 1972
in the back of my friend's van
I achieved nirvana. Kathy
asked me if I wanted a blow job.
Peter said, wow, look,
the stars are so beautiful
and tough but I knew
he meant we can't reach them.
It was just another way of
dressing up an old cliche.
I have always been one to
hold onto advanced ideas
until they become stale
in the embrace.

There was this scientist once
who was so tough he substituted
wire mothers for the real mothers
of these monkeys and discovered
that they became very neurotic
if not psychotic because they
needed to be touched and caressed.
It made me want to bust his jaw open
as if nobody knew that.
But I'm losing the train of my thought.
I was talking about my maiden aunt
who was as tough as a body could be.
She wore army boots and grey wool slacks
and showed me a vial of acid
she kept in her purse
for muggers. Then she smiled at me
like one of those beautiful girls
who want to sell you a car
and said I shouldn't look so much
like a victim. She lived in the city
by herself and at forty
took up the violin and ice skating
against the orders of her doctor.

I have this illusion
of myself being desired
for my muscular body
but my muscles are so thick
and hard I can't feel
the simple touch of another hand.
I live day to day knowing
the average sensory deprivation
of one not loved
as entirely as I would wish.
I have a dream that my aunt
cuts open my chest with an ice skate
her mind in the rhapsody
of a circle eight.

January 1, 1982

WHAT SHOULD LOVE BECOME?

I've been in love with another person
several times in this life. None of these times
has succeeded but that doesn't mean
I'm not a success. I've learned a thing or two

about building bridges, burning them in a wake
for something that has died and will never cross
them again. The river below the flames, however,
never ceases to be lovely, no matter what

it reflects. If there is no man, there is,
nevertheless, the world and poems and other things
I am too small to destroy. In these things alone
do I live with any peace. Because of this

I am independent, poor but not unwise and
still available. An emotional possibility
persists to curb my cynicism. I build bridges now
of paper, thread, a few words, nothing

to compare to the bridges Whitman desired.
But sometimes two men can walk across one
and make it to the other side and there become
what, all too often, we are afraid of, even to dream.

June 14, 1982

INNOCENCE

for Tom, Walt, and Harry

It seems
innocent, doesn't it, that a body
still needs a cause
                    —*Hugh Seidman*

I.

Innocence
kills us all,
said my friend, Waldo
speaking of Anita Bryant
and Christianity
and Faggots
and the Imperialist Fascists Racists Assholes
still gripping power
as if, if for one moment,
they let go and relax,
they'd shit.
Of course, they'd make us
clean it up,
because we are the black mammies
of the Patriarchy.
We can coif their hair
and decorate their pavillions
and paint pictures
and write poems
without them even shrugging,
so long as it's all
Art for ART's sake
and amusing
in a delicately pornographic way,
but Waldo says,
it's people like Andy Warhol
who are selling us out,
people like Dave Kopay
and Gotham and Carol Burnett
who ignore our suffering
even when their motives are innocently pleasurable.
Like the Brahmin says
walk in my shoes a while.
It's a killer.
Walk in my barefeet
over the still burning ashes

of our so-so, chi-chi brothers
and sisters. Back when they called us
witches and lunatics
they were more true
to themselves and
we couldn't afford kinky innocence.
We were too busy hiding ourselves.
Back in Berlin.
Back in Babylon.
Back in Sodom and Gomorrah.
Those were all kinky days.
Now everything is show business
and even the liberals
are wearing beads
and handkerchiefs in their back pockets.
But I still know
we all got here
the hard way.
College dorms and restrooms
and the streets, the same streets
that eat up little black kids,
keep churning us out,
and Stonewall was just the beginning
because our fathers
are still watching us
out of the corners of their eyes
and Mom still cries sometimes
afraid we'll get beat up
if we keep going to those discos
out in the ghetto. And they still pray
if we are only teenagers
that we'll outgrow it.
We are always teenagers.
Out grow what? My being?
My sexuality?
My desire?
I still find myself whispering
in my sleep, my dream,
I can't help it Mom,
I'm stuck
being a faggot
and most of my friends are faggots.
This may be the end of the line, Dad,
because I'm not going to give you
a male child or a female child.
All I can give you is myself
and you are afraid of me.

2.

This cat named Jesus bops up to me
and says he can save me
if I read this little pamphlet
about the evils of Communism.
I say I'm not altogether into Communism either
though I sucked this Marxist cock
for two and a half years
and jumped on it with my ass hole
and rimmed his ass hole
and even french kissed.
I don't think Jesus liked this
because he snatched his pamphlet
out of my hand and waved it
at this black dude
who was also cruising,
but in a much lower key.
Waldo said, "don't let it get you down.
He's not rejecting your soul.
He's got a place for it.
It's just that if he kills you on the spot
he hasn't got anyplace
to stash your body."
Waldo likes to talk brutally
but we both know
it's righteous anger.
Christians and Anti-Communists
can openly solicit your soul
but watch a faggot
openly solicit another faggot's body
and heads spin.
In the Super City you can forget about this,
lose yourself in the casual promiscuity
of the bars, forget,
forget,
forget that
we still have friends
sleeping in closets
and silos
and not even asking for a name
or a cigarette
or gentleness.

I kneel down at Waldo's feet
and dig with my fingernails
until I have a hole maybe

an inch and a half wide
and seven inches deep.
Waldo rubs his crotch
casually in my face
so as not to attract attention
and I pull down my zipper
and stick my cock into the earth,
and begin fucking
and fucking
and fucking
waiting for a cop to come by and
ask me what I'm doing.
I'm sorry officer,
but I was horny
and the earth looked
so beautiful today
I just got this overwhelming urge
like Scarlett O'Hara.
You've seen *GWTW*, haven't you, officer,
when she kneels down and
eats dirt.
Well, I'd call that fellatio
and she did it on the big silver screen
for every one to see.
I haven't got those gigantic aspirations
to exhibit myself like she did
but I've been horny
for days now and
well,
look at it this way,
the earth was here
and so was I
and like Steve Stills says,
if you can't love the one you love,
love the one you're with.
What are you going to arrest me for anyway,
fucking with the earth?
Maybe you ought to get some of those
fucking Industrialists
who are poisoning everything.
Cum's biodegradable, I think.
If it isn't I may have some problems
shitting in a few years.
You see, I usually take it
up my asshole.
I'm not really into fucking that much
but it's a beautiful day

and I just want to have a good time
like anybody else.

The officer doesn't find anything innocent about it.
He pierces me with his eyes
and I come, just like that,
then he grabs both Waldo and me
and whisks us down to the station
where they frisk us a couple times
though I insist the only gun I have
is empty. I request that the arresting officer
frisk me again. I even promise
to pay child support for the child
if I accidentally impregnated the earth.

3.

But even this is fantasy.
I'm afraid of hard work.
I want the revolution to happen
without me. I don't know what to do.
I'm afraid. I can't imagine
a homosexual army
unless we find a really tough lesbian
to be general. We really are
delicate people. The wrong kind of look
sends us fleeing into the streets.
We are still afraid, all too often,
to hold each other. I still hear friends say
this one's too fem, that one's too butch,
this one's conceited and that one's too needy.
Our masks hide us even from ourselves.
We carry ourselves
with the innocence of a costume ball
floating through another night
and another night,
on and on wherever desire carries us,
to the discos and porno houses
and gay liberation meetings.
Everyone tells me
the times have already changed.
We should be loose,
forget politics
unless there's a gay or pro-gay candidate
in the running . . . Capitalism's still in.
Cash in. Watch more tv.
Go to the movies.

But I still have friends
who write songs
with the word "she" in them.
I still know people who are fired
because they are faggots.
I still know people who can't quite
make it all hang together.
I still can't
quite.
Remember, it's usually your dad
telling you you have to become more realistic,
toe the line,
get a job,
join the forces of Capitalism.
And it is still your momma
who listens to your dreams
and wants you to be happy.

IRON MIKE

Mike had white teeth
Which snarled like a wolf's warning.
I recall, he stripped himself naked
And rolled in the new snow,
And pelted us, blue and cold,
While his teeth laughed.
Once he told me
He had climbed the girder
Of the big bridge
And spilled his seed, as the Bible says,
Over the cars passing unaware
And far below.
When he came back from the Marines
He had "Iron Mike" tattooed
On his left arm
As if denying man's utter vulnerability
To any casual sliver of steel.
His mother's wits were addled.
All day she went, mumbling,
Straightening chairs and picking up
Microscopic bits of paper.
And I've often seen his father
Spend all of a free evening
Rechecking his insurance policies
And putting his securities
In order.

TRAIN STATIONS AND BROKEN HEARTS

Why is it I always fall in love,
then have to say good-bye?
I try to stick around
but then I look down
at my hand and
what do I see but
                  a ticket
marked "destination
of a broken heart,"

and I cry.

I've cried in the mountains,
and down on the beach.
I've climbed a tree
and cried for my broken heart.
I've cried in the rain,
I've expressed my pain,
but nobody wants to hear.

I cried.

I go away
on long train rides.
I start a new life.
in Des Moines, Iowa.
I start a new life
in Boise, Idaho.
I start a new life
in Chicago, Illinois.
I start a new life
in Indianapolis, Indiana.
I flee to Iraq.
Istanbul.
Idlewilde Airport.
I go on an Iliad.
I idolize aloofness.
I'll never fall in love again.
I take the train to Alexandria,
Virginia, not Egypt.
Ithaca. Illyrium. Back to the Iroquois.
I discover new sources of energy.
Ill health. I begin to make
an impression. Somebody's got
eyes for me but I play it coy.

Jim Everhard

I cried and

I'm not going to cry again.
I won't cry tomorrow
because I cried yesterday.
I cried like a train.
I cried like Camille.
I cried like onions.
I cried my dues.

I'm tired of trains.
I'm tired of having
no place to run.
I won't give up on love
as long as I've got my music.

Take me away from this pain,
train. Silver streak,
be the silver thread
that can mend my broken heart.

I'll sit in the train station
and wait for you.

ca. 1978/82

A BEAUTIFUL DREAM

for orry

we meet on an ocean crossing steamer,
adapted to the rhythms of the work,
sweating generously but normally austere,
quiet and sincere, like lumber jacks
but without a forest. the ocean
is quite enormous and written home about.
it is also monotonous, like anything
beautiful, like eyes, for instance.
eyes are fascinating and boring simultaneously.
they are also blue or brown or green (hazel).
like my eyes. your eyes are as wide as
austrailia where they first opened.
you tell me stories about the outback
and girls in sidney and boys also.
the stories about the boys were by far
the most exotic. but you wanted to be safe.
you wouldn't kiss me with your tongue.
consequently, i yearn for it to enter my body
anyway it can. i have never felt
the absence of anyone's tongue more than this,
as if you shouldn't be speaking,
though i love to listen to your stories.
you are a beautiful dreamer.
your coppery golden hair
is so soft to the touch
i recline into a dream about it.
i am no longer on a ship.
i am not with you.
i am in a vast pasture land
listening to unseen shepherds
playing with flutes.
then it begins to rain, each drop
like a tear
leading me astray. i will only awaken
to the taste of your tongue.
my mouth is smooth like a shell, but soft, empty.

4 June 1984

DAY AND NIGHT WITHOUT YOU

When we met it was like other halves
becoming whole. I was a beautiful pear,
golden fruit hanging from the limb
of a winter bare tree
in the dead of night. I was in my magical peak.
I stood out strong in the night
because I followed my heart
and my heart was stronger than myself, again.
But the heart, unlike a pear,
does not grow on a tree or fall to the ground.
The heart is not held in your hand.
It has no core. It's not a miracle or magic.
It grows strong through sorrow
and wise as a rainbow is wise. It is the sign
that cannot be seen, the map
of a land that is the land itself.
It is four dark rooms in a house
where no one lives. No one lives in the heart;
the heart lives inside the soul.
The soul is the home of the heart.
I have been lost many times. I have walked
across daylight with my hands before me
like a blind person. The soul can see
but it does not speak of what it sees.
The soul lives in a house where there are no words.
The silence in your soul is your heart.
What beats is only a motion,
layers of muscle, as if the bricks of a house
were filled with blood. And outside
in the orchard behind the house
I watch the pears turn to light, speechlessly.
They are the fruit of sunlight
and at night they live light
they have stored in little lanterns
that burn in windowless rooms.
When I look at the pears I think about you,
how we might have ripened
if we had given each other as much chance
as the light gives each pear. In the natural world
there are courses which cannot be averted;
there are catastrophes which cannot be accounted for;

and there is never a moment that light,
in some form, is not given and received.
Two people burn in the night
and escape with the light.
It happened to us. As sunlight struck
through the opened window
or the memory of light called you away,
we let go
and the light stored in our hearts
has carried us farther than we had planned to go.
Already it is spring
and we have carried on like trees in bloom.
Then the blooms disappear
and the long, long summer approaches
when the branches are hidden behind leaves
and I will remember the pear
which hung from the branch
one last cold night,
how we picked it and ate it
and walked back into our separate houses
and, expectantly, stared out the window
watching light splatter like rainbows
on all the dew,
and there was hope and the eerie fear
that the orchard would outlive what we found
hidden in our hearts,
unnatural hearts in the natural world.
There is no darkness
that is absolute
save the darkness we each carry in our heart
when we think that a pear
was found in the snow
meant for us.

April 13, 1982

A POEM

to be empty
is to be moral
the angel
is always empty
to be empty
is to be infinitely deep
take off the mask
and see yourself
in eyes
without surfaces
to be empty
is to be swallowed
the angel rises
out of the throat
to be empty
is to have been created
to be empty
is to know of a world
where
when
you did not exist
an angel
stands in your place
until you arrive
and fill its mouth
my life
is the mouth of an angel
a mirror
is an angel
with closed wings
a mirror
is the contemplation
of flight
such beauty
cannot be moral
but like a lake
like the eye
of a dead man
in seeing all
in reflecting the sky
is empty
is empty

February 20, 1978

THE BOATING PARTY

Renoir believed life is a banquet,
and somebody else should get the tab.
He was an uncanny freeloader most of his life
and he hoarded liqueurs and lap dogs. His favorite brand
of cigarettes was O.P.'s.
Never a pessimist, he was
the exact opposite of Vincent Van Gogh,
he always got what he begged for. His palette was a veritable
rainbow of cool lights and casual ecstasies.
His favorite
brand of cigarettes was somebody else's Salem Menthols.
He was close friends with Oscar Wilde until the famous trial
whereupon he commented he'd never suspected
such a dark day would befall upon his canvas.
He scratched a series of black canvases
for fear of the avant garde and began
"The Boating Party" in response to Wilde's homosexuality.
A clear transfusion of heterosexual sensuality spreads across the canvas,
which does not answer the question, "Which sex do you prefer"
but necessitates an encounter with the possibility that neither sex
is preferable though both are available.

Why was Renoir so attracted to women with lap dogs?

Answer: penis envy.

Renoir never painted a nude male. One wonders if he secretly
felt women were born nude and men fully dressed. Today his work
glamorizes galleries around the globe of a bourgeois world never to return.
Nostalgia weeps upon his grave. If Renoir were alive today
he'd probably want to bum a cigarette off you unless
he thought you were queer.

1970s

GAY FREEDOM

It's not easy to make plain statements
about freedom, much less "gay freedom."
What does it mean? My mother always said
freedom was the other side of responsibility. For a mother,
she wasn't dumb. Am I free? No.
No, I am not free. To be
perfectly truthful, I don't think
anyone's free. It's not a matter
of being free. Maybe it's more like
taking on the responsibility of a life?

I was proud in the seventies.
Whenever I wrote something gay
I used my real name, though no one
ever believes it is my real name.
"Everhard" is pretty funny for a faggot.
I'm sure my father wasn't thinking,
or his father, or his, or, at least,
the o-o-h w-e-e-l-l of history.
It sounds like something mythological,
something Nordic like
the great everhard slouched in his tree
with horrendous wing span and
that funny crooked beak.

He's my love affair with anarchy
and its kindly prince, the fairy tale
anarchist, Peter Kropotkin.
I have always loved Peter Kropotkin.
Mutual Aid is one of the world's
most beautiful books. He talks about
the herding instinct not like we'll
follow each other into doom but
as if we need each other
to even begin to see
the shape of our doom.
I believe we can see it

as clearly as we see what we use
to build ourselves from it.
The world is built up against doom.

I don't mean doom as an opposite
of freedom. Freedom. Doom.
Now I lay me down to sleep.
I pray the Lord my soul to take
if I should die before I wake.
I want to go there, too, but
it can't be much better than this world
or I wouldn't be entirely happy
if I could only make contact to you.

We should defend each other's freedom
by acting responsible for it,
as if it had to be created or
if it's already here, be found, discovered.
My friend, Blake, thinks freedom
is a bird, a living possibility, a body.
He likes to think of it as flying,
a capable response
to the beauty and the terror
of a broken china cup.
How do you respond to something broken?

What if you broke your arm
and no one would help you?
What if all your plants died
and no one offered to give you some more?
What if you were attacked on the street
by a gang of hate-filled youths?
What if you saw someone else
being attacked? Once I saw a young man
being shoved into his doorway
by a large, vicious looking man.
There was a gun. A woman in front of me
saw it also. We walk side by side
not sure if we are trying to
comfort each other while we ignore
what's happening or if we are really
trying to work something out. We decide
to walk to the corner of the block and
look for a policeman. By the time
we get to the end of the block
the thief has fled. The young man
walks inside, closes his door.

Who was free to do what he wanted?
Certainly not the thief. He wasn't free.
Nor the victim. They were made
for each other. And the witnesses?
Were we free? Who can run away
from himself? Who can find another world?
Gay freedom is the other person's freedom.
That's what we're responsible for.

August 23, 1982

THE MYSTICAL LIFE

There comes a day when all of us
disappear as completely as
the mystic with his rope trick.
Some of us climb old sheets.
Some climb the wind. No matter
how we get there, we all end up
in the same place. We are more
rootless than life seems, except
in the All. Even the tiny fly
carries part of us into the sky.
We rub off on the rose bush.
We drape across the grass.
We cross that bridge before we
get to it. You may think you know
where you're going, at least which
alternatives you have, but you don't.
When you die you will lose your will.
Being a mystic means accepting
what it is like to be dead
before you are dead, but with your will.
Embrace the mystical life.
Pray for the ability to no longer ask
for anything. Volunteer poverty.
Eat soup from a pot that stays
on a fire of eternal flames,
a soup poor in substance
yet rich and warm.

December 22, 1978

Only the Living Haunt this World

When a man dies
he leaves a world filled with holes.
The one hole he slips into
belongs only to himself. It is filled
with his heaviness
for he is no longer filled with
the lightness of breath.

A world full of holes
is left behind. There is a hole
in the chair where he sat,
and a hole at the desk where he wrote,
and a hole in the closet
where he hung some clothes.
Those left behind soon begin to discover
the holes in their world.

At first they remember,
he sat here or stood there or
wrote a letter there. But after awhile
they forget and yet still sense
the holes everywhere. But they forget
that the holes belonged to their friend.
They are trying to be happy again but
the effort seems greater.

They have discovered a world
full of holes. But the holes
are not really in the closet or the desk or the bed.
The holes are in the living
where a little fear has been planted.

ca. 1983

PREPARING FOR DEATH

Mama is the first word.
By the time you arrive at the last word
it will be something entirely different.
Very few people die crying "mama, mama."
In the natural course, your mother
is already dead. Sometimes when you see

a white bird on a window ledge, you think
about her, but at death most of us
do not see a white bird on a window ledge.
The bird on the ledge has flown away
and with it have flown all preparations.
Left only, is the anxiety of having locked

yourself out of the house. If you have a friend
who keeps a copy of your keys, you may
get back inside. If not, you'll have to
find a crow bar but the bird knows nothing
about crow bars. You are only really locked
outside of a house if someone you know

remains within and won't let you join him.
This is the sudden return to nature
that a mother can enforce with ridicule.
How far you have come in so few years.
Locked out of the house you were born in
a white bird sitting on a window ledge

too high up for you to reach,
your only recourse is to talk it over with someone.
This is when you begin to suspect the white bird
is a spy for your mother. No matter where you are
when you die, you will not see the white bird
fly back to that house with the awaited message.

At death, the key to the mystery of your life
is in the belly of this sharp-eyed bird.
We are often told that the answer we have sought
lies back at the beginning we no longer remember.
She took it with her to her grave.
In the end it is returned without a struggle.

January 13, 1983

AIDS

our enemies
want to blame our love

we tend to blame
each other

our friends want to
blame the system

and all too often
we end up blaming ourselves

perhaps i shouldn't
have slept with so many men

or avoided certain
gathering places

maybe i shouldn't have
come out at all

but i can't erase what's happened

consequences are paid
for ignorant mistakes

if only i'd known
perhaps i'd have been somebody else

but i'm somebody else now
and if i'm still well

i'm lucky
and if i'm not

what debilitates the body
debilitates the soul

if i am going to die
but i was always going to die

if i feel the pain
give me the strength

to weep
for myself

and blame no one
it was easier to ask someone

to give me a blow job
than to hold me through the night

[*This poem was written in 1986, the very year of Jim Everhard's own death from AIDS*]

GAY ROOTS is published in paperback and limited hardcover editions.
There is also a special edition of 26 lettered copies,
handbound in boards and signed by editor Winston Leyland.